PRINT CULTURE AND THE BLACKWOOD TRADITION,
1805–1930

PRINT CULTURE AND THE BLACKWOOD TRADITION, 1805–1930

Edited by David Finkelstein

UNIVERSITY OF TORONTO PRESS
Toronto Buffalo London

ISBN–13: 978-0-8020-8711-9
ISBN–10: 0-8020-8711-6

Printed on acid-free paper

Library and Archives Canada Cataloguing in Publication

Finkelstein, David, 1964–
    Print culture and the Blackwood tradition, 1805–1930 / David Finkelstein.

(Studies in book and print culture)
Includes bibliographical references and index.
ISBN 0-8020-8711-6

1. William Blackwood and Sons – History.   2. Publishers and publishing –
Great Britain – History.   3. Great Britain – Intellectual life.   I. Title.
II. Series.

Z325.B63F46 2006   070.50941'09041   C2006-902575-4

University of Toronto Press acknowledges the financial assistance to
its publishing program of the Canada Council for the Arts and the
Ontario Arts Council.

Contents

Illustrations follow p. 166

Illustrations

Acknowledgments

This essay collection has been the result of great collaborative effort between contributors, and first acknowledgments go to them for the collegial spirit in which they engaged with the subject and helped to bring this volume to fruition. Thanks go to Leslie Howsam for agreeing to include the collection in her Studies in Book and Print Culture Series, and to Jill McConkey at the University of Toronto Press for her editorial and production support. I am grateful to Queen Margaret University College, Edinburgh for providing the sabbatical term in early 2004 that enabled me to complete work on this project, and to the QMUC Faculty of Health and Social Sciences and the principal, Professor Anthony Cohen, for providing relevant and timely funding for necessary book production and indexing costs. I am also extremely grateful to York University, Toronto, and the contributors to this volume for timely supply of extra funding to cover indexing costs. For permission to reuse previously published material by Michael Michie in chapter 6, we are grateful to McGill-Queen's University Press (publishers of Michie, *An Enlightenment Tory in Victorian Scotland: The Career of Sir Archibald Alison*, 1997*)*, and the editors of *The Bibliotheck* (publishers of Michie, '"Mr. Wordy" and the Blackwoods: Author and Publisher in Victorian Scotland,' *The Bibliotheck*, 1996 (21), 39–54). Finally, I'd like to thank Alison for patiently putting up with the Blackwood relics and papers that have taken over too much of the study and loft, and far too much of our time together.

PRINT CULTURE AND THE BLACKWOOD TRADITION,
1805–1930

Introduction

DAVID FINKELSTEIN

A theme recurs throughout the 1897 house history of the Edinburgh publishing firm William Blackwood and Sons, one that portrays its directors as romantic literary enthusiasts and supporters, daring adventurers seeking nuggets of gold in the mines of Literature. As the firm's chronicler, Margaret Oliphant, exclaimed about the founding of the firm in the early nineteenth century, 'The Revival of Literature was like the opening of a new mine: it was more than that, a sort of manufactory out of nothing, to which there seemed no limit. You had but to set a man of genius spinning at that shining thread which came from nowhere, which required no purchase of materials or "plant" of machinery, and your fortune was made.'[1]

William Blackwood I and his successors were portrayed as Scots able to set the men (and women) of genius at work spinning literary threads of gold, befriending, encouraging, and gathering together a coterie of authors to form engaged and directed literary circles, and enveloping these individuals under a common 'Blackwoodian' identity. In chronicling the heady, early days of the firm's development, from early bookselling and publishing initiatives in Edinburgh in the first decade of the century, the founding of the famous *Blackwood's Edinburgh Magazine* (a title later simplified in 1905 to *Blackwood's Magazine* after years of it being informally referred to as such) and its publication of the infamous Chaldee Manuscript in 1817, to its published attacks on Coleridge, Wordsworth, and the Cockney School of Poetry, and onwards into mid-Victorian maturity and support of key authors such as George Eliot, Charles Lever, and Anthony Trollope, Oliphant's late-century appraisal offered us the Blackwoods as central players in locating and sustaining a specific late-Victorian vision of nineteenth-century British literary culture.

This collection of essays offers a reappraisal and re-evaluation of this picture, and of the place of the Blackwood firm and its monthly magazine in British literary, political, and social terms between 1805 and 1930. It revisits and contextualizes the relevance and role of the Blackwood firm in shaping the literary, political, and social discourse of its time, both through the range of books and authors it published, and through the literary, critical, political, and journalistic content it featured in its monthly *Blackwood's Magazine*. The volume also continues what has been a renaissance of work over the past fifty years dedicated to the history and place of the Blackwood firm in Romantic, Victorian, and Edwardian literary culture.

Central to this revival of interest in the history of this Edinburgh firm was the Blackwood family's decision to deposit in the National Library of Scotland in 1942 and 1961 their extensive archives of correspondence and publishing records (one of the most complete records of British literary and publishing activity in existence, since added to with further bequests and purchases). Early beneficiaries of this treasure trove of primary material were two pivotal works published in 1958 and 1959 that neatly encapsulated a century of Blackwood publishing activity: Alan Lang Strout's pioneering study of contributors to the early issues of *Blackwood's Magazine*, and Douglas Blackburn's groundbreaking work on Joseph Conrad's correspondence with the Blackwood firm. Both drew on the untapped archival material to demonstrate the centrality of the firm in shaping the trajectory of two distinctive literary movements – Romanticism and Modernism.[2] Since then, determined work has resulted in more than two hundred books and articles being published on Blackwood's general role in British cultural history, with contributors to this volume also playing significant roles in sparking continuing debate on the firm's legacy.[3]

Over the past ten years an avalanche of general studies of the periodical press have appeared, locating literary journals in Romantic, Victorian, and Edwardian cultural history.[4] The Blackwood firm and its magazine are apposite subjects for placing within this context of recent academic interest in print culture and media history. Work in this field has been particularly strong in examining the place of the periodical press in shaping nineteenth-century cultural values. The result has been the application to periodical studies of what D.F. McKenzie termed the 'sociology of texts,' where, as the editors of one recent essay collection acknowledged, 'meanings stem both from texts treated as artefacts of material culture and from their functions in society.'[5] Doing this allows us to acknowledge that publishing firms and journal editors created material that was not static. Though they might have sought to impose an editorial consistency on the material they produced for publication in their lists or journals, competing voices could be seen jostling for space within particular periodical and print culture contexts.

We see points like these addressed in the contributions to this volume. The pieces here re-evaluate the place of Blackwood's in cultural terms. The firm was established in late 1804/5 in Edinburgh by William Blackwood I, and by the turn of the century its books and monthly magazine could be found in official residences, military barracks, and naval ships in Britain and across the world. Who read what it produced, how did it get there, and what did these texts offer potential readers? What were some of Blackwood's key contributions to British literary culture? Who were some of the major figures nurtured through contact with the firm and its directors? This collection offers possible answers to these questions, linked by a common, overarching theme: to examine the extent to which editorial functions, publishing practices, and critical/literary activity coalesced to shape and direct work emerging under the Blackwood imprint or in the pages of its magazine. The collection contests simplistic conceptions of the editorial function (and the Blackwood family's editorial abilities) shifting, as Patten and Finkelstein summarize, 'from modest, coterie beginnings in Edinburgh at the turn of the century into the triple paradigms of high Victorian periodical management that then sloped downward to the rag-tag assemblages of *Tit-Bits*, penny papers, and the awful journalistic pandering of Jasper Milvain and his ilk.'[6]

The collection also offers a re-evaluation and appraisal of the role of the Blackwood firm and its magazine in shaping Romantic, Victorian, and Edwardian print culture and periodical literature, and enquires to what extent their perceived decline was a result of social, cultural, and economic factors, a supplanting 'by the mechanization of printing, the hugely enlarged scale of production, the expansion and professionalization of journalism, and the substitution of news and entertainment for the magisterial essays, reviews, and literature of the preceding decades.'[7]

The Periodical Context: From Quarterlies to Monthlies

William Blackwood I laid down the foundations of the firm at the turn of the nineteenth century, during a period of great change and development in the Scottish publishing and book trade. Blackwood and his contemporaries benefited from Edinburgh's long-standing reputation and tradition as a centre for publishing and printing. The general diffusion of ideas in the late eighteenth century, during what has been characterized as the Scottish Enlightenment, was in great part due to the access Scottish authors had to an efficient and localized print network that could generate and disseminate their texts on a wide scale.

The development of the concept of copyright following the 1774 landmark ruling in the case of the Scottish bookseller Donaldson versus his London-based counterpart Becket (a case that can be read also as a politicized struggle between Edinburgh and London print culture centres for control over literary production and dissemination), created the circumstances through which authorship could be practised as an established and lucrative profession. Scottish publishing firms (and their periodicals) subsequently made and sustained literary careers, as well as shaped the dominant literary discourses of their times.

As Lee Erickson has argued in *The Economy of Literary Form*, between 1800 and 1850 the literary periodical became the dominant publishing format in British culture.[8] The founding of groundbreaking and profitable journals such as the *Edinburgh Review* (founded in 1802) and *Blackwood's Edinburgh Magazine* (founded in 1817) consequently affected the development and relative cultural importance of poetry, the essay, and the novel.[9] The *Edinburgh Review* established the template for subsequent quarterly periodicals of this type. Founded in Edinburgh in 1802 by four disaffected Whig lawyers with literary ambitions (Francis Jeffrey, Henry Brougham, Francis Horner, and Sydney Smith), under Jeffrey's management, the *Edinburgh Review* achieved such eminence that, for a long time, it set the standards and parameters by which most nineteenth-century periodical publications were measured and judged. Contributors were well paid (initially up to £10 sterling per sheet of letterpress), an innovation the publisher Archibald Constable insisted on, despite Jeffrey's opinion that contributors should be 'all gentlemen and no pay.'[10] The format, paper wrapper, the length and style of articles, were all much copied, particularly by rivals such as the *Quarterly Review*, founded in 1809. Contributions to the *Edinburgh Review* were unsigned, a practice that remained almost universal in British literary periodicals until the 1860s.

Among those who had charge of literary journals prior to the emergence of the *Edinburgh Review*, trying to provide great breadth of coverage and comment on all new publications had been the dominant editorial standards. Some of those editors had direct links to encyclopedic compendia: Macvey Napier, for example, started his literary career revising the *Encyclopedia Britannica* in the early part of the century before assuming editorship of the *Edinburgh Review* in 1829. Many of these early miscellanies, such as the *English Review* (1783–96) or the *Analytical Review* (1788–99), did not last beyond ten to fifteen years, a direct result of their eagerness to be viewed 'as instalments of a continuous encyclopaedia, recording the advance of knowledge in every field of human enterprise.'[11] As Joanne Shattock notes in her study *Politics and Reviewers: The 'Edinburgh' and the 'Quarterly' in the Early Victorian Age*, these review journals failed because of their ambitious editorial commitment to cover as many publications as possible, 'even to the extent of cramming what could not be reviewed into a series of short notices.'[12] Such a commitment could not cope with the ever-increasing number of titles in all fields being issued by the turn of the nineteenth century.

As the lead editor, Francis Jeffrey dominated the *Edinburgh Review* for over twenty-five years, from 1803 to 1829. It was he who steered the *Review* to unashamedly selective and elitist practices. When he and his collaborators Brougham, Horner, and Smith met in Buccleuch Place, Edinburgh, in 1802 to discuss their new venture, they declared that their prospective journal should offer commentary only on *select* books of the moment. More important, a commitment to the highest *quality* in reviewing was their fundamental principle. As the advertisement for the opening number made clear, the *Review* aimed to pluck out the best from the torrent of work emanating from the publishing capitals of London and Edinburgh: 'Of the books that are daily presented to the world, a very large proportion is evidently destined to obscurity, by the insignificance of the subjects, or the defects of their execution ... The very lowest order of publications are rejected, accordingly, by most of the literary publications of which the Public are already in possession. But the contributors to the *Edinburgh Review* propose to carry this principle of selection a good deal further; to decline any attempt at exhibiting a complete view of modern literature; and to confine their notice, in a very great degree, to works that have either attained, or deserve, a certain portion of celebrity.'[13]

The editors drew for initial inspiration on long-standing eighteenth-century traditions of Scottish debate in philosophy, politics, economics, evolution, and revolution, while consistently upholding the superiority of the Scottish educational and legal systems. They were, however,

careful to contain the *Review*'s cultural profile as a 'national and nationalist' review within the safe framing of a 'North Briton' identity, thus
balancing Scotland's unique traditions with the political realities of
Scotland's evolving place within the Union.[14]

Competition quickly sprang up from both London- and Scottish-
based quarters. The London publisher John Murray, for example, began
issuing the rival *Quarterly Review* in 1809, and eight years later, in 1817,
William Blackwood I launched the monthly journal *Blackwood's Edinburgh
Magazine*, which he both edited and published. The market soon grew
more crowded, with the founding of periodicals such as the *London
Journal* in 1820 and the *Westminster Review* in 1824. When William
Maginn and *Blackwood's* parted company, Maginn, Hugh Fraser, and
the young publisher James Fraser drew up plans for a half-crown
monthly, *Fraser's*, which capitalized on its greater frequency to exploit
topical materials and a quicker, hipper metropolitan style. Moreover,
the steam-presses used to print the journal allowed for much tighter
deadlines and last-minute improvisations of copy.[15] Many successful
imitators followed.

The influence of the august quarterlies declined further in the 1850s
and 1860s, when they were challenged and eclipsed by monthlies such
as the *Cornhill Magazine* in 1860, the *Fortnightly Review* in 1865, and the
Contemporary Review a year later. Although the *Edinburgh Review* lasted
until 1929, its final years were marked by an overwhelming seriousness
and lack of resilience that grew more antiquated in face of the exuber-
ant dynamism of its competitors. As Mark Pattison would remark
acidly in 1877, 'those venerable old wooden three-deckers, the *Edinburgh
Review* and the *Quarterly Review*, still put out to sea under the command,
I believe, of the Ancient Mariner.'[16] Jeffrey's 'principle of selection' and
stolid, sluggish format could not keep pace with the changing conditions of the periodical market. While visionary, powerful editors created an influential model in the early nineteenth century, their successors
could not adapt that model effectively to new times, markets, and
reading practices.

William Blackwood as Publishing Entrepreneur

When William Blackwood I founded the Blackwood firm in late 1804,
he set in place innovative and highly influential practices that followed
patterns set by the *Edinburgh Review* but also enabled the Blackwood
firm to establish and maintain a central position in the promotion and

dissemination of nineteenth-century textual production. The rise of Blackwood's during the nineteenth century is a narrative of a rise from local to national and then international prominence. At the time of William Blackwood's death in 1834, he was at the head of a publishing company that sold popular books by leading authors worldwide, and the editor for seventeen years of *Blackwood's Edinburgh Magazine*, the most famous monthly publication of the day. Under the direction of his son John Blackwood between 1845 and 1879, the firm and its magazine moved to the forefront of Victorian textual production, becoming one of the leading 'houses' of the period. John's nephew William Blackwood III maintained John's legacy into the twentieth century. Yet as Robert Morrison explores in 'William Blackwood and the Dynamics of Success,' it was William Blackwood I's decisive, hard-nosed commercial instincts, a keen sense of opportunity, and a remarkable ability to determine who and what would please the market that proved crucial in raising the firm from provincial obscurity to enduring prominence during the first thirty years of its existence.

The firm's most valuable textual commodity for ensuring maximum publicity and exposure for its authors was its successful monthly magazine. When William Blackwood I relaunched *Blackwood's Edinburgh Magazine* in October 1817 (after an initial lacklustre six month start), Blackwood utilized the talents of two members of his literary coterie (John Gibson Lockhart and John Wilson) to realize the vision of a marketing campaign that made *Blackwood's* one of the most successful magazines in literary history.

The first few issues of *Blackwood's Edinburgh Magazine*, with their attacks on local and national literary figures, their brand of personalized satire, and their blend of anonymously authored literature, politics, fiction, and poetry, established the reputation of the Blackwood firm across the country. But Blackwood's did not aim solely at mainstream literary targets such as the 'Cockney School of Poetry,' S.T. Coleridge's poetry, or prominent Scottish intellectuals and political figures. As John Strachan suggests in '"The mapp'd out skulls of Scotia": *Blackwood's* and the Scottish Phrenological Controversy,' William Blackwood also ventured into popular science areas to promote and position 'his magazine within post-Napoleonic British literary culture as the most controversial, troubling and entertaining journal of the day,' in this case utilizing a combination of satire and orthodox criticism to deride and attack phrenology, then all the rage in nineteenth-century British and European society.[17] 'Maga' (by which name *Blackwood's*

Magazine was also known) was not the first to aim its critical venom at the 'skull readers': the *Edinburgh Review*, which Strachan argues Maga drew on in formulating its stance on phrenological activity, had often inveighed weightily against the pseudo-scientific approach of phrenologists. But Maga would end up replacing the *Edinburgh Review* as the particular *bête noire* of British phrenologists by its 'particular gift for appropriating the most memorable critical techniques of rival journals and journalists and then raising them to new heights.'[18] Strachan entertainingly demonstrates how Maga made a distinctive mark on contemporary appraisals of head-measuring 'science.'

At the same time, as Ian Duncan in 'Blackwood's and Romantic Nationalism' and Charles Snodgrass in 'Blackwood's Subversive Scottishness' highlight, throughout the first twenty years of its existence, *Blackwood's Edinburgh Magazine* consciously drew on Scottish Enlightenment traditions of philosophical discourse to construct a Scottish identity contained with larger political, social, and critical frameworks. Ian Duncan highlights how the tensions and conflicts of partisan politics, and particularly of Blackwood's Tory-inflected opposition to the Whig reformist tendencies of such journals as the *Edinburgh Review*, manifested themselves in the role the firm and its magazine played in the professionalization of literary production (and what recent critics have called 'literary authority'), and the canonization of the figure of the national author – in this case Walter Scott. Duncan uses in particular John Gibson Lockhart's *Peter's Letters to his Kinsfolk* as a case study to explore in more detail what distinguished the Blackwoodian reconstruction of national identity during the first thirty years of the nineteenth century. Charles Snodgrass complements Duncan by arguing that *Blackwood's* appropriation of a Scottish national identity during pre-Reform era years and its successful subsumation of such appropriations into wider cultural debates and national identities (in particular through the dialogues of the long-running series *Noctes Ambrosianae*) are central to understanding how the firm (through its publications) was able to succeed on a national and international scale where its competitors (such as Archibald Constable) could not.

Consolidating Reputations

Equally important to understanding the relevance and importance of Blackwood's to British literary culture are the editorial policies and publishing innovations the firm used to maintain its place as a dominant force in publishing. From its inception in 1817, *Blackwood's Edinburgh Magazine* was used as a showcase for new talent and as a method of attracting potential contributors to the firm's lists. A technique pioneered by William Blackwood I was the publication in book form of works first serialized in the magazine, predating Henry Colburn and Richard Bentley's use of such marketing strategies by several years. Works featured in this way included John Galt's *The Ayrshire Legatees* (1820–1) and Douglas M. Moir's *The Autobiography of Mansie Wauch* (1824–8).

As noted elsewhere (in my *House of Blackwood*), a key factor in the sustaining of the firm's fortunes throughout much of its history was the editorial self-image promoted by its directors. The House of Blackwood, as many of the essays in this collection point out, 'represented a specific social space as well, an invisible arena that accommodated shifting bands of contributors and authors who were encouraged to meet and mingle, imbibe a common 'culture', and share common, unspoken assumptions about their identities within this large, all-embracing Blackwoodian ecumene.'[19] Michael Michie in '"On behalf of the Right": Archibald Alison, Political Journalism, and *Blackwood's* Conservative Response to Reform, 1830–1870' explores one mid-century realization of this model in the political material published by the firm from the 1830s to the 1870s, both in the magazine and in the firm's book lists. Long serving and committed early key contributors and authors included George Croly and W.E. Aytoun, and later journalists such as Charles Mackay and military officers such as E.B. and William Hamley and G.R. Gleig. As the leading political contributor to Maga during this period, conservative commentator Archibald Alison played a key role in reinterpreting and shaping representations of the political causes of the period to fit within the conservative framework of the magazine and the firm's publications. A case study comparison of his work with other Maga contributors allows us, Michie notes, 'to determine to what extent Blackwood's conservatism remained in sympathy with the changing fortunes and profile of the Conservative party.'[20]

Whether or not the firm's conservative politics adhered to the publishing and editorial predilections of its founder, what is certain is that innovative patterns of textual production were continued by William's successors, and in particular by John Blackwood, whose tenure as editor of *Blackwood's Magazine* (from 1845 to 1879), and as head of the firm (from 1852 to 1879) was marked by a successful and rapid expansion of the firm's lists and interests. It is under John Blackwood that successful associations were made with authors such as Margaret Oliphant, Alexander Kinglake, Charles Reade, and George Eliot. But Blackwood's use of personal relations and appeals to a common house identity to negotiate access to valuable literary property was not always successful, particularly concerning those individuals more keenly attuned to the value and use of literary property to sustain literary careers.

The increasing professionalization of authorship from mid-century onwards and tensions in author–publisher relations created by battles over literary property played their part in the history of British publishing and the Blackwood firm. Throughout the nineteenth century, the firm continued to link serial publication rights in *Blackwood's Magazine* with subsequent hard cover publication options. In part this was due to the editors' unwillingness to seek 'names' for the sake of a literary coup – sensible prices for long-term prospects was part and parcel of their approach to commissioning work (in particular for the magazine). 'Experience of past years goes to show that no special article from some popular idol of the day or hour repays the extra premium that has to be paid,' one of them noted in a late memorandum on this issue.[21]

The Blackwood firm was not the only one to see the benefits of utilizing an eponymously named literary periodical to promote its works and earn intangible literary capital in the process. *Bentley's Miscellany* (founded in 1837), *Macmillan's Magazine* (founded in 1859), and *Longman's Magazine* (founded in 1882) were just some of the journals created like Blackwood's to keep their firm's names in front of the reading public. Reasons for so doing, as William Tinsley declared on finding his losses for *Tinsley's Magazine* (launched in 1867) running at around £25 a month, were quite plain: 'What cheaper advertisement can I have for twenty-five pounds a month? It advertises my name and publications; and it keeps my authors together.'[22]

Keeping one's 'authors together' was an important reason for maintaining the Blackwood firm's house identity and literary networks. The editors of *Blackwood's Magazine* offered a textual network deliberately shaped by editorial policy to produce maximum returns on authorial investments, while concerning themselves with holding aloft 'the twin banners of sound criticism and Tory politics.'[23] Paying for and managing such textual production, however, became a more complicated business as the century progressed. In particular, the role of the editor in shaping material for consumption by a multiplicity of readers became crucial to the success of such textual production. Robert L. Patten's and David Finkelstein's 'Editing *Blackwood's*; or, What Do Editors Do?' explores general nineteenth-century editorial practices and contextualizes the management of *Blackwood's Magazine* in an increasingly competitive literary marketplace. The role of anonymity, the use of serialization, and the configuration of magazine content to reflect perceived patterns of reading all contributed to complicating the role of the editor. As partial answer to the question posed in the title (What do editors do?), Patten and Finkelstein consider how the editor function at *Blackwood's* during the later decades of the century shifted towards the aesthetic of journal design, to considerations of the material function of the contents page, and towards reflecting in that design both the political and jour- nalistic significance of particular articles and the preference of the assumed reading public.

Similarly, Laurel Brake in 'Maga, the Shilling Monthlies, and the New Journalism' examines the impact on Blackwood editorial activity of new markets and formats (weeklies and illustrated journals), and the advent of new journalism and the 'star' author in the late nineteenth century. How did the firm meet the challenges and shifts in patterns of production, consumption, and journalistic activity exemplified by the arrival of cheap weekly rivals and a brighter, racier, more demotic new journalism? Part of the answer lies in the essays offered in the final section of this collection.

Preserving Status

Analysis of the firm's publishing archives suggests that by the turn of the twentieth century the financial fortunes of the Blackwood firm had begun to deteriorate, along with its reputation as a leader in the literary marketplace.[24] The financial downturn owed much to a devastating drop in income from the overextended marketing of George Eliot's texts in multiple formats, upon which the firm relied to a dangerous extent. The downturn in literary reputation reflected critical disdain of the highly profitable material the Blackwood firm began aligning itself with as part of its strategy to meet the challenges of the period. The material, in this case, covered critically unfashionable literary arenas such as colonial fiction, 'popular' novels, and best-selling new journal- ism narratives. As the essays in this section demonstrate, however, the authors championed by the firm during the first three decades of the twentieth century included uniquely talented individuals whose works in *Blackwood's Magazine* and the firm's lists ran counter to Orwell's assessment that 'If you were a patriot you read *Blackwood's Magazine* and publicly thanked God that you were "not brainy."'[25] Such a generalization overlooks an important aspect of the firm's production and the magazine's contents during this period: their reflection of the 'static, diffuse nature of contemporary Edwardian literary and cultural tastes.'[26]

Linda Dryden's 'At the Court of *Blackwood's*: In the Kampong of Hugh Clifford' focuses on the imperialist leaning tendencies of Blackwood's at the turn of the century, which created circumstances whereby the proto-modernist works of Joseph Conrad, such as *Heart of Darkness* and *Lord Jim*, were accepted and featured in *Blackwood's Magazine* as part of the imperial world portrayed by Blackwood stalwarts such as Sir Hugh Clifford and Sir Frank Swettenham. Hugh Clifford's career with Blackwood's, however, is worthy of evaluation for the manner in which his chronicles of life in the Malay Archipelago during the period of British governance in the province both reflected and contended with the British colonial experience. Why his work led both William Blackwood III and John Murray to consider Clifford 'to be in the first rank of practicing writers' is an issue raised for consideration here, with a view that perhaps now is the time for a re-evaluation of Clifford's career and work.

Likewise overlooked have been the firm's connections with 'New Journalist' George W. Steevens, whose dramatic journalistic narratives *With Kitchener to Khartum* and *Capetown to Ladysmith* were Blackwoodian best-sellers in 1899 and 1900 respectively. Steevens's contributions to *Blackwood's Magazine*, and the literary negotiations over his book publications, as Laurence Davies points out in '"A sideways ending to it all": G.W. Steevens, Blackwood, and the *Daily Mail*,' tell us a good deal about the house's literary and economic practices in the 1890s. Davies convincingly makes the case that Steevens's best-selling works and periodical contributions should be reassessed for their role in shifting and shaping the direction of English prose at the opening of the twentieth century.

In contrast, but with similar rehabilitation in mind, Stephen Donovan's 'The Muse of *Blackwood's*: Charles Whibley and Literary Criticism in the World' makes a case for restoring the reputation of ultraconservative literary critic Charles Whibley, whose contributions to *Blackwood's Magazine* between 1895 and 1930 T.S. Eliot ranked as 'the best journalism,' a bulwark of journalistic standards, as Donovan notes, which, Eliot asserted, had been in sharp decline since the epochal rise of the New Journalism thirty years previously. Whibley's monthly 'Musings Without Method,' which closed each issue of the journal for over thirty years, documents the part Whibley played in defining the cultural and political 'public face' of Maga during a period of tremendous social change.

Conclusion

This collection makes the case for rethinking and repositioning Blackwood's place in nineteenth- and early-twentieth-century literary and print culture. Inevitably, all the essays in this collection return to the firm's magazine as a central definer of 'Blackwoodian' values throughout the first century of its existence, as well as to the place of the Blackwood firm as an important conveyer of cultural signifiers reflecting, refracting and shaping discourse in various cultural arenas – literary, journalistic, political, critical – in the nineteenth and early twentieth century. The results confirm what Joseph Conrad told his literary agent J.B. Pinker when recalling his connection with the firm's flagship journal: 'One was in decent company there and had a good sort of public.'[27]

NOTES

1 M.O.W. Oliphant, *Annals of a Publishing House: William Blackwood and Sons*, vol. 1 (Edinburgh: William Blackwood and Sons, 1897), 25.
2 See William Blackburn, ed., *Joseph Conrad: Letters to William Blackwood and David S. Meldrum* (Durham, N.C.: Duke University Press, 1958); Alan Lang Strout, *A Bibliography of Articles in Blackwood's Magazine, 1817–1825* (Lubbock: Texas Technological College, 1959).
3 Some recent examples of Blackwood-focused work include J. Lasley Dameron, Pamela Palmer, and Kenneth J. Curry, compilers, *An Index to the Critical Vocabulary of Blackwood's Edinburgh Magazine 1830–1840* (West Cornwall, Conn.: Locust Hill, 1993); David Finkelstein, *The House of Blackwood: Author–Publisher Relations in the Victorian Era* (University Park: Pennsylvania State University Press, 2002); Donald Gray, 'George Eliot and Her Publishers,' in George Levine, ed., *The Cambridge Companion to George Eliot* (Cambridge: Cambridge University Press, 2001), 181–201; Carol A. Martin, *George Eliot's Serial Fiction* (Columbus: Ohio State University Press, 1994); Robert Morrison, '"Abuse Wickedness, but Acknowledge Wit": *Blackwood's Magazine* and the Shelley Circle,' *Victorian Periodicals Review* 34, no. 2 (Summer 2001), 147–64; Mark Parker, *Literary Magazines and British Romanticism* (Cambridge: Cambridge University Press, 2000); Charles Snodgrass,

'Advancing a Jacobite Patina: Hogg's Relics in Blackwood's House,'
Studies in Hogg and His World 10 (1999), 27–39; D.J. Trela, ed., *Margaret
Oliphant: Critical Essays on a Gentle Subversive* (Selinsgrove, Pa.:
Susquehanna University Press, 1995). For a full online bibliographic listing
of other Blackwood-related publications, see the *Blackwood's Magazine*
webpage at: http://mcs.qmuc.ac.uk/Blackwoods/blackbib.html.

4 Notable examples include: Laurel Brake and Julie Codell, eds., *Encounters
in the Victorian Press: Editors, Authors and Readers* (Basingstoke: Palgrave
Macmillan, 2005); Laurel Brake, *Print in Transition, 1850–1910: Studies in
Media and Book History* (Basingstoke: Palgrave, 2001); Laurel Brake, Bill Bell,
and David Finkelstein, eds., *Nineteenth-Century Media and the Construction
of Identities* (Basingstoke: Palgrave, 2000); Geoffrey Cantor, Gowan Dawson,
et al., eds., *Science in the Nineteenth-Century Periodical: Reading the Magazine
of Nature* (Cambridge: Cambridge University Press, 2004); Massimiliano
Demata and Duncan Wu, eds., *British Romanticism and the Edinburgh Review: Bicentenary Essays* (Basingstoke: Palgrave Macmillan, 2002); Marysa
DeMoor, *Their Fair Share: Women, Power and Criticism in the Athenaeum, from
Millicent Garrett Fawcett to Katherine Mansfield, 1870–1920* (Aldershot,
Hants.: Ashgate, 2000); David Finkelstein and Douglas M. Peers, eds.,
Negotiating India in the Nineteenth-Century Media (Basingstoke: Macmillan,
2000); Kate Jackson, *George Newnes and the New Journalism in Britain, 1880–
1910: Culture and Profit* (Aldershot, Hants: Ashgate, 2001); Graham Law,
Serializing Fiction in the Victorian Press (Basingstoke: Palgrave, 2000);
Barbara Onslow, *Women of the Press in Nineteenth-Century Britain*
(Basingstoke: Macmillan, 2000); Parker, *Literary Magazines and British
Romanticism*; and Kim Wheatley, ed., *Romantic Periodicals and Print Culture*
(London: Cass, 2003).

5 Laurel Brake and Julie F. Codell, 'Introduction,' in *Encounters in the Victorian
Press*, ed. Brake and Codell (Basingstoke: Palgrave Macmillan, 2005), 3.

6 Robert L. Patten and David Finkelstein, 'Editing *Blackwood's*; or, What Do
Editors Do?' below, 151.

7 Joel H. Wiener, ed., *Innovators and Preachers: The Role of the Editor in Victorian England*, Contributions to the Study of Mass Media and Communications 5 (Westport, Conn.: Greenwood, 1985), xvi–xvii.

8 See Leslie A. Marchand, *The Athenaeum: A Mirror of Victorian Culture*
(Chapel Hill: University of North Carolina Press, 1941); Jon Klancher, *The
Making of English Reading Audiences, 1790–1832* (Madison: University of
Wisconsin Press, 1987); and Lee Erickson, *The Economy of Literary Form:
English Literature and the Industrialization of Publishing, 1800–1850* (Balti-
more, Md.: Johns Hopkins University Press, 1996).

9 Lee Erickson, *The Economy of Literary Form: English Literature and the Indus-trialization of Publishing, 1800–1850* (Baltimore, MD: Johns Hopkins University Press, 1996), 6.

10 Joanne Shattock, *Politics and Reviewers: The 'Edinburgh' and the 'Quarterly' in the Early Victorian Age* (Leicester: Leicester University Press, 1989), 4.

11 Derek Roper, *Reviewing before the 'Edinburgh,' 1788–1802* (London: Methuen, 1978), 36–7.

12 Shattock, *Politics and Reviewers*, 4.

13 *Edinburgh Review*, 1 October 1802, n.p.

14 Katie Trumpener, *Bardic Nationalism: The Romantic Novel and the British Empire* (Princeton, N.J.: Princeton University Press, 1997), 16; see also Peter Womack, *Improvement and Romance: Constructing the Myth of the Highlands* (Basingstoke: Macmillan, 1989).

15 Fuller details of the magazine's production and its relationship to speedier printing and copy-writing appear in Patrick Leary, '*Fraser's Magazine* and the Literary Life, 1830–1847,' *Victorian Periodicals Review* 27, no. 2 (Summer 1994), 105–26.

16 Mark Pattison, *Fortnightly Review* 22 (1877), 663.

17 John Strachan, '"The mapp'd out skulls of Scotia": *Blackwood's* and the Scottish Phrenological Controversy,' below, 50.

18 See below, 64.

19 Finkelstein, *The House of Blackwood*, 17–18.

20 Michael Michie '"On behalf of the right": Archibald Alison, Political Journalism, and *Blackwood's* Conservative Response to Reform,' below, p. 119.

21 Undated memorandum, MS 30071, Blackwood Papers, National Library of Scotland.

22 Quoted in Barbara Quinn Schmidt, 'Novelists, Publishers, and Fiction in Middle-Class Magazines: 1860–1880,' *Victorian Periodicals Review* 17, no. 4 (Winter 1984), 143.

23 Charles Whibley, 'A Retrospect,' *Blackwood's Magazine* 201 (April 1917), 433.

24 See Finkelstein, *The House of Blackwood*, appendix 1, 159–66.

25 George Orwell, *The Lion and the Unicorn* (Harmondsworth: Penguin, 1982), 64–5.

26 David Finkelstein, 'Literature, Propaganda and the First World War: The Case of *Blackwood's Magazine*,' in *Grub Street and the Ivory Tower: Literary Journalism and Literary Scholarship from Fielding to the Internet*, ed. Jeremy Treglown and Bridget Bennet (Oxford: Oxford University Press, 1998), 93.

27 Frederick R. Karl and Laurence Davies, eds., *The Collected Letters of Joseph Conrad*, volume 4, *1908–1911* (Cambridge: Cambridge University Press, 1990), 130.

SCOTTISH BEGINNINGS

William Blackwood and the Dynamics of Success

ROBERT MORRISON

'This active, energetic, and in every way remarkable man ... has never been properly understood nor appreciated, either abroad or at home, owing to circumstances the public are unacquainted with.'[1] So wrote John Neal of William Blackwood I in 1865, and Blackwood has remained a shadowy and undervalued figure, despite his enormous impact on his age, and the outstanding longevity and international success of the publishing house he founded. Blackwood rose from humble beginnings to become the publisher of some of the most famous writers of the day, and to found and edit the most influential and exciting magazine of the age. He was at the heart of a great network of authors, readers, critics, and competitors, and the texts in his magazine were produced through a flurry of contending demands, requests, and opportunities. His magazine is notorious for its aggressive and narrow Toryism, but Blackwood sought always to balance consistency against variety, and his magazine is equally remarkable for its satire, innovation, and irreverence, its groundbreaking treatment of fiction, and its penetrating reviews of contemporary poetry. The popular *Noctes Ambrosianae* series is one of the crowning achievements of Blackwood's editorship, and fully encapsulates the range, insight, inconsistency, and energy of the magazine during his seventeen years as editor.

William Blackwood I was born in Edinburgh on 20 November 1776, the middle son in a family of silk mercers. There is no record of his education or schools, but at fourteen he entered into a six-year apprenticeship with the Edinburgh booksellers Bell and Bradfute. He gained further training as the manager of the Glasgow branch of the Edinburgh publishers Mundell and Company, and as a partner with the Edinburgh bookseller and auctioneer Robert Ross. Blackwood then worked in

London for two years in the employ of the antiquarian bookseller Cuthill, but in 1804 he returned to Edinburgh and established a shop at 64 South Bridge, where he specialized in the sale of rare books and began to experiment in publishing. His edition of James Grahame's *The Sabbath* (1805) was followed by an eclectic series of titles, including John Boyd Greenshields's *Home. A Poem* (1806), Arthur Edmondston's *A Treatise on the Varieties and Consequences of Ophthalmia* (1806), a reprint of John Holden's *An Essay Towards a Rational System of Music* (1807), Grahame's *The Seige of Copenhagan* (1808), and Hector MacNeill's *Town Fashions, or Modern Manners Delineated, a Satirical Dialogue* (1810). Blackwood's breakthrough came in 1811 when he published Thomas McCrie's celebrated biography of John Knox, commenced publication of Robert Kerr's eighteen-volume *General History and Collection of Voyages and Travels*, and became the Edinburgh agent for John Murray's eminent London publishing firm, a connection which brought him into close contact with the English book trade, and linked his name to authors such as Jane Austen, Lord Byron, George Crabbe, and Robert Southey. Blackwood's relationship with Murray reached its highest point in 1816 when they co-published Walter Scott's *Tales of my Landlord*, which contained the novels *The Black Dwarf* and *Old Mortality*. In April 1817 Blackwood founded the *Edinburgh Monthly Magazine*, reconstituted six months later as *Blackwood's Edinburgh Magazine*, and with the help of writers such as John Wilson, John Gibson Lockhart, James Hogg, Thomas De Quincey, and William Maginn, he soon turned it into one of the most controversial and highly marketable publications of the day. In the 1820s Blackwood consolidated his place as one of the leaders of British publishing, while his magazine's unrepentant blend of slander, buffoonery, sensationalism, erudition, and truculent High Toryism continued to attract important writers and ever-widening circles of readers. 'Your Magazine is everywhere,' Samuel Taylor Coleridge told Blackwood in 1832.[2] The Scottish travel writer John MacGregor announced that *Blackwood's Magazine* was readily available in the newsrooms of Quebec, while David Macbeth Moir recorded that Blackwood's publication of Samuel Warren's *Passages from the Diary of a Late Physician* 'was truly a hit' and extended Warren's reputation 'not only through France and Germany, but, as a lady from Moscow informed me, to the most northern extremities of Europe.'[3] From modest beginnings, Blackwood built his publishing firm into a dynamic and highly successful business with an international reach and reputation.

Blackwood was a frank, energetic, shrewd, and strong-willed man who placed himself at the centre of his business and fashioned it in his own image. 'He is a nimble active-looking man of middle age,' Lockhart observed in 1819, 'and moves about from one corner to another with great alacrity, and apparently under the influence of high animal spirits. His complexion is very sanguineous, but nothing can be more intelligent, keen, and sagacious, than the expression of the whole physiognomy.'[4] In 1825, John Neal found Blackwood 'a short, "stubbed" man, of about five feet six, I should say, with a plain, straightforward business air, – like that of a substantial tradesman, – with a look of uncommon though quiet shrewdness. You could see at a glance that he was a man to be trusted, – frank and fearless, without being either boastful or aggressive.'[5] Blackwood's great energy is evident in his correspondence to contributors and other people concerned with his publishing house, for it totals nearly four thousand pages in ten letter-books, and to this mass of outgoing mail must be added the task of reading the letters coming into the firm.[6] Blackwood was a proud man. His third son William recollected well the day he and his father went into a circulating library on the Isle of Wight, and a lady entered asking for Susan Ferrier's novel *Inheritance*, which Blackwood had published. 'His countenance lightened up in a moment,' William recalled, 'and the sparkle of the eye with which he looked at ... me [is] all as vividly before me as though the event had happened but yesterday.'[7] Blackwood was an emotional but decisive man, happy to the point of glee when things were going his way but quick to act when the tide turned against him, 'morbidly sensible on the subject of the magazine'[8] but bellicose in its defence. George Combe relates how *Blackwood's* 'vile attack' on a Glasgow writer named John Douglas brought Douglas himself to Edinburgh, where he 'bought a great horsewhip, went to seek Blackwood at his shop, met him in Princes Street by chance, and gave him a sound horsewhipping.' Characteristically, Blackwood fought fire with fire. That same day 'at four,' Combe continues, '[Blackwood] appeared armed with a great stick, supported by John Wilson, James Wilson (John's brother), and Hogg the Ettrick Shepherd and poet, at his back, and he commenced an attack on Douglas. Douglas still had the whip and defended himself with it till he got into the coach, and there the row terminated for the time.'[9] Details of the incident soon spread. Thomas Carlyle spoke amusingly of 'the flagellations of Bill Blackwood & the as paltry antagonist of Bill Blackwood,' and three years later John Scott referred to 'our Scotch friends' and 'the pleasures of caning and being caned, – or cudgelling, and being cudgelled.' Neal concluded that Blackwood had 'a big heart, and ... interwoven steel springs.'[10]

As a publisher of books, Blackwood had a great deal of faith in his own judgment, and he gave it candidly. Famously, he let it be known that he thought Scott should revise the conclusion of *The Black Dwarf* and went so far as to outline what seemed to him a stronger resolution of the plot. Scott's tart reply – 'My respects to the Booksellers & I belong to the Death-head Hussars of literature who neither *take* nor *give* criticism'[11] – is the low point in a relationship that was never very amicable, though Blackwood was again to serve as Scott's publisher for the *Letters of Malachi Malagrowther*. In 1820, John Galt submitted the manuscript of *The Annals of the Parish* to Blackwood, who liked it very much but feared 'there will be some parts which would require a gentle pruning.' Galt consented and later admitted that he was 'much satisfied with the omissions.'[12] When, however, Galt was working on *The Last of the Lairds*, he and Blackwood exchanged an increasingly angry series of letters, as Blackwood worried about charges of vulgarity and came to insist on substantial changes. Galt accused him of 'interference,'[13] but Blackwood felt he knew what the reading public wanted, and 'the Laird must not only be a good book, it must be a first sale one.'[14] Galt again capitulated, and the manuscript was turned over to Blackwood's friend and advisor David Macbeth Moir, who thoroughly recast and sanitized it before Blackwood published the book in 1826.[15] Four years later, when William Godwin wrote to ask if Blackwood might be interested in publishing his *Thoughts on Man*, Blackwood by rule asked to see the manuscript. 'I know that I take a great liberty in making this last request,' he explained to Godwin, 'but little qualified as I may be to judge of such a work as your's [sic], still it would be a satisfaction to be able to form some opinion for myself.' Not surprisingly, Blackwood's opinion was that Godwin's work 'might unsettle the minds of some of it's [sic] readers on matters which I believe to be important,' and the manuscript was rejected.[16] When Blackwood received De Quincey's manuscript of his gothic romance *Klosterheim*, he sent it to Moir, who found it failed 'to come up to my imaginary standard.'[17] But Blackwood himself was impressed and decided to publish *Klosterheim*, though he asked De Quincey to lengthen it, a request De Quincey duly obliged.[18] In 1813, when Lord Byron had only recently become famous with the publication of *Childe Harold's Pilgrimage*, he wryly described how Blackwood had sent Murray 'an order for books, poesy, and cookery, with this agreeable postscript – "The *Harold* and *Cookery* are much wanted."'[19] Blackwood's judgment was much more penetrating than such an anecdote suggests. 'I would trust his opinion of a book sooner than that of any man I know,' John Wilson declared. 'If his opinion had been against my own, and it had been my own book, I should believe he was in the right and give up my own judgment. He was a patron of literature and it owes him much.'[20] Blackwood relied extensively on his own opinion to choose and shape the books he published, and under his direction the firm issued volumes by Scott, Lockhart, Hogg, Galt, De Quincey, Susan Ferrier, and Felicia Hemans.

Blackwood ran his magazine with the same determination and incisiveness that governed his management of book publishing. He undoubtedly recognized that the magazine format itself, which had remained essentially unaltered since Edward Cave introduced his *Gentleman's Magazine* in 1731, was ripe for change, and he seems clearly to have realized the untapped potential of Edinburgh's rich literary, political, and cultural traditions. But more directly, Blackwood founded his magazine as part of his ongoing battle with Archibald Constable, his senior by only two years, a fellow Scot, a Whig, and the high-profile publisher of the *Edinburgh Review*, the *Encyclopedia Britannica*, and most of Scott's novels. The relationship between the two men seems to have soured as early as 1801, when Blackwood left his partnership with Robert Ross, and Constable was slow to pay a debt.[21] Blackwood launched his own publishing business only a few years later, and Constable's prominence and politics made him an obvious rival. When in 1816 Blackwood was able to wrest Scott from Constable's clutches by becoming the publisher of *The Black Dwarf*, he could not hide his elation: 'I have been occupied with this for years,' Blackwood told Murray, 'and I hope have now accomplished what will be of immense service to us.'[22] Subsequent negotiations with Scott, however, did not go as smoothly as Blackwood had hoped, and Constable was able to win Scott back, much to Blackwood's irritation. During these same months Blackwood founded his *Edinburgh Monthly Magazine*, with James Cleghorn and Thomas Pringle as editors, and when they both proved listless liberals, he quickly had them removed, whereupon both went over to Constable's side and worked for him on his *Scots Magazine*. Enough was enough. Blackwood had grown tired of running second to Constable – in both book and periodical publication – and he determined on scathing and scandalous reprisal. 'The Chaldee Manuscript,' written by Wilson, Lockhart, and Hogg, was published by Blackwood in the first number of his new

magazine, and was an immediate *succès de scandale*. 'It relates,' reported
Carlyle, 'in an emblematical manner, the rise, progress, decline & fall of
the late Edin*r* magazine. Constable & the Editors as well as most of the
Edin*r* Authors are bitterly lampooned.'[23] Like many other Edinburgh
Whigs, Constable was apoplectic, but Blackwood wanted to move into
the first rank, and he had clearly decided that the best way to drive
Constable from the field was an open declaration of hostilities. 'Behold I
will call mighty creatures which will comfort thee,' the veiled editor
tells Blackwood in 'The Chaldee Manuscript,' 'and destroy the power of
thy adversary.'[24] The 'history' of *Blackwood's Magazine*, wrote Lockhart
in 1819, 'may be considered ... as the struggle ... of two rival booksellers, striving for their respective shares in the profits of periodical
publications.'[25]

   Blackwood's magazine aimed itself squarely at the authority and
prestige of the *Edinburgh Review*, a publication that had shown him
the immense possibilities of periodical literature. On the one hand,
Blackwood's very deliberately appropriated the *Edinburgh's* arrogance,
selectivity, vitriol, intelligence, and locality, and plainly modelled itself
on central features of the *Edinburgh's* success. Strikingly, the *Edinburgh*
commenced its career in October 1802 by inventing and then assaulting
the Lake School of William Wordsworth, Samuel Taylor Coleridge, and
Robert Southey. *Blackwood's* commenced its career exactly fifteen years
later, in October 1817, by similarly inventing and then damning the
Cockney School of Leigh Hunt, John Keats, and William Hazlitt, for
Blackwood had easily discerned the cultural and economic capital to be
derived from this kind of emulation and commodification. Yet on the
other hand, Blackwood found Constable's profits and whiggery equally
abhorrent and, as J.H. Alexander argues, 'countless references in the
early volumes of *Blackwood's* make it clear that the young magazine
sought to define itself principally in opposition' to the *Edinburgh*.[26] Two
of the key figures in *Blackwood's* campaign were the *Edinburgh's* editor
Francis Jeffrey, whom the *Blackwood's* critics delighted to call the 'Small
Known' (beside the 'Great Unknown,' Walter Scott), and Wordsworth,
the poet Jeffrey castigated and *Blackwood's* repeatedly celebrated. Jeffrey's
'"failure" to appreciate Wordsworth's genius,' observes David Higgins,
'was used as a prime example of his own weakness as a critic, the
inadequacies of the *Edinburgh Review*, and the lamentable ignorance
and partisanship of Edinburgh Whigs.'[27] Blackwood's battle with Constable continued until 1825, when the great financial collapse brought
about Constable's bankruptcy. *Blackwood's* endorsement of Wordsworth

was a forceful and representative way of both formulating its opposition to the *Edinburgh*, and championing its own critical methodology and political affiliations.

The editorship of *Blackwood's Magazine* has been much discussed. Critics still routinely credit the position to John Wilson, or observe that 'the evidence is sketchy, but it tends to support the idea of a trusted individual (like Lock[hart] or Wilson) taking the role of editor but accepting the interventions of the publisher rather freely.'[28] Blackwood's role was far more fundamental and significant. Lockhart and Wilson were crucial partners in the *Blackwood's* project, particularly during its first three years. Lockhart sometimes behaved as though he himself were in charge, as when he sent a letter to Coleridge representing himself as 'The Editor of Blackwood's Magazine.'[29] Wilson too often cast himself in the position of editor, recruiting friends like De Quincey to write for the magazine[30] and gradually assuming the role of 'Christopher North,' the fictive editor of *Blackwood's*. Indeed, Wilson was widely regarded as primarily responsible for the magazine's distinctive tone and identity. 'Wilson is so first rate a fellow that you ought never think for a moment of letting him slip out of your fingers,' Maginn instructed Blackwood. 'He is the greatest attraction a Magazine can have, and is worth the whole of us.'[31] Moir acknowledged that 'however good Maga may in general be, there is a lack of her peculiar and distinguishing excellencies when [Wilson's] pen is not within her.'[32] Blackwood himself described Wilson as 'the Genius and the Living Spirit which has animated the work.'[33]

Yet despite his debts to Lockhart and Wilson, the great bulk of the evidence strongly suggests that Blackwood was his own editor, and as he shaped and chose the books he published, so too he was centrally responsible for making *Blackwood's* the most controversial and influential magazine of the age. Alan Lang Strout asserts that from 1818 until 1820 Lockhart and Wilson might be seen as 'literary editors,' but that Blackwood himself always retained 'veto power.'[34] Certainly by 1820 he was firmly seated in the editor's chair, for when Charles Lloyd sent a submission to Wilson, Blackwood swiftly wrote back that 'much as I respect the Professor's opinion, I do not on many accounts wish to trouble him or any one but I wish always myself to be the medium of communication.'[35] In 1826 Blackwood told his main political commentator David Robinson, 'I am the Manager of the Magazine myself.'[36] When asked by a friend in 1828, Wilson asserted that he was 'not editor,' and wrote to Blackwood that to claim otherwise 'would be taking credit to myself for what I do not deserve, and defrauding you of the merit of capacity and spirit in the conduct thereof.' 'You are your own Editor,' he stated flatly, '& a good one.'[37] In the August 1830 number of the magazine Blackwood is toasted as a man who unites 'in himself two – shall I say – three characters – such as were never before united in one man – PROPRIETOR – PUBLISHER – shall I add ... EDITOR of BLACKWOOD'S MAGAZINE!'[38] Blackwood told Coleridge that the magazine was 'my darling child, to which my whole heart and soul are devoted.'[39] In 1850 De Quincey described Wilson as the magazine's 'intellectual Atlas,' but 'he was not the editor of that journal at any time. The late Mr Blackwood, a sagacious and energetic man, was his own editor.'[40] Wilson's oldest friend Alexander Blair knew that Wilson 'had no part in *governing* the publication.'[41] David Masson declared that 'Wilson's connection with the magazine' became so close that he was 'by universal repute regarded as the editor,' but 'Blackwood himself always retained the ultimate right in the management.'[42] By 1897, George Douglas found it 'necessary to caution the reader against the oft-repeated error that Wilson was at any time editor of the Magazine.'[43] Wilson was an indispensable ally and a powerful source of ideas, but Blackwood himself was primarily responsible for giving the magazine its 'capacity and spirit.' *Blackwood's Magazine* was Blackwood's magazine.

Part of the reason Blackwood's role has been so frequently overlooked is his own wilful obfuscation of it. 'The Chaldee Manuscript' features Blackwood as 'the man whose name is as ebony', and another mysterious 'man clothed in dark garments' who acts as the veiled editor.[44] In *Peter's Letters to his Kinsfolk*, Lockhart writes that 'it is not known who the editor is ... but my friend Wastle tells me that he is an obscure man, almost continually confined to his apartment by rheumatism.'[45] In September 1819 *Blackwood's Magazine* announced – spuriously, of course – that William Blackwood was soon to publish *The Autobiography of Christopher North, Esq. Editor of Blackwood's Edinburgh Magazine*, and when the *Noctes Ambrosianae* series began in 1822 Christopher North appeared as *Blackwood's* fictive editor. All this smoke and misinformation was deliberate: as Hazlitt put it, 'Seeing is believing, it is said'; but when it comes to *Blackwood's*, 'Lying is believing, say I.'[46] Blackwood naturally found the fiction of Christopher North convenient and highly serviceable, for it enabled him to deflect scandal and the rebukes of disgruntled contributors while at the same time maintaining tight editorial control over the direction and contents of his magazine.

'The Editor took his own way and I cannot interfere with him,' he complained typically (and disingenuously) to Walter Scott.[47] Part of Blackwood's strategy was to keep the uninitiated at a good distance from his magazine: 'I knowing as I do Forbes's history and connections, I do not feel comfortable at the idea of his entering as it were into the very Sanctum of Maga.'[48] Blackwood also ensured that production was shrouded in secrecy: 'The getting up of Maga is at best a mystery to all,' Moir assured him in 1832, 'and any thing tending to increase it can only operate in doubling the wonderment.'[49] Blackwood, declared Neal, exercised 'despotic power, in all that concerned the management' of his magazine, but he was 'careful to keep out of sight himself,' and to 'thrust' Christopher North 'forward, upon all occasions.'[50] Such an arrangement brought Blackwood security, flexibility, and hidden but pervasive editorial control, though it has very often meant that credit for *Blackwood's* enormous success has gone to others when it belongs to him.

The task of both publishing and editing a monthly magazine was a daunting one, and successfully combining the two roles required enormous energy, insight, and business savvy. The other leading periodical publications of the day divided the position. Constable published the *Edinburgh Review*, but left the editing to Jeffrey. Murray published the *Quarterly*, but it was edited by William Gifford. The *New Monthly Magazine* was published by Henry Colburn but he hired Thomas Campbell and Cyrus Redding to do the editing. Robert Baldwin published the *London Magazine* but John Scott was his editor. *Fraser's Magazine* was published by James Fraser but edited by William Maginn. 'You and I are not editors, but publishers,' Murray insisted to Blackwood in 1818, but Blackwood's ambitions and abilities extended well beyond Murray's.[51] By way of comparison, John Taylor was for a time co-owner and editor of the *London Magazine*, and while De Quincey declared that 'a literary *Pleiad* might have been gathered out of the stars connected with this journal,'[52] Taylor's pride, reserve, and indecision drove contributors away and badly damaged sales. After only a year of Taylor's editorship, Charles Lamb felt the momentum slipping away: 'The Lond. Mag. wants the personal note too much,' he declared. 'Blackw^d owes everything to it.'[53] In another year Lamb found himself lingering among the *London's* 'creaking rafters, like the last rat.'[54] Within four years Taylor had abandoned ship and sold his interest. Most of Blackwood's major competitors divided the roles of publisher and editor, while Taylor soon found himself unequal to the task of doing both. But

Blackwood embraced the dual role, and the magazine went from strength to strength under his leadership.

In his capacity as publisher and editor, Blackwood placed himself at the centre of a vast nexus of cultural, social, legal, economic, political, and interpersonal forces, and a study of his publications and correspondence reveals the highly collaborative and heavily mediated conditions of cultural production. The texts in *Blackwood's Magazine* were forged amidst the diverse and often contradictory demands of authors, co-authors, fellow contributors, critics, printers, lawyers, readers, and rival publications, and each month the contending discourses of these various groups impinged on Blackwood in specific and unpredictable ways, structuring, disrupting, and refining the texts that appeared in his magazine. Contributors asked for personal favours. 'Barry Cornwall is about to publish,' George Croly informed Blackwood. 'May I beg of you, if you are not inclined to praise him – not to notice him at all.'[55] They pushed hard for the inclusion of their own articles: 'If ever there was any of my things,' Moir insisted to Blackwood, 'which from any species of intrinsic merit seemed to me to have a shadow of *right* to be inserted it was that poem.'[56] They lobbied for reviews of their own work: when Alaric Watts published his *Literary Souvenir* he wrote pointedly to Blackwood that he would 'be much disappointed if I do not see some notice of it in your next Magazine.'[57] Blackwood had often to balance competing allegiances. 'The attack upon that driveller [William] Roscoe, is most just and capitally done,' Blackwood reported to Maginn, 'but for two reasons I would leave it to yourself to say if it would be prudent for me to publish it. In the first place, he is a very old friend of the Professor's [Wilson's] ... in the second place such an article would absolutely horrify my poor friend Cadell.'[58] Blackwood was the recipient of a great deal of advice: some of it sought, much of it unsolicited; some of it heeded, much of it ignored. Typically, the faults of *Blackwood's*, declared Maginn, 'are 1st Too much locality of allusion ... 2dly Occasional coarseness which annoys the Englishmen. 3dly The attempts of minor correspondents to imitate the audacious puffery of the Magazine, which can be done by W[ilson] only.'[59] Famously, Coleridge urged Blackwood to think of his magazine's 'characteristic plan and purposes; which may, I think, be comprised in three terms, as a Philosophical, Philological, and Aesthetic Miscellany.'[60] Blackwood had constantly to worry about libel suits. Theodore Besterman calculates that Blackwood's legal expenses for the whole period of his proprietorship 'cannot have been far below £3000.'[61] Sometimes Blackwood was encouraged to attack: a violent assault on the *Edinburgh* is needed, Wilson writes, 'because it would attract notice & excite anger,' and because 'there are no attacks in the magazine' of this month.[62] But on other occasions Blackwood was told to retreat. 'The John Bull magazine is going on,' Maginn asserted. 'Why are you fighting with it?'[63] Sometimes Blackwood was inclined to take the chance on legal action: 'Your cutting up of Kean is very savage, and in some parts I would almost think libelous,' he tells Maginn; 'however we shall see.'[64] But on other occasions he made it plain that he had had enough of lawsuits: 'Nothing would delight the Whigs ... so much as getting me into the jury court again,' he objected to Maginn in 1825. '... I would really beg of you to weigh consequences when you are cutting left and right.'[65] In 'The Chaldee Manuscript' Blackwood is surrounded by counselors, and 'behold, when they began to speak, they were too many, neither could the man know what was the meaning of their counsel, for they spake together, and the voice of their speaking was mingled.'[66] Fifteen years later Blackwood remarked, 'What a difficult task I have in managing the various and powerful minds who are at work for Maga.'[67] In Blackwood's magazine, texts made their way to publication through a complex matrix of enthusiasm, recrimination, alliance, litigation, and opportunism, and Blackwood's monthly task was to mediate and exploit these forces in the production of a magazine that delivered propaganda, pleasure, and profit.

Blackwood created his magazine with two primary – and rival – objectives in view: the desire for unity and the demand for variety. On the one hand, Blackwood felt a strong pull toward category, generality, and a clear meta-narrative of tradition, stability, loyalty, reverence, continuity, and the apodictic truths of Toryism. Yet on the other hand, he knew he could not expect readers to buy a new issue of the magazine if it simply reiterated what it had already said many times before. He required novelty and innovation, for his product had to be at once familiar and unusual, recognizable and unexpected, consistent and contradictory. Politics thus warred with economics, for Blackwood's deep-seated need to promulgate Tory dogma was frequently confounded by his intense desire to produce an exciting and highly marketable magazine that challenged and surprised its core audience, and that colonized and attracted new readers and contributors. Blackwood's tight embrace of both sides of this equation produced a magazine of bewildering and often stark inconsistencies. Irene Mannion remarks that '*Blackwood's* shows, as in a double-headed mirror, the traditional community of taste giving way to the modern community of ideas, the old respect for character and information vying with the modern urge to colonize Opinion.'[68] The magazine was omniscient in tone but heterogeneous in substance, mixing authority and elitism with frankness and audacity. It mobilized coruscating wit and invasive irony, but called repeatedly for stability and submission. Moir concisely summarized the situation: 'no other existing periodical has like Maga a character so various, and yet so indisputably its own.'[69] More recently, Jon Klancher explores how in *Blackwood's* 'a powerful transauthorial discourse echoes through its protean collocation of styles, topics, and voices.'[70]

Blackwood imposed unity on his magazine in a number of different ways. He relied extensively on a small number of highly productive authors. During his seventeen-year tenure, six writers – Wilson, Lockhart, Maginn, Moir, David Robinson, and Archibald Alison – wrote 42 per cent of the magazine, and of this figure Wilson and Lockhart wrote a staggering 29 per cent.[71] *Blackwood's* also introduced a series of well-liked and highly recognizable fictive characters, many of whom were represented as contributors to the magazine, including 'Christopher North,' 'The Ettrick Shepherd,' 'Morgan Odoherty,' 'Timothy Tickler,' and 'Mordecai Mullion.' Blackwood featured several different long-running serials, including Lockhart's and Wilson's 'The Cockney School of Poetry' (eight instalments), Hogg's 'The Shepherd's Calendar' (thirteen instalments), Allan Cunningham's *Recollections* (twelve instalments), Galt's *The Ayrshire Legatees* (eight instalments), Moir's *The Autobiography of Mansie Wauch* (twelve instalments), Caroline Bowles Southey's *Chapters on Churchyards* (eighteen instalments), Michael Scott's *Tom Cringle's Log* (twenty-three instalments), and Samuel Warren's *Passages from the Diary of a Late Physician* (eighteen instalments). Energy pervades *Blackwood's*, an 'intense and fervent spirit that breathes through all its pages,' as the *Athenaeum* put it in 1828.[72] There is a strong sense of collaboration and camaraderie. Blackwood's writers endorse and promote one another. They reappear to the same themes, images, events, characters, and ideas. Patterns emerge, messages are reinforced, connections multiply and recur. In 1879, Alexander Shand observed that the 'strength' of Blackwood's magazine was 'very much in the close union of its supporters. The directing mind was bound to the working brains by the ties of personal intimacy and friendship.'[73]

These unifying factors were of course underwritten and consolidated by Blackwood's belligerent Toryism, which surged through the magazine from the scabrous Cockney School attacks to the near hysterical condemnations of the Reform Bill, and shaped articles from across the range of the magazine. *Blackwood's* exalted the constitution, the monarchy, and the Church and bellicosely opposed Catholics, democracy, free trade, reform, and the abolition of the slave trade. When the Tory party itself began to deviate from this line in the late 1820s, and the Duke of Wellington and Robert Peel went so far as to pass Catholic Emancipation in 1829, *Blackwood's* attacked with a malice that sometimes outdid the vitriol it had previously meted out to the Whigs. Typically, De Quincey labelled the hero of Waterloo an 'old withered pantaloon,' and Maginn urged Tories to 'come spit upon *Peel*.'[74] David Robinson was Blackwood's chief political writer from 1824 until 1831, during which time he contributed over ninety articles that, according to Blackwood himself, did more than almost anything else 'to raise the character and sale of the Magazine.'[75] Yet when Robinson refused to damn Reform, Blackwood dropped him. In 1832 Wilson visited Cyrus Redding and asked him if he would review an 'excellent' volume of poems inscribed to Henry Brougham, then Whig Lord Chancellor. Redding replied that he would, but he wondered why Wilson did not mention it himself in *Blackwood's*. 'I dare not,' Wilson responded. Blackwood 'would fall into hysterics.'[76] For Edgar Allan Poe, *Blackwood's* political articles were rigid to the point of parody. In order to produce a political article 'of the genuine Blackwood stamp,' he remarks, 'Mr Blackwood has a pair of tailor's-shears, and three apprentices who stand by him for orders. One hands him the "Times," another the "Examiner," and a third a "Gulley's New Compendium of Slang-Whang." Mr B. merely cuts out and intersperses. It is soon done – nothing but Examiner, Slang-Whang, and Times – then Times, Slang-Whang, and Examiner – and then Times, Examiner, and Slang-Whang.'[77] The construction of a *Blackwood's* political article was perhaps a little more complicated than Poe suggests, but his mockery emphasizes the fact that political commentary in the magazine adhered closely to the formulaic repetition of Tory dogma. What is more, while narrowly defined in terms of specific political articles, Blackwood ensured that his Toryism was an overarching concern of his magazine, and permeated discussions ranging from history, philosophy, economics and art to travel, literature, biography, and the military. When De Quincey wrote political articles for the magazine, he eagerly tailored his opinions to Blackwood's wishes. 'With respect to the suggestion as to the higher grounds of religious principle,' he informed Blackwood in 1830, 'I assure you that I have of late years most sincerely held such views myself.'[78] When De Quincey wrote book reviews, politics remained a central concern. The object of his 1831 assessment of the clergyman and classicist Samuel Parr is, as Barry Symonds notes, 'to offer an emblem of the type of ideological construct valued by the new, apparently liberal, Whig government ... Parr accordingly has to be shown up as a man of second-rate attainments.'[79] Parr's whiggery means that as an author he is 'ridiculous.' De Quincey later admitted that his *Blackwood's* essay was *'partisan,'*[80] but so were scores of articles on a myriad of topics. *Blackwood's* politics, declared Barry St Leger, were 'interwoven with its whole texture.'[81] F.D. Maurice agreed, and more emphatically: 'There is no allowance to be made for any adverse friction in [*Blackwood's*] movements, there is no diversity of operation to destroy the harmony of the result; all moves in obedience to one impulse, all tends to one object.'[82] Blackwood demanded the political allegiance of his writers, and politics harmonized articles throughout his magazine.

Yet despite *Blackwood's* emphatic unity, Lockhart was right to assert that 'we are not the drones of Toryism.'[83] The magazine frequently contained discordant and rebellious voices that challenged and perplexed its strident insistence on the status quo. Like no other periodical publication of the day, it privileged instability, candour, variety, irony, and contradiction. This was after all a magazine that was founded in scandal, that wilfully cloaked its operations in fiction and disguise, and that often seemed hell-bent on disrupting the world of public discourse through tergiversation, audacity, satire, and character assassination. *Blackwood's*, writes Peter Murphy, 'was a kind of extended language-experiment ... that tested the coherence of the world of writing,' and that was repeatedly destabilized by 'the apparently insane struggle' between its 'destructive and irresponsible practice ... and its social philosophy' of time-honoured Toryism.[84] *Blackwood's* was new. Its format established an innovative pattern for magazines by gradually removing all formal departments, and mixing together fiction, reviews, correspondence, poetry, and essays. 'A Berkshire Rector has been pleased to wonder,' writes Lockhart (and perhaps others):

> Why we've dismissed the primitive arrangement,
> He hates, he says, from verse to prose to blunder,
> Our quick transitions seem to him *derangement*.
>
> Begging our good friend's pardon, we prefer
> To mix the *dulce* with the *utile*,
> And think it has in fact a charming air
> Such different things in the same page to see.[85]

The magazine's 'style and manner' were described by Robert Mudie in 1825 as 'altogether new,' and three years later Henry Stebbing celebrated *Blackwood's* iconoclasm: 'There is a recklessness, a sinning against, and breaking through of rules, a spirit of wild revelry, or desperate despite, throughout its composition.'[86] Washington Irving considered the magazine 'a daringly original work' that was 'too much for his delicate nerves.'[87] In 1850 De Quincey looked back on *Blackwood's* opening years, and praised it for 'that great innovating principle … under which it oscillated pretty equally between human life on the one hand and literature on the other.'[88]

Blackwood's was highly various. It openly scorned consistency: Lockhart asserted bluntly that 'the notion of unity of mind, in a Journal like this, is a thing quite below our contempt.'[89] Writers were given freedom to express their ideas: 'the great superiority of Blackwood's Magazine over all other works of our time is, that one *can* be allowed to speak one's mind there.'[90] Blackwood wrote proudly to Neal in 1825: 'I hardly know any work except "Maga" where you could have felt yourself so much at your ease in most fearlessly saying what you thought right of men and things.'[91] *Blackwood's* allowed for changes of direction and opinion. The magazine's Cockney School attacks were still ongoing in 1823, when Wilson described Leigh Hunt as 'a fool and a liar,' and sneeringly asked 'who would spit upon a toad crawling in its unwieldy and freckled putrefaction?' Yet by 1834 the Cockney School battles had been forgotten, and Wilson enthusiastically described Hunt's *London Journal* as 'not only beyond all comparison, but out of all sight, the most entertaining and instructive of all the cheap periodicals.'[92] *Blackwood's* encouraged debate. In the early years there were contributions from non-Tories and even self-proclaimed Whigs: 'I wish my friends to follow the bent of their genius,' Blackwood told the Whig Thomas Doubleday in 1820, 'and the miscellaneous character of our work admits of every description.'[93] In May 1831 the *Blackwood's* writers were given a forum to debate the advantages and disadvantages of the Reform Bill: 'Not a few, and these not inconsiderable, differences in opinion exist among Ourselves,' observed Wilson; 'and as they have been, so they will be expressed in Maga, without subjecting her to any reproach.'[94] *Blackwood's* was defiantly satirical, and it used humour both to ravage and mollify. The scurrilousness was often inexcusable, but the wit made it difficult to stay mad. The *Blackwood's* critics were widely blamed for hastening John Keats's death, but after Percy Shelley's death by drowning in 1822, Maginn made a characteristically clever return to the attack. 'What a rash man Shelley was, to put to sea in a frail boat with Jack's poetry on board!,' he cried. 'Why, man, it would sink a trireme ... Seventeen ton of pig-iron would not be more fatal ballast. Down went the boat with a "swirl!" I lay a wager that it righted soon after ejecting Jack.'[95] Eyre Evans Crowe remarked that 'the characteristic beauty of Maga, the *ideal* of her character has been a powerful mixture of acrimony & good humour,' while Henry Crabb Robinson noted that in *Blackwood's* 'the fun makes one overlook the knavery, even culpably.'[96] Blackwood prized diversity. 'What I require is not what has been before, to publish again & again,' he declared, 'but something which bears the impress of the times.'[97] He was keenly aware of the 'danger of palling the public with too much even of a very good thing,' and insisted that 'Novelty, variety, and interest [were] the great charms of a magazine.'[98] 'I need hardly tell you that I have always a superabundance of what may be called good articles,' Blackwood explained to William Mudford in 1828, 'and that what I want are articles which have some distinctive or superior cast about them ... The great curse of the London periodicals is their eternal sameness.'[99] Dullness was inexcusable and *Blackwood's* convincingly proclaimed itself a 'perpetual "Magazin de Nouveautés," – a perfect "Theatre de Variétés,"' a 'real Magazine of mirth, misanthropy, wit, wisdom, folly, fiction, fun, festivity, theology, bruising and thingumbob.'[100] Coleridge lauded both the 'continuity' and 'variety' of the magazine, championing the 'deep importance' of its 'moral and political truths' but equally enthusiastic about its 'long, never-flagging Height and Sustainedness of irony.'[101] *Blackwood's* hard political line emerged through a welter of wit, liberality, mirth, contradiction, and squibbery.

Blackwood's regressive political opinions stand in marked contrast to his innovative attitude towards fiction. In *The English Novel in the Magazines*, Robert Mayo remarks that the vast majority of original fiction published in the magazines between 1740 and 1815 was 'trashy, affected, and egregiously sentimental.'[102] Blackwood changed all that. He valued fiction. 'To pay writers of fiction at rates roughly on par with those paid to many essayists and reviewers,' notes William Kilbourne, 'and to make fiction a regular and important feature of an intellectually sophisticated magazine were bold and progressive policies – so bold and progressive that until a few months before William Blackwood's death in September 1834, *Blackwood's* was practically unrivalled as the leading publisher of good magazine fiction.'[103] From 1820 onward fiction accounted for an average of over 300 pages per year, or roughly one-fifth of the total of *Blackwood's* annual contents.[104] There was of course a long tradition of serializing novels in the magazines – Tobias Smollett's *The Life and Adventures of Sir Launcelot Greaves* appeared in the *British Magazine* in 1760–1. But Blackwood gave the idea vigorous new life when he serialized John Galt's *Ayrshire Legatees* in 1820–1, and followed this success with the serialization of six other novels, including Moir's *Autobiography of Mansie Wauch* and Michael Scott's *Tom Cringle's Log*. Blackwood's publication of these works played a key role in the rise of the serialized novel to such enormous prominence in the Victorian era, and established his magazine as a leader in contemporary fiction. *Blackwood's* later featured novels by George Eliot, Anthony Trollope, and Joseph Conrad, among many others. Blackwood also had a keen interest in shorter fiction, and published tales ranging from Caroline Bowles Southey's highly sentimental *Chapters on Churchyards* (1824–9) to seminal narratives of the fantastic like Robert Macnish's 'The Metempsychosis' (1826). But Blackwood was most interested in 'the exciting, the terrible, and the grisly,'[105] and during his editorship he published tales of terror by Galt, Hogg, Maginn, Walter Scott, Warren, and Wilson. These tales were sensational and shamelessly commercial, but their immediacy and concision gave them a remarkable ability to startle, dismay, and unnerve. They had a powerful influence on writers such as Robert Browning, Charles Dickens, and all four Brontës,[106] and laid the groundwork for the emergence of the modern short story as an internationally significant form in these decades – in the writings of Nikolai Gogol, Aleksandr Pushkin, Honoré de Balzac, Prosper Mérimée, Nathaniel Hawthorne, and of course Poe, who emulated, parodied, and reworked *Blackwood's* tales throughout his career.[107] Blackwood's fascination with and respect for fiction was a highly distinguishing feature of his magazine, and one that had an enormous impact on the publication and reception of fiction in the nineteenth-century and beyond. While Blackwood's politics looked to the past, his attitude towards fiction saw far into the future.

An equally innovative feature of Blackwood's magazine was its literary criticism. In its attitude towards continental literature, J.H. Alexander finds that *Blackwood's* 'makes living contact, that it cares deeply about what it finds (especially in Germany), and that it explores some of the possible implications for British literature.'[108] *Blackwood's* reviewed the novel with pioneering insight, for it has 'risen to a rank in the world of letters, little, if at all inferior to the most dignified productions of scholars and poets,' as an anonymous reviewer observed in 1818.[109] Michael Munday argues that the 'improved status of the novel is seen most clearly' in *Blackwood's* pages, and offers Lockhart's 1817 commentary on Godwin's *Caleb Williams* as a representative example. The essay demonstrates both that *Caleb Williams* has 'played a part in Lockhart's imaginative life,' and that criticism of the novel has come a long way since the days when 'the whole genre' could be dismissed 'by a reference to the Minerva Press.'[110] Blackwood published the finest poetry reviews of the age. The magazine's treatment of Coleridge was sometimes slanderous but most of its comments on him are positive and perceptive, as when Wilson observes that Coleridge 'is the prince of superstitious poets; and he that does not read Christabel with a strange and harrowing feeling of mysterious dread, may be assured that his soul is made of impenetrable stuff.'[111] *Blackwood's* was the great champion of Wordsworth at a time when many assessments were negative or indifferent. 'With all the great and essential faculties of the Poet,' writes Wilson, '[Wordsworth] possesses the calm and self-commanding powers of the Philosopher.' He is 'the first man that stripped thought and passion of all vain or foolish disguises, and shewed them in their just proportions and unencumbered power.'[112] *Blackwood's* treatment of Byron was uneven, but Byron himself thought Wilson's insightful assessment of *Manfred* had 'all the air of being a poet's, & was a very good one,' while an 1823 'letter' of Lockhart's has been described as 'the best of all the accounts of the spirit and status of *Don Juan* printed in any periodical of the time.'[113] 'I maintain, and have always maintained,' asserts Lockhart, 'that Don Juan is, without exception, the first of Lord Byron's works.'[114]

Most strikingly, *Blackwood's* was a keen supporter of Percy Shelley, and though it featured a spiteful review of *Adonais*, no other contemporary periodical quoted him so extensively, or defended him so staunchly. Leading magazines like the *London* and the *New Monthly* steered largely clear of him, while the *Edinburgh* ignored him altogether during his lifetime and the *Quarterly* was notoriously malicious. *Blackwood's* alone was forthright and generous, in part because Shelley was so highly regarded by *Blackwood's* reviewers such as Lockhart and De Quincey,[115] but also undoubtedly because Blackwood himself was an admirer. 'I hope whenever you hear from Mr Shelley you will let me know how he likes the Magazine,' Blackwood wrote in a letter to Charles Ollier in 1820. 'I still flatter myself he will be enduced to send something first ... I am anxious to hear when his next work will be out.'[116] John Scott censured *Blackwood's* for a number of excesses, but acknowledged that it had 'vindicated with ability, energy, and effect, several neglected and calumniated, but highly deserving poetical reputations.'[117] John Sterling put the matter in a nutshell when he declared of *Blackwood's* that while there was 'no political work in Europe so entirely and shamelessly bad,' there was 'certainly no English periodical work, the criticism in which is, on the whole, so original, profound and eloquent.'[118] John Stuart Mill observed that 'whatever may be in other respects our opinion of *Blackwood's Magazine*, it is impossible to deny to its principal writers ... a certain ... geniality of temperament ... Genuine powers of mind, with whatever opinions connected, seldom fail to meet with response and recognition from these writers.'[119] For many *Blackwood's* means blackguard, but even its detractors recognized that it published some of the most open-minded and far-sighted reviews of the age, and many of them directly at odds with its own professions of Toryism. Even the Cockney School attacks, so long regarded as evidence of *Blackwood's* 'critical irresponsibility, political bias, and personal slander,'[120] are more accurately seen as penetrating indicators of just how clearly *Blackwood's* critics recognized the burgeoning radical impulses that were soon to exert such inexorable pressure on their cherished notions of constancy and conformity. As Nicholas Roe remarks, 'in their acute response to forces at work in contemporary literary, social, and political spheres, the [Cockney School] essays are comparable to – and certainly as significant as – the "Prefaces" to *Lyrical Ballads*.'[121] Blackwood's old-school politics did not prevent him from publishing dynamic and sympathetic assessments of the speculative Coleridge, the democratic Wordsworth, the scandalous Byron, and the radical Shelley, even as the Cockney School essays lashed out at these same impulses. Blackwood's single-minded adherence to a narrow Tory line is countered by his broad-minded embrace of variety, debate, novelty, and dissent. He was divided between partisanship and profit, iteration and innovation, tradition and novelty, dogma and diversity, solemnity and satire, stability and subversion, and these paradoxes repeatedly energized and disrupted his magazine.

Perhaps the most characteristic feature of Blackwood's magazine is the *Noctes Ambrosianae* series, a collection of seventy-one dialogues that appeared in *Blackwood's* between 1822 and 1835, and that were written in large part by Wilson, with a good deal of help in the early years from Lockhart and Maginn, and incidental assistance along the way from Hartley Coleridge, Letitia Landon, Galt, Hogg, Moir, and several others. The series featured four principal characters: Christopher North, *Blackwood's* fictive editor and an older and infirm version of Wilson;

Timothy Tickler, based on Wilson's uncle Robert Sym, and an elderly conservative; Morgan Odoherty, younger and Irish, and based on Maginn; and the Ettrick Shepherd, who spoke in Scots and was based on Hogg. In the *Noctes*, Blackwood's magazine performed its own production. Blackwood, Hogg, Lockhart, Maginn, and Wilson spent an enormous amount of time discussing *Blackwood's*, and the *Noctes* mythologized and condensed these dialogues, for they featured fictive contributors to the magazine in fictionalized conversations about the magazine that frequently shaped and exposed the actual production of the magazine. Wilson told N.P. Willis that he and Lockhart 'used to sup together with Blackwood, and that was the real origin of the "Noctes."'[122] Blackwood himself is occasionally a character in the dialogues, as when he enters the fifth 'Noctes' and torments a Highland Chieftain for an article. The magazine's production is a central concern throughout the series. 'Ebony may jaw as he pleases,' writes Lockhart in the first *Noctes*. 'The Number will do well enough as it is. If there is not enough, let him send his devil into the Balaam-box.'[123] In the sixtieth *Noctes*, Wilson has Christopher North declare that *Blackwood's* is 'THE CURSE OF MY EXIST-ENCE,' and allude to Blackwood himself as an 'Ingrate' for rejecting one of North's own contributions.[124] The *Noctes* gave trenchant expression to Blackwood's political views. 'I like their Toryism,' declared Hartley Coleridge of the *Noctes* interlocutors, 'because it is of the old, hearty, cavalier, fox-hunting, beef and port kidney, such as Ben, and Shakespeare, and Dick Corbet (pride of the *lawn*), would have chimed in with.'[125] Yet the series as a whole was remarkable for its extravagance, range, and disputatiousness. 'My Cabinet,' cried Christopher North in the nineteenth *Noctes*, 'is completely a divided one.'[126] More tellingly, the Shepherd announced in the twentieth-fourth *Noctes* that he was ready to dispute 'on ony subject, sacred or profane ... What sall it be?,' he demanded: 'History, Philosophy, Theology, Poetry, Political Economy, Oratory, Criticism, Jurisprudence, Agriculture, Commerce, Manufactures, Establishments in Church and State, Cookery, Chemistry, Mathematics ...?'[127] The *Noctes* celebrate both the camaraderie and the contentiousness at the heart of *Blackwood's*, and in Maginn's memorable formulation revealed the 'THE EDITOR'S MOST EXCELLENT MAGAZINITY, IN COUNCIL.'[128] Blackwood inscribed his personality on every level of his magazine, and the *Noctes* are the most dynamic representation of its character under his direction: prescient, outrageous, diverse, consistent, cutting, fictive. William Blackwood died on 16 September 1834 and Wilson brought the *Noctes* to a close in February 1835, for the series that had so fully represented Blackwood's editorship now undoubtedly seemed misplaced and inappropriate without him. Further material on the *Noctes*, and in particular on its Tory-centred idealization of Scots identity, can be found in Charles Snodgrass's contribution elsewhere in this essay collection.

In the summer of 1834, as Blackwood lay on his deathbed, he received a letter from Michael Scott, whose hugely popular *Tom Cringle's Log* had been both serialized in *Blackwood's* and published by the firm as a book. Coleridge declared the sketches 'most excellent,' and Lockhart thought Cringle 'perhaps the most brilliant series of Magazine papers of the time.'[129] Scott was deeply distressed to hear of Blackwood's illness. 'When you were well, and at the helm,' he wrote, 'I used to carry sail fearlessly, for I knew you would always keep me in the right course.'[130] Scott's confidence in and concern for Blackwood were typical of these months. Though he kept himself deliberately out of sight and has been largely overlooked since his death, those closest to Blackwood recognized what he had accomplished, and the debts they owed to him. Blackwood published the books of some of the most eminent and influential authors of his age and edited a monthly magazine that operated from a provincial centre but reached an international audience, and that bristled always with confidence and contradiction. The Blackwood firm went on to enormous and enduring success but, as Maginn put it, 'The first pluck was shown, William Blackwood, by thee.'[131]

NOTES

I acknowledge with gratitude a grant from the Social Sciences and Humanities Research Council of Canada for research into *Blackwood's Magazine*.

  1 John Neal, 'William Blackwood,' *Atlantic Monthly* 16 (December 1865), 660.
  2 *Collected Letters of Samuel Taylor Coleridge*, ed. E.L. Griggs, 6 vols. (Oxford: Clarendon Press, 1956–71), 6:912 (hereafter, Coleridge, *Letters*).
  3 John MacGregor, *British America*, 2 vols. (Edinburgh: Blackwood, 1832), 2:512; Thomas Aird, 'Memoir,' in *The Poetical Works of David Macbeth Moir*, ed. Thomas Aird (Edinburgh: Blackwood, 1852), lxiv.
  4 John Gibson Lockhart, *Peter's Letters to his Kinsfolk*, 3 vols. (Edinburgh: Blackwood, 1819), 2:188.

5 Neal, 'William Blackwood,' 670.
6 See Maurice Milne, 'The Veiled Editor Unveiled: William Blackwood and His Magazine,' *Publishing History* 16 (1984), 100.
7 Margaret Oliphant, *Annals of a Publishing House*, 2 vols. (Edinburgh: Blackwood, 1897), 2:400.
8 'Richard Woodhouse's *Cause Book*: The Opium-Eater, the Magazine Wars, and the London Literary Scene in 1821,' in *Harvard Library Bulletin*, ed. Robert Morrison, 9, no. 3 (Fall 1998), 15. Cf. Dale Hepker: 'During his lifetime, Blackwood cared for the *Magazine* as he would have cared for a baby' (Dale Hepker, 'Early Nineteenth-Century British Author–Publisher Relations (unpub. PhD diss., University of Nebraska, 1978), 150).
9 Charles Gibbon, *The Life of George Combe, Author of 'The Constitution of Man,'* 2 vols. (London: Macmillan and Co., 1878), 1:112. I would like to thank John Strachan for this reference.
10 *The Collected Letters of Thomas and Jane Welsh Carlyle*, eds. Charles Richard Sanders, Clyde de L. Ryals, Kenneth Fielding, et al., 29 vols. (Durham, N.C.: Duke University Press, 1970–), 1:130 (hereafter, Carlyle, *Letters*). John Scott, 'Lord Byron: His French Critics: The Newspapers; and The Magazines,' *London Magazine* 1 (May 1820), 495. Neal, 'William Blackwood,' 660.
11 *The Letters of Sir Walter Scott*, ed. H.J.C. Grierson, et al., 12 vols. (London: Constable, 1932–7), 4:276.
12 Ian A. Gordon, *John Galt: The Life of a Writer* (Toronto: University of Toronto Press, 1972), 34.
13 'The Letters of John Galt,' ed. George Spencer Beasley (unpub. PhD diss., Texas Technological College, 1951), 159.
14 Gordon, *Galt*, 80.
15 Ian A. Gordon, 'Plastic Surgery on a Nineteenth-Century Novel: John Galt, William Blackwood, Dr. D.M. Moir and *The Last of the Lairds*,' in *The Library*, 5th Series, 32, no. 3 (September 1977), 251–5.
16 Irene Elizabeth Mannion, 'Criticism "Con Amore": A Study of Blackwood's Magazine 1817–1834' (unpub PhD diss., University of California at Los Angeles, 1984), 107–8.
17 'The Letters of David Macbeth Moir to William Blackwood and His Sons,' ed. Eugene A. Nolte, 2 vols. (unpub. PhD diss., Texas Technological College, 1955), 2:566 (hereafter, Moir, 'Letters').
18 Thomas De Quincey, 'Klosterheim,' in *The Works of Thomas De Quincey*, volume 8, ed. Robert Morrison (London: Pickering and Chatto, 2001), 224.

19 *Byron's Letters and Journals*, ed. L.A. Marchand, 12 vols. (London: Murray, 1973–1982), 3:238 (hereafter, Byron, *Letters and Journals*).
20 N.P. Willis, *Pencillings by the Way*, 3 vols. (London: Macrone, 1836), 3:205–6.
21 Milne, 'Veiled Editor,' 88.
22 Peter Garside, 'Essay on the Text,' in Walter Scott, *The Black Dwarf*, ed. Peter Garside (Edinburgh: Edinburgh University Press, 1993), 126.
23 Carlyle, *Letters*, 1:116.
24 F.D. Tredrey, *The House of Blackwood, 1804–1954* (Edinburgh: Blackwood, 1954), 250.
25 Lockhart, *Peter's Letters*, 2:226.
26 J.H. Alexander, '*Blackwood's*: Magazine as Romantic Form,' *Wordsworth Circle* 15, no. 2 (Spring 1984), 57.
27 David Higgins, '*Blackwood's Edinburgh Magazine* and the Construction of Wordsworth's Genius,' in *Romantic Periodicals and Print Culture*, ed. Kim Wheatley (London: Cass, 2003), 126–7.
28 Mark Parker, *Literary Magazines and British Romanticism* (Cambridge: Cambridge University Press, 2000), 199. See Robert Morrison, 'John Wilson and the Editorship of *Blackwood's Magazine*,' *Notes and Queries* 46, no. 1 (1999), 48–50.
29 Coleridge, *Letters*, 4:943.
30 Robert Morrison, 'De Quincey, Champion of Shelley,' *Keats-Shelley Journal* 41 (1992), 36–7.
31 'Maginn-Blackwood Correspondence,' ed. Ann Kersey Cooke, 2 vols. (unpub. MA thesis, Texas Technological College, 1955), 1:196.
32 Moir, 'Letters,' 1:197.
33 Oliphant, *Annals*, 1:308.
34 Alan Lang Strout, *A Bibliography of Articles in Blackwood's Magazine* (Lubbock: Texas Technological College, 1959), 3.
35 Mannion, 'Criticism,' 97.
36 Maurice Milne, 'The Politics of Blackwood's, 1817–1846' (unpub. PhD diss., University of Newcastle, 1984), 97.
37 Oliphant, *Annals*, 1:302–3. M.A. Hassan, 'The Major Romantic Poets and Their Critics in Blackwood's Magazine: 1817–1825' (unpub. PhD diss., University of Edinburgh, 1971), 11.
38 John Wilson and John Gibson Lockhart, 'Noctes Ambrosianae, No. LI,' *Blackwood's Magazine* 28 (August 1830), 420.
39 Milne, 'Politics,' 28.
40 Thomas De Quincey, 'Professor Wilson,' in *The Works of Thomas De*

Quincey, volume 17, ed. Edmund Baxter (London: Pickering and Chatto, 2001), 36 (hereafter, De Quincey, 'Professor Wilson').

41 Elsie Swann, *Christopher North <John Wilson>* (Edinburgh: Oliver and Boyd, 1934), 238.

42 David Masson, 'The Noctes Ambrosianae,' *National Review* 3 (1856), 177.

43 George Douglas, *The Blackwood Group* (Edinburgh: Oliphant, Anderson, and Ferrier, 1897), 34.

44 Tredrey, *The House of Blackwood*, 252, 250.

45 Lockhart, *Peter's Letters*, 2:225–6.

46 William Hazlitt, 'On Public Opinion' in *The Complete Works of William Hazlitt*, ed. P.P. Howe, 21 vols. (London: Dent, 1930–4), 17:308.

47 Milnes, 'Veiled Editor,' 93.

48 'Maginn–Blackwood,' 2:499.

49 Moir, 'Letters,' 2:592.

50 Neal, 'William Blackwood,' 660

51 Samuel Smiles, *A Publisher and His Friends: Memoir and Correspondence of the late John Murray*, 2 vols (London: Murray, 1891), 1:481.

52 Thomas De Quincey, 'Sketches of Life and Manners [December 1840],' in *The Works of Thomas De Quincey*, volume 11, ed. Julian North (London: Pickering and Chatto, 2003), 273.

53 *The Letters of Charles and Mary Lamb*, ed. E.V. Lucas, 3 vols. (London: Dent, 1935), 2:323.

54 Ibid., 2:394–5.

55 'The Letters of George Croly to William Blackwood and His Sons,' ed. William Ross Thompson, 2 vols. (unpub. PhD diss., Texas Technological College, 1957), 1:65–6.

56 Moir, 'Letters,' 1:390.

57 'The Letters of Alaric Alexander Watts,' ed. Estus Cantrell Polk (unpub. PhD diss., Texas Technological College, 1952), 299.

58 'Maginn–Blackwood,' 2:588–9.

59 'Maginn–Blackwood,' 2:386–7.

60 Samuel Taylor Coleridge, 'Selections from Mr Coleridge's Literary Correspondence,' *Blackwood's Magazine* 10 (October 1821), 254.

61 Milne, 'Veiled Editor,' 94–5.

62 Hassan, 'The Major Romantic Poets,' 20.

63 'Maginn–Blackwood,' 2:510.

64 'Maginn–Blackwood,' 2:471.

65 Ralph Wardle, 'William Maginn and Blackwood's Magazine' (unpub. PhD diss., Harvard University, 1938), 50.

66 Tredrey, *The House of Blackwood*, 249.

67 Mannion, 'Criticism,' 154.
68 Ibid., 80.
69 Moir, 'Letters,' 1:270.
70 Jon Klancher, *The Making of English Reading Audiences, 1790–1832* (Madison: University of Wisconsin Press, 1987), 52.
71 Mannion, 'Criticism,' 155.
72 Henry Stebbing, 'Periodical Literature,' *Athenaeum* 1 (8 April 1828), 336.
73 Alexander Shand, 'Contemporary Literature. III. Magazine-Writers,' *Blackwood's Magazine* 125 (February 1879), 227.
74 Thomas De Quincey, 'Political Anticipations,' in *The Works of Thomas De Quincey,* volume 7, ed. Robert Morrison (London: Pickering and Chatto, 2000), 215. Wardle, 'William Maginn,' 299.
75 Milne, 'Politics,' 143.
76 Cyrus Redding, *Fifty Years' Recollection, Literary and Personal,* 3 vols. (London: Skeet, 1858), 3:46.
77 Edgar Allan Poe, 'How to Write a Blackwood Article,' in *Collected Works of Edgar Allan Poe,* ed. Thomas Ollive Mabbott, 3 vols. (Cambridge: Belknap Press of Harvard University Press, 1969–78), 2:338.
78 Barry Symonds, 'De Quincey and His Publishers: The Letters of Thomas De Quincey to His Publishers, and Other Letters, 1819–1832' (unpub. PhD diss., University of Edinburgh, 1994), 394.
79 Ibid., 400.
80 Thomas De Quincey, 'Dr Parr and his Contemporaries,' in *The Works of Thomas De Quincey,* volume 8, ed. Robert Morrison (London: Pickering and Chatto, 2001), 35, 443.
81 Mannion, 'Criticism,' 125.
82 F.D. Maurice, 'The New School of Cockneyism, No. 1,' *Metropolitan Quarterly Magazine* 1 (1826), 50.
83 Claire Cartmell, 'The Age of Politics, Personalities, and Periodicals: The Early Nineteenth-Century World of the "Noctes Ambrosianae" of Blackwood's Edinburgh Magazine' (unpub. PhD diss., University of Leeds, 1974), 55.
84 Peter Murphy, 'Impersonation and Authorship in Romantic Britain,' *ELH* 59 (1992), 626, 636.
85 Alexander, 'Romantic Form,' 63.
86 Robert Mudie, *The Modern Athens: A Dissection and Demonstration of Men and Things in the Scotch Capital* (London: Knight and Lacey, 1825), 247; Stebbing, 'Periodical Literature,' 336.
87 Neal, 'William Blackwood,' 668.
88 De Quincey, 'Professor Wilson,' 36.

89 John Gibson Lockhart, 'Lord Byron,' *Blackwood's Magazine* 17 (February 1825), 132.

90 William Maginn and John Gibson Lockhart, 'Maxims of Mr Odoherty,' *Blackwood's Magazine* 15 (May 1824), 605.

91 Neal, 'William Blackwood,' 668.

92 John Wilson, 'The Age of Bronze,' *Blackwood's Magazine* 13 (April 1823), 458, 460. John Wilson, 'Noctes Ambrosianae, No. LXVII,' *Blackwood's Magazine* 36 (August 1834), 273.

93 Mannion, 'Criticism,' 98–9.

94 John Wilson, 'Reformers and Anti-Reformers,' *Blackwood's Magazine* 29 (May 1831), 725.

95 William Maginn, 'Letters of Mr Mullion to the Leading Poets of the Age,' *Blackwood's Magazine* 16 (September 1824), 288.

96 'Three Irish Contributors to Blackwood's Magazine: Eyre Evans Crowe, George Downes, and Horatio Townsend,' ed. Nell Wayne Carlisle Bennett (unpub. MA thesis, Texas Technological College, 1958), 24. *Henry Crabb Robinson on Books and Their Writers*, ed. E.J. Morley, 3 vols. (London: Dent, 1938), 1:316.

97 Mannion, 'Criticism,' 89.

98 Neal, 'William Blackwood,' 666. Mannion, 'Criticism,' 98.

99 Mannion, 'Criticism,' 102.

100 'Pyne's History of the Royal Residences,' *Blackwood's Magazine* 5 (September 1819), 690; this pseudonymous review was by 'Berzelius Pendragon.' William Maginn, 'Noctes Ambrosianae, No. IV,' *Blackwood's Magazine* 12 (July 1822), 106.

101 Coleridge, *Letters*, 6:912.

102 Robert Mayo, *The English Novel in the Magazines, 1740–1815* (Evanston, Ill.: Northwestern University Press, 1962), 351.

103 William Kilbourne, 'The Role of Fiction in Blackwood's Magazine from 1817 to 1845' (unpub. PhD diss., Northwestern University, 1966), 67–8.

104 Ibid., 46.

105 Ibid., 157.

106 Robert Morrison and Chris Baldick, 'Introduction,' in *Tales of Terror from Blackwood's Magazine* (Oxford: Oxford University Press, 1995), vii–xviii.

107 For further discussion, see Robert Morrison and Chris Baldick, 'Introduction,' in *The Vampyre and Other Tales of the Macabre* (Oxford: Oxford University Press, 1997), xxi–xxii.

108 J.H. Alexander, 'Learning from Europe: Continental Literature in the *Edinburgh Review* and *Blackwood's Magazine*, 1802–1825,' *Wordsworth Circle* 21, no. 3 (Summer 1990), 122.

109 Kilbourne, 'The Role of Fiction,' 40.

110 Michael Munday, 'The Novel and Its Critics in the Early Nineteenth Century,' *Studies in Philology* 79, no. 2 (Spring 1982), 211.

111 John Wilson, 'Essays on the Lake School of Poetry. No. III. Coleridge,' *Blackwood's Magazine* 6 (October 1819), 9.

112 John Wilson, 'Essays on the Lake School of Poetry. No. I. Wordsworth's *White Doe of Rylstone*,' *Blackwood's Magazine* 3 (July 1818), 371. John Wilson, 'Wordsworth's Sonnets and Memorials,' *Blackwood's Magazine* 12 (August 1822), 175.

113 Byron, *Letters and Journals*, 5:269. Theodore Redpath, *The Young Romantics and Critical Opinion* (London: Harrap, 1973), 48.

114 John Gibson Lockhart, 'Odoherty on *Don Juan*,' *Blackwood's Magazine* 14 (September 1823), 282–3.

115 Robert Morrison, '"Abuse Wickedness, but Acknowledge Wit": *Blackwood's Magazine* and the Shelley Circle,' *Victorian Periodicals Review* 34, no. 2 (2001), 147–64.

116 Charles E. Robinson, 'Percy Bysshe Shelley, Charles Ollier, and William Blackwood: The Contexts of Early Nineteenth-Century Publishing,' in *Shelley Revalued*, ed. Kelvin Everest (Leicester: Leicester University Press, 1983), 197–8.

117 John Scott, 'The Magazines,' 496.

118 John Sterling, 'The English Periodical Press,' *Athenaeum* 1 (27 August 1828), 695.

119 John Stuart Mill, '*Poem, Chiefly Lyrical [1830]* and *Poems [1833]*,' in *Tennyson: The Critical Heritage*, ed. John Jump (London: Routledge and Kegan Paul, 1967), 85.

120 John O. Hayden, *The Romantic Reviewers, 1802–1824* (Chicago: University of Chicago Press, 1969), 258.

121 Nicholas Roe, 'A Cockney Schoolroom: John Keats at Enfield,' in *Keats: Bicentenary Readings*, ed. Michael O'Neill (Edinburgh: Edinburgh University Press, 1997), 24.

122 Willis, *Pencillings*, 3:210.

123 John Gibson Lockhart, 'Noctes Ambrosianae, No. I,' *Blackwood's Magazine* 11 (March 1822), 369.

124 John Wilson, 'Noctes Ambrosianae, No. LX,' *Blackwood's Magazine* 31 (February 1832), 261, 262.

125 Alan Lang Strout, 'The *Noctes Ambrosianae*, and James Hogg,' *Review of English Studies* 13 (January 1937), 49.

126 John Wilson, 'Noctes Ambrosianae, No. XIX,' *Blackwood's Magazine* 17 (March 1825), 380.

127 John Wilson, 'Noctes Ambrosianae, No. XXIV,' *Blackwood's Magazine* 19 (February 1826), 227.
128 William Maginn, 'Noctes Ambrosianae, No. VI,' *Blackwood's Magazine* 12 (December 1822), 695.
129 Samuel Taylor Coleridge, *Table Talk*, ed. Carl Woodring, 2 vols. (Princeton, N.J.: Princeton University Press, 1990), 2:278. John Gibson Lockhart, 'M.G. Lewis's *West India Journals*,' *Quarterly Review* 50 (January 1834), 377.
130 Oliphant, *Annals*, 2:43.
131 'Maginn–Blackwood,' 2:669.

'The mapp'd out skulls of Scotia': *Blackwood's* and the Scottish Phrenological Controversy

JOHN STRACHAN

In September 1814, amidst considerable public interest in phrenology – the 'science' of delineating character from an examination of the shape of the skull – Lord Byron was visited by the German practitioner Johann Spurzheim. After the physician had pronounced upon the significance of the contours of the poet's head, Byron confessed himself 'a little astonished' by Spurzheim's assessment that 'every thing developed in & on this same skull of mine has its *opposite* in great force so that to believe him my good & evil are at perpetual war.' '[P]ray heaven,' he continues, 'the last don't come off victorious.'[1] Byron's joshing admiration notwithstanding, few of his literary and satirical peers were as charitable, and phrenology – or 'craniology' to use Spurzheim's favoured term – became highly contentious during the late Georgian period, praised as the master-science capable of unlocking the secrets of human personality by its adherents and condemned as the hare-brained ravings of absurd German theorists by its opponents. The debates over the science of skull-reading were particularly heated in North Britain, and this essay examines the reception of phrenology in Scotland, focusing on the three Scottish periodicals in which most heat was generated: *Blackwood's Edinburgh Magazine*, the *Edinburgh Review*, and the *Phrenological Journal*. In particular, I want to explore the withering response to phrenology in *Blackwood's*. As the *Phrenological Journal* noted in 1823, it was *Blackwood's* – or 'Maga,' as it was known – which was the most antipathetic of all of the craniology-baiters: 'Blackwood's Edinburgh Magazine has distinguished itself as the most persevering, and, of course, the most absurd of the assailants of phrenology, and enemies of phrenologists.'[2]

This essay has three sections. The first part introduces phrenology and discusses its reception in Scotland: in the attacks in the *Edinburgh* and the apologia in the *Phrenological*. The second part offers a detailed account of *Blackwood's* rough handling of phrenology, demonstrating how it utilized both satire and more orthodox critical writing to condemn the skull-readers. The third and final part moves from *how* the magazine attacked phrenology to *why*. I want to suggest that the ferocity of *Blackwood's* attack was more than simply a matter of intellectual conviction, that it was part of a conscious marketing ploy to launch the magazine as a *succès de scandale*. Adding the phrenologists to the roster of hapless victims mauled in the early numbers – the Cockney School, the Edinburgh Whig establishment, S.T. Coleridge and so on – served William Blackwood's purpose of positioning his magazine within post-Napoleonic British literary culture as the most controversial, troubling, and entertaining journal of the day.

I

From 1800 onwards, the founder of phrenology, Franz Joseph Gall and his foremost disciple Johann Kaspar Spurzheim (St Paul to the former's Jesus), proselytized for the cause of cranial analysis in a series of books which were quickly translated into English. Gall argued that an individual's mental attributes consisted of separate faculties: 'Adhesiveness,' 'Destructiveness,' 'Combativeness,' and so on, each of which has its location or 'organ' in a region upon the surface of the brain. The larger the size of the organ, the greater one's manifestation of that characteristic. As the skull hardens in childhood, it is shaped by the protuberances of the brain; hence the importance of the external form of the cranium. Through an analysis of the skull, the phrenologist can determine the nature and personality of any individual. Figure 2 shows an early nineteenth-century craniological map.

From its first appearance in English, phrenological thought was highly contentious in Great Britain. That said, though there are antipathetic reviews in the first decade of the nineteenth century, it was not until the 1810s and 1820s that the debates over the validity of phrenology really developed. The 1814 visit to England by Spurzheim, during which he examined the skull of the author of *Childe Harold*, was principally responsible for sparking these controversies, most notably in the Scottish anatomist John Gordon's fearsome 1815 assault in the *Edinburgh Review*. 'The writings of Drs Gall and Spurzheim,' declared Gordon, 'have not added one fact to the stock of our knowledge,' and phrenology is 'thorough quackery from beginning to end.'[3] To quote more fully,

'The writings of Drs Gall and Spurzheim have not added one fact to the stock of our knowledge, respecting either the structure or the functions of man; but consist of such a mixture of gross errors, extravagant absurdities, downright mis-statements, and unmeaning quotations from Scripture, as can leave no doubt, we apprehend, in the minds of honest and intelligent men, as to the real ignorance, the real hypocrisy, and the real empiricism of the authors.'[4] In the face of the *Edinburgh*'s opposition, as *Blackwood's* noted, Spurzheim 'resolved to visit Edinburgh ... to repress the voice of opposition,'[5] and confronted his adversaries in 1816, demonstrating in Dr Gordon's dissection rooms at the university.

Despite his encounter with Spurzheim, Gordon remained unconvinced, publishing his antipathetic *Observations on the Structure of the Human Brain* in 1817. Nonetheless, though Gordon and his *Edinburgh* colleagues remained implacably opposed to phrenology, Spurzheim's stay in Edinburgh, which lasted for over six months, made at least one significant convert, the indefatigable George Combe, a man of law (a writer to the signet) rather than a medical man, who gave up his profession to become the most notable British propagandist for phrenology, and who produced a series of increasingly elephantine craniological books, most notably *A System of Phrenology* (which runs to well over 1,000 pages by the fifth edition). Building upon Spurzheim's tendency to illustrate phrenology by reference to the heads of monarchs, statesmen, and warriors, Combe's work is littered with references to contemporary artists, musicians and, in particular, authors. He might be said to be the father of what I would label 'craniocriticism,' an interpretive practice taken up with enthusiasm by contributors to the most important British craniological publication, the *Phrenological Journal*, which Combe edited from its foundation in 1823 until 1847. Like *Blackwood's* and the *Edinburgh*, the *Journal* was based in Scotland's capital. (Edinburgh was, throughout the craniological controversies, the site of the most intelligent, engaged, and rancorous debate. Indeed, the Edinburgh Phrenological Society, founded in 1820, predated its London equivalent by three years.) In both the *Phrenological Journal* and the *System of Phrenology*, literary criticism and phrenology go hand in hand, and the cranial formations of great writers are cited in analyses of their work. Thus the well-developed organ of Combativeness evident on the head of Walter Scott inspires the 'love of battles'[6] demonstrated in the Waverley novels. And Philoprogentiveness, 'the love of children,' is Wordsworth's defining characteristic. In his *System of Phrenology*, Combe declares that the poet's simplicities are a direct consequence of this:

'Some of the faults of his manner is clearly attributable to an excess of its influence.'[7] Phrenological thought is, of course, often decidedly racist and Combe illustrates the difference between European and non-European culture by a comparison between the skull of an anonymous Peruvian and, though some might think that this is loading the dice somewhat, Robert Burns (figure 3).

Combe also cites Burns in his discussion of Benevolence. The humanitarianism of Burns's poetry is due to the influence of the poet's sizable organ of Benevolence. Combe demonstrates this by a contrast between Burns and one Griffiths, a kind of late Georgian serial killer (figure 4). Burns, you will observe, demonstrates a huge organ of Benevolence, while in 'the cold-blooded and deliberate murderer'[8] Griffiths it is next to non-existent.

Combe's *Phrenological Journal* was a conscious response to the hostile reception afforded phrenology in Edinburgh. Consistently in the red, the periodical, sponsored by its editor and his disciples, served as a loss-leader designed to salvage the reputation of phrenology in the face of the systematic attacks in reviews and literary magazines, most notably, if initially, in the *Edinburgh*, and thereafter, and worst of all, in *Blackwood's*. The 'Introductory Statement' to the first number, published in December 1823, declared that phrenology's literary enemies relied upon 'falsehoods and malignities – impertinencies and insolencies – dull jokes – indecencies – nastinesses and brutalities.'[9] While the *Journal* can engage with responsible criticism, it consciously sets out to defend phrenology from the assaults of crude attackers:

While we pledge ourselves to honour and respect all candid, fair, and philosophical opponents, whose object, like our own, is scientific truth, and not mere victory – above all, that most worthy opponent who has never yet blessed our sight, an inductive adversary, who shall scrutinise our facts – while we shall ever approve in others the utmost caution in assenting to our observations and propositions, and leave to their own self-satisfaction all who do us no possible harm, by merely resolving not to believe – we mean to repel all offensive operations of those we designate eminently our enemies, and to brand their attacks as disgraceful to the age in which we live, and its certain reproach in the next ; and we trust that no instance of our retaliation, for retaliation every iota of it will be, of attacks made with perfect impunity for several years past, shall lack the entire sympathy, nay, the hearty approbation of our impartial readers, who, in their love of justice, do not object to witness punishment condign.[10]

The *Journal* is right to lament the 'impertinencies,' 'insolencies,' and, most particularly, the 'dull jokes' directed at phrenology. A significant part of the attack on phrenology took the form of satire. T.L. Peacock's famous portrayal of Mr Cranium in *Headlong Hall* (1816) is but one of a large body of satirical ripostes to phrenology, in which *Blackwood's Edinburgh Magazine* played a significant part. From the first stirrings in Isaac D'Israeli's 1805 'A Dissertation upon Skulls,' satirists were quick to point the finger of scorn at phrenology. Quite apart from graphic satire such as George Cruikshank's *Phrenological Illustrations* (1826), and dramatic satire such as Thomas Wade's *The Phrenologists* (1830), there is a large body of satirical writing in both prose and poetry, from the anonymous *Craniology Burlesqued* (1816) and *The Craniad* (1817) onwards. Satirical treatments of phrenology most commonly lambaste it for its physiological determinism, denial of free will, and 'pseudo-scientific' jargon. And its being foreign of course adds to the mirth, with the phrenologist portrayed as, to use *Blackwood's* phrase, a 'crack-brained [German] theorist,'[11] peddling crude and reductive explanations for human diversity.

A section of Robert Montgomery's Juvenalian satire *The Age Reviewed* (1828) stresses the importance of Scotland in contemporary controversies over craniology, and of George Combe's role as the British standard bearer for the science. Montgomery traces the history of phrenology from Germany to Scotland:

> Soon spread the mapp'd-out skulls thro' Scotia's towns,
> And Glasgow sawnies bump'd their dirty crowns;
> Then foggy Spurzheim croaked in bungling tomes,
> Till gaping Scotland hugg'd her crack-brain'd momes! –
> Last, Combe, the printing jobbernowl for all,
> In half a thousand pages grubb'd for Gall;[12]

Such acidulous treatment of phrenology is not uncommon in its early reception. The chorus of jeers from scientists and intellectuals was complemented by satire on phrenology as a hare-brained pseudo-science, and on phrenologists as quacks and charlatans. As ever in the Romantic period, contemporary satire echoes wider social debate. The best testimony of how the two prongs of the attack are interlinked lies in the widespread, if not certain, attribution of the first significant Scottish satire on craniology, *The Craniad; or Spurzheim illustrated. A Poem in two parts* (published in Edinburgh in 1817), to John Gordon and Francis

Jeffrey of the *Edinburgh Review*. In heroic couplets, the satire is an extended exercise in verbatim parody, with the source of each section in
Gall and Spurzheim footnoted with full quotation and acerbic commentary throughout. For example, the poem opens by citing Spurzheim:
'Man participating in the nature of all other beings – of minerals, plants
and animals, and being therefore a microcosm, must possess all the
properties common to him and to other beings.' This is rendered thus in
the main body of the poem:

> Man is a microcosm – a little earth!
> And turns revolving from his very birth;
> Hence endless revolutions in the mind;
> And in the feelings of the human kind[13]

The poem concludes thus, in its trademark doggerel pentameter:

> Thus have we sung, in craniologic strains,
> The marks of character, – the laws of brains;
> Thus have we proved what ne'er was proved before,
> But which, once proved, can ne'er be doubted more,
> That every faculty is born and bred,
> And rear'd to full perfection, in the head.
> That mind depends on brains we've clearly shown,
> For when the brains are out, the mind is flown;
> That skulls contain the laws of human life,
> Which often are with human laws at strife.[14]

This passage illustrates a central problem with *The Craniad*: it is not very
good, either as satire or, indeed, as poetry. *Blackwood's* was probably
aware of the rumours as to its antecedents and the antipathy demonstrated in its review of the poem may have been prompted by a wish to
engage in its favourite pastime – baiting the *Edinburgh* – but there is
some truth in its two-sentence review, attributed in Alan Lang Strout's
A Bibliography of Articles in Blackwood's Magazine 1817–1825 to either J.G.
Lockhart or John Wilson: 'The Craniad is the worst poem we have now
in Scotland. The author has it in his power at once to decide the great
craniological controversy: let him submit his skull to general inspec-
tion, and if it exhibit a single intellectual organ, Spurzheim's theory is
overthrown.'[15]

The attack on *The Craniad*, a satirical poem widely supposed to be associated with the *Edinburgh Review*, was published in the third number of William Blackwood's magazine, in June 1817. It might be seen as a moment where Lockhart or Wilson squares up to the *Edinburgh*, an early skirmish in the campaign which was to explode with such ferocity four months later, in the October relaunch number of *Blackwood's Edinburgh Magazine*, in the notorious 'Chaldee Manuscript,' which offers allegorical lampoon on Constable, Jeffrey, Gordon, and the *Edinburgh* cohorts, as well as the more plain-speaking 'Strictures on the Edinburgh Review' published in the reprinted number. Though *The Craniad* is, like *Blackwood's* itself, deeply anti-phrenological, the opportunity to blaspheme against the *Edinburgh*, 'the Koran of the reading public'[16] in contemporary Scotland, was too good to miss. Indeed, it might be argued that these two sentences serve as a declaration of intent. If the Spurzheimites were troubled by the attacks in the *Edinburgh*, much worse was to come in William Blackwood's magazine. The review marks the moment Wilson or Lockhart wrests the anti-phrenological mantle from the *Edinburgh*. It implies that Gordon and Jeffrey were little better than the phrenologists and that, before 1817, the phrenologists had only to face the lumpen and slow-witted abuse of the Edinburgh Reviewers; now they would understand what it was to feel the lash applied by genuine practitioners of the art.

Within a short space of time *Blackwood's* had outdone its rival in phrenology-bashing, and had become, in the words of the *Phrenological Journal* 'the most persevering ... of the assailants of phrenology.' As Charles Gibbon wrote of *Blackwood's* in 1878, 'Although opposed to the *Edinburgh Review* in most things, it surpassed that periodical in abusing and ridiculing phrenology and its professors.'[17] This 'surpassing' is exactly what William Blackwood wanted. I argue below that much of *Blackwood's* success and notoriety consisted of taking existing strands in contemporary literary journalism to hitherto unheard of extremes, and its handling of phrenology is a classic example of that tendency. The review of *The Craniad*, whether it be by Wilson or by Lockhart (the ambiguity is pleasingly Blackwoodian, if *status quo ante*), signifies an intention to outdo and supersede the *Edinburgh*. It anticipates the manner in which, four months later, after William Blackwood had given free rein to the 'Leopard' and the 'Scorpion,' Wilson and Lockhart would roast the *Edinburgh* in the infamous, venomous, and magnificent October 1817 relaunch number of *Blackwood's Edinburgh Magazine*.

II

From its foundation, *Blackwood's* carried animadversions on phrenology. Even back in the days of the *Edinburgh Monthly Magazine*, the journal was offering vigorous repudiations of craniology. Indeed, the very first number of Blackwood's periodical, published in April 1817, contains a sprightly correspondent's letter by 'A.M.,' 'The Craniological Controversy. Some Observations on the late Pamphlets of Dr Gordon and Dr Spurzheim.' The 'Observations' see phrenology as an epiphenomenal fancy, a late Georgian whim which will not long survive the departure of Spurzheim from Edinburgh: 'Craniology has almost "lived its little hour." In this city we are certain, that, with the absence of Dr Spurzheim, and the introduction of some other novelty, as a French-dance or a new beauty, it will be very soon forgotten. There is nothing which can make us regret the fall of this ill-fated system. It seems to have been a mere exhalation of human thought, which has risen, and is passing away before us, in all its native duskiness; with no rainbow tinge to allure our Gaze by its beauty – not one celestial hue to lighten the dull materiality of its aspect.'[18]

In a manner which anticipates the later, two-pronged attacks of *Blackwood's* which combine satire with more conventional prose polemic, A.M. attempts satire, parodying craniology by hypothesizing a new physical science, 'cardiology,' in which the heart replaces the skull as the object of physiological analysis:

Since the brain has had its day as the basis of a system, we see no reason why that organ in the human body, which is popularly supposed to be the seat of passion, shall not in its turn serve to amuse the credulity of mankind. Why may not the human heart be registered in a good sized quarto volume, with plates and references, and be made the basis of a system of cardiology? Some enquirer may arise, who is fond enough of travelling, and sufficiently anxious for a transient reputation to run over Europe, and give lectures on its fibres and emotions. He may surely discover such a difference in the twisting of these fibres; – in the curvature of its valves; – the sweeping of its arteries; – or the arrangements of its nerves; as may afford a very amusing explanation of human passion. The heart, indeed, is not just as open to examination in the living subject as the skull; and we doubt that any lady could be found sufficiently in love with science, and a new system, to expose her heart for the sake of either, to the manipulation of a cardiologist.[19]

Unamusing as this is, and superseded as it is by the similar but brilliant 'Noseology' ('A Dissertation on the intellectual faculties, as manifested by the various configurations of the nose') of May 1819, this is significant as the first example of the magazine's use of 'wretched jokes' against phrenology. Inevitably, *Blackwood's Edinburgh Magazine*, the most significant repository of post-Napoleonic satirical writing, participated fully in the comic nose-thumbing of phrenology evident in the wider satirical culture.[20] It published both straightforward anathematizing essays against phrenology *and* satirical treatments; as ever in Maga, more orthodox critical writing and satire are interlinked. For instance, from May 1818 onwards, the journal, courtesy of the parodic talents of William Howison, featured its own spoof craniological correspondent, 'Doctor Ulrick Sternstare,' inevitably 'a learned German' and clearly a thinly veiled version of Spurzheim, who supposedly pens two series which run in the early volumes: 'The Craniologist's Review' and 'Letters on the National Characteristics of the Scots.' In the 'Scots Letters,' 'Sternstare' declares: 'The superb collection of sculls which I have been accumulating, in reference to Scottish characteristics, is increasing every day. But a covenantor is yet required to form the apex of the pyramid. Meanwhile I must content myself with collecting whatever specimens I can find. I have long had an eye upon an old Scottish snuff-dealer in London, whose head contains some remarkable points. He is now in his last illness and ... I may, [soon] expect to see him here in the dissection room ... If you meet with any thing curious, be so good as to transmit it to me, whether dead in a glass case, or alive with a letter of introduction. No specimen, I promise you, shall ever suspect that I am taking a look of him.'[21]

Such raillery became a key part of *Blackwood's* armoury, as the phrenologists well knew. The 'Introductory Statement' to the first number of the *Phrenological Journal* characterizes the ignoble methods used by its journalistic opponents: their use of mockery, caricatured argument, and satire ('wretched jokes'). Instead of engaging in logical and reasoned debate, the enemies of phrenology, the *Quarterly Review*, the *Edinburgh Review*, and, most notably, *Blackwood's Edinburgh Magazine,* rely upon 'Railing and Abuse,' 'Falsehoods and Malignities,' 'Impertinencies and Insolences,' 'Wretched Jokes,' and 'Indecencies, Nastinesses, and Brutalities' (the latter triumvirate, the *Phrenological* concedes, 'distinguish[ing] the classic page of Blackwood alone'):

These are the ignoble means by which men, who yet style themselves philosophers, and are pleased to hold at naught the power of observation,

and the reasonings of all other intelligent creatures, have deemed it philosophical to treat one of the most important inductive inquiries which
science has yet been called upon to prosecute; – these are the weapons
with which they have endeavoured to annoy and obstruct those who have
given that inquiry their serious attention. To answer such reasonings were
degradation only less profound than to employ them; but it were of the
worst example to allow them to pass unnoticed ... Let us be perfectly
understood. We force our doctrine on no one; but we are well entitled to
say, 'attack it fairly – attack us fairly, or let both alone.' We cannot too often
repeat, that all candid inductive opponents, who love truth better than a
paltry hollow reputation, shall meet with our most perfect respect and
consideration; nay, even speculative a priori reasoners, who are at once
sincere and civil; shall have no reason to complain of our manner to them,
when we perform the easy task of pointing out their errors. But all
falsehood, unfairness, malevolence, impertinence, and folly, we shall drive
back from ourselves, and brush away from our science.[22]

Blackwood's took little notice.

Howison's 'Craniologist's Review,' in the true Spurzheimian manner,
sees Sternstare offering his thoughts on the heads of various historical and contemporary notables, Cromwell, Voltaire and Napoleon
among them. On Bonaparte, Sternstare declares – and the reader is best-
advised to read this aloud in a cod-German accent – 'In the upper back
part of his head, we find an excessive expansion of self-love. [There is]
imperfect development of the organs of veneration [in] the lateral organs which surround the table at the top of his head ... [however,] I
think him a more amiable character than that vile toad Frederick of
Prussia, who had no moral faculties on the top of his head.'[23] Compare
Combe's remarks on the emperor, this time made in earnest, and it is
sometimes difficult to differentiate parody from formal model. This is
Combe: 'let the student of phrenology ... compare the mask of Napoleon ... with those of men of average talents and he will discover the
extraordinary length of the zygomatic arch, indicating the [large] size of
the anterior lobe of the brain [evident] in men of great powers.'[24] The
magazine had little time for Combe, as this mock-encomium from
December 1821 demonstrates:

For our own parts, we think that Gall and Spurzheim, and Combe, have
thrown greater light on the nature of man than all the other philosophers
put together since the world began. Indeed, there is now little or nothing

to discover. The moral and intellectual geography of the head of man, and, we, understand, of all other animals, is laid down with a minuteness of accuracy that must be very galling to the feelings of an Arrowsmith or a Morrison. Aristotle, Lord Bacon, and Locke, are mere impotent ninnies in comparison with Gall, Spurzheim, and Combe; and, indeed, any one page of Combe's great work on Phrenology, is worth 'all that Bactrian, Samian sage e'er writ.' We propose that a collossal and equestrian statue be erected to him on the Calton-hill, instead of that absurd national monument the Parthenon; and that a subscription be forthwith set a-going, under the auspices of Sir John Sinclair.[25]

It is entirely possible that some of *Blackwood's* animus here, rather than reflecting some dispassionate intellectual position, has its roots in the journal's recent history. Given the magazine's fondness for personalities and relish for grudges, one cannot imagine that the legal representative of the dismissed editors of the *Edinburgh Monthly Magazine*, Cleghorn and Pringle, would receive gentle treatment at the hands of its successor, *Blackwood's Edinburgh Magazine*. And, indeed, it was George Combe who acted in that capacity, as his biographer noted:

> He was brought into contact with the literary circles of Edinburgh by acting as agent for James Cleghorn and Thomas Pringle, the editors of the Edinburgh Monthly Magazine, in their dispute with the publisher, William Blackwood. The latter having disagreed with the editors announced the discontinuance of the periodical, and started Blackwood's Edinburgh Magazine. Cleghorn and Pringle, feeling themselves aggrieved, sought compensation for their share in the copyright of the original magazine, and at the same time they joined Blackwood's rival publisher, Constable, in issuing a new series of the Scots Magazine, under the title of the Edinburgh Magazine. There was a good deal of wrangling amongst the editors and publishers, and the vigorous vituperation in fashion in those days was used freely by both sides. Combe displayed his usual discretion in conducting the case, and succeeded in arranging it without going into court. His clients received from Mr Blackwood £125 in payment of all their claims.[26]

Perhaps, given these circumstances, it is small wonder that 'Ebony' called in the dogs of war on Combe: a phrenologist *and* a friend of Pringle and Cleghorn (to add to the catalogue of iniquity, Combe was inclined towards Whiggism, and, worse, had been on the Jacobin side in his youth).[27]

Inevitably, phrenology also figures in the most compendious of all the satirical series in the magazine, the *Noctes Ambrosianæ*. In the 'Noctes' for May 1823, the assembled company's discussion of the recent hanging of the notorious Deacon Brodie develops into a gleeful account of the supposed gulling of the *Phrenological Journal* into publishing a craniological analysis of a turnip:

ODOHERTY: What did your friend Brodie die of, Mr Tickler?

TICKLER: Apoplexy, I suppose. His face was as black as my hat.

HOGG: Lucy Mackinnon's bonny face was black too, they were saying.

DR MULLION: Yes; 'black, but comely.' I saw her a day or two afterwards, – very like the print.

TICKLER: These infernal ideots, the phrenologists, have been kicking up a dust about her skull, too, it appears. Will those fellows take no hint?

ODOHERTY: They take a hint! Why, you might as well preach to the Jumpers, or the Harmonists, or any other set of stupid fanatics. Don't let me hear them mentioned again.

DR MULLION: They have survived the turnip. What more can be said?

HOGG: The turnip, doctor?

DR MULLION: You haven't heard of it, then? – I thought all the world had. You must know, however, that a certain ingenious person of this town lately met with a turnip of more than common foziness in his field; he made a cast of it, clapped it to the cast of somebody's face, and sent the composition to the Phrenological, with his compliments, as a *fac-simile* of the head of a celebrated *Swede*, by name Professor Tornhippson. They bit, – a committee was appointed, – a report was drawn up, – and the whole character of the professor was soon made out as completely *secundum artem*, as Haggart's had been under the same happy auspices a little before. In a word, they found out that the illustrious Dr Tornhippson had been distinguished for his inhabitiveness, constructiveness, philoprogenitiveness, &c. – nay, even for 'tune', 'ideality', and 'veneration.'

ODOHERTY: I fear they have heard of the hoax, and cancelled that sheet of their Transactions. What a pity!

HOGG: Hoh! hoh! hoh! The organization of a fozey turnip! Hoh! hoh! hoh! hoh! the like o' that! The Swedish turnip – the celebrated Swede! – [28]

Blackwood's continued its assault on phrenology in its May 1819 satirical essay on 'Noseology,' 'A Dissertation on the intellectual faculties, as manifested by the various configurations of the nose.' The nose being visible to all, 'Noseology' has one key advantage over its rival science:

'With all due deference to craniology ... the present forms of politeness forbid the freedom of handling the skulls of others in search of the development of their organs.'[29] *Blackwood's* constructs a new Slaw-kenbergian science which, inevitably, draws its examples from the noses of the great. A 'convex apex of the nose is indicative of courage'; thus 'the personal valour of his grace the Duke of Wellington is [exemplified] in the projective character of his nose.' 'Noseology' also targets the analogical method whereby, in Spurzheim's terms, 'the brains of the lower animals can be compared with the human brain by the reflected light of analogy.' According to 'Noseology,' 'A nose forming a right angle at the base, is also a negative characteristic indicating cupidity and curiosity ... in elucidating ... this proposition, we shall adduce the analogies of various inquisitive animals. The [sharp-nosed] fox prying into a hen roost and the ferret in a rabbit's burrow ... combin[es] curiosity with cupidity ... Similarly [human] docility is in proportion to nasal flexibility; and here we shall again draw our inferences from the brute creation. The extreme docility of the elephant can only be attributed to the wonderful flexibility of his proboscis, [and] the rhinoceros derives a character of stubbornness from his inflexible snout surmounted by a horn.'[30]

Blackwood's returned to the attack in August 1821, in the 'Essays on Cranioscopy, Craniology, Phrenology, &c. By Sir Toby Tickletoby, Bart.' Tickletoby begins by arguing that his 'chief objection to [phrenology] is that it does not go far enough ... For instance, we know that there are dull, ... stupid, and even insane people in the world; yet there is no organ of stupidity, or bump of dullness, – no ridge or depression to designate the sane from the insane, the crack-brained theorist from the cool investigator. [However,] there must be tremendous bumps of folly and gullibility (*gullibilitiveness*, I believe, should be the word) ... Spurzheim and his followers offer abundant and most melancholy proof.'[31] Like the Noseologist before him, Tickletoby proposes a new physiological science to replace phrenology, one derived from the analysis of the buttocks, which draws on the practical researches of the schoolmaster Edward Clyster, who has made 'repeated examination of the bottoms of nearly 800 boys, while usher of the Grammar School of Kittlehearty.' Caning these posteriors, discovers Clyster, tends to 'stimulat[e]' the 'intellectual powers' of the boys concerned; as a consequence it follows that 'the bottom is more intimately connected with the mind than preceding investigators have supposed.'[32]

Tickletoby also offers a marvellously Swiftian modest proposal, arguing that the soft heads of infants who demonstrated unpromising bumps might be refashioned into more agreeable shapes: 'As all the organs of thought and volition are distinctively laid down in the cranial map [and given] the practicability of compressing the cranial bones at an early age ... nothing more is required ... than to mould the infant head to a given form, by the simple application of an unyielding metal head-dress, formed so as to permit the development of the required organs.'[33] This procedure at a stroke can solve the problems of crime, war, and famine: '[by] repressing the [bump] of *furtiveness* ... the cause of crime would be instantly done away. Allow not the organs of destructiveness and combativeness to expand ... and war and ruin will be banished from the land. When the means of subsistence becomes too scanty for the existing population, let the organs of amativeness and philo-progentiveness have no room for display ... and the next generation would live and die in ... celibacy.'[34] Splendid as this is, it should be noted that the game of *reductio ad absurdum* is sometimes not easy to play with phrenology; Richard Gregory has demonstrated that several nineteenth-century phrenologists actually advocated the reshaping of the soft infant head into more propitious shapes.[35]

III

Why did *Blackwood's* attack phrenology with such entertaining venom? And why did the magazine so quickly replace the *Edinburgh* as the phrenologists' principal *bête noire*? The first number of William Blackwood's journal noted that 'The Edinburgh Review stood foremost in opposition to this new system, and pointed out more fully and clearly than the rest, the anatomical errors on which it was founded,'[36] but six years later, the first number of the *Phrenological Journal* saw Maga as its chief tormentor: 'Blackwood's Edinburgh Magazine has distinguished itself as the most persevering, and, of course, the most absurd of the assailants of phrenology, and enemies of phrenologists.'[37] To my mind, *Blackwood's* consciously stole the clothes of the *Edinburgh* as part of its tendency to appropriate and accentuate the most controversial contemporary journalism. How did the magazine make its name? Certainly by being consciously provocative, but also, and in large part, by taking existing strands within the age's journalism to extremes: by being even more spiteful than the *Quarterly* about Leigh Hunt and the Cockney School, by purloining William Hone's brand of politically pointed biblical allegory to attack Edinburgh Whiggism in the 'Chaldee Manuscript,' and by outdoing the *Edinburgh* in traducing phrenology.

Antipathetic critics of the magazine have condemned its ferocity and venom as indicative of the worst and most splenetic kind of contemporary reaction ('convinced Tories' and 'inveterate bullies' as Ian Jack has it)[38] or as the work of a gang of near-deranged malevolents ('it is difficult to believe that Wilson was wholly sane' – Jack again);[39] J.G. Lockhart had 'a disgusting mind'[40] and so on. But it might be argued that the splendid extremity of *Blackwood's* has material antecedents, and derives from a conscious need to rescue a failing magazine from oblivion by any means necessary. The story is familiar to all devotees of the magazine, and amply covered in Robert Morrison's piece for this collection. The *Edinburgh Monthly Magazine* dropped, if not stillborn, but sickly, from the press in April 1817, and when its proprietor relaunched the magazine six months later, he did all he could to ensure that its successor, *Blackwood's Edinburgh Magazine,* would be the talk of the town.

Blackwood, Wilson, and Lockhart's relaunch was as deliberately provocative as could be imagined in early nineteenth-century Edinburgh, a conscious decision to court controversy, to provoke discussion, and, undeniably, thereby to boost sales. It is worth tarrying over the nature of the October 1817 number, which contained the 'Translation from an Ancient Chaldee Manuscript,'[41] the mock-biblical allegorical attack on the Scottish Whig establishment, Constable and the *Edinburgh* reviewers most particularly, the first of Lockhart and Wilson's animadversive onslaughts, 'On the Cockney School of Poetry,' and an entertaining but spectacularly bilious review, probably by Wilson, of Coleridge's *Biographia Literaria* which led the poet to consider a libel suit. While Coleridge refrained from litigation, the lawyer and naturalist John Graham Dalyell, recognizing himself in the 'Chaldee' as the beast whose face was 'like unto the face of an ape' did sue Blackwood in a case which 'Ebony' settled out of court. This of course provided even more publicity; Blackwood had his *succès de scandale* and the fortunes of his failing magazine were restored.

Though the modern reader might see Z's splendid if spectacularly unfair assault on the Cockney School as the most notable aspect of the October 1817 number, it should not be forgotten that the *Edinburgh Review* is the principal target of the relaunch issue. It contains the 'Chaldee' with its *ad hominem* assaults on Constable, Jeffrey, and their cohorts, and when Blackwood was forced to withdraw the satire in the reprinted number he remained on the attack, replacing it with the forthrightly titled 'Strictures on the Edinburgh Review.' The number sees *Blackwood's* taking on the *Edinburgh*; *The Craniad* challenge writ large, an upstart challenging orthodoxy. Modern critics who depict *Blackwood's* as the voice of the Tory establishment mistake British for Scottish politics. Scotland, then as now, was more liberal in its politics than England, and in challenging the *Edinburgh* and Whiggism *Blackwood's* saw itself as subverting the status quo rather than endorsing it. *Blackwood's*, in Scottish terms an oppositionalist journal, remade itself in Oedipal strife with the *Edinburgh Review*. Though real political disagreement underlies the conflict between the two journals, their similarity should not be underestimated. *Blackwood's* had the same literary DNA as the *Edinburgh*, and made itself, in part, by imitating the *Review*. The temper of the journals is close; for both the nineteenth-century and the modern reader the most memorable and controversial portions of the *Edinburgh* are when it wields the assassin's knife, rather than in its interminable essays on economics or anthropology. Francis Jeffrey jocularly admitted that every number of the *Review* should contain one 'tickler,' a stinging, ill-natured, or lacerating review.[42] *Blackwood's* learned from the *Edinburgh* that controversy is good for business, and borrowed its rival's manner, as for example in John Wilson applying the lash to the *Biographia* in October 1817 in a fashion clearly indebted to Jeffrey's 1814 demolition of *The Excursion*.

    William Blackwood satisfied the public appetite for ritual humiliation to an even greater extent than the *Edinburgh Review*, garnishing his dishes with character assassination and the most mordantly effective political satire since the days of the *Anti-Jacobin*. The new *Blackwood's* had a particular gift for appropriating the most memorable critical techniques of rival journals and journalists and then raising them to new heights (some would say lowering them to new depths, of course). Attacking the obscurantism of the Lake school? Jeffrey and the *Edinburgh* were famous for it. Lampooning the 'Cockney School'? That was the job of the *Quarterly*, which, for Shelley and others, sent John Keats to his grave as a consequence of its ill-natured strictures. Cod-biblical allegory? That was the province of William Hone, whose February 1817 anti-governmental liturgical parodies had caused so much controversy. As the October 1817 number demonstrates, Blackwood's intention was to outdo his rivals: be nastier to Hunt, Keats, and the Cockney School than the *Quarterly* and savage the Laker Coleridge in a way which would have made even Francis Jeffrey blush. *Blackwood's* attitude to phrenology can be seen in a similar light; the magazine, in Charles Gibbon's phrase, 'surpassed' the *Edinburgh* in its venom, becoming the market leader in abusing the phrenologists, part of its wider drive to achieve dominance in the competitive world of late Georgian print journalism.

NOTES

1 *Letters and Journals of Lord Byron*, ed. Leslie A. Marchand, 12 vols. (London: John Murray, 1973–94), vol. 4 (1975), 182.
2 *Phrenological Journal* 1 (December 1823), xvii–xviii.
3 *Edinburgh Review* 25 (June 1815), 227. Later Gordon returns to this theme: 'Such is the trash, the despicable trumpery, which two men, calling themselves scientific inquirers, have the impudence gravely to present to the physiologists of the nineteenth century, as specimens of reasonings and induction' (250).
4 *Edinburgh Review* 25 (June 1815), 263. Commenting on this notice in 1823, the *Phrenological Journal* declared, decidedly optimistically given that the *Review* was still running anti-phrenological articles in the late 1820s, that 'We have not a shadow of doubt that, if the editor of the Edinburgh Review could, he would gladly recall this most imprudent manifesto. Our belief is, that he will not again meddle with the subject, although he will thereby be placed in an awkward predicament, if phrenology becomes, as it cannot fail to do, a subject of general interest. The old refutation will not suit the present state of the science. A new attempt by the Edinburgh Review would be good fortune quite beyond our hopes' (*Phrenological Journal* 1 (December 1823), xvii).
5 *Edinburgh Monthly Magazine* 1 (April 1817), 35.
6 George Combe, *A System of Phrenology*, 5th ed., 2 vols. (Edinburgh: MacLachlan and Stewart, 1853), 1:248.
7 Ibid., 1:199. At least Wordsworth could console himself that William Hazlitt fared little better at Combe's hands: 'Hazlitt's head indicated a large development of Ideality [imaginativeness], sometimes to excess, and the faculty glows in his compositions. It was the sustaining power which gave effect to his productions; for he was eminent for neither sound principles, correct observations, nor extensive knowledge. He seems to have relied chiefly on his imagination and language for success; and his works are already sinking into the shades of oblivion' (*A System of Phrenology*, 1:485–6).
8 Ibid., 1:387.
9 *Phrenological Journal* 1 (December 1823), xiv.

10 Ibid.

11 *Blackwood's Edinburgh Magazine* 10 (August 1821, pt. II), 74.

12 Robert Montgomery, *The Age Reviewed* (London: William Charlton Wright, 1828), 122. Montgomery develops his attack in a footnote: 'Gall and Spurzheim esteem themselves greater philosophers than Locke, Hartley, &c, &c. Who shall set the bounds to human ingenuity? We may, without presumption, shortly expect that flying will be fashionable. Some mountebank has already commenced a prelude: and when the Mechanics are enlightened, no doubt wings will have their turn. It will be a pleasant day's jaunt to fly over to brother Jonathan, and at once settle about the North West passage. "But this is preposterous"; – not a bit reader: it is not half so wonderful as Phrenology – the Bump Philosophy. If Gall or Spurzheim would but sacrifice their own brains for dissection, it would be a capital method to ensure immortality. Thus it would be recorded: – "That scientific martyr Mr"'(ibid.). Within a decade Combe's 'half a thousand' had become a thousand pages and more.

13 *The Craniad; or Spurzheim illustrated. A Poem in two parts* (Edinburgh, 1817), 14.

14 Ibid., 87.

15 *Edinburgh Monthly Magazine* 1, no. 3 (June 1817), 288.

16 *Phrenological Journal* 1 (December 1823), iv.

17 Charles Gibbon, *The Life of George Combe, Author of 'The Constitution of Man,'* 2 vols. (London, Macmillan and Co., 1878), 1:110.

18 *Edinburgh Monthly Magazine* 1 (April 1817), 38.

19 Ibid.

20 And its contributors did not confine themselves to phrenological-related mirth in the magazine alone. J.G. Lockhart's *Peter's Letters to his Kinsfolk*, 3 vols. (Edinburgh: William Blackwood, 1819) features an amusing description of the Hunterian museum in the University of Glasgow: 'This Museum is chiefly remarkable for [its] very fine collection of anatomical preparations ... In one corner I saw an Egyptian mummy ... [Unfortunately], as it was entirely enveloped in the original swaddling-bands, I had no opportunity of investigating the organ of combativeness in the lower lateral part of the forehead, which is said by Spurzheim to be large in most mummies' (J.G. Lockhart, *Peter's Letters to his Kinsfolk*, 3 vols., Edinburgh: William Blackwood, 1819, vol. 1, 194–5). Lockhart notes that the mummy was 'shut up in a huge wooden case, strongly clasped with iron bars, as if to prevent it from coming out and chasing any of the professors up stairs, when they happen to visit that apartment at a late and dreary hour' (Lockhart, *Peter's Letters to his Kinsfolk*, 1:195). I am grateful to Philip Dundas for drawing this passage to my attention.

21 *Blackwood's Edinburgh Magazine* 4 (December 1818), 329–30.
22 *Phrenological Journal* 1 (December 1823), xxvii–xxix.
23 *Blackwood's Edinburgh Magazine* 3 (May 1818), 147.
24 Combe, *A System of Phrenology*, 2:28.
25 *Blackwood's Edinburgh Magazine* 10 (December 1821), 690.
26 Gibbon, *The Life of George Combe*, 1:109–10.
27 'A demagogue and reformer' by his own account (Gibbon, *The Life of George Combe*, 1:15).
28 *Blackwood's Edinburgh Magazine* 13 (May 1823), 593. According to the *Phrenological Journal*, 'the true tale ... was as follows':

In April 1821, a medical gentleman in Edinburgh, aided by a landscape painter, fashioned a turnip into the nearest resemblance to a human skull which their combined skill and ingenuity could produce. They had a cast made from it, and sent it to Mr G. Combe, requesting his observations on the mental talents and dispositions which it indicated; adding, that it was a cast from the skull of a person of an uncommon character. Mr C. instantly detected the trick, and returned the cast, with the following parody of 'The Man of Thessaly' pasted on the coronal surface :
There was a man in Edinburg,
And he was wond'rous wise
He went into a turnip-field,
And cast about his eyes
And when he cast his eyes about,
He saw the turnips fine;
'How many heads are there' says he,
'That likeness bear to mine?
So very like they are, indeed,
No sage, I'm sure, could know
This turnip-head that I have on
From thora that there do grow.'
He pull'd a turnip from the ground ;
A cast from it was thrown :
He sent it to a Spurzheimite,
And pass'd it for his own.
And so, indeed, it truly was
His own in every sense;
For cast and joke alike were made
All at his own expense.
The medical gentleman called on Mr Combe next day, and assured him that he meant no offence, and intended only a joke. Mr C. replied, that

he treated the matter entirely as such; and that if the author of it was satisfied with his share of the wit, no feeling of uneasiness remained on the other side. The story got into the Caledonian Mercury, at the time, so that the above misrepresentation must have proceeded on the faith that the real facts were by this time forgotten. For nearly six months past, the opponents of phrenology have been chuckling over this story, as a delightful specimen of the accuracy of our science; and we have been equally amused with the proof it affords of their own gullibility (*Phrenological Journal* 1 [December 1823], xix–xx).

29 *Blackwood's Edinburgh Magazine* 5 (May 1819), 158. In his famous essay in the *Edinburgh*, John Gordon had tried a similar, though decidedly less amusing, kind of lampoon:

we have observed that persons who have a lurking affection for port-wine have uniformly a certain redness of nose; and yet we are far from conceiving ourselves warranted to infer from this, that the nasal hue is the cause of the vinous partiality. Some, on the contrary, are disposed to maintain that it is rather the effect; but this we hold to be quite wicked and calumnious. Again, it is a remark, which we have never found to fail, that all great lawyers have long and very mobile fingers, 'digiti prehensiles,' as Linnaeus would have called them, with a remarkably smooth cuticle or epidermis on the palms of their hands. Shall we therefore conclude that this length and flexibility of finger, and this exceeding smoothness of palm, are the cause of eminence in the law? No; this may be a 'case of mere coincidence; nay the professional eminence may indirectly be the cause of some of these phenomena; but this is dangerous ground' (*Edinburgh Review* 25 [June 1815], 247).

30 *Blackwood's Edinburgh Magazine* 5 (May 1819), 159.
31 *Blackwood's Edinburgh Magazine* 10 (August 1821, pt. II), 74.
32 Ibid., 74.
33 Ibid., 75.
34 Ibid., 76.
35 Richard L. Gregory, *The Oxford Companion to the Mind* (Oxford: Oxford University Press, 1987), 619.
36 *Blackwood's Edinburgh Magazine* 1 (April 1817), 35.
37 *Phrenological Journal* 1 (December 1823), xvii–xviii.
38 Ian Jack, *English Literature 1815–1832* (Oxford: Oxford University Press, 1963), 18.

39 Ibid., 336.
40 A contemporary opinion quoted in ibid., 239.
41 The most extensively annotated edition of the 'Chaldee' is in *Parodies of the Romantic Age*, ed. Graeme Stones and John Strachan, 5 vols. (London: Pickering and Chatto, 1999), 3:95–118.
42 Samuel Smiles, *A Publisher and His Friends: Memoir and Correspondence of the Late John Murray*, ed. Thomas Mackay (London: John Murray, 1911), 87.

Blackwood's and Romantic Nationalism

IAN DUNCAN

It is a melancholy fact, that a single generation of abstract reasoners is enough to vitiate the pedigree of national sentiment and association; and although the ancient literature and history remain, they cannot resume their influence so extensively as before. Perhaps, in England, nothing has contributed so much as the host of periodical publications to obliterate sentiment, and substitute metaphysical restlessness in its place.

– 'Remarks on Schlegel's History of Literature,'
Blackwood's Edinburgh Magazine 3 (1818), 18

I

Scottish periodicals and fiction, the products of an Edinburgh publishing boom, dominated British literature during the first third of the nineteenth century. The decade after Waterloo (1815–25) was distinguished by the international success of Scott's Waverley novels, the rise of a rival school of Scottish fiction associated with the publisher William Blackwood, and a 'culture war' waged between Edinburgh Whig and Tory periodicals that accompanied the escalation of Reform agitation and government repression throughout Great Britain. *Blackwood's Edinburgh Magazine*, ferociously Tory, pitched itself into the midst of the fray. In its key early years, 1818–19, *Blackwood's* generated a Romantic discourse of cultural nationalism in opposition to the liberal political economy of the *Edinburgh Review*. The discourse received its full development in book-length publications accessory to the magazine, notably John Gibson Lockhart's translation of Friedrich Schlegel's *Lectures on the History of Literature* (1818) and the same author's semi-fictional anatomy of the modern Scottish scene, *Peter's Letters to his Kinsfolk* (1819). Although neglected by literary historians outside the field of Scottish studies,[1] *Peter's Letters to his Kinsfolk* offers the first programmatic, book-length account of the ideological formation of a national culture in Great Britain. It articulates the doctrinal emergence of a modern aesthetic conception of national culture, polemically defined against an Enlightenment discourse of sceptical rationality and represented by the symbolic techniques of romance revival.

William Blackwood financed Lockhart's visit to Germany in 1817, enabling him to scout the advance-guard of the European counter-enlightenment recently popularized by Germaine de Staël.[2] Lockhart also followed in the footsteps of Coleridge, who had visited Germany in his radical youth but was at this moment harnessing German metaphysics for a right-wing clerisy of church and state in the two *Lay Sermons* (1816–17). From Friedrich Schiller and Friedrich Schlegel, whose *History of Literature* he translated on his return to Scotland, Lockhart derived the cultural theory with which, together with John Wilson and the other Young Turks of *Blackwood's Edinburgh Magazine*, he would scourge Edinburgh's Whig literary establishment. In May 1818 this *enfant terrible* was introduced to Walter Scott, who had discreetly supported the new magazine while maintaining an official neutrality in the rivalry between Blackwood and Archibald Constable. Impressed by Lockhart's account of the German literary scene, Scott quickly drew him into his patronage network. In October, Lockhart and Wilson visited Scott's country house at Abbotsford. Anxious that this gifted protegé should distance himself from the by now scandalous orbit of *Blackwood's*, Scott had offered Lockhart the historical portion of the *Edinburgh Annual Register*, which he was too busy to continue himself. *Peter's Letters to his Kinsfolk* appeared the following year. Lockhart's first book, a testament to the maturity and respectability accompanying his new association with Scott, performs an elaborate homage to the future father-in-law, beginning with its titular echo of Scott's account of a tour to the field of Waterloo, *Paul's Letters to his Kinsfolk* (1815). As the lavish, ceremonial centrepiece of *Peter's Letters*, Lockhart recreates his visit to Abbotsford, casting Scott as the tutelary guardian of an ancestral Scottish culture.

In *Peter's Letters to his Kinsfolk* Lockhart combines Schlegel's schema of national literary history and the aesthetic pedagogy prescribed by Schiller (in *On the Aesthetic Education of Man*) with the counter-revolutionary tropes of an organic constitutionalism devised by Edmund

Burke. Lockhart applies this Coleridgean synthesis of German theory and Burkean politics to the topos of a Scottish, rather than English, national tradition. In so doing, no doubt paradoxically, *Peter's Letters* founds the modern tradition of nationalist critiques of Scottish culture. Critics inveterately hostile to the discourse of imperial Tory Unionism founded at *Blackwood's* have tended nevertheless to repeat its main rhetorical strategy, which brings a Scottish tradition to light by exposing its inauthenticity or lack in relation to an 'organic' English standard. Adopting and extending Schlegel's anti-Enlightenment polemic, Lockhart brands a modern, liberal tradition of 'speculative philosophy' or 'Scotch metaphysics,' running from Hume to the *Edinburgh Review*, as the defective and false version of a national culture. Lockhart rejects popular Presbyterianism on the same grounds, as an alien, divisive force. The new nationalist ideal of a mystic secular totality, combining past, present, and future generations, relies on a polemical repudiation of the Whig tradition that empirically constituted much of modern Scottish cultural history. As so often seems to be the case, the foundational speech-act of national tradition is a sentence of banishment.

With this rejection of the modern past, Lockhart brings the 'Post-Enlightenment' epoch of Scott's novels and *Blackwood's Magazine* into critical focus as the opening of a new cultural stage or period.[3] The critique of enlightenment provides the dialectical fulcrum of a new – 'Romantic' – ideological formation, as it adapts the radical themes of an earlier generation (the elevation of sentiment over reason, the location of collective identity in a deep ancestral past) and applies them to the case of Scotland. (It also involves the misrecognition of those themes insofar as they are products of the Enlightenment culture under attack.) *Peter's Letters to his Kinsfolk* prescribes a modern nationalist cultural politics in which culture absorbs politics and an aesthetic investment in tradition constitutes national identity. Following Schiller, paving the way for Carlyle, Lockhart personifies national tradition in the authoritarian archetype of the 'hero as man of letters,' whom we engage in pious reverence rather than critical dialogue. The great man restores, in his own example, the organic, synecdochic relation between individual and society that constitutes national character. Lockhart represents his patron Scott as the incarnation of national tradition, and Scott appears to have authorized Lockhart's representation, which would turn out to be decisive in the later fortunes of his reputation.[4] Nevertheless, Lockhart's version of Scott was only one among many contemporary renditions of a powerful figure, and in certain key respects it was a misconstruction, detaching Scott from the Enlightenment philosophical matrix he shared with the Edinburgh reviewers.

II

Lockhart's essay 'On the Revival of a Taste for our Ancient Literature' (appearing in *Blackwood's* in December 1818, between his Schlegel translation and *Peter's Letters*) summarizes the half-century of British antiquarian and poetic revival – later to be given the title Romanticism – as evidence of a modern 'revolution of sentiment.'[5] Lockhart echoes Schlegel's claim that the late eighteenth-century British and German romanticisms constitute 'a mighty change' in European literature.[6] In Scotland in 1819 that epochal shift appears as an effect of political opposition, the ideological reproduction of party strife across the institutions of literature in a period of acute economic and social turbulence. Lockhart's essay participates in a larger debate in the Edinburgh periodicals about the institutional status and social function of 'literature' in relation to what were perceived, in the aftermath of the French Revolution, as the dangerously totalizing forces of politics and commerce in modern society. The debate traces the disintegration of the eighteenth-century idea of a 'republic of letters' supposed to regulate civil society and its replacement with a new, transcendental figure of national culture.[7]

From its 1802 foundation, the *Edinburgh Review* committed itself to a rehabilitation of the Moderate Whig ethos of the Scottish Enlightenment, discredited in the Anti-Jacobin reaction, and to a political program in which the Enlightenment discourse of political economy would provide scientific legitimacy for electoral reform. The intervening catastrophe of the French Revolution had to be acknowledged, however. Following the conservative critique of modernization formulated in Adam Ferguson's *History of Civil Society*, the *Edinburgh Review* diagnosed the potential corruption of the republic of letters by its subjection to market forces. The progress of civilization has meant the substitution of 'enthusiasm' and 'enchantment' – traditional modes of identification with a symbolic order – with not simply 'knowledge' but a restless, groundless, 'metaphysical' desire, stimulated by the proliferation of periodicals and other literary commodities in an industrializing print culture. The *Edinburgh Review* set itself above this predicament by identifying critical judgment, its signature performance, with the assumption of a professional status analogous to that of the Scots judiciary.[8]

The Blackwoodian attack on the *Edinburgh Review*, led by Lockhart, fastened on the journal's immersion in the commercial conditions it criticised – deconstructing the professional exceptionalism with which the reviewers attempted to secure their disinterestedness. An effective opposition to the *Edinburgh* required, thus, a discursive and formal articulation – defining an alternative relation between literature and society – in addition to the assertion of a rival politics. The genre of monthly miscellany assumed by *Blackwood's* (ostensibly in rivalry with *Constable's Edinburgh Magazine*, and provoked by the appearance of a pro-Reform newspaper, the *Scotsman*) provided a nimbler and fitter medium for intervention in cultural debate, addressing the expanding population of middle-class readers, than the stately quarterlies – the Tory *Quarterly Review* as well as the Whig *Edinburgh*. This formal and class-based rather than strictly political determination is evident in Radical critiques that reiterate the Blackwoodian stance, from James Mill's complaint (in the first number of the utilitarian *Westminster Review*, 1824) that both the *Edinburgh* and *Quarterly* alike represent an 'aristocratic' establishment, to the Reform-era remark in *Tait's Edinburgh Magazine* (a Radical monthly formally patterned on its political antagonist *Blackwood's*) that the 'Whig Coterie' of the *Edinburgh Review* had founded, 'if anything, a Tory publication.'[9]

Jon Klancher describes the technique by which the heterogeneous styles and genres of the miscellany produce the reflexive figure of a transcendental subject – a 'national mind': 'such a writing machine will produce a self-reflexive, desiring reader conscious of the expansive mental power that extrudes through his reading of any particular content … Shaping the *Blackwood's* reader demands an inexhaustible panoply of stylistic resources so that it can demonstrate a "power of thought" which is doubled and redoubled in an endless intellectual exertion.'[10] *Blackwood's* rhetoric, in other words, transforms the restless and recursive, 'metaphysical' modality of modern desire into a purposive dynamic of intellectual labour in order to fashion a transcendental subject. But this 'intellectual exertion' remains a rhetorical illusion, the mirroring effect of a florid and opaque stylistics rather than of critical reason, and subjectivity remains solipsistically confined within the temporality of its individual act of reading. The question remains open as to the objective, collectively recognized figure that will satisfy this 'endless intellectual exertion' – lest it turn outwards in a dangerous political discontent.

'The real and radical difficulty,' as Francis Jeffrey himself had acknowledged, 'is to find some pursuit that will permanently interest, – some object that will continue to captivate and engross the faculties.'[11] The very first number of the *Edinburgh Monthly Magazine* – preceding its scandalous mutation into *Blackwood's* – featured a series of articles ('On the Sculpture of the Greeks,' 'On Greek Tragedy') that turn a Fergusonian admiration of the Athenian republic towards an argument for substituting aesthetics for politics as the modern discipline of national virtue. The Attic theatre 'was not merely a place of public amusement, but rather a temple for the purification of the national manners, and the worship of the gods.'[12] Now, in a commercial, cosmopolitan, proto-democratic age, the arts are all the more important 'in a *moral* point of view, for the animation of virtue and of patriotism.'[13] Works of art acquire the status of relics of ancestral excellence – effigies of a lost organic relation between individual subject and national community. Contact with them becomes an act of reverence in which the psyche is replenished with the virtue they contain. But it is far from apparent how modern literary production, bought and sold in the market and fragmented by partisan politics, can reproduce this sacralizing function. Lockhart takes up the question, but does not answer it, in a *Blackwood's* essay on the state of modern periodical criticism: 'It is a bold thing to compare Shakespeare with a Reviewer; but if ever the world shall possess a perfect Reviewer, be assured that he will bear, in many respects, a striking resemblance to this first of poets. Like him he will be universal–impartial–rational.'[14] Such a reviewer is not at present to be found. Lockhart's own persona, the 'Baron von Lauerwinkel,' deplores the politicization of culture in the two major quarterlies and exhorts the reviewers to mend their ways – without any admission of the militant escalation of those cultural politics being undertaken in his own magazine at that very moment.

Lockhart found his answer in the cultural nationalism promoted in Germany by Friedrich Schlegel. Schlegel argued at the beginning of his *Lectures on the History of Literature* that the transformation of literary culture at the end of the eighteenth century brought the recovery of an integrated national character out of the abyss of scepticism excavated by the philosophical reasoning of Voltaire, Rousseau, and Hume. Schlegel read this scepticism as the fatal intellectual symptom of a modern social fragmentation, in terms derived from Schiller and reminiscent of Adam Ferguson: 'A separation ... between the men of letters and the courtly society, and again between both of these and the common people, is destructive of all national character.'[15] The *Blackwood's Magazine* review of Lockhart's translation ('by far the most rational and profound view of the history of literature which has yet been presented to Europe') did not hesitate to apply Schlegel's diagnosis to the local ('English,' i.e., British) case, identifying 'the host of periodical publications' – the *Edinburgh Review*, implicitly, foremost among them – as transmitters of the destructive Enlightenment legacy of 'metaphysical restlessness': 'It is a melancholy fact, that a single generation of abstract reasoners is enough to vitiate the pedigree of national sentiment and association; and although the ancient literature and history remain, they cannot resume their influence so extensively as before. Perhaps, in England, nothing has contributed so much as the host of periodical publications to obliterate sentiment, and substitute metaphysical restlessness in its place.'[16] Schlegel however proposed a solution. Literature, reinterpreted 'in its widest sense, as the voice which gives expression to the human intellect – as the aggregate mass of symbols in which the spirit of an age or the character of a nation is shadowed forth' (I. 274), reconstitutes the nation both as a collectivity and at the level of individual psychology, as it recombines the severed faculties of reason and sentiment. 'The formation of a national character requires a combination of all those powers and faculties, which we too often keep distinct and isolated,' due to the division of labour (I. 7). 'Literature' may resolve the ideological predicament of modernity, in other words, and reconstitute a fragmented national identity, by itself representing, and so performatively reintegrating, the vital, totalizing homology between nation and psyche.

III

Lockhart and his fellow reviewers mystified the relation of *Peter's Letters to his Kinsfolk* to its Blackwoodian matrix, in a strategy that included pseudonymous disguises for Lockhart's authorship ('Peter Morris,' a Welsh physician) and his political views ('William Wastle,' an antiquarian laird), and even the pretence that the first edition of *Peter's Letters* was a second edition. In fact *Peter's Letters* made its first appearance in the pages of *Blackwood's Magazine*, which serialized substantial extracts in the numbers of February and March 1819 under the pretext of reviewing the hard-to-find first edition (allegedly printed in Aberystwyth).[17] Lockhart represents his native Scotland in the character of a Welshman addressing English readers. The figure of the protagonist as ethnic stranger, adapted from *Waverley* and the Irish national tales of Sydney Owenson and Maria Edgeworth, provides a doubled trope for the articulation of what Mary Louise Pratt has called autoethnographic authority.[18] Crucially, an alien interpreter – in ethnographic parlance, a 'participant observer' – constructs the objective field of national culture as a total, closed set of relations. The work of interpretation constitutes that totality as a virtual coherence of parts and internal differences; while the interpreter's alienation from the field is the condition that makes it visible as a totality. As James Buzard has argued, the device of the participant observer resolves the 'hermeneutic circle' problematic of ethnographic interpretation, which requires both entry into the field and engagement with its social relations in order to be able to understand them, and a stance outside the field in order to see it as a whole.[19] Lockhart derives the ethnic cast of his protagonist, the Scotsman-as-Welshman, from Smollett's epistolary novel *Humphry Clinker* (1771), the early prototype of Romantic national fiction, and beyond that from an older (Elizabethan) discourse of British nationalism. The Welsh Briton typifies an originary ethnicity – a primitive Britishness – that has been so thoroughly colonised that it can now function smoothly as a naturalized representative of the modern United Kingdom. In other words, the subject belongs to a modern national culture by virtue of an original historical alienation within it. In this way nationality is made the badge or trophy of empire: the sign of a specifically imperial formation of subjectivity in the modern state. As critics have argued, Scott had used the technique in *Waverley* (constructing the synecdochic series Highlands = Scotland = Great Britain), while his most virtuoso exploration of the principle would occur in *Ivanhoe*, published at the end of 1819.[20] *Peter's Letters* makes an important, polemical adjustment to the scheme in order to convert the national tale from the mode of romance to criticism. The protagonist is not an Englishman but a Celt: the ancestral depth of whose subjection enables him to read the inner fragmentation that constitutes modern Scotland's failure of national identity.

This judgment relies on an all-important relocation of national character from the empirical, ethnographic domain, where it is found to be defective, to its mystic supplement and synecdochic totality, *tradition*: a virtual construct (something *else* or *more* which constitutes wholeness) that restores the lost homology between individual and nation. Lockhart's fiction yields the powerful crux of the Unionist ideology of nationality: that a national culture is the product of an imperial tradition, and Scotland only acquires its integrity once it becomes the synecdoche for an Anglo-British empire. The integrated Briton 'Peter Morris' interprets (for 'English' readers) a broken Scotland in the ideal shadow of a tradition defined, as it turns out, by Anglo-British tropes of cultural hegemony. The 'dissociation' diagnosed as a psychological attribute of the tradition is in fact an invention of the critic, who splits the actual tradition in order to invoke a lost, mystical whole. Here, the nationality that Scotland by itself cannot provide is supplied by English models. Oxford, rather than the Scottish universities, preserves 'the steady and enduring radiance of our [sic] national past.'[21] And despite the corrosive scepticism of the *Edinburgh Review*, 'an immense majority of the people of Scotland' are still 'enlightened patriots – men who understand the value of national experience, and venerate those feelings of loyalty and attachment to the more formal and external parts of the English constitution' – that is, the 'Glorious Revolution' constitution that Scotland acquired with the Union (II. 139).[22]

Lockhart's critique of periodical journalism, reiterated and amplified in *Peter's Letters*, shifts its focus to become the critique of a national tradition. In the psychological synecdoche of national character, tradition is the organicist trope that absorbs politics into culture. Peter Morris denounces no longer the politicization of culture as such but the Whig 'temper,' manifest in a recursive and levelling relation between the 'mad and ferocious scepticism' of the reviewers ('envy in disguise'), and the 'vulgar and envious insolence' of middle-class dissenters. In this light (according to Morris's informant Wastle) Jeffrey and the Whig literati are 'the legitimate progeny of the sceptical philosophers of the last age' (II. 128). Lockhart mounts a sustained critique of the intellectual culture of the Scottish Enlightenment, personified by David Hume, throughout the first volume of *Peter's Letters*, which he summarizes in an essay on Scottish literature and national tradition that concludes the second volume. This essay contains nearly all the themes that reappear in twentieth-century Scottish nationalist criticism: the linguistic division between written English and spoken Scots, the social gulf between literati and folk, and even the castigation of 'Puritanism,' as well as Enlightenment scepticism, as alienating doctrinal systems. Lockhart imports Schlegel's scheme to found, in effect, the nationalist topos of the Scottish literary tradition, the notorious 'Caledonian Antisyzygy' or dissociation of sensibility, in its classic definition of a split between intellect and feeling:[23] 'The generation of Hume, Smith, &c., left matters of feeling very much unexplored, and probably considered Poetry merely as an elegant and tasteful appendage to the other branches of literature, with which they themselves were more conversant. Their disquisitions on morals were meant to be the vehicles of ingenious theories – not of convictions of sentiment. They employed, therefore, even in them, only the national intellect, and not the national modes of feeling' (II. 360). Although Hume's genius fitted him 'for seizing and possessing an extensive dominion over Scottish intellect,' the 'defect of feeling in his composition' (a term which conflates writing and character) disabled an authentically national representation: 'He was very nearly the *beau ideal* of the national understanding, and had he stood in any thing like the same relation to some other parts of the national character, without all question he might have produced works which would have been recognised by them as complete pictures of their mode of thinking and feeling, and which would, therefore, have obtained a measure of influence exactly coincident with the extent of their national existence' (I. 85). Hume not only promoted, through his influence, the splitting of national tradition, but personifies it in his own literary character: 'in spite of all that nature and art could do, the devil has been too strong for David; and the Prince of Sceptics has himself been found the most potent instrument for diminishing, almost for neutralizing, the true and grave influence of the Prince of Historians' (I. 88).[24] Riven by a psychomachia between radical philosopher and conservative historian, Hume becomes a character in a fable by Hogg or Stevenson. This metaphysical and psychological split within the self constitutes the cultural schism of the nation between cosmopolitan literati and pious folk. Restoring the homology between individual and collective in the diagnosis of a division within each of them, Lockhart thus integrates the dismembered tradition at the level of critique. The critique, in other words, constitutes the nation as a virtual or ideal term by perpetuating division as its empirical foundation.

In a critique of the Scottish university curriculum, Lockhart appeals to history as the discipline that can unite the severed faculties: 'If Philosophy (strictly so called) grapples chiefly with our reason, and the Fine Arts with our feelings and imagination, History, on the other hand, claims a more universal possession of us, and considers the whole man, and all the powers of his soul, as alike within her control' (I. 165). Lockhart harnesses the traditional content of an Enlightenment historicism ('the outward and visible effects, which the various modifications of society and education have already produced upon man') to a new spiritual technique of *Bildung* or subject formation: '[History is] the only study which presents to all our endeavours and aspirations after higher intellectual cultivation, a fast middle-point, and grappling-place, – the effects, namely, the outward and visible effects, which the various modifications of society and education have already produced upon man, his destinies, and his powers' (I. 163). Here and elsewhere Lockhart's word 'grapple' designates the process, called *suture* by Althusserian theorists, by which the individual mind is joined to a collective ideological formation. (Lockhart's term, with its admission of friction and resistance, seems more apposite than the other, with its misleading connotation of surgical precision.)

Above all, as Schiller had recommended, the new technique of culture is *aesthetic*. Its interpretive strategy yields 'the link and bond of connection which fastens the whole mighty structure together': whole person and whole nation (I. 165). Schlegel, once more, had defined history as a 'national consciousness, expressing itself in works of narrative and illustration.'[25] Lockhart's election of history as spiritual technique, rather than register of information, anticipates Carlyle and even Emerson:

> History ... when she is not confined to the mere chronicling of names, years, and external events, but seizes and expands before us the spirit of great men, great times, and great actions, is in herself alone a true and entire philosophy, intelligible in all things, and sure in all things; and above all other kinds of philosophy, rich in both the materials and the means of application. The value of the fine arts, in regard to the higher species of mental cultivation, is admitted by all whose opinion is of any avail. But even these, without that earnestness of intention, and gravity of power, which they derive from their connection with the actual experience of man, his destiny, and his history – would be in danger of degenerating into an empty sport, a mere plaything of the imagination. The true sense and purpose of the highest and most admirable productions of the imitative arts, (and of poetry among the rest,) are then only clearly and powerfully revealed to us, when we are able to transport ourselves into the air and spirit of the times in which they were produced, or whose image it is their object to represent. (I. 164)

As cultural technique, the study of history recovers – or creates – a spiritual identity with a lost past, abolishing the material differences between then and now. The act of 'transport' also abolishes the distinction between history as a condition of representation and history as an object of representation: we are at once inside and outside the text. This hermeneutic sublime is antithetical to the scientific historicism of the

Enlightenment, which measured diachronic differences ordered by synchronic analogies within a materialist developmental continuum. The past provides that mystic foundation of the transcendental subject, the imaginary Archimedean point from which the present may be criticized as well as inhabited: 'The remembrance of the great *past*, – the knowledge of its occurrences and its spirit, is the only thing which can furnish us with a fair and quiet point of view from which to survey the *present* – a standard by which to form just conclusions respecting the comparative greatness or littleness of that which passes before our eyes' (I. 165). Once more, we read the formulae of a Victorian pedagogy of culture and tradition at their moment of transmission and assembly.

   Peter's Letters is explicit enough about the aesthetic strategy of interpretation that underwrites its autoethnographic ruse. The participant observer, standing back from the empirical text of culture, can read it, criticize it and imaginatively complete it, because he occupies the viewpoint of tradition, an ideal construct that belongs to him rather than to the natives of the scene. In Peter Morris's visit to a country sacrament at the conclusion of the third volume, the narrator descends, at last, among the folk. His aloofness from the ceremony enables him to harmonize its parts and situate it teleologically in a tradition, thereby reconstituting it virtually and synecdochally as an epiphany of national character. Such a meaning is emphatically not available to the participants: 'In surveying these pious groupes [*sic*], I could not help turning my reflections once again upon the intellectual energies of the nation to which they belong, and of whose peculiar spirit such a speaking example lay before me. It is in rustic assemblages like these that the true characteristics of every race of men are most palpably and conspicuously displayed, and it is there that we can best see in multiplied instances the natural germs of that which, under the influence of culture, assumes a prouder character, and blossoms into the animating soul and spirit of a national literature' (III. 326). The scene exhibits, in other words, a potentiality which the reader finds completed in the virtual medium of national literature. This completion substitutes the communicants' expectation of salvation as the purpose of the sacrament. 'Culture,' in its old meaning of cultivation, improvement, education, at once alienates the scene (from 'culture,' an empirical way of life belonging to the natives) and brings it into its own (as 'culture,' the property of our reading, the 'soul and spirit of a national literature'). Accordingly, the meaning of the sacrament has to be rescued from the doctrinal hold of Presbyterian theology: 'You would have seen (for who that has eyes to see, and heart to feel, could have been blind to it?) that the austerities of the peculiar doctrinal system to which they adhere, have had no power to chill or counteract the ardours of that religious sentiment which they share with all that belong to the widespread family of Christians' (III. 332). Once again, 'theory' is detached from 'sentiment' in order for the latter term to signify a restored totality. In the present case the 'doctrinal system,' which happens to be that of the main radical and reforming tradition in early modern Scottish history, is an attribute of the relative insensibility of the natives of the scene, while 'religious sentiment' turns out to be an aesthetic property of the connoisseur who can view and appreciate 'the orderly and solemn guise of [the people's] behaviour,' 'the deep and thrilling harmony of their untaught voices,' 'the low and affecting swell of [the psalm's] own sad composing cadences,' and so forth.

Not only does Lockhart expropriate popular religion for his version of national tradition by throwing out its doctrines and reducing it to a repertoire of forms and impressions, but he subjects 'national literature' itself to a similar colonizing operation. The virtual, teleological projection of national literature takes place upon an allusive evocation of its empirical manifestation in the form of Robert Burns, who haunts the scene. The first volume of *Peter's Letters* had featured a rescue of Burns's reputation from Whig misprision to make it one of the modern cornerstones of a national literature. Now Morris examines the faces in the crowd 'to see if I could trace any countenance resembling that of Burns' (III. 329), who had demonstrated 'that within the limits and ideas of the rustic life of *his* country, he could find an exhibition of the moral interests of human nature, sufficiently varied to serve as the bread and sure foundation of an excellent superstructure of poetry' (III. 330–1). But the Burns embedded in an actual social history is a vexing character. He had already turned the field sacrament into a literary property in one of his best poems, 'The Holy Fair.' Peter Morris admits that the verification of Burns's description in 'The Holy Fair' is a principal motive for his visit. Lockhart, who would play a decisive role in the posthumous canonization of Burns, was troubled by 'The Holy Fair': far from inculcating a tender reverence, the poem unleashes an exuberantly satirical, lewd, and carnivalesque depiction of the country sacrament. 'That the same man should have produced the "Cottar's Saturday Night" and the "Holy Fair" about the same time,' Lockhart later wrote, 'will ever continue to move wonder and regret.'[26] The historical Burns, in short, was another schizoid figure, like Hume, and admission to the national tradition required a drastic surgical intervention.[27]

Lockhart's representation of the field sacrament thus corrects Burns's most vivid account of popular life by, in effect, transforming 'The Holy Fair' into 'The Cottar's Saturday Night' – the showcase of a pious peasantry for gentle readers. Lockhart takes the logic of the alienated observer some steps beyond the poet of the 'Cottar.' The aesthetic mode of representation, having banished doctrine as the source of piety, must replace it with a past emptied of positive social meaning – in short, with death: 'There was a breath of sober enduring heroism in [the psalm's] long-repeated melancholy accents–which seemed to fall like a sweet evening dew upon all the hearts that drank in the sacred murmurs. A fresh sunset glow seemed to mantle in the palest cheek around me – and every old and hagard [*sic*] eye beamed once more with a farewell splendour of enthusiasm, while the air into which it looked up, trembled and was enriched with the clear solemn music of the departed devout. It seemed as if the hereditary strain connected all that sat upon those grassy tombs in bonds of stricter kindred with all that slept beneath them–and the pure flame of their Christian love derived, I doubt not, a new and innocent fervour from the deeply-stirred embers of their ancestral piety' (III. 333–34). 'Ancestral piety' signifies death instead of the radical zeal of Covenanting forefathers, in an extended allusion (via Gray's 'Elegy Written in a Country Churchyard') to Walter Scott's *Old Mortality* (published by Blackwood in a short-lived appropriation of Scott from Constable in 1816). 'O, rake not up the ashes of their fathers!' the editor of *Tales of My Landlord* had quoted from John Home's *Douglas*, as he surveyed the tranquil graves of Covenanters in a country churchyard (before going on in the novel to do exactly that).[28] As Lockhart glosses it, his favourite among Scott's novels has made the Covenanting heritage safe ('a new and innocent fervour') for the national tradition by purging it of its radical political energies and turning it into an object for aesthetic contemplation: in effect (as Scott's title hinted), a National Monument. Absence and death constitute tradition, the mystic bond of connection. The aesthetic gaze is thus inevitably elegiac: death is the condition of the figures it looks upon, their separateness and stillness. Yet there is something uncanny about dead figures that return. National tradition is not so much a mausoleum as a haunted house. Lockhart's purple prose metamorphoses the erotic vitality of Burns's Holy Fair into a hectic, vampirical illusion – 'a fresh sunset glow seemed to mantle in the palest cheek around me' – as it relegates 'enthusiasm' to 'a farewell splendour,' covenant with the dead. Through Peter Morris, we read the mystic link between mourners and ancestors in the death they share; that is to say, their elegiac gaze becomes ours, and we read the figures in the landscape as already dead. The end of this declension is our own death, the authentic content of the scene as it is of national tradition.

The field sacrament shows how Lockhart's construction of national culture performs the dismemberment of the empirical body of Scottish literature and history that is its critical theme. Lockhart invokes history as the discipline that constitutes a national culture; but the past recovered is an ideal one, a spectral dimension parallel to the record of actual utterances, events, and deeds. Such history is, in fact, a romance revival, which converts the scientific representation of a primitive other, in an evolutionary relation to ourselves, to an imaginary identification with ancestral origins separated from us by death (but which we will join in our death). Those origins remain lost, expired, ghostly, only recuperable in an aesthetic relation, as a fiction; yet that aesthetic relation works as an imaginative possession, as though the revival of the past renders *the present* spectral, unreal – in Slavoj Žižek's formulation, undead: 'The ambiguous and contradictory nature of the modern *nation* is the same as that of vampires and other living dead: they are wrongly perceived as "leftovers from the past"; their place is constituted by the very break of modernity.'[29] National culture turns out to be a textual system of phantom relations, a dialectical construction of loss, pathos, and influence, and it originates, accordingly, not anywhere in the world, in social and economic relations, but in literature – in a relationship between reader and romance.

IV

The romance-revival tropes of national culture and tradition converge most powerfully upon the figure of Scott, 'Patriarch of the National Poetry of Scotland' (II. 351), in the extended account of the visit to Abbotsford that closes the second volume of *Peter's Letters to his Kinsfolk*. Peter Morris's journey down from Edinburgh and subsequent tour of the countryside, guided by his host, allegorize the subject's entry into the ideological formation of national culture. An initially alien, 'bare and sterile' landscape begins to blossom and to acquire 'picturesque' features, including relics of a feudal past, as Morris approaches Abbotsford. Literary and historical associations thicken around the estate. Scott informs Morris that he is 'treading on classical ground – that here was *Huntly Burn*, by whose side Thomas the Rhymer of old saw

the Queen of Faery riding in her glory' (II. 318). Through Scott's mediation a kind of cognitive re-mapping takes place, in which the strange
landscape becomes familiar – becomes (for this pseudo-Cambro-Briton,
and in language that echoes Wordsworth) *home*: 'The name of every hill
and every valley all around is poetical, and I felt, as I heard them
pointed out one by one, as if so many old friends had been introduced
to my acquaintance after a long absence, in which I had thought of them
all a thousand times' (II. 320). Scott's nation-making authority resides in
his joint character as proprietor and interpreter. His ability to reanimate
the landscape by reviving (or creating) its national associations, for
Morris and for us, is inextricably tied up with his role as landlord.
Scotland, Abbotsford, and Scott's poetry all stand metonymically for
one another. The figure of the laird as *genius loci* is in striking contrast
with the national-tale convention, carried over into *Waverley*, which
casts the native informant and national spirit as a maiden whom the
visiting protagonist ends up marrying. All the more so that this would
constitute the author's, Lockhart's, biographical plot. Sophia Scott
herself makes no appearance in *Peter's Letters*, which surrounds the
patriarch with his feudal retainers.[30] The appearance of the national
father-in-law announces the completion of the historical process
of Union, the topic of the national tale; the troping of his wealth
and power as cultural capital marks the extent to which he has taken
possession.

   Morris crowns the account of his visit with an essay on national
literature in which Scott definitively occupies the station elsewhere
granted to Burns:[31] 'At a time when the literature of Scotland – and of
England too – was becoming every day more and more destitute of
command over everything but the mere speculative understanding
of men – this great genius seems to have been raised up to counteract, in
the wisest and best of all ways, this unfortunate tendency of his age, by
re-awakening the sympathies of his countrymen for the more energetic
characters and passions of their forefathers' (II. 348).

   Scott enacts the programme of aesthetic education that Lockhart had
described under the rubric of history, decisively establishing it as a
technique of *historical romance*. The national author 'grapples boldly
with the feelings of his countrymen' (II. 361), 'making them acquainted
with the various courses of thought and emotion, by which their forefathers had their genius and character drawn out' (II. 350). He transports
his readers by a genial force: his, not theirs, is the sublime agency of
sympathetic reawakening. In Scott's recital of the ballad of Otterbourne,

Lockhart describes the process at work. First, like a vatic medium, Scott undergoes a physiognomic transformation, as the verse possesses *him*: 'It seemed as if one single cadence of the ancestral strain had charm enough to transport his whole spirit back into the very pride and presence of the moment, when the White Lion of the Percies was stained and trampled under foot beside the bloody rushes of Otterbourne. The more than martial fervours of his kindled eye, were almost enough to give to the same lines the same magic in my ears; and I could half fancy that the portion of Scottish blood which is mingled in my veins, had begun to assert, by a more ardent throb, its right to partake in the triumphs of the same primitive allegiance' (II. 303–4). The romance revival is oddly qualified, however, by the time it reaches its audience: 'almost enough to give to the same lines the same magic in my ears ... I could half fancy.' Ours can only ever be a partial imitation or reflection of the author's transport, as though his mediumship shields us from the full violence of the energy he channels. 'Primitive allegiance' remains, for the reader still more than for the listener, a representation realized by the heroic labour of an author, whose 'authentic' connection with his sources we are required to take on faith.

NOTES

1 The most detailed and perceptive account of *Peter's Letters to his Kinsfolk* remains that of F.R. Hart, who reads it as an experiment in 'national biography': *Lockhart as Romantic Biographer* (Edinburgh: Edinburgh University Press, 1971), 46–75.
2 De Staël's *De l'Allemagne* was translated into English in 1813. Lockhart attended Fichte's lectures and met with Goethe. Detailed information about his German tour is hard to come by.
3 On the Romantic discourse of periodization or 'the Spirit of the Age,' see James Chandler, *England in 1819: The Politics of Literary Culture and the Case of Romantic Historicism* (Chicago: University of Chicago Press, 1998), 105–14.
4 Scott advised and encouraged Lockhart in the composition of *Peter's Letters*, applauding 'the exquisite Dr Morris and his compeers' and supplying information on 'the state of our Scottish literature about twenty five years since.' On the book's publication he acknowledged Lockhart's 'kind and delicate account of his visit to Abbotsford.' See H.J.C. Grierson, ed., *Letters of Sir Walter Scott*, 12 vols. (London: Constable, 1932), 5: 323, 332,

431. At the beginning of 1820 Lockhart was formally engaged to Scott's daughter Sophia, and shortly afterwards appointed his father-in-law's literary executor.

5 'On the Revival of a Taste for our Ancient literature,' *Blackwood's Edinburgh Magazine* 4 (December 1818), 264–6.

6 Frederick Schlegel, *Lectures in the History of Literature, Ancient and Modern*, trans. J.G. Lockhart, 2 vols. (Philadelphia: Dobson, 1818), 1:2.

7 For a fuller account of the debate, see Ian Duncan, 'Edinburgh, Capital of the Nineteenth Century,' in *Romantic Metropolis: Cultural Productions of the City 1770–1850*, ed. James Chandler and Kevin Gilmartin (Cambridge: Cambridge University Press, 2005), 45–64 .

8 See Biancamaria Fontana, *Rethinking the Politics of Commercial Society: The Edinburgh Review 1802–1832* (Cambridge: Cambridge University Press, 1985); Francis Jeffrey, 'On Literature, Considered in its Relationship to Social Institutions,' *Edinburgh Review* 41 (1813), 1–25; Ina Ferris, *The Achievement of Literary Authority: Gender, History, and the Waverley Novels* (Ithaca, N.Y.: Cornell University Press, 1991).

9 Marilyn Butler, 'Culture's Medium: The Role of the Review,' in *The Cambridge Companion to British Romanticism*, ed. Stuart Curran (Cambridge: Cambridge University Press, 1993), 120–47 (137); *Tait's Edinburgh Magazine* 11 (1833), 58–9.

10 Jon Klancher, *The Making of English Reading Audiences, 1790–1832* (Madison: University of Wisconsin Press, 1987), 52–3.

11 Jeffrey, 'On Literature,' 17.

12 *Edinburgh Monthly Magazine* 1 (1817), 39.

13 Ibid., 13.

14 [John Gibson Lockhart], 'Remarks on the Periodical Criticism of England, by the Baron von Lauerwinkel,' *Blackwood's Edinburgh Magazine* 3 (1818), 670–9 (672).

15 Schlegel, *Lectures on the History of Literature*, 1:6.

16 'Remarks on Schlegel's History of Literature,' *Blackwood's Edinburgh Magazine* 3 (1818), 479–511 (510).

17 'Observations on "Peter's Letters to his Kinsfolk,"' *Blackwood's Edinburgh Magazine* 4 (1819), 612–21, 745–52.

18 Pratt, *Imperial Eyes: Travel Writing and Transculturation* (New York: Routledge, 1992), 7. See also James Buzard, 'Translation and Tourism: Scott's *Waverley* and the Rendering of Culture,' *Yale Journal of Criticism* 8, no. 2 (1995), 31–7. On the national tale, see Katie Trumpener, *Bardic Nationalism: Romantic Novel and the British Empire* (Princeton, N.J.: Princeton University Press, 1997), 128–57.

19 Buzard, 'Translation and Tourism,' 35; see also Christopher Herbert, *Culture and Anomie: Ethnographic Imagination in the Nineteenth Century* (Chicago: University of Chicago Press, 1991), 1–28.

20 See, e.g., Buzard, 'Translation and Tourism.'

21 [John Gibson Lockhart], *Peter's Letters to his Kinsfolk*, 3 vols. (Edinburgh: Blackwood, 1819), 2:206. Future references will be cited in the text.

22 On the role of 'the English constitution' in the Enlightenment tradition of Scottish historiography that Lockhart is adapting here, see Colin Kidd, *Subverting Scotland's Past: Scottish Whig Historians and the Creation of an Anglo-British Identity, 1689–c.1830* (Cambridge: Cambridge University Press, 1993).

23 The diagnostic term 'Caledonian Antisyzygy,' coined in 1919 by G. Gregory Smith and taken up by Hugh MacDiarmid, signified the internal contradictoriness of Scottish national character. For its literary-historical manifestation as a 'dissociation of sensibility,' see Edwin Muir, *Scott and Scotland: The Predicament of the Scottish Writer* (London: Routledge, 1936). For recent critiques see Tom Nairn, *The Break-Up of Britain: Crisis and Neo-Nationalism* (London: New Left Books, 1981), and Cairns Craig, *Out of History: Narrative Paradigms in Scottish and British Culture* (Edinburgh: Polygon, 1996), 82–118.

24 Compare Schlegel's argument that Hume's philosophical scepticism, 'by no means becoming in a great national historian,' undermined his literary influence: *Lectures on the History of Literature*, 2:221.

25 Ibid., 1:16.

26 J.G. Lockhart, *Life of Robert Burns* (1828); repr. in *Robert Burns: The Critical Heritage*, ed. Donald A. Low (London: Routledge and Kegan Paul, 1974), 343.

27 On Burns's reputation in the generation following his death, see Leith Davis, *Acts of Union: Scotland and the Literary Negotiation of the British Nation 1707–1830* (Stanford, Calif.: Stanford University Press, 1998), 124–48.

28 Walter Scott, *The Tale of Old Mortality*, ed. Douglas Mack (Edinburgh: Edinburgh University Press, 1993), 14.

29 Slavoj Žižek, *Tarrying with the Negative: Kant, Hegel, and the Critique of Ideology* (Durham, N.C.: Duke University Press, 1993), 222.

30 Andrew Lang reproduces a watercolour sketch of Sophia by Lockhart that shows her in the classic harp-playing pose of the national heroine: *The Life and Letters of John Gibson Lockhart*, 2 vols. (London: John C. Nimmo, 1897), vol. 1, facing p. 288. For the convention, see Trumpener, *Bardic Nationalism*, 18–19.

31 Compare Lockhart on Burns: 'The political circumstances of Scotland
were, and had been, such as to starve the flame of patriotism; the popular
literature had striven, and not in vain, to make itself English; and, above
all, a new and cold system of speculative philosophy had begun to spread
widely among us. A peasant appeared, and set himself to check the creep-
ing pestilence of this indifference.' Low, ed., *Robert Burns: The Critical
Heritage*, 345.

Blackwood's Subversive Scottishness

CHARLES SNODGRASS

Introduction

From the beginning of the Scottish Enlightenment down to the Age of Scott, there occurred a transfer of an important philosophical enquiry about what can be known and thought of *in common* with others. The notion of common sympathy, or a sympathy or *sense* of the common, became an intellectual nexus in early-nineteenth-century Scotland for coalescing not only a Scottish national identity – through common cultural heritage, traditions, and rituals – but also a pro-British, Union-ized identity. Arguments about the issue of sympathy and common sense ranged across philosophical, political, economic, and intellectual terrains, with battle lines fixed along political lines. On the one hand, there were those with liberal sympathies like David Hume and Adam Smith who, following a long line of Lockeian empiricism, held that sympathy was an 'idea' or concept that could only be discerned through our minds, i.e., our imaginations (hence, Hume's ultimate scepticism about the external world). On the other hand, conservative followers of the Scottish philosopher Dugald Stewart (among them the writers later dubbed 'The Blackwood Group') ascribed to his view that sympathy was an 'idea' or concept only discernable by intuiting the external world. Stewart gave no credence to the power of the imagination in forming a genuine perception of the world; only a 'common sense' of the world as each of us knows it can be discernable. In short, 'Common Sense takes common-sense beliefs as certain.'[1] The difficulty in seeing this philosophical argument through to a logical conclusion resulted from a precariousness upon which the School of Common Sense philosophy rested. For example, if asked by a Humeian sceptic whether

George IV ever set foot on Scottish soil during his August 1822 state visit to Edinburgh, followers of the Common Sense school of philosophy must necessarily take 'the metaphysical *character* of the beliefs of common sense for granted as something manifest.'[2] Whether a common sense that the visit may have occurred or the character of a common Scottish national identity exists, the Blackwood Group took the beliefs of common sense in Edinburgh, and indeed Lowland Scotland in general, 'for granted as something manifest.'

The common ideological agenda of the conservative Scottish Tories in Edinburgh, coupled with the pervasive sense of national longing for a restoration of a *Scottish* monarch, provided the Blackwood Group with the ability to marry these two impulses into a fresh identity of a romantic Scot and Scotland. This essay probes into the matter to analyse to what extent this approach to Scottish national identity underpinned the intellectual philosophy associated with William Blackwood I and his magazine during the first third of the nineteenth century.

One important influence in crafting this Scottish national identity was Walter Scott. In his undergraduate days at the University of Edinburgh taking courses under Dugald Stewart (holder of the Chair of Moral Philosophy), Walter Scott would be influenced by common sense philosophy later evidenced in his deployment of Stewart's principles throughout his historical novels. As early as the winter of 1789, at age eighteen, Scott submitted in Stewart's Moral Philosophy class an essay entitled 'On the Origins of the Feudal System.' In it Scott argues that, according to biographer Edgar Johnson, 'the feudal organization of society appeared *in all nations* under certain *common* circumstances.'[3] One only needs to look at Scott's *Marmion* (1808) or any Waverley Novel to see this ideology of communal sympathy at work. Moreover, Johnson observes of Scott that 'in Stewart's eloquent panegyric of moral philosophy based on common sense analysis of man and society he found the germ of his own practical ethics.'[4] Later in 1808, Scott was at work on the Dryden portion of *The Lives of the Poets* in which his analysis surpasses both Edmund Malone's and Samuel Johnson's accounts by 're-lating Dryden to his *character* and showing how his writings both mold and were molded by the climate of the age.'[5]

Scott would come to harness these interests in communal identity in his interaction with the Blackwood Group, and in particular in his interaction in the private sphere of Edinburgh literary and intellectual clubs. One such private circle was the fairly elite Friday Club. Formed in June of 1803, the Friday Club counted among its original members

Professor Dugald Stewart, Walter Scott, Francis Jeffrey, Henry Cockburn, Henry Brougham, and Henry Mackenzie.[6] As Cockburn recalls in his *Life of Lord Jeffrey* (1852), the Friday Club was 'so called from the day on which it first used to meet. It was entirely of a literary and social *character*, and was open, without any practical limitation of numbers, to any person generally resident in Edinburgh who was supposed to combine a taste for learning and science with *agreeable* manners; and especially with perfect safety. "The idea was Scott's," Jeffrey says in a letter to Murray.'[7] The club 'first assembled at Bayle's Tavern in Shakespeare Square,'[8] around the corner from Edinburgh's Theatre Royal (since demolished) where in August 1822 George IV attended a special 'Command' performance of a dramatized version of *Rob Roy*, supervised by Scott.

For the next 'sixteen or eighteen years,' the Friday Club then 'went to Fortune's [Tontine Tavern], in the Eastmost division of Princes Street'; Cockburn fondly recalls Fortune's as 'the very best tavern that has ever been in Edinburgh; and was particularly remarkable for having, to an extent that few establishments of the kind have anywhere, the quietness of a private house.'[9] Fridays at Fortune's tended to cost a fortune. As Cockburn reflects: 'I don't think it was till the Peace of 1814, that, the continent being opened, we soared above prejudice, and ate and drank everything that was rare and dear ... It is needless to add that our bills have always been high, or that their tendency has always been to get higher. Upon an average each dinner cost [*sic*] to those who partake of it from £1.18s. to £2.5s ... For costliness is a good thing in such an association. It makes it more comfortable, and more select.'[10] Fortune's Tontine Tavern, officially the Caledonian Coffee Room, used to be located at No. 5 Princes Street, seven doors down and across the street from No. 17, the home of *Blackwood's Edinburgh Magazine*.[11] Margaret Oliphant chronicles that Blackwood relocated his book-selling firm from his Old Town South Bridge quarters – across the street from the David Hume Tower of Old College – to No. 17 Princes Street in New Town in 1816, 'an address soon made memorable as the headquarters of a literary group unequaled in Edinburgh or within the limits of Great Britain.'[12] So, in effect, from 1816 to 1820 or 1822, Edinburgh's select literati – particularly, but not exclusively, Stewart, Scott, and Mackenzie – convened on a monthly basis 'as a social institution' to discuss '[l]earning, and talent, and public reputation' during 'the private hours of conspicuous men,'[13] where the public (individual) commingled with the private (group/club). Appearing on a monthly basis as well, *Blackwood's* contributed to such discussions by publishing historical, political, fictional, local, scientific, agricultural, (Scottish) national, commercial, and meteorological articles of interest, all in miscellany style. 'Maga,' as it became known colloquially, also published a 'Monthly List of New Publications,' categorized by London and Edinburgh publishing houses, and (intermittently) 'Works Preparing for Publication' – all courses upon which the Friday Club feasted during its monthly soirées.

I would be remiss, however, to insinuate that clubbing is unique to Edinburgh. In fact, having originated as a coffee house, Fortune's Tavern mirrored a number of early eighteenth-century precursors, including the Scriblerus Club, The (Literary) Club, the Kit-Kat Club, and the Brothers Club. One only needs to peruse the pages of the *Tatler* (1709–11), the *Spectator* (1711–12), and Pope's the *Dunciad* (1728) for allusions informing these texts regarding these clubs' personalities, agendas, and events.[14] As Jürgen Habermas has argued, the sociability of the tavern club became a key locus in creating common connections and circles which branched out into affairs of state administration and politics. These clubs, Habermas explains, provided for a kind of 'social intercourse that, far from presupposing equality of status, disregarded status altogether,'[15] as we see with the Friday Club, in an attempt to establish a common, levelling bond among its members. The club functioned as a web of discourse for the Blackwood Group, providing a forum for the construction of a common sense of both local (Edinburgh) and national (Scottish) identity.

My point, therefore, in recapturing an elite Edinburgh literati nightlife is to illustrate how the materiality of Edinburgh's relatively small, close-knit proximity contributed to a sense of common sympathy within literary, social, and political minds during the early years of William Blackwood's publishing career. And while Hume and Smith did not belong to the Friday Club (having died before its founding), a common sense of Scottish Enlightenment philosophy pervaded the Friday Club, for as Cockburn, its long-time secretary, labelled it, Fortune's was 'our philosophic Tavern.'[16]

Convivial Criticism in Ambrose's Tavern

In *The Making of Classical Edinburgh*, A.J. Youngson maintains that the Friday Club was by no means a singular phenomenon during the Golden days of Edinburgh. I concur with Youngson and would take his assertion one step further by arguing that the most famous, or more appositely cacophonous, assembly of Edinburgh literati existed not physically but fictionally. That is to say, the *Noctes Ambrosianæ* were a series of quasi-satirical articles published intermittently in *Blackwood's Edinburgh Magazine* between March 1822 to February 1835, and 'no Magazine articles won more attention or favor.'[17] Set in Ambrose's Tavern,[18] these pieces were dramatized parodies of Edinburgh's literati scene, complete with acts, stage directions, and sometimes musical scores. As Trevor Royle notes, these night talks 'took the form of imaginary conversations, usually over gargantuan suppers, in Ambrose's Tavern at 15 Picardy Place, Edinburgh. Some of the participants were fictitious but most of them were real: John Wilson as "Christopher North," James Hogg as "The Ettrick Shepherd," Robert Sym as "Timothy Tickler," Thomas De Quincey as "The Opium Eater," and William Maginn as "O'Doherty" [*sic*].'[19] Over the years, the range of topics, events, and literary works discussed left few in Edinburgh free from the 'Noctes' group's caustic criticism and witticisms, including Hogg himself, who became a frequent target for North's arrow and the Scorpion's sting.[20]

The emergence of the *Noctes Ambrosianæ* coincides with the dissolution of the Friday Club. While we should bear in mind that the Friday Club was a historical club with real members, the 'Noctes' group is an entirely fictional club with imagined characters that typically were modelled on real people. I would argue, then, that the 'Noctes' group mirrors the common sympathy found in such prominent circles as the Friday Club but used satire and parody to construct a 'sympathetic' identity among Scottish literati. The 'Noctes' group deploys humour – albeit historically specific and often arcane to non-Edinburghers of Scott's Age – which functions as a relief valve for potentially libelous and alarming treatments of historical personages and events. And a particularly revealing example of how the 'Noctes' group harnessed its Menippian satire to secure the favour of Edinburgh literati and obscure the historical nature surrounding the events discussed occurs in 'Noctes Ambrosianæ No. VI,' which appeared in 'The Royal Number' of September 1822, two weeks after George IV's visit.[21]

This particular 'Noctes' is worth closer examination not merely for its crafty or 'pawkie' conflation of fiction and reality, but also because, as J.H. Alexander aptly observes, 'it is at very least an important historical document and a remarkable curiosity.'[22] Perhaps more importantly, Alexander continues, 'It gives wholehearted expression to a high Tory way of imagining: Whigs are physical as well as moral weaklings, unable to hold their drink or tolerate tobacco smoke; the aristocracy play their part, and the poor know their place, being loyal and religious as well as full of physical vitality; the Highlanders are willing and honoured participants as well as traditional figures of fun. The Kingdom is United in friendly rivalry.'[23] Against this backdrop and the awareness of this 'Noctes' number being written in the wake of the well publicized pageantry surrounding George IV's visit just weeks before, we should be attuned to the curious common sympathy that Wilson and Lockhart – who are largely responsible for the production of this 'Noctes' – construct for their readers in order to laud the king on the one hand and admonish 'true' Highlanders, such as Alastair Randalson Macdonell of Glengarry (1773–1838), on the other. So, imagine the following scene.

Just after Mr Ambrose has set 'Cold Supper' for this convivial group, Act I of this 'Noctes' opens with 'Old Kit' ('Christopher North,' i.e., John Wilson) announcing that 'The King has left Theatre, and we all shall be here in a few seconds. I made my escape from the Manager's box, just before the row and the rush began.'[24] The theatre to which North refers is, of course, the Theatre Royal at which George IV attended his command performance of *Rob Roy*, just down the street from the House of Blackwood and in the same square in which the Friday Club first convened. North is joined immediately by 'Odoherty, Tickler, Seward, Buller, Highland Chieftain, and Mr. Blackwood' (*BM*, 369). J.H. Alexander conjectures that 'the fictitious Oxonians Harry Seward of Christ Church and Buller of Brasenose, who first appear in 'The Twelfth of August' (*BM*, 5.604), were probably 'embodiments ... of [Wilson's] old Oxford reminiscences' ... ; Buller was probably based on John Hughes (1790–1857) of Oriel College.'[25] In either case, it is important to note that Seward and Buller take up the role of loyal and somewhat self-righteous high-Tories in service to the 'new' Hanoverian king of Scotland. To anonymise and further confuse readers in this shifting pseudonymous exchange, Odoherty introduces the Highland chief as simply 'the Chief of the Clan —— ' (*BM*, 369). In a tongue-in-cheek reworking of Adam Smith's view that a 'man of rank ... is observed by all the world' which is 'eager to look at him,' Seward cheerily remarks, 'Why, did not he look every inch a King, this evening? A King of Great Britain, France, and Ireland, ought, if possible, to be a man worth looking at. His subjects expect it, and it is reasonable that they should' (*BM*, 369). Here is a prime example of the *Noctes'* damning with faint praise.

While the explicit comparative compliment of George IV to the epony-mous hero of *King Lear* (4.6) would not have been lost on most readers of Maga, the image of a rather rotund sixty-year-old monarch – arrayed at the theatre in a field marshal's uniform that had never seen a battle-field – would have caused most readers to blush or wince. This parodic conflation was due in large part to an early nineteenth-century British infatuation with George IV's bulky body. For instance, in a letter of 18 February 1822 to John Morritt, Sir Walter Scott estimates that '[i]f *our Fat Friend* makes good his word there will be plenty of gaieties for Miss Morritt and Gathering of the Gael and cocking of bonnets and waving of plaids and masques in Holyrood with much more that will not be seen every day.'[26] Another, more immediate, example outside of this 'Noctes' text of attention given to the king's body appears in George Cruikshank's caricature of George IV and Sir William Curtis in High-land dress during the visit, a cartoon entitled 'The Sovereign and Sub-ject —— Equipt for a Northern Visit.'[27] Alluding to the king's age, now sixty years hence, and exaggerating his kilted corpulence, the caption's epigraph reads: 'Folly as it grows in Years / The more extravagant appears.'[28] Cruikshank's sexually allusive cartoon satirizes an exchange between George IV and Alderman and former London Mayor Curtis:

[GEORGE IV:] What my Knight of the Calipash, have you got into the Highland Costume? Poh 'doff that man it don't become you, you are to [sic] old for such freaks. I am every inch a Scot –
   'Leave those to tryfle with more grace and ease,
   'Whom Folly pleases, or whose Follies please.
[SIR WILLIAM CURTIS:] As a loyal Subject I follow your —— Example! by Gale tho we must take care of the Lassies, for this dress is but little better than Achilles's fig leaf. If I don't take care I shall lose the little I have got speedy and soon.

This cartoon appeared in both colour and black and white soon after the Royal Visit. Thus, the 'Noctes'' allusion to 'every inch a king' operates within textual and fictive (*King Lear* and the 'Noctes' itself) as well as political (the king's body) spheres simultaneously. It must necessarily do so in order to succeed as a light-hearted joke, or *jeu d'esprit*, as the Blackwoodians were fond of calling such repartee. A common sense of current events, undergirded by a common sympathy for Scotland's 'ain king,' produced a common ideological ground upon which the 'Noctes' group was able to taunt George IV while simultaneously remaining loyal to his Hanoverian government.

After more lauding of the king's bodily, as well as sovereign, presence, a most curious exchange occurs between Mr Blackwood, the titular editor (pseudonymously dubbed 'Ebony'), and Mr North, the actual co-editor (along with Lockhart) of *Blackwood's*:

MR BLACKWOOD: Do you think, sirs, that the King would become a contributor to the Magazine? I have sent his Majesty a set splendidly bound, by –
MR NORTH: Hush, Ebony, leave that to me. You must not interfere with the Editorial department. (*BM*, 369)

Apart from this amazing moment of William Blackwood's self-referentiality *within* his own publication (a rare phenomenon) and slyly soliciting George IV as a contributor to his Tory Maga, this speculation actually pre-dates by a year a letter of 12 September 1823 to George IV's private librarian, in which Blackwood gives terms for the 'price of the 13 Vols' of the 'Maga' at '£9.12.6.'[29] Moreover, this September 1822 'Noctes' passage echoes John Wilson's 29 October 1817 letter to Blackwood that cautioned, amidst 'The Chaldee Manuscript' crisis, 'above all, let *us* [i.e., Wilson and Lockhart] speak & act for ourselves, without any *record* of deed of *yours*.'[30] To complicate Blackwood's editorial role in Maga, in this 'Noctes' Wilson claims that 'I am Editor of Blackwood's Magazine, of which you may have heard' (*BM*, 386); however genuine this claim might have been is impossible to discern absolutely.

While there remained throughout the Age of Scott a translucent veil over the genuine editorship of *Blackwood's*, there also existed a thin and well worn mask over the real author of *Waverley*, the orchestrator of George IV's visit. It was, in fact, fairly well known among Edinburgh literati that Walter Scott was the 'Author of Waverley,' as James Ballantyne printed on the novels' title-pages. However, it was not until 23 February 1827, at a dinner of the Edinburgh Theatrical Fund, that Scott publicly acknowledged his authorship of the Waverley Novels.[31] This 'Noctes' participates early on in that thinly disguised masquerade of authorship when – in an embedded poem addressed 'TO CHRISTOPHER NORTH, ESQ.' and with which 'North'/Wilson almost lights his pipe! – it jests of 'the great poet, who writes in prose ; / Sure I mean the Author of Waverley, / Whoe'er he be, if any one knows' (*BM*, 376). The 'Noctes' group, including Scott's son-in-law Lockhart, knew very well who the 'Author of Waverley' was, yet played out the *jeu d'esprit* in order to maintain a sense of ambiguity and uncertainty about the real author, who had much to lose as an advocate, sheriff, and baronet by this unmasking.

If 'Ebony's'/Blackwood's call for a contribution from the king is not enough of an overtly political gesture by itself – publicly reaffirming Maga's 'good [Tory] cause' engendered by Smithian 'fellow-feeling' – then soliciting an article from the anonymous Highland Chieftain clearly is. The exchange between the editor and the Chieftain is worth some consideration in light of both contemporaneous local and national occurrences:

MR BLACKWOOD: I beg your pardon, sir, but I should wish much to have a sound, sensible, Article on the State of the Highlands of Scotland. I suspect there is much misrepresentation as to the alleged cruelty and impolicy of large farms. Dog on it, will any man tell me, sir, that –

CHIEFTAIN: Mr Blackwood, I wish I could write an article of the kind you mention. You are a gentleman of liberal sentiments. In twenty years the Highlands will be happier than they ever have been since the days of Ossian. Lowland Lairds have no right to abuse us for departing from the savage state.

MR BLACKWOOD: Could you let us have it for next Number, sir? We stand in need of such articles prodigiously – sound, sensible, statistical articles, full of useful information. We have wit, fun, fancy, feeling, and all that sort of thing in abundance, but we are short of useful information. We want facts – a Number now and then, with less fun and more facts, would take, and promote the sale with dull people. Yes, it is a fact, that we want facts. (BM, 372)

The adamancy surrounding Blackwood's pre-Gradgrind demand for facts only momentarily lightens the reference by the chieftain to the ongoing, pugnacious Highland Clearances. The 'State' of the Highlands had been undergoing economic and geographical Balkanization since the late 1770s, in what began as a genuine if not misguided attempt at 'improvement' of ostensibly backward Gaelic culture. Rosalind Mitchison has argued succinctly that '[s]ince the eighteenth century all recommendations for improvement had considered that the population, which at the time all wished to retain, would be of greater economic use on the coast than inland. So policy was to shift the population to the coast and to encourage it to mix farming with other activities. The inland area could then be used for sheep farming which would bring in a large rent.'[32]

The most notorious example of Highland Clearances remains the 'improvement' to the Sutherland Estates beginning in 1813 and reaching a fever pitch in 1819. The Duke and Duchess of Sutherland (who also held the title of Lady Stafford) commissioned economist James Loch to reorganize and 'improve' their Sutherland Estates, a large portion of the Northern Highlands that spanned from Ullapool on the west coast to John O'Groats on the east coast.[33] As John Prebble points out in *The King's Jaunt*, in 'human terms ... the [Sutherland improvement] meant the eviction or removal of men, women and children in favour of sheep. It meant the demolition or burning of ancient townships in the mountains, and the merciless destruction of the culture that had once sustained their inhabitants.'[34] More than an economic and geographical reformation, the clearances took on a sinister ideological nature when Loch, in his *Account of the Improvements on the Estate of Sutherland*, envisioned that 'the *character* of this whole population will be completely changed ... The children of those who are removed from the hills will lose all recollection of the habits and customs of their fathers.'[35]

When Ebony/Blackwood claims in this 'Noctes' that 'facts' are what his 'dull' readers (read: Whigs and Highlanders) need, the hidden message is that 'statistics' of how much better off the Highlanders, and in turn Scotland as a whole, would be from these 'improvements' are what will settle once and for all the controversy surrounding the Sutherland clearances. Because Lady Elizabeth Stafford had been instrumental in suppressing rebellions and ignoring tenant petitions against clearances on her estates, she viewed the Royal Visit as 'an opportunity to refute the slanders upon her family, to re-establish it in public esteem, and to demonstrate the loyalty it inspired among the young men of her clan.'[36] As the Countess of Sutherland in her own right by the age of six when her father died, Lady Stafford earned a deep and abiding animosity from her tenants and, in turn, from other quarters in Scotland that were sympathetic to the established Highland culture. So caustic was hatred for Lady Stafford that threats against her life were not unheard of, as revealed by the following anonymous 1819 letter reprinted in the *Gentleman's Magazine*: 'You damned Bitch. You are a damned Old Cat and deserve to be worried and burnt out for burning out the poor Highlanders. If you dont [sic] make a public apology & explanation I will brave you.'[37]

Against this turbulent and dangerous backdrop, Lady Stafford deliberately chose to appear during the visit as a self-exonerating gesture. While her attempt was certainly successful and welcomed with the pageant-master himself – in fact, Scott and Lockhart were lifelong friends of Elizabeth Sutherland – there was little common sympathy for her among Scots at large. Therefore, the 'Noctes' group having the Highland Chieftain, as opposed to any other character present, claim that '[i]n twenty years the Highlands will be happier than they ever have been since the days of Ossian,' functions as a genuine endorsement from one who ought to know. If we view 'the days of Ossian' not as the third century but as the latter eighteenth in which they were written, then the Chieftain's comment serves to 'officially' amputate that romanticized, noble savage limb long grafted onto the Highlander's character by James Macpherson's counterfeit Gaelic translations. Characterizing the chieftain as an economic 'improver' serves to underscore Blackwoodians' commercialism – as well as Adam Smith's *laissez-faire* economics that inform it – and thereby sanctions the Anglicization of the *Gaeltacht*, or Gaelic culture. The overarching effect of such a manoeuvre on the part of the Blackwood Group becomes one of ideological containment at the expense of a viable Highland culture that should now be read, literally and metaphorically, as merely a nostalgic, romanticized culture reminiscent of uncouth Ossianic days gone by.

In solidifying, again both literally and figuratively, this pro-Union, high-Tory sentiment throughout Scotland, yet particularly in Edinburgh, the 'Noctes' group speculates on the relevance of current erections of monuments in the city. That is, further into this 'Noctes' the conversation shifts slightly from the king and politics in Act I to a discussion of two monuments situated on Calton Hill: the Lord Nelson Monument, an inverted telescope constructed in 1807–17, and the National Monument, begun in 1822. An event key to this discussion was George IV's sanctioning of the laying of the foundation and cornerstone of the National Monument,[38] a monument to Scottish soldiers who had fallen during the Napoleonic Wars and intended to be an exact Parthenon replica. The sanction occurred on 27 August 1822, just before he attended the *Rob Roy* performance at the Theatre Royal. The 'Noctes' group, full-flushed with the events of that day, reconsiders that culturally significant moment while aboard the duke of Atholl's barge docked at the nearby Newhaven Harbour's Chain Pier:

MR NORTH: Again [a gas-light] blazes forth, and tinges Nelson's Pillar with its ruddy splendour.

MR TICKLER: Nelson's Pillar – ay – may it stand there for ever! Did they not talk of pulling it down for the Parthenon? *We* held it up. Pull down a Monument to the greatest of all British admirals! Fie – fie.

MR BULLER: We Englishmen thought the proposal an odd one. But the Pillar, it was said, was in bad taste, and disfigured the modern Athens.

MR NORTH: It is in bad taste. What then? Are monuments to the illustrious dead to lie at the mercy of Dilettanti? But, as Mr Tickler said, *we* preserved that Monument.

MR SEWARD: I admire the Parthenon. Most of you will recollect my prise poem on that subject. I am glad the foundation-stone has been laid.

MR NORTH: So am I. Let Scotland shew now that she has liberality as well as taste, and not suffer the walls to be dilapidated by time before they have been raised to their perfect height.

ODOHERTY: The Parthenon will be an elegant testimonial. Is it not, too, a national testimonial? Why then should not the Scottish nation pay the masons? ...

MR TICKLER: The Standard-Bearer speaks nobly. We admire the Parthenon. We resolve to build it. We call ourselves Athenians, and then implore Parliament to pay the piper. Poor devils! we ought to be ashamed of ourselves.

MR BULLER: Mr Odoherty, I agree with you. A rich nation does well to be magnificent. Up with towers, temples, baths, porticos, and what not ; but for one nation to build splendid structures, and then call on another for their praises and their purses, is, in my opinion, not exactly after the fashion of the Athenians.

MR BLACKWOOD: I have no objection to publish an additional Number any month in behoof of the Parthenon. I think Mr Linning deserves the highest praise for his zeal and perseverance. (*BM*, 377–8)[39]

The cosmic, or calculated I would argue, irony of George IV's dedication of a monument to fallen Scottish soldiers can be located in the very idea of such a structure. On the one hand, we have a monument to fallen *Scottish* (and largely Highland) soldiers,[40] many of whom, as Colonel David Stewart of Garth details in his two-volume *Sketches of the Character, Manners and Present State of Highlanders of Scotland* (1822), earned such military prowess by fighting in skirmishes against the crown after the Jacobite Rebellion of 1745–6. However, this monument, in Gayatri Spivak's terms, attempts to 'bury its undead past' by eliding that turbulent pro-national history in favour of a pro-union one.[41] On the other hand, we have a Hanoverian monarch, with the 'auld royal bluid o' Scotland ... in his veins,'[42] paying tribute to Scottish soldiers whom he and his forefathers were instrumental in suppressing. The laying of the cornerstone of the National Monument, then, becomes another, yet highly significant, incremental move toward rehabilitating the 'savage,' 'uncouth' Highlander into an acceptable member of the Union, based predominantly on his martial dexterity. In a masterstroke of policy, Highland chiefs were given military commissions to promote enlistment through clan loyalty. As Robert Clyde has cogently argued,[43] this rehabilitation of Scottish *character* was completed during the mid-Victorian period, as is evident in such romanticized imperial exploits as Tennyson's 'The Charge of the Light Brigade' (1854) and the Scottish Tartans Society's current motto 'Bring Forrit the Tartan,' commemorating the 1857 siege of Secundrabagh, India, a victory – in more ways than one – for the 93rd Regiment (the Sutherland Highlanders).

Refashioning Edinburgh as 'the Athens of the North' was a critical step in this rehabilitation, a step that Blackwoodians, including Scott, helped to materially and fictionally construct. In the Age of Scott, a common sense pervaded Edinburgh as a self-stylized 'Modern Athens.' Edinburghers' self-perception operated on more than a conceptual level; they envisioned their own modern-day acropolis atop Calton Hill. Tickler and Buller's anxiety regarding the funding of the National Monument interestingly anticipates the fleeting rise and fall of this 'Modern Athens.'[44]

In a certain sense, then, the fragmented, failed project of constructing a National Monument memorializes in stone a testament to the haphazard and incomplete nineteenth-century project of Scottish national identity reconstruction. A once glorified vision of Scottish history and culture now stands as an absurd ruin of the Scottish Enlightenment's project of coalescing a common sympathy among its disparate Highland and Lowland cultures. In George IV, Scotland finally had its 'ain king' again; a *British* constitutional monarchy had subverted the Jacobitical pretence to the throne, and, as Susan Ferrier narrates in *Marriage* (1818), the Act of Union had at last been consummated, with Scotland in the role of bride. Playing off of William Playfair's comment that the National Monument had become 'the pride and poverty of Scotland,'[45] this eerie and persistent reminder of the glory that was (and potentially once again could become) Scotland is now known commonly to Scots, somewhat fittingly, as 'Scotland's disgrace.'

Blackwoodian Toryism vs Scottish Whiggism

It was not until some historiographical complexity was refashioned that the children of the Scottish Enlightenment were able to manoeuvre the foregoing bifurcated yet intrinsically interconnected project of establishing a Scottish nationalist common sympathy in the service of a unified, homogeneous Scotland. This complexity, for Scotland anyhow, has its origins in the Scottish Whiggism of George Buchanan (1506–82).

In this same Royal Number 'Noctes,' Wilson and Lockhart work in a reminder in the third and final act – as if the Maga's readers needed reminding – of *Blackwood's* patron saint, as it were:

GIRNAWAY: Gudewife [read: Glaswegian Everywoman], you ken that buik our son sends us every month, wi the face of Geordie Buchanan on't. – Would ye believe that we hae under our roof-tree the very lads that write it. Here's the cock o' the company, Mr North himself.

GUDEWIFE: I jaloused something wonderfu', whene'er I saw the face of him, and that Adjutant ane. Siccan a buik I never read afore. It gars ane laugh, they canna tell how ; and a' the time ye ken what ye're reading is serious, too – Naething ill in't, but a' gude – supporting the kintra, and the King, and the kirk. (*BM*, 387)

From its renaissance in October 1817, *Blackwood's* sported 'the face of Geordie Buchanan on't.' To answer why Blackwoodians chose to represent themselves under the aegis of Buchananite Whiggism, we need first to sketch how it was that the high-Tory Blackwoodians hailed Buchanan as their Scottish historian exemplar.

In terms of Scottish historiography, Colin Kidd points out that Buchanan was an 'influential Protestant ... who had reformed the Church in defiance of their Catholic Queen ... Thus he constructed an ancient constitutional history of Scotland, relying on a theory of popular sovereignty in which 'people' meant an assembly of the nobles and clan chiefs, or in the Aristotelian-Livian terminology of this eminent classicist, the virtuous men of the community ... In time Buchananite ideology became the dominant mode of political argument among Scottish Presbyterians, and Buchanan's works were alternately banned and republished in accordance with the vicissitudes in Scotland's turbulent and monarchical and ecclesiastical politics between the author's death in 1582 and the Revolution of 1689.'[46] There are three key ideas to keep in mind when viewing Buchanan through a Blackwoodian lens. First, while we have seen the principle of *common* sympathy at work in the service of forging a renewed Scottish national identity from the Scottish Enlightenment onward, its political and constitutive element has is roots in Buchanan's theory of *popular* sovereignty. This popular sovereignty functions as a common sympathy – Walter Scott encouraged his fellow Scots to view George IV within the relationship of 'we are THE CLAN, and our King is THE CHIEF'[47] – and a popular sovereignty upon which Blackwoodians further propagandize and capitalize. Second, it should be noted carefully that the term Scottish Whig did not have the same meaning and ideological connotations as it did later in Francis Jeffrey and Henry Cockburn's era; that is, while Scottish Whiggism in Buchanan's day signified a status quo politics of ancient constitutional monarchy via oligarchical power, Whiggism during the Age of Liverpool was virtually synonymous with a liberality of Reform – a designation Blackwoodians certainly eschewed. Yet, in view of the Blackwood Group's clever political positioning and subtle reconstruction of national identity, it became apropos that they allied themselves with a defunct ideology. In one sly move, the group managed to embrace this ancient constitutional monarchy – reifying George IV's position within a revered Scottish cultural heritage – while *simultaneously* rousing 'Whig' affinities with all of that term's polyvalences, a pawkie move indeed. Finally, it is not far-fetched to read 'the virtuous men of the community' of Buchanan's age as the 'Noctes' group during the Age of Scott, a self-stylized politically, aesthetically, and morally virtuous group modelled on the Friday Club's elitism and proffering its own revision of Scottish constitutional monarchy via George IV à la Bonnie Prince Charlie. In terms of the moral posturing, we cannot overlook Blackwood's involvement and the group's pride during Wilson's appointment to the Chair of Moral Philosophy at the University of Edinburgh, a post he held from 1822 to 1851, but for which he had no qualifications. Thus, the monthly reiteration of Buchanan's 'eminent classicist' head on *Blackwood's* served a multiplicity of functions. Furthermore, I would argue that there is a more artful employment of Buchanan by Blackwood, who as an antiquarian bookseller not only knew Buchanan's works but sold them to his friends and colleagues.

Born in Killearn, Stirlingshire – what has later come to be known as 'Rob Roy Country' largely through the efforts of Scott – Buchanan effected a number of significant historical and political roles during his life, including James VI and I's tutor, Member and then Keeper of the Privy Council (Scotland), Moderator of the General Assembly, and – after Rizzio's murder in 1566 and Lord Darnley's the following year – an implacable foe of the Catholic Mary, Queen of Scots. Moreover, he was the author of *Rerum Scoticarum Historia* [*History of Scotland*] (1582), and a number of tragedies and satires. Of the latter, the most curious in terms of how Buchananism informs the Blackwood Group is *The Chamæleon, or the Crafty Statesman* written in 1570 but not published until 1715.[48] As the Latin scholar's biographer Ian McFarlane notes, Buchanan opens the *Chamæleon* with 'a description of the animal which can change to any colour.'[49] He virulently attacks William Maitland for his apostasy, labelling him 'a changeable coloured enemie to the Kings Grandmother ... and to his Country.'[50] In terms of sovereign succession, with George IV sitting in the Theatre Royal's audience watching a dramatized version of *Rob Roy*, one cannot help but be reminded of *Hamlet* when the prince remarks slyly to Claudius that he fares 'of the chameleon's dish: I eat the air.'[51] With the deliberate pun of feeding on the air/heir, Blackwoodians similarly both fed upon the commercially frenzied air that pervaded George IV's visit as well as fed upon his ideologically charged accession to the Scottish crown.

Apart from the obvious connection of George Buchanan's grim visage on the front cover of every monthly issue of *Blackwood's*, the use of satire in Maga facilitates our understanding of masking in both the 'Noctes' as well as the magazine's editorial practices. In other words, satire, particularly the masque – or 'mask' as it is often and deliberately printed in the magazine – became not merely a generic device by which these Scottish authors taunted and teased their readership, but, more importantly, masquerading became a literary group practice through which Blackwoodians deployed a comically complex *jeu d'esprit* reconstruction of national identity. The main tactic used in this literary manoeuvre was that of pseudonyms. Although the practice of pseudonymic writing has been commonly viewed as a cheap attempt 'to disguise the true nature or intent of the person,' I am more inclined to agree with Margaret Ezell that the practice can be read as a literary technique 'to enhance and to announce the values and characteristics upheld by the group' and that 'the use of the device of a mask or pseudonym also permit[s] the happy interplay of the worlds of fiction and reality,'[52] as we have seen in the above 'Noctes.'

The importance of capitalizing on Buchanan as the Blackwood Group – and by extension a 'Noctes' sub-group – figurehead takes on symbolic and literary signification when considering the pseudonymous nature of their writings. As Margaret Oliphant notes in *Annals of a Publishing House*, there developed a 'sworn brotherhood' among these Blackwoodians with respect to maintaining their masks.[53] In a curious and undated letter to Blackwood – Oliphant rightly notes that these letters regarding the 'Noctes' are often (deliberately?) undated – Lockhart discloses the highly collaborative, malleable nature of the 'Noctes': 'Your idea of the "Noctes" is most capital; but the thing must be done at leisure, and I rather think when Wilson and I are together. Meantime trust it to the Doctor ["Odoherty"/Maginn], and let me have his hints.

This would be the far best vehicle for discussing the Periodical Press. Never having seen Gifford, I could not do him very well. I think I could do "John Bull" and Jeffrey. Get hold of Theodore's old farces, that I may steal *his own puns*. Hogg told me he had been writing a "Noctes." Let me see it when it is in type, that I may put in a few cuts at himself.'[54] Oliphant reiterates this type of coterie authorship in her description of the production process of *Noctes*: 'It would not seem that these Symposia were under any regular system at first or subjected to any editorship. When they began it was frequently Lockhart who was the author, sometimes Maginn ... : occasionally Hogg had, or was allowed to suppose that he had, a large share in them. Finally they fell into the hands of Wilson.'[55] Though prudence be our best guide in reading *'Christopher North': A Memoir of John Wilson*, written by his daughter Mrs Mary (*née* Wilson) Gordon, the Blackwood's Group is pictured here adopting a 'system of mystification practised in the management, which has never been carried so far in any other publication, and undoubtedly contributed very greatly to its success. The illustrious example of Sir Walter Scott [the "Great Unknown"] had given encouragement to this species of deception, and the editor and writers of *Blackwood* [*sic*] thought themselves quite at liberty, not only to perplex the public by affixing all sorts of fictitious names and addresses to their communications, but to put forth their *jeux d'esprit* occasionally under cover of the names of real personages who had never dreamed of so distinguishing themselves.' In effect, 'these conspirators had made up their minds to act on O'Doherty's principle, of never denying anything they had *not* written, or ever acknowledging anything they *had*.'[56] The upshot is that while Alan Lang Strout's efforts of meticulously cataloguing individual articles published in *Blackwood's* from 1817 to 1825 are a welcome and valuable contribution to the study of Romantic periodical publication,[57] we cannot fix with any certainty a good deal of the articles submitted during Wilson and Lockhart's editorial tenure; much less can we be certain of 'North's' or 'Tickler's' or the 'Shepherd's' dialogues in the *Noctes*.

A more revealing example of how Buchananite satire operates within the Blackwood Group is 'Hogg's Royal Jubilee, &c.,' which falls after John Galt's novella *The Gathering of the West; or, We're Come to See the King* and before this Royal Number 'Noctes.' Although presented in this issue in condensed review form, Blackwood had published this masque as a single volume entitled *The Royal Jubilee: A Scottish Mask* earlier in 1822; the abridged version in *Blackwood's* elides several Jacobite songs and scores. As the title-page of the original indicates, this masque was authored by 'The Ettrick Shepherd,' the well-known pseudonymous 'Noctes' mask for Hogg. Hogg's masque employs the courtly nature and spectacle expected of a work commemorating George IV's visit, featuring such curious characters as the Queen of the Fairies as well as Geniuses of the Ocean, Gaels, the West, and Holyrood. In keeping with the conventional revelry – both of a masque and of George IV's visit – Hogg pits the Fairy Queen (with her Spencerian echo), against the Genius of the Gael. Left to their own devices, Hogg's pro-union Fairy Queen and the decidedly Highland/Celtic Genius of the Gael come to such a critical reckoning over the suppression and glossing over of Highland cultural memory that they are soon 'in the act of seizing one another.'[58] In the original text William Blackwood published, the Fairy Queen attempts to reawaken the Genius of the Gael's long dormant memory of the Jacobite pretence to sovereignty. [59] Published in time for the Royal Visit, this original masque ostensibly prophesies George IV donning the Garb o' the Gaul. However, Hogg, a close and lifelong friend of Scott, was well aware of the pageant-master's plans for the king's progress and visit.

Taken at face value, this masque becomes a humorous parody of Scotland's acquiescence to its Southern sister. While the Jacobite songs such as 'Killiecrankie,' 'When the King Comes O'er the Water,' and '*MacGregor na Raura*' [sic] clearly invoked a political undercurrent,[60] the comic current cleansed the categories of Highlander and Jacobite with nostalgic cultural memory. Hogg's – and, in turn, Blackwood's (who published and re-published it) – chameleon-like masque maintains a semblance of deference to an independent Scottish identity reminiscent of Jacobitism while *simultaneously* shrouding that identity within the chequered-tartan woven of 'progressive' pro-Union principles. However, the re-published version in the Royal Number distilled and distorted these categories to a laughable absurdity. That is, as the Blackwoodian reprints of excerpts of their 'Ettrick Shepherd's' satirical masque show, anonymous and masked reviewers editorialize throughout, providing post hoc commentary on the visit while simultaneously glossing over the potentially painful remembrance of things past and diverting their audience's and George IV's attention by proclaiming: 'In the verses which we have quoted, whimsical and absurd as many of them are, there is much that denotes the true poet. May we venture to hope, that the King's eye may be directed from them towards another work of the Ettrick Shepherd's, the Queen's Wake? That is, indeed, a work of genius, and proves the Ettrick Shepherd to be, beyond all doubt, the most original poet whom Scotland has produced from among the people, since the death of Burns' (*BM*, 349).

Walter Scott took no offense at this good-natured repositioning of the Scottish laureate, especially since his class origins and recent baronetcy allowed him to rise above the *jeu d'esprit*, not to mention his near sole devotion to prose rather than poetry since *Waverley* in 1814. Yet the curious point in redirecting George IV's attention away from the nervous hilarity of Hogg's *Royal Jubilee* (1822) to *The Queen's Wake* (1813) is that while both works are tributes to sovereigns, the latter lauds a *Scottish* monarch, Mary, Queen of Scots, Buchanan's moral, ethical, and political rival.[61] Just as Scott's 'Hints Addressed to the Inhabitants of Edinburgh, and Others' pamphlet functioned as a deft piece of Scottish historiographical revisionism – obscuring complicated genealogical differences between the Houses of Stewart and Hanover by promoting George IV as 'CHIEF of the Clans' and directing the Scottish nation's, and by 'chief' extension George IV's, attention backward – Hogg's *The Queen's Wake* helped to shift the colour of Scottish patriotism from White Rose or cockade of Jacobitical Catholicism to the Black Rose of the Hanoverian Protestantism. As I have been trying to demonstrate through this close reading of this 'Noctes' within the context of the Blackwood Group's promotion of pro-Union ideology, by feasting upon the ambrosian air pervading their heir's apparent succession to a Scottish crown, the 'Noctes' group cleverly deployed a Buchananite chameleon slippage in both their pawkie politics and libellous literature.

In recording the use to which the Blackwood's Group put the 'Noctes,' Oliphant observes that 'the "Noctes" always remained (sometimes disastrously) a safety-valve for the heat of jest or satire or almost irrestrainable impulse of slaughter ... and in this lucky medium they had always each other to spend a stray jibe upon' (Hogg receiving more than his fair share). [62] Whereas Buchanan's attack on the Reformation's chameleon-like apostasy would have been grounds for imprisonment again or his own murder,[63] the Blackwood Group's attack on significant Edinburgh and London literati in 'The Chaldee Manuscript' was '*actionable*' grounds (to use Wilson's terms) for libel charges. What helped to save the Blackwoodians from conviction, and thus ruin, was the inability of the courts to determine precisely who was responsible for the 'profane' and vitriolic attacks. Pseudonymous writing provided the necessary camouflage for Blackwoodians during their enactment of a subtle yet far-reaching realignment of Scottish national identity. That was exactly how the Blackwood Group wanted it.

Bella Caledonia

What we have seen thus far, then, is how the progress of an epistemo-logical treatment of sympathy and common sense during the Scottish Enlightenment becomes repossessed in order to function as 'the far best vehicle' for promoting and publishing George IV's progress within the succession of Scottish sovereignty and citizenry. Thus we arrive at the close of the Scottish Enlightenment, which became the neo-Jacobitical Age of Scott (ca. 1800–32), an age both bound up in retracing its own painfully treacherous past while simultaneously romanticizing and, in turn, depoliticizing it. Replacing a common sympathy of loss that oc-curred from both the Acts of Succession and Union with a renewed, albeit pro-Union qualified, common sense of *national* identity engen-dered a fertile intellectual, political, and cultural climate *sympathetic* to a nostalgic, tartan-clad Scottish identity.

If we keep in mind David Hume's notion in his *Treatise on Human Nature* that 'the minds of men are mirrors to one another, not only because they reflect each others emotions, but also because those rays of passions and sentiments and opinions may be often reverberated, and may decay away by insensible degrees,'[64] then in the pages of *Blackwood's* what we witness is the unfolding pageantry of this common sympathy for a renewed, vibrant Scotland. While the 'Noctes' group allows us to read how this transformation of epistemological common sense operates at a local level, the Blackwood Group authors provide us with a richly textured expression of the same sense of common sympathy writ large at the national and Union levels. Taken in condensed form, the 'Noctes' group's expression can be portrayed as overwhelmingly vitriolic, per-haps too localized and myopic in intention. Yet these authors individu-ally, and as a coterie, designed a piece that provided a grand expression of contemporary puzzlement over Scots national identity. This essay has attempted to throw open the doors of Ambrose's Tavern to hear exactly how the 'Noctes' group's auld song rang out at a national level.

NOTES

1 Alexander Brodie, *The Tradition of Scottish Philosophy: A New Perspective on the Enlightenment* (Edinburgh: Polygon, 1990), 87.
2 Ibid., 255; emphasis added.
3 Edgar Johnson, *Sir Walter Scott: The Great Unknown*, 2 vols. (New York: Macmillan, 1970), 1:77; emphasis added.

4 Ibid., 1:75.
5 Ibid., 1:291; emphasis added.
6 For a detailed list of the Friday Club members, see Henry Cockburn's 'Account of the Friday Club,' National Library of Scotland, MS 15943. I am grateful to the Trustees and Staff of the National Library of Scotland for their kind permission to rely upon this manuscript.
7 Quoted in Henry Cockburn, *Memorials of His Time*, ed. Karl F.C. Miller (Chicago: University of Chicago Press, 1974), 290–1n.; emphasis in original.
8 Henry Cockburn, quoted in Alan Bell, 'Cockburn's "Account of the Friday Club,"' in *Lord Cockburn: A Bicentenary Commemoration 1779–1979*, ed. Alan Bell (Edinburgh: Scottish Academic Press, 1979), 181–97.
9 Ibid.
10 Ibid., 187.
11 As A[lexander]. J[ohn]. Youngson notes, '[n]umbers one to nine were on the south side of the street,' (*The Making of Classical Edinburgh, 1750–1840* (Edinburgh: Edinburgh University Press, 1966), 230).
12 Margaret Oliphant, *Annals of a Publishing House: William Blackwood and His Sons, Their Magazine and Friends*, 2 vols. (1987; repr. New York: MAS, 1974), 1:36.
13 Cockburn, quoted in Bell, 'Cockburn's, "Account,"' 184, 181.
14 On the sociality and coterie nature of literary clubs, see Timothy Raylor, *Cavaliers, Clubs, and Literary Culture: Sir John Mennes, James Smith, and the Order of the Fancy* (Newark, DE: University of Delaware Press, 1994); Anne Ruggles Gere, 'Common Properties of Pleasure: Texts in Nineteenth-Century Women's Clubs,' *Cardozo Arts and Entertainment Law Journal* 10 no. 2 (1992), 647–63; Davis McElroy, *Scotland's Age of Improvement: A Survey of Eighteenth-Century Literary Clubs and Societies* (Pullman: Washington State University Press, 1969); Lewis Perry Curtis, *Esto Perpetua: The Club of Dr. Johnson and His Friends, 1764–1784* (Hamden, Conn.: Archon, 1963); and Robert Allen, *The Clubs of Augustan London* (Cambridge, Mass.: Harvard University Press, 1933).
15 Jürgen Habermas, *The Structural Transformation of the Public Sphere: An Inquiry into a Category of Bourgeois Society* (1962), trans. Thomas Burger (Cambridge, Mass.: MIT Press, 1989), 37.
16 Cockburn, quoted in Bell, 'Cockburn's "Account,"' 196.
17 R. Shelton Mackenzie, 'History of Blackwood's Magazine,' in *Noctes Ambrosianæ*, 5 vols., ed. R. Shelton Mackenzie (New York: Redfield, 1854), 1:xiv.

18 As J.H. Alexander clarifies in the introduction to his *Tavern Sages: Selections from the 'Noctes Ambrosianæ'* (Aberdeen: Association of Scottish Literary Studies, 1992), 'Most of [the *Noctes*] are set in the actual tavern run by the Yorkshireman William Ambrose at 1 Gabriel's Road, and from No. 29 (November 1826) in his superior establishment, Ambrose's North British Hotel, Tavern, and Coffee-House at 15 Picardy Place' (vii).

19 Trevor Royle, 'Noctes Ambrosianae,' in *Companion to Scottish Literature* (Detroit: Gale, 1983), 228. The typical spelling for this *Noctes* character in Maga is O'Doghterty, rather than Royle's O'Doherty.

20 Ever since the publication of 'The Chaldee Manuscript' (October 1817) in which a proto-Noctes group virulently satirized virtually all Edinburgh literati to the point of libel charges, John Gibson Lockhart became known pseudonymously as 'Scorpion.' The epithet has its origin in 'The Chaldee' when it prophesies that '[t]here came also, from a far country, the scorpion, which delighteth to sting the faces of men, that he might sting sorely the countenance of the man which is crafty, and of the two beasts' (quoted in Mackenzie, 'History,' 1:xxiii). The 'two beasts' are Thomas Pringle and James Cleg-horn, the original and ostensibly ineffective co-editors of the magazine, before they went to work for Scott's publisher, Archibald Constable, whose cunning earned him both Scott's Waverley Novels and the Blackwoodian derisive epithet 'Crafty.'

21 This 'Noctes' misprinted as 'VI' instead of 'V.'

22 Alexander, *Tavern Sages*, x.

23 Ibid.

24 'Noctes Ambrosianæ No. VI' (369–91), in *Blackwood's Edinburgh Magazine* 12 (September 1822), 369; hereafter cited parenthetically in the text and abbreviated *BM*.

25 Alexander, *Tavern Sages*, 196. See also, *Noctes Ambrosianæ by Professor Wilson*, ed. J.F.F. [James Frederick Ferrier], 4 vols. (Edinburgh: W. Blackwood, 1855), 2:115n.

26 *The Letters of Sir Walter Scott*, 12 vols., ed. Sir Herbert J.C. Grierson (London: Constable, 1932–7), 6:70; my emphasis; hereafter cited parenthetically in the text and abbreviated as *Letters*. John Bacon Sawrey Morritt (1771–1843), educated at St John's College, Cambridge, was a classical scholar and English traveller who served intermittently as MP from 1799 to 1820. He was a lifelong friend of Scott, and he supplied Scott with information for *Rokeby: A Poem* (1813) and classical Greek monuments.

27 I am indebted to Professor Robert L. Patten for accurately identifying this as a George Cruikshank cartoon.

28 See lines 29–30 of 'An Heroical Epistle of Hudibras to Sidrophel,' in
    Samuel Butler's *Hudibras* (London: John Martyn and Henry Herringman,
    1678).
29 National Library of Scotland, MS 30002, fols.130–1. This unpublished letter
    is addressed to 'The Right Honourable The Lord Register,' George IV's
    Windsor Palace Librarian. I am grateful to the Trustees and Staff of the
    National Library of Scotland for permission to quote from this manuscript.
30 National Library of Scotland, MS 4002, fols. 281–2; emphasis in original.
    This letter, postmarked '29 Oct 1817,' from John Wilson to William
    Blackwood was written during the scandal surrounding both 'The
    Chaldee Manuscript' and the first attack 'On the Cockney School of
    Poetry.'
31 As Scott recalls in his journal, his mask of anonymity was removed
    somewhat unwillingly by Lord Meadowbank (Alexander Maconochie,
    1777–1861) at the Theatrical Fund dinner:

> Besides the joke had lasted long enough and I was tired of it. I had not
> however the most distant intention of chusing the time and place
> where the thing actually took place for mounting the confessional.
> Ld. Meadowbank who is a kind and clever little fellow but somewhat
> bustling and forward said to me in the drawing room 'Do you care any
> thing about the mystery of the Waverley novels now' – 'Not I' I replied
> 'the secret is too generally known' – I was led to think from this that he
> meant to make some jocular allusion to Rob Roy ... But when instead of
> skirmish of this kind he made a speech in which he seriously identified
> me with the Author of Waverley I had no opportunity of evasion and
> was bound either to confess or deny and it struck while he was speak-
> ing it was as good and natural occasion as I could find for making my
> avowal (Sir Walter Scott, *The Journal of Sir Walter Scott*, ed. W.E.K. Ander-
> son [Oxford: Clarendon Press, 1972], 282).

32 Rosalind Mitchison, 'The Highland Clearances,' in *A Companion to Scottish
    Culture*, ed. David Daiches (London: Edward Arnold, 1981), 68. For a more
    comprehensive account of the complexities involving the clearances, see
    Eric Richards, *A History of the Highland Clearances: Agrarian Transformation
    and the Evictions, 1746–1886* (London: Croom Helm, 1982). ·
33 London-born George Granville Leveson-Gower (1758–1833) was dubbed
    the First Duke of Sutherland in 1803. His wife, Elizabeth Sutherland (1765–
    1839), later Lady Stafford, was the Countess of Sutherland in her own
    right but became the Duchess of Sutherland upon their marriage in 1785.

34 John Prebble, *The King's Jaunt: George IV in Scotland, August 1822: 'One and twenty daft days'* (London: Collins, 1988; repr. Edinburgh: Birlinn, 2000), 26.

35 Quoted in Prebble, *The King's Jaunt*, 33; emphasis in original. Economist James Loch (1780–1855) was commissioned as the Sutherlands' steward and in 1815 wrote *An Account of the Improvement on the Sutherland Estate, Belonging to the Marquis and Marchioness of Stafford* (London: E. Macleish). In 1820 he published *An Account of the Improvements on the Estates of Marquess of Stafford, in the Counties of Stafford and Salop* (London: Longman, Hurst, Rees, Orme, and Brown). This account, from which Lady Stafford liberally borrowed excerpts, was meant to serve as both a justification for Sutherland 'improvements' as well as a how-to manual for other Highland land managers. 'The "Sutherlandshire clearances" of the second Marquis of Stafford, by which between 1811 and 1820 fifteen thousand crofters were removed from the inland to the seacoast districts, were carried out under his supervision. The policy of these clearances was bitterly attacked, and they were said to have been harshly carried out' (*DNB*).

36 Quoted in Prebble, *The King's Jaunt*, 31.

37 Donald Sutherland, Letter to Lady Stafford, quoted in Prebble, *The King's Jaunt*, 31. As Prebble observes, 'Donald Sutherland' is a name as pervasive in Scotland as John Smith in the United States and, thus, is the 'equivalent of anonymity' (31).

38 See Gerald Finley, *Turner and George the Fourth in Edinburgh* (London: Tate Gallery, 1981), in which Finley rightly notes that '[w]hile the King was not present at this ceremony, he did send his representative' (37). Nonetheless, the grandiose pomp and circumstance and officiousness surrounding this ceremony reassert the king's imprimatur whether or not his body was present.

39 The controversy about the Nelson Monument being unaesthetically pleasing, and therefore in need of demolition, began when Sir Archibald Alison (1792–1867) published his article on the 'Proposed National Monument at Edinburgh' in *Blackwood's* 5 (July 1819, 377–87). It continued when he again proposed that a Parthenon replica should replace the Nelson Monument in his *Blackwood's* article 'Restoration of the Parthenon as the National Monument' (no. 5, November 1819, 137–48). 'Mr Linning' was Michael Linning, Secretary to the National Monument Committee (Alexander, *Tavern Sages*, 199).

40 The National Monument was 'designed upon the model of the celebrated Parthenon, and consecrated to the Deity, in testimony of the nation's gratitude for the signal success of British arms during the late war' (Prebble, *The King's Jaunt*, 330).

41 Gayatri Chakravorty Spivak, 'Problem with Thinking Ethics for the Other Woman,' Lecture to the Interdisciplinary Group for Historical Literary Studies, 'History and Ethics: The Question of the Other' Lecture Series, Texas A&M University, 20 February 1997.

42 This line is spoken by a 'Mr Gudeman' in this 'Noctes' (*BM*, 386) and is a paraphrase of Sir Walter Scott claiming (anonymously) that 'King George IV. Comes hither as the descendant of a long line of Scottish Kings. The blood of the heroic Robert Bruce – the blood of the noble, the enlightened, the generous James I. is in his veins' [Sir Walter Scott], 'Hints Addressed to the Inhabitants of Edinburgh, and Others, in Prospect of His Majesty's Visit' (Edinburgh: Manners and Miller, Archibald Constable, William Blackwood, Waugh and Innes, and John Roberston, 1822), 6.

43 See Robert Clyde, *From Rebel to Hero: The Image of the Highlander, 1745–1830* (Lothian: Tuckwell Press, 1995).

44 The funding for this National Monument ran out sixteen months after subscriptions began in January 1822. For example, Youngson reports that just eight months before George IV's August Royal Visit in January 1822 that: 'an appeal was launched for £42,000 "to erect a facsimile of the Parthenon," an appeal signed by, among others, Sir Walter Scott, Francis Jeffrey, and Henry Cockburn. There were to be "catacombs," and at one point it was suggested that the Monument might be a burial place for the famous and great, a sort of Westminster Abbey on the top of Calton Hill. But alas! sixteen months later only £16,000 had been subscribed, although a Parliamentary grant of £10,000 was hoped for. The promoters were disappointed. (Youngson, *The Making of Classical Edinburgh*, 159).

45 Quoted in Youngson, ibid.

46 Colin Kidd, *Subverting Scotland's Past: Scottish Whig Historians and the Creation of an Anglo-British Identity, 1689–c.1830* (Cambridge: Cambridge University Press, 1993), 20–1.

47 Scott, 'Hints,' 7.

48 According to Ian McFarlane, the *Chamæleon* is precisely datable because the 'last event specifically mentioned in the text is the assembly at Linlithgow of 29 April 1570' (*Buchanan* [London: Duckworth, 1981], 336). Because this satire directly implicates William Maitland (ca. 1525–73) of Lethington in both Rizzio's and Darnley's murders, the text of *Chamæleon* 'circulated *sub rosa*' until the Jacobitical Thomas Ruddiman (1674–1757) included it for his *Georgii Buchanani Scoti* [*George Buchanan, Scot*] in 1715.

49 Ian D. McFarlane, *Buchanan* (London: Duckworth, 1981), 337.

50 Ibid., 336, n. 44.

51 See, William Shakespeare, *The Tragedy of Hamlet, Prince of Denmark* 3.2.

52 Margaret J.M. Ezell, 'Reading Pseudonyms in Seventeenth-Century English Coterie Literature' (14–25), *Essays in Literature* 24 (Spring 1994), 23.

53 Oliphant, *Annals*, 1:201.

54 Quoted in ibid., 1:202; emphasis in original.

55 Ibid., 1:201.

56 Mary Gordon, *'Christopher North': A Memoir of John Wilson*, 2nd ed. (Edinburgh: Grange Publishing, 1879), 193, 194.

57 See, Alan Lang Strout, *A Bibliography of Articles in Blackwood's Magazine, 1817–1825* (Lubbock: Texas Technological College, 1959).

58 James Hogg, *The Royal Jubilee: A Scottish Mask* (Edinburgh: W. Blackwood, 1822), 38.

59 The full exchange at this point in *The Royal Jubilee* reads:

> QUEEN: Dost thou remember?
> GENIUS OF GAEL: Lady, no:
>   But why recall the days of woe,
>   To mar the roving spirits' bliss
>   In such a jubilee as this?
> QUEEN: Because that then, in uncouth rhyme,
>   You mumbled something of this time:
>   Of a tartaned King that should appear,
>   The only stem of a house held dear,
>   Who should give loyalty its due,
>   And the honours of the Gael renew. (Ibid., 22)

60 The first two songs appear as Song XIX and XXVII, respectively, in Hogg's anthology of Jacobite songs published by Blackwood and entitled *The Jacobite Relics of Scotland; Being the Songs, Airs, and Legends, of the Adherents to the House of Stuart*, 2 vols. (Edinburgh: W. Blackwood, 1819–21), 2:32–3, 2:45–7. The air 'Killiecrankie' commemorates, of course, the defeat of the Jacobite army (under Major General Hugh Mackay) by King William III's army (under Viscount Dundee, John Graham of Claverhouse, who later died from battle injury) at the Battle of Killiecrankie, 27 July 1689. 'When the King Comes O'er the Water,' whose final refrain line proclaims that 'I will sing a rantin sang, That day our King comes o'er the water,' resonates on at least two levels; that is, it explicitly blusters with Jacobite enthusiasm for 'King' James VII and later Bonnie Prince Charlie, when they sailed from France to Scotland to reclaim their right to the Scottish throne. However, this song implicitly signifies George IV's Royal Visit since his arrival via Greenwich was by sea on his yacht the *Royal George*. The air

'MacGregor na Raura,' which should read 'MacGregor o' Ruara,' laments the death of MacGregor of Glen Lyon (d. 1570), ancestor of Rob Roy MacGregor; although the original author is unknown, the song was translated from Gaelic into English by the Islay poet Thomas Pattison and published in Alexander Campbell's *Albyn's Anthology; or, A Selection of the Melodies and Local Poetry Peculiar to Scotland & the Isles, Hitherto Unpublished*, 2 vols. (Edinburgh: Oliver and Boyd, 1816).

61 See, James Hogg, *The Queen's Wake: A Legendary Poem* (Edinburgh: Longman, Hurst, Rees, Orme, Brown, 1813).

62 Oliphant, *Annals*, 1:206.

63 While in Portugal teaching theology at the University of Coimbra, Buchanan was arrested by the Lisbon Inquisition on 15 August 1550, tried and interrogated intermittently until the Inquisitor General's dismissal on 28 January 1552. The burden of the inquisition rested not on his theological teaching, but rather on his previously published satirical poems (see, McFarlane, *Buchanan*, especially chapter 4: 'Coimbra,' 122–58).

64 David Hume, *Treatise on Human Nature: Being an Attempt to Introduce the Experimental Reasoning into Moral Subjects* (1739), 2nd ed., ed. Sir Lewis Amherst Selby-Bigge and Peter Harold Nidditch (Oxford: Clarendon Press, 1978), 365.

CONSOLIDATING REPUTATIONS

'On behalf of the Right': Archibald Alison, Political Journalism, and *Blackwood's* Conservative Response to Reform, 1830–1870

MICHAEL MICHIE

Equality is the dream of democracy – inequality is the law of progress.
Archibald Alison Jr, 'Democracy Beyond the Seas,'
Blackwood's Magazine (February 1870), 220

The year 1867 marked something of a political turning point for the House of Blackwood. The Second Reform Act, while not seriously threatening the political power of the landed classes, did make the threat or promise of democracy more tangible, and accelerated the eventual arrival of a permanent change in the political and social landscape: the cleavage between owning property and the right to vote. Also, the death of Sir Archibald Alison in that year marked the demise of one of the most steadfast defenders of the old order. 'The oldest Tory' had been perhaps the most consistent and reliable political contributor to *Blackwood's Edinburgh Magazine* with over 171 contributions in some thirty years.

In what follows, I will focus on Blackwood's response to reform and class politics in the mid-nineteenth century, in order to examine the ways in which the publishing house tried to uphold conservative values, if not the fortunes of the Conservative Party itself. I also discuss the relationship between editors and political journalists. I argue that Blackwood's tried to uphold what it saw as the key values of respectable society and the balanced constitution. Alison, who looked back for his model to the agrarian commercial society envisaged by Adam Smith, was the most representative High Tory figure who set the tone for at least the period covering the first two reform acts and possibly beyond. His example was followed by writers who, while pursuing careers as lawyers, journalists, critics, or military officers, shared his catholic interests and willingness to write with confidence, if not always authority, on a wide range of subjects. While the magazine and the publishing house generally maintained a 'rare consistency' over this period in defence of the broad values of conservatism, their polemical ardour waned somewhat after 1868.

The overriding concern for nineteenth-century conservatives was 'deciding how much political and social reform could be accommodated within the mixed or balanced constitution in which Burke had found the key to the reconciliation of order and liberty.'[1] The various attempts to go beyond Burke resulted in a wide variety of attitudes, and some distinct Tory groups, differentiated by their responses to industrialization, urbanization, and political economy. In the early part of the century when conservatism emerged as an identifiable affiliation on the level of practical party politics, positions were taken around such issues as parliamentary reform, Catholic emancipation, free trade and the Corn laws, and currency. Here Tories divided into Liberal and Ultra or High camps, depending on how far they were prepared to accept the new political economy and its view of the 'free' market. Liberal Toryism became the most influential conservative tendency at the level of government from the end of the war under the Liverpool administration until Peel split the party over the repeal of the Corn Laws. Many Liberal Tories drifted into the Liberal Party, while the remaining High Tories, including Blackwood's stalwarts Alison and William Aytoun, renamed themselves the Protectionist Party.

Authors and Politics

As is well known, *Blackwood's Edinburgh Magazine* was formed to vigorously promote broad conservative principles and to do it with style. Positions might be taken against this or that Tory ministry or politician, but the broad cast of 'Maga''s allegiance remained clear. Blackwood's were consistently able to call upon a loyal group of contributors.

Political opinion at *Blackwood's* was sustained over a remarkably long period because editorial control was tight. John Blackwood's 'familiarity with the history of modern English and Continental politics ... included an intimacy with ... the "inner life" of the Conservative Party.' This made him something of an 'authoritative book of reference' with regard to conservative politics. Blackwood's obituary writer noted that he 'subordinated mere party considerations and personal predilections to what he conceived to be the true interests of the country.' An instance of this was in 'making the best of' the 1867 Reform Bill.

The key point is that John Blackwood's political opinions were 'expressed continually and accurately in the pages of the magazine.'[2] Blackwood himself contributed only a few pages, but political contributions by others rarely strayed from the publisher's line. Indeed, it was frequently noticeable when a writer was regarded as politically suspect, or had somehow let the side down. For example, Bonamy Price, a political economist, wrote an article for Maga in 1868 on religious equality. Robert Hogarth Patterson (speaking as Blackwood's manager) noted that Price had 'got the *entrée* to your magazine,' but went on to caution that while Price was 'an able and fresh thinker, and a forcible writer, . . . at the same time I understand your sentiment of mistrust, for although prizing his articles <u>highly</u>, I had always to keep an eye on them, lest some views or expressions of his did not square with mine. Price moves in good political society, and has opportunities of conversing freely with men in high position.'[3] Price, for his part, felt some unease. 'I find myself in a very awkward position as to political writing,' he confided to John Blackwood. 'I am a very moderate Liberal and none of my old friends, who have grown very immoderate will publish what I have to say on politics. I cannot exactly go the full length of absolute Conservatism: but I know that on important points, my feelings and views coincide with those of pure conservatives.'[4] Price then sought the support of Patterson, not knowing the latter was keeping an eye on his political trustworthiness: 'If you are so minded you may help me with Mr. Blackwood. I feel he half likes & half mistrusts me: so that any word of [praise] for what I write may assist me with him ... I am a sort of wandering Jew, my Liberal allies having long ago far outdistanced me.'[5] In 1881, Alexander Allardyce's verdict on a piece by A. Innes Shand (a literary rather than a political writer) pointed to not just editorial oversight, but Party oversight as well: 'Shand's paper reads like a second rate London letter supplied to a weekly provincial journal. His remarks about the Conservative depression are quite out of keeping with the tone of Lord John [Manners]'s article, and would very justly draw down upon the Magazine the indignation of the party.'[6]

Looking through the lists of contents for *Blackwood's Magazine* in the *Wellesley Index* one is struck by the consistency of format and content. An edition typically had a few political pieces commenting on events in the House or with the ministry or opposition during the previous month. It would also include one or two literary pieces, and something on travel, the military, or foreign affairs. Quite frequently the political commentary would be augmented by a longer paper on a political figure or event. This pattern was remarkably consistent over many years. Scottish affairs received coverage but not as much as one might expect; this was often interpreted as a merely local topic and thus of less consequence. Alison wrote only four pieces on Scottish politics. In 1832, clearly spelling out editorial policy, he felt obliged to provide a justification for his 'local' topic: 'Destined as our pages are to carry the conservative principles, and attachment to the constitution, to the remotest corners where the English language is spoken in the world, it is with great reluctance that we mingle with such momentous disquisitions, anything of a local or provincial nature; and our readers must long have perceived, that our pages are, in general, as free from the details of Scotch transactions as if they were written in Nova Zembla. But while this is the general rule, there must be some exceptions; occasions on which the conservative principles themselves call upon us to give publicity, and confer merited celebrity, on patriotic services.'[7] In 1869, William Blackwood remarked that an essay by John Skelton (who contributed many of the Scottish-themed articles from the 1860s to the end of the century) 'might have been better it has as you remarked a decided local tone about it.'[8]

It was the struggle over reform in the early 1830s which gave a sharp and not infrequently alarmist edge to Maga's political writing. Archibald Alison was largely responsible for not only providing an eighteenth-century pedigree for conservative principles, but also applying them to unfolding events. Alison was a criminal lawyer and sheriff-depute of Lanarkshire from 1834 until his death. He wrote a best-selling history of the French Revolution; a critique of Malthus and political economy; and an influential text on the principles and practice of Scottish criminal law. Between 1830 and 1852 Maga featured 171 articles written by Alison, on topics ranging from contemporary politics and foreign policy to literary and artistic criticism and history. Blackwood's also published a collection of his miscellaneous essays and a two-volume life of Marlborough. As a lawyer with a strong political bent, Alison early on looked for the right vehicle for his opinions. William Blackwood, so vigorous a champion of conservative principles, was an obvious choice of publisher for someone who aspired to be the conservative conscience of the age. Alison's first foray into print was as the anonymous author of a pamphlet published by Blackwood in 1825. *Remarks on the Administration of Criminal Justice* was a critique of the imposition of English practices upon the Scottish criminal justice system, a critique which Alison was asked to write by the solicitor-general, John Hope. The fall of the conservative ministry in 1830 meant Alison was without a patronage appointment, but with increased opportunity to write. He told Blackwood, 'I shall furnish you with a paper regularly every month.' In 1834 Alison did find a career post: as sheriff of Lanarkshire. His workload was extremely heavy, in court appearances, circuit work, dealing with Chartist and working class unrest, committees, and official correspondence. But he nonetheless managed to produce his *History of Europe* and a regular supply of papers for Blackwood.

It is fortunate that Alison's long correspondence with his publisher exists (and that his handwriting is legible).[9] These letters contain numerous examples of his very close, at times obsessive, stewardship of all his works through the process of revisions, corrections, publication, and sales. For instance, in several letters he proposed politically opportune times for the appearance of the first two volumes of the *History*, such as the 'opening of the first session of the Reformed parliament'; or to catch the 'Christmas vacation' in Edinburgh 'when the lawyers are all in town.' Alison even gave his publisher a detailed timetable for the printers. It would be interesting to know how Blackwood responded to these promptings. There is some indication in Alison's letters that Blackwood was not entirely happy about the ever-increasing size of the work. Alison had to plead that 750 pages was the minimum length of volumes, but that in subsequent editions he could reduce this to 600 pages by making the entire work ten or twelve volumes.[10] The sheer size of the work, as well as Alison's somewhat plodding style, became a frequent object of amusement in literary circles, the most well-known instance being Disraeli's parody in *Coningsby* of Alison as 'Mr. Wordy.'[11] The year 1840 saw the publication of *Principles of Population*, Alison's critique of Malthus, as well as the printing of the eighth and ninth volumes of the *History*. In the spring and summer of 1842, Alison pushed to complete his massive work. He described the last hours, in a passage remarkable if true, for the view it gives us of his endurance, if not of the quality of the product: '[The]concluding passages were written in [the sheriff's] office one fore-noon, including the whole parallel of Napoleon and Wellington & his internment at Paris, while I was taking as commissions a long Proof under a Permit from the court of Session and when my pen was stopped every five minutes to decide a disputed point of evidence, or dictate a contested passage – The last forty-eight pages ... to the internment of St Helena was written at a stretch in

Eighteen hours without stopping, and finished at six o'clock on Tuesday morning the 7th June.'[12] The almost immediate success of the *History* was gratifying. Reprinting the first edition alone involved a total of 18,550 volumes. As early as 1843 volumes one and two were into their fifth reprint. In 1848, the year the second edition began to appear, Henry Cockburn was 'assured by a person who certainly ought to know that including the current new edition, the author has already realized £20,000 ... there seems to be no satiating the public with it ... America devours it.'[13] Earl Grey apparently read it aloud to his wife by the fireside to pass the wintry evenings.

From then on it was a matter of putting out as many new additions as public response dictated. Alison added material from more recent reading and responded to reviews and correspondence. He was quite willing to make changes suggested by reviewers and plain readers; from Peel and the *Edinburgh Review* to 'an extraordinary number of correspondents.' In 1844 Alison was forced to postpone a publication deadline because of the 'cast additions.' He told Blackwood this was especially desirable because of the 'nibbling' of the critic John Wilson Croker, in the *Quarterly Review* (Maga's more staid conservative rival). Alison detailed all the mistakes Croker had made and all the authorities Alison had used of which Croker 'does not seem to have had the least Idea.' Alison thought, 'it would be well to cut up that style of reviewing in your magazine; & I could furnish materials for crucifying him as completely as Macaulay did his edition of Johnson.'[14]

Always acutely aware of audience, Alison hoped that his work would appeal to 'scholars and men of reflective habits, the chief class on whom in any form we must rely upon for our sales.' But he and Blackwood had their eyes on other classes as well. By 1852 the *History* appeared in a luxury Library edition and an octavo 'crown edition' aimed at middle-class readers. Further, Blackwood suggested, why not use the work to help enlighten the working class, now that the Chartist threat was over? Ten thousand copies were printed of a People's edition 'for the use of the working classes.' Several months later it appeared as if the sales of the People's edition had not adversely affected sales of the more expensive editions. This showed, claimed Alison, 'that the throwing open the one shilling Gallery has not lessened the Sales of the Tickets for the Boxes & Pit.'[15]

Alison had a good deal of clout with regard to his contributions. His letters certainly give the impression that he took for granted whatever he sent to Maga would be published. Only twice in a forty-two-year relationship did Alison experience rejection. The first involved an article on reform of town corporations that was left out of the February 1836 number. Alison complained that this was an issue of paramount political importance. Corporations all over the country were in danger of falling into Radical hands. Blackwood's had 'lost the immense credit of taking the Lead of all the Conservative Journals and periodicals, in enforcing the just and practical view of this subject: and thereby irrevocably forfeited the opportunity of guiding the public mind.' The day Maga began to abandon the 'Elevated' course of truth and shaped its articles not according to force of argument or justice, but to the interested and partial desires of particular political men however Elevated or important, will be the first of the decline.' Alison acknowledged the need of the magazine to have a veto over articles submitted. However, his was a special case: 'I feel that as applied to myself we should come to an understanding ...' Alison felt a sense of public duty to aid Maga 'in a period of democratic excitement,' but the burdensome and complicated nature of his work as sheriff meant that he had great difficulty finding time 'for Literary Pursuits.' Therefore if Blackwood, for whatever reason, was not going to publish at once Alison's articles, he should be informed of this, and 'would henceforth attempt nothing unless I specially hear from you that a paper is desirable and will be inserted.'[16]

This compromise seems to have worked well, but was not immune to political differences. The second and more serious rejection Alison experienced was in late 1850 for a critical article on Peel; too critical apparently for Blackwood. Alison stated that he was not prepared to 'slave' at an article only to have it 'thrown back on my hands.' An 'eminent London bookseller' had asked him to name his own terms for such a work. Henceforth he would not write for *Blackwood's* on political topics. 'Time will show,' he concluded, 'whether your journal will lose or gain credit by its Rejection – But rely upon it, the fact of its having been rejected shall be made public.'[17] Perhaps this threat was not carried out, as Alison continued to publish in the magazine, although not, however, on politics.

After Alison had ceased writing political articles for the magazine (while still availing himself of the opportunity to put forward conservative principles), other writers gradually took his place, although very much in his shadow. Robert Hogarth Patterson, commenting on Alison's *Autobiography* in 1882, pronounced Alison 'a truly great man: also not in the least a Party man ... but most candid & outspoken on behalf of the

Right. How he scorches up both the landowners of Lanarkshire & town councilors of Glasgow! Alison was a true friend of the Poor, & of even handed justice all round.'[18] Alison's all-round presence as social commentator on economics, politics, history, finance, literature, and art, was not to be seen again, although some of his successors attempted to emulate him.

Writing about politics for Blackwood's (principally for the magazine) seemed to be initiated on a relatively informal basis. Some writers suggested papers and topics themselves; in other cases, the Blackwoods suggested possibilities or were told of prospects by their many contacts. In 1854, John Blackwood wrote to his brother William with the intention 'to ask Bulwer [Lytton] to do something on politics & [I] mean to go & call upon him tomorrow morning. I really do not know any body else who could say anything effective.' A week later he reported that Lytton 'will not be able to write anything on Politics for this month but entered very warmly into the idea of popularizing Conservatism in the Magazine. I do not think there is any man in the country who has better conservative ideas & is so well able to express them in a way likely to please people of all shades of opinion.' Lytton in this instance suggested contacting 'J.W. Hamilton late of the treasury' who could give them the most accurate details of the Reform bill 'and so I shall lay hold of him tomorrow and see if I can get anything.'[19] This last comment suggests the extreme familiarity that the Blackwoods and indeed most of their contributors had with the political scene and its players. Paths crossed in London, in Edinburgh, at fox-hunting, the Garrick Club and Ascot, and in the case of John Blackwood, at the Royal and Ancient Golf Club of St Andrews. Patterson, in an incidentally revealing comment about the class distinctions within the magazine (although he seemed generally to disregard these and address the editors with much familiarity), observed once to William Blackwood: 'I saw you today driving to Ascot, I suppose, as I was coming into town on the top of a bus.'[20]

Herbert Cowell, who contributed pieces for the magazine from 1869 to 1900, wrote in 1854 thanking the Editor for publishing his first article ('Conservative Ascendancy Considered'). He had, he confided, never contributed to any public magazine. Cowell's relationship with the Blackwoods remained formal and reserved. Four years later, Blackwood offered him the chance to publish 'political and other articles.' Cowell's piece, sent in response, was accompanied by this comment: 'I have made it of a purely party description and entirely retrospective' but perhaps Blackwood might 'think that a more decided tone with respect to future policy necessary under existing circumstances.' Cowell was planning another article 'which might offer opportunity for delineating conservative principles.'[21] In 1868, Cowell again contacted the editors, noting that he had 'already some years ago been admitted as a contributor & therefore take the liberty to address you.' The editors heard nothing from Cowell until 1872, when he returned from practising law in Calcutta. He referred to Blackwood's offer in 1868 to publish an article and noted his 'desire to connect with political publications.'

Patterson recommended himself as someone already seasoned in the printing business and as a fledgling newspaper editor (*Edinburgh Advertiser*). He rapidly became one of Blackwood's key authors especially in politics, economics and finance, and foreign policy. Blackwood's published at least three of his books: *The Economy of Capital; or, Gold and Trade* (1865; a collection of his magazine articles), *The Genius of Nations* (1867), and *The New Golden Age and Influence of Precious Metals Upon the World* (1882). Patterson worked mainly in the newspaper business, as editor and proprietor of the *Press* in 1859 and, in 1865, editor of the *Globe*, later editor, in 1872, of the *Glasgow News*. His aim for the *Globe* was that of 'a moderate Conservative journal ... It is not the Party of course, which has bought the paper: they never do anything so extravagant, except in bribery at elections. But if the public choose to believe the C[onservative] C[lub] is the proprietor, good and well,[22] Patterson's interest in chemistry and in finance led him to other occupations. He played a leading part on a board of referees appointed by Parliament to report on the best means of purification of coal-gas in London and participated in the discovery of a process for the elimination of sulphur and ammonia impurities from gas. He also rapidly gained a reputation as a financial expert, being consulted by both the Bank of England and the Bank of France, and was elected a member of the Council of the Statistical Society.

Patterson's range of interests is sometimes reminiscent of Alison's, and indeed there was an element of discipleship involved. One key difference between them was that Patterson rarely had security of employment. For all his expertise in financial matters, Patterson was frequently short of money and considered various positions such as a magistrate in Jamaica, Assistant Postmaster in Ceylon and railway agent in India. In the mid-1860s he asked John Blackwood to support Lytton's intervention for a permanent government office, also adding for good measure: 'Does old Sir Archibald know any of the new government Ministers well? I am quite sure he would write very strongly on my behalf ... No Man knows him as an author as I do. He used to say so. If I am to succeed at all, it must be <u>now</u>.'[23]

In contrast to the restrained and formal relationship maintained by Cowell, Patterson kept up a sustained correspondence with John and William Blackwood, fairly aggressively at times stewarding and promoting his articles. A typical letter from Patterson noted that he was forwarding an article on monetary policy and would complete one on foreign policy and concluded:

> There are a lot of things you have to write to me about: –
> The Alison article: what about it?
> Selections from Sir E.B.L [ytton]. What of <u>it?</u>
> My Poem[24]

Five days later, Patterson observed: 'How awfully busy you must be! Or else how sublimely indifferent to the lapse of Time –.'[25] Patterson too, had a somewhat petulant run-in with William Blackwood, as had Alison. This was over the inordinate amount of time (in Patterson's view) he had to wait for an editorial decision to publish his articles. He had, he complained, given Blackwood 'first offer of these articles very willingly.' Patterson pointed to his record since 1854, especially in articles on foreign policy: '<u>no others</u>, <u>without exception</u>, have been anything like equally correct.' Normally, an editorial decision, he pointed out, is almost always given within a fortnight, – I have sometimes got a <u>proof</u> within a week.' William Blackwood, annoyed, replied that this was 'fault-finding' and Patterson apologized.[26]

Blackwood's Takes on Reform

The rest of this chapter looks more closely at the content of the political writing itself, focusing on the conservative response to reform. By 1831, when Alison began writing articles on current affairs for the magazine on a regular basis, the earlier nineteenth-century period of responding to issues by shifting governmental coalitions was coming to an end. The passing of the 1832 Reform Act hardened party organization as well as its ideological position. Alison took an unmistakably High Tory and protectionist position.[27] His eighteenth-century sceptical whiggism led him to distinguish 'personal liberty' from 'political liberty.' The former emphasized the security of individuals guaranteed by law, on order, and on the protection of property, whereas 'political liberty' (or 'democratic ambition') could easily lead to the 'love of system' and the desire for wholesale political innovation. For Alison, the desire to share in the enactment of laws, if indulged, opened the door to excessive innovation and probably terror. While the Whigs of his own day may have been sincere in their benevolence, he felt their principles led them inevitably to become political bedfellows with radicals and chartists.

Alison claimed that the basic principles of a balanced constitution and government had been established in the seventeenth century and reinforced in the eighteenth and should not be tampered with. The balanced constitution required that the 'people' keep government honest: 'The natural check in a free country upon this corrupt system, into which every constitutional monarchy has a tendency to run, is found in the vigorous opposition and incessant watchfulness of the people.' What had happened in France after about 1790, and again under Louis Phillipe, and what had been happening in Britain 'during the ten years of Whig power which succeeded the downfall of the Tories in 1830' was precisely that the 'popular party' – that is, 'numbers' – ruled unchecked.[28] While Alison's *History* was primarily an account of the battles of the revolutionary wars, it did have an overt political purpose: to warn his contemporaries of the dangers of excessive democratic reform. The urgency of this was heightened at the beginning of the 1830s by Alison's perception of the political and economic state of Britain. He thought 'a revolution was approaching in Great Britain,' fuelled by what he saw as mistaken expectations of the benefits of rapid social change, and by the post-war distress and commercial crisis.[29] He was, of course, not alone in this kind of hyper-vigilance; Thomas de Quincy contributed a paper to Maga in 1830 entitled 'Revolution in Great Britain.' Alison thought a study of the disastrous revolutionary experiment in France might help stem the tide and cause some to reflect on the consequences of hasty 'projects of alteration in institutions.' Also he was anticipating that the 1830 revolution in France would eventually degenerate into violent excess as 1789 had done. Beginning in January 1831, *Blackwood's* featured a series of twelve articles by Alison (probably the longest series of papers by one author they ever published) drawing parallels between the French revolutions of 1789 and 1830, and the demands for reform in Britain. While Alison's ideological agenda was to analyse and publicize the dire consequences for society of drastic political reform, his desire to uphold professional values in his work was strong; he believed that he was an objective historian, not a party hack.

In warning of the dangers of the Reform Act, Alison's analysis and his expectations of revolution, though widely shared by fellow conservatives, were wildly alarmist. Even though 'the Act's chief significance was its acknowledgement of urban, middle class status,' notes a recent commentator, 'it did not usher in a period of middle class political ascendancy over, nor even parity with, the landed elite.'[30] Not only did the landed elite continue to dominate the House of Commons and the Cabinet, the Conservatives, benefiting from superior electoral organization as well as from traditional deference, and in Scotland especially from Whig ineptitude, recovered sufficiently to win the 1841 election although much less convincingly in Scotland than in England. Alison's immediate response to the act was a message in Maga to the Conservative Party to wake up and organize; prescient advice as it turned out, from the party's 'best propagandist.' As low as the franchise has been fixed, he argued, 'in order to let in the meanest class of householders, in too many places to overwhelm the suffrages of men of education and property, we feel convinced, that almost every where, except in the large and manufacturing towns, the Conservative party could by proper exertions, still at the next election secure the return.' The main target should be the trading classes 'who think that the reform they have got is to save them from all calamities.' But having cast down 'the barrier of the aristocracy ... the middling classes will speedily find' their commercial interests were at risk from the revolutionary tempest which the passing of the bill had surely set in motion. Conservatives should therefore sign and publish a declaration to support 'only a member of conservative principles.' Also the party should boycott all tradesmen in their employ who did not support the Conservative candidate.[31]

Four years after the Reform Act, *Blackwood's* published Alison's evaluation of its effects. This was one of his most polemical and mean-spirited pieces of political journalism, certainly preserving the magazine's early reputation for acerbic commentary, but without its early wit and verve. While Alison never disguised the fact that all his writing including his *History* aimed to further the conservative cause, he generally claimed to maintain a distance from direct political partisanship, striving for a more scholarly, professional disinterestedness (and no doubt, increased sales). However, this 1836 article betrayed a bitterness and sense of defeat. His main targets were 'the rapacity of the Popish priesthood and the cupidity of the liberal swarm.' The latter accompanied their displacement of legislative talent and wisdom in Parliament, and the proliferation of offices. Municipal and corporate reform seemed most alarming. Too many boroughs had 'fallen under the curse of the

Penny Rate suffrage'; jobbing and hasty, crude legislation attested that 'we have taken filth out of the gutter to perform our ablutions.' Property would increasingly come under assault from 'the ten pounders and the two-pounders.' Alison could only hope that this might open the eyes of those property-holders who had blindly supported the Whigs. Failing that, only the House of Lords remained as a barrier to democracy; the 'representatives of property, Intelligence, and rational thought' in a nation were in the great towns and in many counties, 'property and knowledge are altogether unrepresented.'[32]

It was not that Alison ignored the necessity for change. He had been extremely critical of the pre-Reform 'abuse' of direct election of town councillors 'out of members of the same craft which they represented.' There was a political principle at stake here: the proper principle of representation in a popular constitution 'was that the whole body should be chosen by the different industrial classes of society.' This corporatist model, according to Alison, would have assured 'an ample representation of all the interests of the community.' Instead of such a reform, there had been a revolution which 'overturned the old and fundamental condition of European society, the representation of classes ... trades [and] professions' and instituted the '*indiscriminate* election of the ten-pounders.' Generally speaking, burgh reform seemed to Alison to violate a vital conservative principle of the balanced constitution: '*property was the directing, and numbers the watching and controlling power.*' To Alison, the most calamitous effect of the Reform Act was the rise in the number of Irish members of Parliament. He was wrong about this: Irish representation in the House of Commons remained at 100 as set out in the Act of Union of 1801.[33]

The political and social progress of the United States had long been an object of great interest in Britain, and the rise of 'democracy' there fuelled by manhood suffrage was studied as a harbinger of things to come, for good or for ill, by all political persuasions. Alison had given a brief sketch of the United States in his social economy work on Malthus (1830). He labelled the United States, a country where acquisition of landed property was combined with a strong propensity for internal migration, as a 'nomad agricultural state.' Democracy, which provided an infusion of energy into modern states (and in which the United States had produced a generally high standard of living) would also cause society to be perpetually split into separate interests and would 'chafe against all the restraints of law and justice.' The 'furious popular passions,' for now channelled into random violence, 'will gradually but certainly induce the curse of civil warfare.' Echoing Tocqueville, Alison claimed the irreconcilable difference between blacks and whites would involve the Southern states 'in the horrors of a servile war.'[34]

Alison's reaction when the Union and the Confederacy did in fact go to war is not known. But we do know that many in Britain, especially conservatives, supported the South, even though the British government remained neutral (a fact which angered the North). At first, the war was frequently seen as a war of independence, and the Southern claims on this basis were taken to be of similar legitimacy as the claims of, say, Poland. The fact that the South won several early battles probably reinforced, in the minds of many, the rightness of their cause. Charles Mackay, writing on the 'American Struggle' in 1866 argued that an inevitable result of democracy and manhood suffrage was the domination of politics by the ignorant and corrupt masses. Only the Southern planters had maintained the true aristocratic vocation of politics, to 'study politics on principle and serve the state for the glory and duty of the work.' Such a huge country, Mackay suggested, could be governed only as a decentralized republic. However, central government became too strong, especially as it was 'fuelled by the dictatorial assumptions of 'Northern Puritanism.' Puritanism was revolutionary and dictatorial and it 'threw down a gauntlet which Conservatism [the Southern planters] was compelled to lift.'[35] And what of slavery? Many conservatives in Britain no doubt regarded this as an entirely suitable form of labour for the climate. Many, like Mackay, argued that slavery should be abolished gradually and with compensation to the slave owners. Archibald Alison Jr. considered that the North won only by dint of 'superiority in numbers and in wealth.' It could hold the Southern states by 'military despotism or slave despotism.' Concluding that the North chose the latter course, Mackay (and Patterson in another article) regarded Lincoln's Emancipation Proclamation of 1862 as entirely cynical and as a terrible weapon unleashed on the South.[36]

1867, Reform, and the Working Classes

The Conservative Party endured 'twenty years in the wilderness' following Peel's attempt to modernize it in the 1840s.[37] Palmerston's death in 1865 unleashed both inter- and intra-party conflict which had been relatively dormant since 1859. Russell's and Gladstone's modest reform bill in 1866 received strong opposition from Liberals while Radicals were themselves divided around options ranging from household suffrage to manhood suffrage. The Liberal government was defeated and Derby formed his third ministry. Unable to completely avoid the issue of reform, and 'despite Disraeli's initial indifference to the question, Derby insisted, in October 1866, that the government must deal with the reform issue.' As debate progressed, Disraeli 'abandoned many of his earlier restrictions' and a Conservative bill was passed with the aid of rebel Liberal back-benchers and Radicals. According to Hawkins, '[w]hen the much-altered measure passed through Parliament in August 1867 it effectively almost doubled the electorate, enfranchising about a third of the adult male population in England and Wales.'[38]

The editors handed the main task of elucidating the reform crisis to the military chaplain, Napoleonic War veteran and stout contributor George Gleig. Gleig was one of a group of writers with military connections, such as E.B. and William Hamley and Alison's son Archibald Jr (who had served in India). These writers served Blackwoods well through the second half of the century. In several articles published in 1866 and 1867, Gleig explained the crisis and supported the course of action taken by Derby and Disraeli. Gleig attributed the crisis in government to three factors: Russell's conceited assumption that there was support for reform among all classes, especially 'the great Whig families'; Gladstone's hold over the Liberal Party and his radicalization on the suffrage question; and 'the expansion of ultra-Liberalism in high places.' The consequence of this for Gleig in 1866 was that the reform legislation proposed threatened both to perpetuate 'the ascendancy of Liberalism in the House of Commons' and to break the balanced constitution to inflict 'glaring injustice ... upon the landed interest' and its 'legitimate interest.'[39]

Almost a year later, the picture had changed completely and a minority Conservative government had to decide whether to propose reform and if so, how much. Gleig suggested that there were 'noblemen and gentlemen of standing' among the Liberal benches who had never really approved of the reform legislation they had voted for (under the party control of Gladstone). Derby and Disraeli 'therefore arrived at the conclusion that if to these noblemen and gentlemen a better scheme of Parliamentary Reform could be proposed, they might be induced to accept it, especially if the proposal were accompanied by an offer to share with them the honours and responsibilities of office ... Neither Lord Derby nor Mr. Disraeli were pledged to an anti-reform policy, having proposed a measure of their own.'[40] Further, Derby realized that 'the people were determined to have a change in the electoral system of the country.' The main question therefore was 'How far shall we go?'

While the Conservatives did have to contend with defections by Carnavon and Cranbourne, Gleig claimed that Gladstone's blunders, in drawing 'day by day the connection between himself and the Reform League and the Trades-unions' made the Tory task a little easier. Disraeli on the other hand, seized the hour; 'he arranged his movements with such consummate skill ... without sacrificing a single principle.' The upshot was, as Gleig announced in the opening sentence of his August 1867 article, 'The Reform Bill may now, we presume, be considered to be safe to pass.'[41] In comparing the Liberal leaders of 1831–2 with those of 1866–7, Gleig admitted to a certain admiration for the former, who 'understood what they were about ... They went in boldly for a great revolution, – a bloodless one – ... a revolution which would even spare the outward forms of things.'[42] Gleig appeared to be speaking for the magazine on the 1832 reforms: 'It is too late now to ask the question whether the Constitution of 1832 has ceased to satisfy the just requirements of the country. For our own part, as we resisted the introduction of that Constitution six-and-thirty years ago, so we have never been able to close our eyes against the many shortcomings with which it was chargeable ... Still, upon the whole, we taught ourselves to be content with what the Whigs had given us; and so we believe, did the people at large.'[43]

Gleig castigated the Liberals and their radical allies for complaining that the Conservative bill would be ruinous; he charged that Disraeli's bill was in fact more liberal than theirs and more in accord with the temper of the times. Disraeli did a wise thing – not for himself alone, nor for the Conservatives generally, but for the country – in so settling the conditions of his Reform Bill, that the political privileges created by it should reach a larger and more independent and reasonable body of persons (respectable workers) than that which had won the favour of Mr Gladstone and Mr Bright (merely the elite of the working classes).[44]

The view of Disraeli is interesting here. As Adelman argues, until fairly recently, the view taken of Disraeli was that he had moved to a principled position of 'Tory democracy,' genuinely trying to make the

Conservative Party the party of the middle and working classes. This view has been criticized; an emerging consensus now is that 'Disraeli's attitude during the Reform crisis was purely opportunist. He neither sought to educate his party, nor displayed either firmness or consistency of purpose in his support for "democracy." Indeed during these months Disraeli had only one major aim: to destroy Gladstone's leadership over a united Liberal Party and, by seizing the initiative in reform himself and promoting a reform bill, to raise the fortunes of the Conservative Party and consolidate his own (hitherto somewhat tenuous) position as party leader.'[45] The Conservatives were indeed forced to come to terms with the new political realities of class and politics, but they did so almost entirely from the narrow perspective of holding on to power.

Gleig's fulsome praise of Disraeli was focused on his view of the latter's brilliance as a political strategist and on his recognition of political realities, with the obligatory claim that he did what he did for the country. Gleig, however, did not present Disraeli as a newborn democrat, an educator of his party. The key thing was that he produced a 'safe' bill. Gleig also tended to ignore Derby's role: Hawkins argues that if any 'educating' of the Conservative Party, and of Disraeli himself, occurred, it was by Derby.

Derby believed there existed a genuine demand for reform, but it was not voiced by the Reform League. If the destructive slide to manhood suffrage and radical fomenting of extreme aspirations was to be prevented, a clear defensible line demarcating a responsible electorate had to be drawn. By December 1866, Derby believed that, in the case of the urban electorate, household suffrage provided such a principle: Disraeli's conversion followed.[46]

The year 1867 also saw intense interest by Blackwood's in the subject of the working class and trade unions. This was prompted partly by the fear that the Second Reform act might irrevocably open the gates to 'democracy' and partly by the growing strength, numerical and legal and political, of trade unions. 1859 saw the emergence of a broad committee of trade union leaders, the London Trades Council was formed in 1860, and the Trade Unionists Manhood Suffrage and Vote by Ballot Association in 1862. Analysis of this topic was entrusted to Charles Mackay, correspondent in the United States for the London *Times*. Mackay wrote thirty-five articles for the magazine between May 1866 and May 1888, many of them comparing society and politics in the

United States (unfavourably) with British society. Mackay also achieved a lasting reputation as a writer of popular social psychology, for his *Extraordinary Popular Delusions and the Madness of Crowds* (1841, 1852). This may explain why the editors thought he should tackle the subject of trade unions.

Mackay was concerned to refute the charge that the working classes were not represented in the political system and that trades unions should adopt a political stance in order to win them such a role. He objected to a 'new cant' that had arisen from the efforts of Radicals such as Bright 'who would Americanize our politics and our manners, and hand over the government of the country to the numerical majority of the whole people, irrespective of property or intelligence.' This would tend, if successful, 'to overwhelm the political balance which vests power in this country in wealth and intelligence as well as in numbers.' Mackay claimed disingenuously that no class was excluded from the suffrage; as far as the working class was concerned, 'any man who labours with his hands for his daily bread may obtain the privilege of a vote for the borough or county in which he resides, if he will become a householder paying a certain amount of rent, or the owner of a freehold of the annual value of forty shillings.' The constitution, in other words, did not ban the political participation of workers, although of course, only few such would be desirous of, or fitted for, exercising the vote.[47] It was understandable why workers had been driven to organize, but it should be realized that the organization of capital and of labour were not the same. Capitalists were not a unit, they competed with each other 'to the great advantage of the public and all the labouring classes.' Labour's organization, on the other hand, had by now become tyrannical for the individual worker. This furthermore was the strongest indication that universal suffrage 'will cultivate a despotism.'[48] Mackay, as the resident expert on America ('and the institutions we are asked to imitate as the perfection of political wisdom') noted that manhood suffrage there, despite being enjoyed for a considerable time, had not seemed to benefit the working classes: 'there is not a single mechanic in either House of Congress.'

In 1870, Maga followed up Mackay's warnings about trade unions with a two-part series on the same subject by the political economist (and ambivalent conservative) Bonamy Price. Claiming that the unions based their program on the principles of political economy, Price proposed that it should be judged on its practicality, as 'economical science.' If the unions aimed to secure a permanent minimum for wages, how was this permanence to be assured, if the 'natural law' of the market was ignored? Labourers must learn to adjust to the available amount of work. They should not increase their families beyond a point where there is no work to sustain them. Wages must depend on the demand for work: 'society naturally arrives at the minimum it needs – it reposes on the basis of a population whose numbers accommodate themselves to the general products of industry and to the share which accrues by natural law to the capitalists and the labourers.'[49] Price was willing to accord legal recognition to trades unions, but only under certain conditions: they must cease to use force and violence against their own members; they should demonstrate a high level of ethical conduct to the rest of society and they should not use funds given for benefits in the struggle for wages. As for possible alternatives, Price recommended instituting 'conciliation courts' for each trade and, echoing Mackay, the establishment of cooperative societies; associations of masters and workers, who would share in profits.[50]

Profit sharing was certainly not on the mind of the Blackwoods' directors a few years after Price's articles appeared. As a response to the printers' strikes for shorter work week and higher wages, at the publishing house in 1872–3, notes Finkelstein, Blackwoods hired scab labour and declared their office non-union. It remained so until the turn of the century: 'As John Blackwood saw it, union meddling merely destroyed the paternalist management style he envisaged in operation under his tenure. "We must put it to them what right have they to look to us in sickness or trouble," he wrote, "if they are to serve us this way in a pinch."'[51]

Icons and Irritants

Blackwoods had a fairly well defined gallery of political heroes and villains. On the heroic side, Disraeli stood almost alone. There was no instance in English history of a political leadership in 'which greater qualities of sagacity, independence of judgment and tenacity of purpose' had been exhibited, wrote Herbert Cowell in Disraeli's obituary. 'Disraeli's authority overshadowed his colleagues and the country and he … centred in himself the whole force and representation of the empire.'[52] Disraeli reconstructed the Tory party; primarily, according to Cowell, by his desire to improve the condition of the masses (unlikely), and to attach them to Conservative policy (more probably); practically settled the principle of parliamentary representation by firmly taking control (Derby notwithstanding) of the reform process and establishing reform on the basis of household suffrage; and reconstituted the South-eastern territories of Europe.

With regard to villains, Gladstone (and Gladstonianism) probably had a special place; particularly as he betrayed his natural origins, lasted so long and continued to flirt with Radicalism. John Bright, along with other Radicals, came in for consistent censure, as did John Stuart Mill. It is not surprising that Mill seemed an easy target for Blackwood's conservatives; after all he had had the temerity to write a savage review of Alison's *History*. Tories usually had little time for theorists of any stripe, preferring to focus on the nuts and bolts of politics. Mill's works on liberty and on women's rights were examples of dangerously ab-stract theorizing divorced from the real world of natural causes.

Herbert Cowell, in an 1873 review, ostensibly of J.F. Stephen's *Liberty, Equality, Fraternity*, but primarily focused on Mill, began by noting the 'unaccountably overweening confidence of philosophers in themselves and the devotion with which their utterances are received by a small circle of admirers.' Cowell conceded that philosophers were needed, but not to attack the very foundations of social life. *On Liberty* appeared to apply to a society 'where all have disciplined tastes and correct judgments' while *On the Subjection of Women* presupposed a society where 'education and artificial life are supposed to have destroyed the natural division of the sexes and the wide separation in their several functions and duties.'[53] Cowell, having noted Mill's 'sanctioning' of the revolt in Jamaica, went on to characterize Mill's 'ideal panorama of society as a scene of one vast Jamaica revolt, in which all sense of duty and subordination is merged in the divine right of every man and woman to do as he pleases.' Present day radicalism was founded upon the rights of man. Toryism on the other hand, 'regards the duties of citizens.' Duties were more easily defined than rights and formed the proper basis for rules of conduct. Cowell mischaracterized Mill's first principle of liberty as allowing the individual to be entirely free of society and social convention.[54]

When Cowell turned to review Mill's *Autobiography* the following year, he found there contextual confirmation of the philosopher's in-ability to engage with the real world. Mill's utilitarian upbringing and education at the hands of his father explained for Cowell 'the inad-equacy of an analytic training and habit of mind to secure accuracy of judgment even in the most ordinary affairs of life.' Added to this was the shocking story of Mill's infatuation with Harriet Taylor. This provided the final evidence, if any more was needed, of Mill's attack on his own society. Not only was John Taylor's life 'embittered,' Mill's 'passionate, idolatrous worship' of Harriet Taylor was 'in violation of duties which society still holds sacred.'[55]

Mill's intellectual and political campaign for women's rights had several years before been the subject of two reviews in the magazine, both by women: the novelist and essayist Margaret Oliphant provided a sardonic reading of the suffrage petition in 1866, while a year later Anne Mozley, who wrote twenty-five essays for Blackwood's mostly on manners, social conventions, literature, and religion, gave a more straightforward anti-feminist critique of the *Subjection of Women*. Mill was sarcastically introduced by Oliphant as 'a champion to avenge our wrongs and procure us our rights.' Her strategy was first to characterize the cohort of women to whom Mill proposed giving the vote – the class of female householders, lone women who paid their own rent and taxes – as 'old enough and stout-hearted enough to take care of themselves' Mill had 'classified us and given us a new place in creation. He has made us out to be something less than women, something almost man. It is a vote that he means to give us – that celestial all but divine privilege which makes the face of the working man to shine prospectively.'

In actuality these women had become anything but envious of men, who 'in fact, required a vast deal of propping up and stimulating to keep them with their front to the world.' It was younger, hot-headed women who desired more importance and thought that could be at- tained through equality with men.[56] Besides, Oliphant continued, the vote was not an especially valued prize: she claimed that 'the further one ascends the social scale the less importance generally does the possessor of the franchise give to his vote.' Independent older women had public opinion in their hands to a considerable extent already, 'why come out of our domestic sphere and descend to the poll with the greengrocer.' Oliphant concluded by reasserting the traditional spheres: women were 'not created for ploughing or voting, – nor to carry guns or make speeches, not even to produce poetry or excel in the fine arts. Equality of place or rights was not the chief thing for our maker.' Male and female were two distinct creatures. Mill's refined contacts were a small group of intellectual women with 'artificial wants and capabili- ties'; he had made the mistake of accepting them as a type of universal womankind. His proposal was therefore 'insulting' to the mass of women whose 'ambition is not of so small a character as to be satisfied with the privilege of voting for an MP.'[57]

Oliphant's strategy, arguing that since the vote had been extended, it wasn't really worth having any more, was a frequent theme among Blackwoods' authors. Archibald Alison Jr, for instance, argued that 'the leveling tyranny of the masses ... drives all the better class of citizens, all men of independent principles to withdraw altogether from public life.'[58] Charles Mackay, giving an example from American democracy, wished to have it both ways: manhood suffrage meant that politics, especially at the State level, was the preserve of the mob; but at the same time, 'no mechanic' was to be found in either House of Congress.[59] Gleig repeated the American lesson: 'the best bred and best mannered citizens shrink ... from the debasing influences of public life.'[60]

Even though conservatives may have come to terms with 'Disraeli's' Reform Act of 1867, they continued to fight rearguard actions against further encroachments of democracy. One such was the important reform to the electoral system, the ballot Act of 1872. Gleig offered a number of traditional objections to this bill as it was being promoted by Gladstone. The MP he argued, is not a 'mere delegate' but rather goes to legislate 'for the whole empire'; therefore the electors share in the responsibility for their public act of electing. The Ballot would put an end to any chance of 'regulating' electoral contests, as parties would no longer be able to judge the 'possible balance of power' before the vote in order to agree to avoid a contest by conceding a share in representation; by extension, the number of candidates would multiply. Confusing campaigning with voting, Gleig claimed that 'the natural disposition of the tenant to make common cause with his landlord' would be ignored. Because men would have to keep their opinions to themselves, secret voting promoted 'stealth' and 'scheming' and promised to 'lower the moral tone of society.' Gleig needn't have worried: Rubinstein suggests that 'in most of Britain, the introduction of the ballot probably had little effect, and the Conservatives resoundingly won the next election [1874] without any help from threats to voters by landlords or factory owners.'[61]

Postscript: 'The End of the Struggle'?

The year 1870 saw Archibald Alison Jr writing a paean to the march of civilization: closely paraphrasing his father, Alison noted that the 'restless spirit of democracy' had impelled 'the Anglo-Saxon race over the sea.' 'It is impossible,' he wrote, 'to contemplate the progress of the Anglo-Saxon race in the New World and in Australia without a feeling of awe.' The 'silent, ceaseless, daily advance of the frontier of civilization in the far west' was 'surely the most wonderful phenomenon of modern times.'[62]

In a more pragmatic vein, Blackwood's Tories were trying in the early 1880s to come to terms with a new political reality, in which 'the preferences of an increasingly democratic electorate decided who should govern the nation.'[63] Allardyce set the scene in 1881. The Whigs were extinct and the liberals were rapidly fading away under the vicissitudes of Gladstone's ego: 'We have, then, in the present day, only two active parties in the State: Conservatism or Toryism and Gladstonianism ["Radicalism"]. On the one side, a powerful code of traditional, well-known and often-tried principles, which the people of Britain have had a great part in formulating; on the other, the will of a Minister who has to shift and trim his sails as the popular breeze blows.'[64]

The conservative task was to win over enough of the new voters in order to claim that 'the people of Britain' were on their side, while trying to portray many of those same voters as a fickle 'popular breeze' when they supported Gladstone. Facing a new round of enfranchisement and redistribution in 1885, Sir John Manners sounded the familiar alarms (against a 'revolutionized' House of Commons and an 'incapacitated political system') but saw hope in the single-member system and the strength of the House of Lords.[65]

David Finkelstein notes elsewhere in this volume that the magazine was losing readership during the 1880s and that this trend continued at least until the First World War. Part of the problem was strong competition from a new avowedly conservative monthly, the *National Review*. Encroaching on 'Blackwoodian space' in its closeness to the London Carlton Club and poaching Maga authors such as Herbert Cowell and Sir Stafford Northcote, the *National Review* flourished for the next seventy years. H.S. Northcote may have been referring to the *Review* in a letter to Blackwood in 1882: 'I believe the real history of ... the new magazine ... is that there is to be a new club after the fashion of the "Cosmopolitan" – a sort of literary conservative club meeting for conversational purposes once or twice a week.' The new magazine was connected 'but not as an official exponent of conservative leaders' ideas.' Northcote thought a 'good evening provincial paper much more wanted.'[66] It is significant that as conservatives were forced to come to terms with the changed class nature of politics from the 1880s on, and as the *National Review* competition started to bite, Blackwoods shifted the focus of its magazine away from tilting at reform windmills and towards the area in which unbridled conservative values could still be located: patriotic accounts of colonial and military adventures.

The House of Blackwood did indeed consistently act 'on behalf of the Right.' For over fifty years Maga's conservative journalists harried liberal, radical, and even conservative reform. To Archibald Alison, William Aytoun, William and John Blackwood, the first combative generation of Blackwood's High Tories, the rot had set in by 1832. Property would all too soon cease to be the commanding principle of politics; class the repository of electoral fitness. They may have found some consolation in the turn towards the welfare state in the early 1900s. Robert Blake notes their 'shadowy prevision of the welfare state and a planned economy.' While Alison and others of the same mind certainly did see a protective role for the state, this was, however, within a strongly hierarchical society dominated by the landed elite and requiring only a passive watchfulness of the labouring classes. Manners, Allardyce, and their colleagues in the 1880s, more at ease with liberal democracy, but unsure of the Tories' future, were not to know that twenty years of Conservative dominance were to follow, resulting in part from the Liberals support of Home Rule, nor that their party would become after the First World War, the party of government in the new century. The House of Blackwood continued to publish 'on behalf of the Right,' but its glory days as 'gatekeeper' of conservative politics were over.

NOTES

1 Noel O'Sullivan, *Conservatism* (New York: St Martin's Press, 1976), 83.
2 Laurence Lockhart, 'The Late John Blackwood,' *Blackwood's Magazine* 126 (December 1879), 772–5.
3 Letter to John Blackwood from R.H. Patterson, 1868, National Library of Scotland (NLS), MS 4238, fol. 164.
4 Letter to John Blackwood from Bonamy Price, 30 August, 1868. NLS, MS 4239, fol. 42.
5 Letter to R.H. Patterson from Bonamy Price, 14 October 1868, NLS, MS 4239, fol. 54
6 Letter to W. Blackwood from A. Allardyce, 19 February 1881. NLS, MS 4415, fol. 44.
7 Archibald Alison, 'The State of Public Feeling in Scotland,' *Blackwood's Magazine* 31 (January 1832), 65.

8 Letter from W. Blackwood, 21 October 1869, NLS, MS 4243, fol. 134.

9 The following discussions of Alison's dealings with his publisher are drawn from my political biography, *An Enlightenment Tory in Victorian Scotland: The Career of Sir Archibald Alison* (Montreal and Kingston: McGill-Queen's University Press, 1997), especially chapter 5, and from my '"Mr. Wordy" and the Blackwoods: Author and Publisher in Victorian Scotland,' *Bibliotheck* (1996), 39–54. I am grateful to the publishers for permission to use this material.

10 Letter to Blackwood from Archibald Alison, 30 July 1838, NLS, MS 4046,

11 Benjamin Disraeli, *Coningsby, or The New Generation*, ed. Sheila M. Smith (Oxford: Oxford University Press, 1982), 110.

12 Letter to Blackwood from Archibald Alison, 7 June 1842, NLS, MS 4058.

13 Henry Cockburn, *Journal of Henry Cockburn* (Edinburgh: Edmonston and Douglas, 1874) 2:232–3.

14 Letter to Blackwood from Archibald Alison, 30 May 1846, NLS, MS 4077.

15 Letter to Blackwood from Archibald Alison, 11 July 1853, NLS, MS 4101.

16 Letter to Blackwood from Archibald Alison, 31 January 1836, NLS, MS 30969.

17 Letter to Blackwood from Archibald Alison, 15 January 1857, NLS, MS 4092.

18 Letter to William Blackwood from R.H. Patterson, 30 January 1882, NLS, MS 4437, fol. 171.

19 Letter to William Blackwood from John Blackwood, February [?] 1854, NLS, MS 4104, fol. 125.

20 Letter to William Blackwood from R.H. Patterson, n.d., 1868, NLS, MS 4214, fol. 59.

21 Letter to Blackwood from Herbert Cowell, 10 August 1858, NLS, MS 4130, fol. 105.

22 Letter to John Blackwood from R.H. Patterson, September 1866, NLS, MS 4214, fol. 47.

23 Letter to William Blackwood from R.J. Patterson, 10 April 1882, NLS, MS 4437, fol. 171.

24 Letter to John Blackwood from R.H. Patterson, 5 April 1866, NLS, MS 4214, fol. 31.

25 Letter to John Blackwood from R.H. Patterson, 10 April 1866, NLS, MS 4214, fol. 33.

26 Letter to William Blackwood from R.H. Patterson, 6 February 1883, NLS, MS 4449, fol. 140–1. Patterson's claim to be prescient as a commentator on foreign affairs had some weight to it as this comment suggests: 'it is not for human intellect to *predict* when the *War* will break out ... But come

when it may, it is the Eastern Question again which will *open the strife* – ... which will probably lead to a Great War, which is due before the century expires.' Ibid., fol. 141.

27 The following section draws upon my *An Enlightenment Tory in Victorian Scotland*, chapter 6.

28 Alison, 'British History during the Eighteenth Century,' *Blackwood's Magazine* 57 (March 1845), 364, 365.

29 Alison, *Some Account of My Life and Writings: An Autobiography by the late Sir Archibald Alison*, ed. L.J. Alison, 2 vols. (Edinburgh: Blackwood, 1883), 1:244–5.

30 Peter Mandler, *Aristocratic Government in the Age of Reform: Whigs and Liberals, 1830–1852* (Oxford: Clarendon Press, 1990), 1.

31 Alison, 'Duties of the Conservative Party,' *Blackwood's Magazine* 32 (July 1832), 140.

32 Alison, 'Experience of Democracy,' *Blackwood's Magazine* 40 (September 1836), 293, 294, 303, 305–6, 308.

33 Ibid., 304.

34 Michie, *Enlightenment Tory*, 110.

35 Charles Mackay, 'The Principles and Issues of the American Struggle,' *Blackwood's Magazine* 100 (July 1866), 17–27.

36 Mackay, ibid.; R.H. Patterson, 'The Crisis of the American War,' *Blackwood's Magazine* 92 (November 1862), 636–46; Archibald Alison Jr, 'Democracy Beyond the Seas,' *Blackwood's Magazine* 107 (February 1870), 234.

37 Paul Adelman, *Gladstone, Disraeli and Later Victorian Politics* (London: Longman, 1997), 18.

38 Angus Hawkins, *British Party Politics, 1852–1886* (New York: St Martin's Press, 1998), 111.

39 G.R. Gleig, 'The Political Crisis,' *Blackwood's Magazine* 99 (June 1866), 773, 781.

40 Gleig, 'The Reform Bill,' *Blackwood's Magazine* 103 (May 1868), 634.

41 Gleig, 'The Bill As It Is,' *Blackwood's Magazine* 102 (August 1867), 245.

42 Ibid., 246.

43 Ibid., 249.

44 Ibid., 251.

45 Adelman, *Gladstone*, 18.

46 Hawkins, *British Party Politics*, 249.

47 Charles Mackay, 'The Working Classes,' *Blackwood's Magazine* 101 (February 1867), 221–2.

48 Ibid., 223.

49 Bonamy Price, 'Trade Unions, Part II,' *Blackwood's Magazine* 107 (June 1870), 745.

50 Ibid., 752, 760.
51 David Finkelstein, *The House of Blackwood: Author–Publisher Relations in the Victorian Era* (University Park: Pennsylvania State University Press, 2002), 41, 47.
52 Herbert Cowell, 'The Earl of Beaconsfield,' *Blackwood's Magazine* 129 (May 1881), 674.
53 Cowell, 'Liberty, Equality, Fraternity: Mr. John Stuart Mill,' *Blackwood's Magazine* 114 (September 1873), 346, 348.
54 Ibid., 350.
55 Cowell, 'John Stuart Mill: An Autobiography,' *Blackwood's Magazine* 115 (January 1874), 90, 84.
56 Margaret Oliphant, 'The Great Unrepresented,' *Blackwood's Magazine* 100 (September 1866), 370–1.
57 Ibid., 376.
58 Alison, 'Democracy,' 235.
59 Mackay, 'Principles and Issues.'
60 G.R. Gleig, 'The Ballot Bill,' *Blackwood's Magazine* 110 (August 1871) 264.
61 Ibid., 161. William Rubinstein, *Britain's Century: A Political and Social History, 1815–1905* (London and New York: Arnold and Oxford University Press, 1998), 141.
62 Archibald Alison Jr, 'Democracy,' *Blackwood's Magazine* 107 (February 1870), 235.
63 Hawkins, *British Party Politics*, 290.
64 Alexander Allardyce, 'The Ethics of Gladstonianism,' *Blackwood's Magazine* 130 (November 1881), 634.
65 Sir John Manners, 'The End of the Struggle,' *Blackwood's Magazine* 137 (January 1885), 151.
66 Letter to Blackwood from H.S. Northcote, 5 December 1882, NLS MS 4437, fol. 32.

Editing *Blackwood's*; or, What Do Editors Do?

ROBERT L. PATTEN AND DAVID FINKELSTEIN

I have now been connected with newspapers over thirty years and I have never yet discovered what an editor is.

— Henry Labouchere[1]

In the spring of 1885 William Blackwood III, editor, 'proprietor' of *Blackwood's Magazine*, and head of the Edinburgh-based publishing firm William Blackwood and Sons, made his annual pilgrimage to the firm's London office. Ever since the base in Paternoster Row had been founded in 1840, it had been a ritual for the director of the firm to travel south during the summer months for an extended period in the City, Westminster, and the West End. This excursion afforded William opportunities to renew political and literary acquaintances, to scout for new authors, and to remind London publishers that the Blackwood firm still commanded a presence in the business of publishing valued texts at reasonable prices.

William interspersed business with pleasure. During the day he attended business meetings and, in the late afternoons, read proofs of forthcoming books and magazines; in the evening he dined out and then attended literary soirées or the theatre. The job of checking proofs for *Blackwood's Magazine* ('Maga' to the trade) was not a difficult or onerous task, but it was one William himself regularly undertook. On reviewing the proofs for the May 1885 issue two weeks before they were due to be printed, something in the front matter of the journal caused him to rush to the telegraph office and fire off an urgent cable to his Edinburgh office manager, Thomas Henderson. Each monthly issue, encased in brown paper wrappers, contained a thirty-two-page advertising supplement inserted before the contents page, as well as advertisements on the inside front wrapper and inside and outside back wrapper. The advertisements ranged from announcements of forthcoming works and small boxed sections extolling the virtues of 'Fry's Cocoa Extract,' 'Brand and Co.'s Preserved Provisions,' and 'Stone's Patent Form Cases for Solicitors,' to advertisements for insurance agents, tea merchants, and other bulk merchandizing specialists. This aspect of Victorian periodical production frequently eludes modern day researchers, whose knowledge of the contents of such journals derives from examining bound library copies, stripped of 'irrelevant' ephemera during rebinding. It is, however, a point increasingly acknowledged by recent scholars studying readers' receptions of Victorian serialized fiction.[2]

William noticed something that, in his role as editor, startled and offended his aesthetic sense: an advertisement for one of Blackwood's latest book publications, Lady Violet Martin's essay collection *Shakespeare's Female Characters*, originally published sporadically in *Blackwood's Magazine* between January 1881 and February 1885, was prominently and incongruously displayed on the inside front wrapper, juxtaposed to touts for common household soap and health products. This would not do! Blackwood called on Henderson to remove notice of Lady Martin's '*great* work' from the offending page and to shift it elsewhere in the supplement. 'To see it above Pears Soap and the Best Tonic would give her Ladyship a fit & certainly I do much object to seeing books ranked amongst quackery adverts,' he added with a note of asperity.[3] The matter was duly taken care of, and Lady Martin emerged none the wiser regarding the near collision of her work with soaps and tonics.

What does this brief moment of editorial activity tell us about periodical discourse in the nineteenth century? For one, it highlights matters most analysts miss in discussing the Victorian period, in particular the activity of nineteenth-century editors. Their office tasks linked the aesthetics, commercial transactions, and contents of their journals to their conceptualization of their readers; and these interrelated considerations determined the manner in which editors set out to shape their periodicals for the marketplace. In this case, the repositioning of advertising material reflected William's anxiety to avoid offending a valued and socially positioned contributor, his attention to the aesthetics of journal production, and his hierarchized and ambivalent attitude towards the type of advertising the journal was increasingly drawing in to offset production costs.

This advertising incident allows us entry into exploring how a nineteenth-century journal was 'conducted'[4] – how decisions were made, how quickly they were carried out, how far in advance the editorial team planned the contents, and what factors influenced changing, omitting, or revising structures and material. In essence, the question we are exploring is, what is the 'editor function'? How does one begin to quantify and speculate on the variety of functions editors of periodicals served in nineteenth-century Britain? So often we refer to someone as 'editing' a magazine, without much thought about what such duties entail. (Usually the reference is made to indicate that the 'editor' 'approved' of the contents of the issue.) How did those duties differ at different magazines and at different times? How has the 'editor function' been obscured by the 'cult of authorship' and its recent deconstruction? What might constitute the editor's role at various points along a spectrum of possibilities?

Blackwood Enters the Literary Marketplace

William Blackwood I established *Blackwood's Edinburgh Magazine* in 1817 when he was forty-one. He was an enterprising and energetic man whose move into publishing at the turn of the nineteenth century had come as a result of opportunities created by his predecessors. He played a key role in both the periodical and book-publishing field, reviving the older Edinburgh tradition of the publishing house as a literary gathering place. From the beginning, he encouraged emerging writers to make his place of business a centre of literary society, a sort of club where men of letters might find a meeting place. One outcome was the building of the 'Old Saloon' when the firm moved to new premises at 45 George Street in 1829 – an oval room where literary portraits stared down upon an oval table, and confirmed 'Blackwoodians' gathered to continue the tradition begun in the early days.

As noted in earlier contributions to this collection, William Blackwood consolidated his initial success by using the journal to attract a core of well-placed writers to the firm. These included the Irishmen William Maginn and Sir Samuel Ferguson, the Scots John Galt, David Macbeth Moir ('Delta'), and George Moir, and the Mancunian Thomas De Quincey. The magazine also featured occasional reviews by Walter Scott, fiction by Samuel Warren and Susan Ferrier, and work by Samuel Taylor Coleridge. Blackwood used Maga both as a showcase for new talent and as a method of attracting potential contributors to the firm's book lists. He pioneered a business model that allowed him to capitalize on the journal's content by republishing the material in book form, predating by several years Henry Colburn and Richard Bentley's use of such marketing strategies in the late 1820s.

Under the editorship of John Blackwood (1845–79) and his nephew William Blackwood III (1879–1912), *Blackwood's Magazine* consolidated its position in British literary culture as a leading representative of Tory thought and bourgeois middle-class cultural production. Its identification with Disraeli was so strong that William, sending an account of a May 1868 debate on Irish disestablishment to his uncle John, used the personal pronoun: 'the Govt. did right in not resigning at first tho' it has caused *us* to appear to be dragged through the mud.'[5] Maga was also a considerable force in publishing important fiction. In its pages appeared significant works by George Eliot (*Scenes of Clerical Life*, January–November 1857), Margaret Oliphant (*Miss Marjoribanks*, February 1865–May 1866), Anthony Trollope (*John Caldigate*, April 1878–June 1879), F. Marion Crawford (*Saracinesca*, May 1886–April 1887), Joseph Conrad (*Heart of Darkness*, February–April 1899; *Lord Jim*, October 1899–November 1900), and Neil Munro (*Children of the Tempest*, 1902–3), as well as shorter work by Oscar Wilde, R.D. Blackmore, Thomas Hardy, Arthur Conan Doyle, John Buchan, and others.

Like the Blackwoods, other British publishers were quick to realize the benefits to be gained from the relationship between commerce and periodical literature. Viewed historically, the formula pioneered by Scottish-based journals can be seen to tie in with the industrialization of Britain, the shift from piecemeal work to mass production. Similarly, refinements in production techniques and the increasing availability of relevant low-cost raw materials fed into the development of British print culture. New technology, such as the invention in the early 1800s of stereotyping, the Fourdrinier papermaking machine, and the Stanhope press, enabled publishers to lower production costs and produce books and periodicals more quickly and more cheaply as the century progressed.[6]

Commercial imperatives and an expanding readership played their part in shaping nineteenth-century publishing approaches to literary production. William Hazlitt highlighted this conjoining of mass markets and mass audiences, and in particular the role of British literary periodicals in negotiating between the two, in 'The Periodical Press,' his well-known 1823 contribution to the *Edinburgh Review*. 'Literary immortality is now let on short leases,' he declared, 'and we must be contented to succeed by rotation.' He continued, 'We exist in the bustle of the world, and cannot escape from the notice of our contemporaries. We must please to live, and therefore should live to please. We must look to the public for support. Instead of solemn testimonies from the learned, we require the smiles of the fair and the polite. If princes scowl upon us, the broad shining face of the people may turn to us with a favourable aspect. Is not this life (too) sweet? Would we change it for the former if we could? But the great point is, that *we cannot*! Therefore, let Reviews flourish – let Magazines increase and multiply – let the Daily and Weekly Newspapers live forever!'[7]

Running parallel to this accelerating and enlarging publishing industry was a shifting focus for writing and marketing: from pleasing patrons and elite opinion makers to pleasing a mass audience. Negotiating a fit between format, writers, and readers preoccupied many publishers and editors seeking to navigate the literary currents of the nineteenth century. As educational opportunities, real income, and leisure increased throughout the century, readership expanded. Periodicals – and their editors – had to invent a range of subjects, copytexts, styles, and marketing strategies to satisfy new audiences.

Shifting Options: Three Types of Editors

Early in the nineteenth century editors, frequently operating through pseudonymous characters, spoke for a set of political, social, and aesthetic values that were often related, in Scotland at least, to nationalism and the middle class (think of *Noctes Ambrosianae* and Christopher North). Moreover, sometimes editorships changed hands without much notable change in the policies of the periodical. For instance, William Maginn, editor of *Fraser's*, wrote much of the editorial statement of purpose for Richard Bentley's rival magazine *Bentley's Miscellany* that Charles Dickens, pseudonymously as 'Boz,' edited; and when Harrison Ainsworth succeeded Dickens as editor there was little change in editorial policy or the stable of authors, excepting the huge loss of Dickens himself.

By mid-century, three types of editorial strategies were being utilized in the periodical productions of the day. First, there was the 'big name' editor, such as William Makepeace Thackeray at the *Cornhill Magazine*, who utilized his – or, in some rare occasions, such as Mrs Henry Wood's editorship of the *Argosy*, her – literary connections to solicit other 'big names' and left most of the day-to-day details to subordinates.[8] Second, there was the 'hands on' editor who oversaw every aspect of production, including the make-up and timing of articles and reviews, as Dickens with his sub-editor W.H. Wills and cadre of dependable contributors such as Wilkie Collins and George Augustus Sala did. And third, there was the publisher–proprietor model, such as George Smith and William Blackwood III, who took an active interest in his property and often through tie-ins with other of his publishing ventures managed to obtain major works that recouped their substantial cost by running both in the periodical and in a variety of volume formats – still later supplemented by reprint licensing at home and abroad.[9] Typical of this practice was the recycling of Maga material through the popular, multi-volume series *Tales from Blackwood's*, first issued in twelve volumes in 1857 and periodically refreshed in new series editions until 1891.[10] In 1879, material culled from the second series was published on the European continent as a two-volume set in the famous Tauchnitz reprint series, for which the firm received a £40 reprint fee from the German firm.[11]

Even though the number of instances is insufficient and our categories are crude, such examples help alert us to the varieties of 'editing' that went on through the century. Speculative postulations about the functions nineteenth-century periodical editors performed have been ventured previously, notably in the essays edited by Joel H. Wiener in 1985, *Innovators and Preachers*. The collection, grouped into three sections, raised some important questions still only partially answered today: to what extent did editors shape public opinion? How did they work with their staffs? What effects did the transition from anonymity to signed articles have on editors and editorial policy?[12] Did editors lead, follow, or get out of the way of progress? What did nineteenth-century editors do during their working days? And how did those tasks change over the century?

A simple formula would be to conceive of the editorial function as shifting from the modest, coterie beginnings in Edinburgh at the turn of the century into the triple paradigms of high Victorian periodical management that then sloped downward to the rag-tag assemblages of *Tit-Bits*, penny papers, and the awful journalistic pandering of Jasper Milvain and his ilk. This is not dissimilar to the rise and fall of the literary editor tracked by Joel Wiener and his colleagues: after the early decades of the nineteenth century, when editors still clung to their amateur status, the Wiener volume argues, there emerged at mid-century strong professional editors who became powerful personalities in the print world –

'distinctive' functionaries, Walter Bagehot called them,[13] and who in the next generation, at the turn of the century, were supplanted by the mechanization of printing, the hugely enlarged scale of production, the expansion and professionalization of journalism, and the substitution of news and entertainment for the magisterial essays, reviews, and literature of the preceding decades.[14]

Job Descriptions: Seven Editorial Functions

But the question of 'what do editors do?' transcends national boundaries as it pretends to transcend temporal ones. The question moves from a historically and nationally conditioned inquiry into the functioning of certain workers in a certain industry to a categorical query presupposing transcendent, transhistorical answers. By 'editing' one could mean almost anything. There seem to be at least seven functions that might be part of an editor's job: (1) overseeing finance and administration, (2) promoting an ideology, (3) commissioning contributors, (4) arranging and perfecting copy, (5) buying and selling advertising, (6) supervising quality, and above all, (7) giving the periodical a distinctive character. Nineteenth-century British editors did and did not do all seven of these things, at various times throughout the century, and under all three editorial regimes just enumerated. We will illustrate instances of each kind of editorial task, contextualizing the Blackwood's firm against its many competitors. And then we will consider the most surprising finding: the correlation between responsible editing and success, or irresponsible editing and failure, is remarkably chancy.

Overseeing Finance and Administration

The most obvious division of labour in editing a journal may be that between the business side and the copytext side. A prevalent arrangement throughout the nineteenth century was for a publisher to finance the journal, often in order to obtain authors, texts, and publicity for his publishing house, and to turn over the editorial responsibilities to a hireling. John Murray published, William Gifford and John Gibson Lockhart successively edited, the *Quarterly Review*; Archibald Constable financed, Francis Jeffrey edited, the *Edinburgh Review*; Henry Colburn published, William Jerdan edited, the *New Monthly*; Alexander Macmillan published, David Masson, and later Mowbray Morris, edited *Macmillan's Magazine*; A.J.B. Beresford Hope published, John Douglas Cook and

Philip Harwood co-edited, the *Saturday Review*. Even at *The Times* in mid-twentieth-century London, the distinguished British literary editor Anthony Curtis tells us, authority was 'divided between the Manager who controlled the money-bags [for the absentee Proprietor, Lord Astor of Hever] and the Editor who controlled the editorial content.'[15]

But there are enough variations on this model of publisher versus editor to make it inadequate as a paradigm. For instance, Robert and William Chambers, booksellers and publishers, inaugurated *Chambers's Edinburgh Journal* in 1832 to provide information for the newly literate middle classes and artisans. William edited for the first year, while Robert tended to the business side; then Robert became joint editor from 1833 to 1837, and sole editor from 1837 to 1858. Other family firms show a similar blurring of the business and editorial sides. From 1808 John Hunt managed the financial affairs of the *Examiner*, while Leigh Hunt supervised the editing; but when Leigh Hunt departed for Italy in 1821 John's son Henry Leigh Hunt assumed the editor's chair, and seven years later, in 1828, became publisher as well. Dickens owned half of *Household Words*, and his publishers owned a quarter; when he broke with them and started a new periodical, *All the Year Round*, he and his subeditor Wills were co-proprietors (Dickens owning three-quarters). '[T]here is no publisher whatever associated with All the Year Round,' he told Edward Bulwer Lytton. 'I, and Wills my sub Editor, are the Sole Proprietors; therefore implicit reliance may be placed in the Journal's proceedings.'[16]

The Blackwoods published their *Blackwood's Edinburgh Magazine* from the first issue, April 1817, but shared distribution with other firms from time to time: John Murray; Thomas Cadell; Baldwin, Craddock and Joy. The family also edited the magazine, after the disastrous initial issues produced by Pringle and Cleghorn. However, as other essays in this collection note, Maga's 'editor' was also sometimes a composite figure, developed out of robust debate among 'collaborators' who included at an early stage Lockhart and Maginn. From 1845 to 1879 the 'editor's office' resolved into a cooperative made up of the dominant figures of John and (from 1861) William Blackwood III, supported by their Edinburgh and London managers George Simpson and Joseph Munt Langford, respectively. They were not the only ones to edit in a collective fashion: George Smith, when Thackeray resigned the editor's chair at the *Cornhill*, formed an editorial committee consisting of himself, Frederick Greenwood, George Henry Lewes, and later Edward Dutton Cook. Various combinations of the *Cornhill* quadrumvirate lasted until

1871, when Leslie Stephen became sole editor. And sometimes when publishers interfered on the editorial side, as Bradbury and Evans did with *Once a Week*, the results were disastrous.[17] So the divide between publishing function and editorial function blurs in many nineteenth-century instances, and the responsibility for success or failure cannot be attributed to editorial practice only.

Although the division between publishing and editing is not always a test for successful management, it would seem that running the office well should be an inescapable measure of editorial competence and responsibility. Not always. Jerdan and Maginn were hopelessly irresponsible, but their journals throve. William Gifford tried to be businesslike, but he was plagued by illness during his editorship of the *Quarterly Review* in the 1820s; issues often came out three to six months late, and in 1824 only two of the four issues appeared. And yet the circulation tripled. John Scott was meticulous about all matters pertaining to the *London Magazine*. Unfortunately, so was his second in the duel he fought in February 1821. P.G. Patmore insisted that the first exchange of shots did not satisfy honour, and that another round had to be fired. It was, and Scott was killed.

Sometimes editors hired their staff, but as often the office manager reported to and was paid by the publisher. W.H. Wills worked as subeditor to Dickens on *Household Words* and *All the Year Round* and owned an eighth of the latter, so technically he reported to himself. Edward S. Morgan worked for Richard Bentley when Dickens and Ainsworth were editing *Bentley's Miscellany*. John Stuart Mill was, for a time in the late 1830s, both proprietor and editor of the *London and Westminster Review*; he was assisted by Thomas Falconer and John Robertson, nominally editors, but in fact subeditors and office managers whose brashness and incivility toward contributors (Falconer even rejected an article by Carlyle that Mill had already approved) precipitated many crises. The Blackwoods had clerks in the Edinburgh and London offices to do all the usual accounting,[18] whereas proprietors William Hall and Frederick Mullet Evans respectively managed payments and proofs for Chapman and Hall and Bradbury and Evans – though Dickens and other writers occasionally complained about their laxness.

Some editors chose to have little to do with details; others, such as Trollope, Mill, Dickens, and Thackeray, wanted final say on the contents of each issue. And Trollope also insisted on the right to set contributors' fees. He told the publisher James Sprent Virtue that he had three conditions for accepting the editorship of *Saint Paul's*: 'firstly, that I should put whatever I pleased into the magazine, or keep whatever I pleased out of it, without interference; secondly, that I should from month to month give in to him a list of payments to be made to contributors, and that he should pay them, allowing me to fix the amounts; and thirdly, that the arrangement should remain in force at any rate for two years.'[19] All the terms were met, and though Trollope signed up an 'excellent literary corps,'[20] returns from circulation never met expenses. By 1869, Virtue was forced to sell out to Alexander Strahan, who immediately reduced the rate of pay for editor and contributors. Trollope was out by mid-1870. After captaining two unsuccessful ventures, the *Fortnightly* and *Saint Paul's*, Trollope concluded ruefully 'that publishers themselves have been the best editors of magazines, when they have been able to give time and intelligence to the work. Nothing certainly has ever been done better than *Blackwood's*.'[21]

Promoting an Ideology

Sometimes publishers were found to finance what we might think of as the editor's responsibility, namely promulgating an ideological or political position. Benthamites got Jeremy Bentham to finance the *Westminster Review*; Anthony Trollope talked Frederic Chapman into investing in a new nonpartisan journal, the *Fortnightly Review*, modelled on the *Review des Deux Mondes*, in which major fiction would be serialized; and for a time the Conservative James Hannay was touted as the editor-in-succession to Edmund Yates for a revamped, politicized *Temple Bar*. And vice versa. A financier/publisher with a strong political view, Thomas Wentworth Beaumont, in 1835 sought out a compliant editor for the *British and Foreign Review*. He wanted someone who would represent his Russophobia, dislike of the existing political parties, and advocacy of moderate constitutional reform. Beaumont went through three such editors in a year, the last two numbers being edited as well as published by himself. Then he settled on the Anglo-Saxon scholar John Mitchell Kemble, who, as K.K. Collins says succinctly, 'changed the review's profile considerably – and helped to bring on its collapse.'[22] When J.W. Parker Jr became editor, and his father the publisher, of *Fraser's* in 1847, policies were altered to accord with his own Christian Socialism. And Thomas Gibson Bowles not only owned, but also edited and wrote most of the copy for the periodical *Vanity Fair* for twenty-one years. It could be argued, in this case, that his co-editor or principal author was not a writer but the succession of brilliant draftsmen, starting with Carlo Pellegrini ('Ape') and Leslie Ward ('Spy'), who supplied those weekly caricatures that illustrated Bowles's notion of verbal and visual satire as 'the unheroic representation of heroes.'[23]

Similarly, the Blackwood family took a proprietorial view of their role in British politics. Their dismay and concern when Alfred Austin launched the Conservative Party backed *National Review* in March 1883, with its similar aims to be 'devoted to political and literary matters ... [and] to be unashamedly committed to Tory principles,' and its roster of contributors drawn from *Blackwood's* own pool of political sources, cut across Maga's self-declared right to represent 'the party.'[24] Circulation figures for *Blackwood's Magazine* dropped as a result, and over the coming years William Blackwood III was forced to mount a counterattack, commissioning costly review essays and opinion pieces by leading Conservative Party figures, in a not altogether successful attempt to regain lost cultural capital and magazine sales.

It might be argued that the careers of many women editors should be considered under the category of ideology. Early in the century, while gift annuals were edited by both men and women, the most successful editor was probably the Countess of Blessington, whose *Gems of Beauty* (1835–40), *Book of Beauty* (1834–48), and *Keepsake* (1841–8), instantiated an upper-class, fashionable, literate, and artistic ideal. She worked tirelessly, not only at the hundreds of tedious details associated with producing lavishly illustrated and gorgeously bound volumes, but also at entertaining her literary, social, and political connections. Driven by a succession of financial crises and impoverished relatives, Lady Blessington combined the occupations of hostess, novelist, historian (her 'Conversations with Lord Byron,' published in Henry Colburn's *New Monthly Magazine*, were acclaimed), editor, and publicist – and all these roles reinforced the 'silver fork' culture she and her principal publishers, Colburn and Charles Heath, promulgated. Other female editors of annuals, such as Letitia Elizabeth Landon and Mary Howitt, served less as editors than as copywriters working to the orders of their publishers.[25]

There were other ways that women editors shaped the ideology of their publications. One model was the husband-and-wife team. Mary and William Howitt founded *Howitt's Journal*, dedicated to providing working-class readers with enlightening and progressive copy. Unfortunately it failed.[26] A more successful collaboration was the partnership of John Maxwell and Mary Elizabeth Braddon. She edited his *Belgravia* from 1867 to 1876 and filled it with her own highly wrought fictions, designed, like the snobbish title, as 'the best bait for the shillings' of the lower-middle-class residents of Brixton and Bow.[27] After serialization, Maxwell repackaged her sensation fictions for sale as three-deckers to the circulating libraries and an eager public. Anna Maria Hall, who trained Braddon in editing, combined some of the characteristics of all the other women editors of her acquaintance. She and her husband, Samuel Carter Hall, editor and publisher, were noted for their 'at homes.' She was a capable and vigorous, if short-lived, editor of several prominent journals, including Maxwell's *St. James's Magazine*, she wrote for her husband's *Art Union Journal* and other periodicals, she churned out novels that somewhat intemperately advocated Christian self-sacrifice, and she was active in philanthropic projects. In these instances the philosophical, political, aesthetic, and social orientations of both spouses were closely aligned and evident in their joint and separate publications. Probably the most successful woman editor was Rachel Beer, who at the end of the century edited her husband's *Observer* and wrote a leader each week for the *Sunday Times*.

Another publishing market women editors developed as a particular ideological niche was magazines overtly directed to other women and to women's issues. With the segmentation of the mass market from the 1860s on, the growth in female literacy, the increase in female employment outside the domestic sphere, and, by the 1890s, women's growing independence in everything from clothing and sports to living alone in the city, the market for women's journals multiplied. Family-oriented publications, such as the *Family Herald* and *Cassell's Family Paper*, reached readers throughout the household, but other periodicals explicitly addressed the homemaker. The *Englishwoman's Domestic Magazine* sold 60,000 copies per issue in 1862.[28] Isabella Beeton joined her publisher husband, Samuel Orchart Beeton, as editor of this magazine, and also of his *Queen*, and she helped design and launch *Young Englishwoman* in 1864. All this while she was also running a household, writing the chart-topping classic *Household Management*, helping to raise her siblings and stepsiblings, and constantly pregnant. She died, aged twenty-nine, of puerperal fever following the birth of her fourth son.

While many of these women's journals were run and written by women for women, the gender of the editor was not a necessary marker of a publication's subject matter. Though never sitting officially in the editor's chair, Harriet Martineau, George Eliot, and Margaret Oliphant were among the most prolific, formidable, and wide-ranging essayists of the century, and none of them confined their writing to 'women's issues' alone. And though one might suppose that as female customers multiplied female editors would also multiply, in fact in the early 1890s there were only two women editing a woman's paper.[29] Oscar Wilde delighted, at this period, in editing *Women's World* (1887–9).

No more than men do women editors share many things in common. But possibly their careers are, for the most part, more implicated in their domestic circumstances: home interests, family, charitable and political work, and editorial tasks are, in many instances, all parts of a whole. Moreover, women, no matter how intelligent, had to overcome the handicaps of self-education, lack of school and university ties to call on in obtaining contributors, and the diminished, often oppressively squashed, expectations they were thought fit to fulfil. To some extent women editors could be shielded by their publisher husbands, or by owning a controlling interest in the publication. But many bounced around, editing for short stints at the whim of proprietors or the public. The surest way to sustain a career, for most women before journalism opened up careers at the end of the century, was to write fiction. In this regard, Ellen Wood's career as novelist and editor of *Argosy* (1867–87) is almost paradigmatic. The journal subsisted largely on her contributions, numerous enough to last for years after her death; and although at the start of their marriage her husband's income as a banker financed a comfortable life, in the last, straitened, decades they depended on her earnings from writing.

Like Ellen Wood, many other women editors were hired not to deal with the business of setting type, obtaining advertising, arranging page make-up, stimulating sales, or addressing politics. Instead, they were hired to provide copy, generally copy of a particular sort – for example, Puseyite, sensational, didactic, or sentimental – to find others similarly inclined, and to orient their periodicals to the imagined interests of developing cohorts of female and increasingly urban consumers, be they suffragettes, homemakers, charity workers, shop girls, or ladies of leisure. We cannot, however, be sure this is the whole story, because only recently has the work of women writers, editors, and publishers begun to receive scholarly attention.

The story about male editors is more familiar. While publishers, from Blackwood to George Smith and Alexander Macmillan, often started or bought up magazines in order to promote their political and social agendas, the ideological side of publishing rarely stayed entirely separate from the business or editorial sides, and thus editors were often drawn into financial, political, and managerial affairs. Trollope relished mixing paymaster with political duties. As he said in his 'Introduction' to the first number of *Saint Paul's*, '[we] intend to be political, – thinking that of all the studies to which men and women can attach themselves, that of politics is the first and the finest.'[30] On the other hand, Christopher Kent reminds us that legally the editor had little status; he or she was the agent of the proprietor. Proprietors rather than editors got sued for libellous content, and an editor's contract with a proprietor could not be enforced by the courts.[31]

Commissioning Contributors

What does seem clear, at least at the outset, is that editors sought to find contributors. The Blackwood family was assiduous in cultivating its links with relevant authorities in a variety of social and cultural spheres. John Blackwood's friendship with John T. Delane (editor of the *Times*), begun when they had roomed together in London early in their respective careers, led Blackwood to important journalistic contacts that he used to develop political and social articles. Through Delane, Blackwood recruited a core of contributors whose general views coincided with the conservative tone he envisaged for Maga. These included stalwarts such as military officers Edward Bruce Hamley and William George Hamley, Frederick Hardman (French correspondent for the *Times*), George Finlay (Greek correspondent for the *Times*), Laurence Oliphant (novelist and war correspondent), Margaret Oliphant, and explorer James Augustus Grant.[32] Equally, John and William Blackwood's robust cultivation of key figures in military and political circles, such as Lord John Manners and John Cecil Russell, yielded commentary when required for Maga's pages.

  The deployment of influential figures as periodical contributors was by no means unique to the Blackwood firm. There were other editors who knew everybody and got very capable writers to contribute on a regular basis. Jerdan in his early years as editor of the *London Magazine*, James Fraser, who secured Thomas Carlyle for *Fraser's*,[33] Dickens when editing *Bentley's Miscellany*, Thackeray spending George Smith's money lavishly to sign up the best authors going for the *Cornhill Magazine* in the early 1860s, all 'edited' in the sense that they found major contributors for their pages. At the *Athenaeum* in the middle decades of the century, Hepworth Dixon had Henry Chorley writing about music and Charles Augustus Sainte-Beuve, Jules Janin, and Heinrich Heine covering European culture. After a slump in the 1860s, Norman MacColl restored the distinction of the *Athenaeum* by securing such luminaries as Dante Gabriel Rossetti, Edmund Gosse, Andrew Lang, W.W. Skeat, Francis Furnivall, and George Otto Trevelyan. Possibly the most unusual regular contributor to a major journal was Thomas Griffiths Wainewright, a dandy, wit, and polymath, who wrote hundreds of articles and notes on art (he championed William Blake) and theatre and gossip for the *London Magazine*. He also poisoned a number of relatives whose fortunes he wished to possess. These murders were not, however, entirely mercenary. Asked why he administered strychnine to his sister-in-law, whose life he had insured, he replied, 'Upon my soul, I don't know, unless it was because she had thick ankles.'[34]

So, we might argue that the editor's principal function was to secure copy. But that's a little too simple. Some editors, Jerdan and Maginn notably in the early part of the century, and Dickens in the early years of *Household Words*, wrote or rewrote a great deal of copy themselves. They functioned, at times, less like commissioning editors and more like ghostwriters. And once a writer had been secured for a journal, sometimes by the editor, sometimes by a generous-handed publisher, generations of editors could be stuck with that writer, whether or not the successive editors liked or agreed with the work. Long-lived journals could in this regard hardly be said to be the product of a single editorial vision. At *Blackwood's*, John Wilson contributed over 500 articles, Archibald Alison and his son were staff writers for a combined total of seventy-five years, and Margaret Oliphant chalked up over 200 contributions during a career of over forty years with John and William.[35] Abraham Hayward wrote for half a century for the *Quarterly Review*, and Sir John Barrow just missed reaching his half-century of continuous contributions to the same magazine.

The line between commissioning editor and contributing author blurs in other ways as well. Not only did some editors blue-pencil extensively; some contributors were collectivities, not individuals. The pseudonymity cloaking contributors' identity throughout much of the nineteenth century also concealed the extent to which more than one hand, even beyond the editor's revisions, might be responsible for a piece, and also concealed the fact that the same pseudonymous author might be the creation of different writers at different times. Christopher North eventually wrote all the voices speaking in *Noctes Ambrosianae*, although that *Blackwood's* series started out with several writers participating. Oliver Yorke, the inebriated figure created to stand as editor of

Fraser's, may have been a collaborative product, mainly by Maginn, but occasionally incorporating ideas or passages by Francis Mahoney and possibly others in Maginn's brilliant stable, which included Thackeray, Lockhart, Theodore Hook, Percival Weldon Banks, Mahony ('Father Prout'), Moir, and the artist-in-residence Daniel Maclise.[36] Perhaps the most famous collective editorial persona was 'Mr. Punch,' who ventriloquized a polyglot assortment of irrepressible wits who quarrelled with one another and modified Punch's personality over many decades.[37]

And finally, the most conclusive counter-example of all: William John Thoms successfully founded (1850) and edited *Notes and Queries* without ever hiring a single contributor. As the subtitle declared, Thoms's print journal provided a 'Medium of Inter-Communication' for 'Literary Men, Artists, Antiquaries, Genealogists, Etc.' It depended on the rapidly improving transportation networks across Britain, and on the penny post, and it allowed a kind of democratic exchange among contributors interested in one or more of its 'threads' of continuing topics, or in some antiquarian fact or question. These correspondents supplied all the copy. And while some were quasi-regulars, Thoms did not solicit their letters nor pay anyone for a contribution. As Patrick Leary shows, *Notes and Queries* anticipates the internet in many ways, not least of which is Thoms's tactful role as 'webmaster,' primarily trying to keep pace with submissions, chivvying writers to curb prolixity and duplication, and only occasionally imposing editorial control over intemperate or endless exchanges. *Notes and Queries* still thrives, and in its Victorian heyday, the publisher George Bell used the journal to bring other antiquarian materials to his firm.[38]

Arranging and Perfecting Copy

When Dickens first edited *Bentley's Miscellany*, he was a hands-on manager. '[O]blige me,' Dickens asked Bentley's office manager Morgan in early September 1837, 'by informing Mr. Bentley ... that I have already arranged the contents of a greater part of the next number; and given the Printer the fullest instructions on the subject which will enable him to make up the magazine from the commencement as it goes on.' Shortly thereafter Dickens quarrelled repeatedly with his co-editor and publisher, decided he was exhausted and over-committed, and lost interest in the day-to-day management: 'Order the Miscellany just as you please,' Dickens told Bentley in December of 1837. 'I have no wish or care about the matter.'[39]

But arranging issues was taken seriously by the Blackwoods, whose views on matters such as the most appropriate placing of work can be found in the daily letters sent between the cooperative of directors and office managers that effectively controlled and orchestrated the journal's production between 1845, when John Blackwood took on the role of editor, and 1879, when William Blackwood III stepped into his shoes. It recommenced in less effective form in the 1890s and 1900s, when William Blackwood was joined by his nephews George William and James Hugh Blackwood and by his literary adviser and London office manager David Storrar Meldrum. Surviving editorial letters from both periods show all participants discussing at length matters such as the literary merit of submissions and the benefits of starting off or ending the monthly issues with particular pieces, exposing a hierarchical ordering of literary production for an implied reader who was expected to read in linear fashion from the front to the back of each issue. (Some twenty-first century magazines are designed to be flipped through from the back forward.)

An example of Blackwoods' customary practice in designing monthly numbers is the serialization of R.D. Blackmore's *Maid of Sker* between August 1871 and July 1872.[40] Blackmore had come to prominence two years earlier with his popular Exmoor romance *Lorna Doone*, published by Samson Low. John Blackwood, keen on Blackmore's popular, broadbrush romance style, promptly recruited his next work, *The Maid of Sker*, for serialization in Maga. 'The Market Gardener,' as the Blackwoods dubbed him in view of his passion for growing fruit and vegetables, was given the honour of leading off the August 1871 issue of *Blackwood's Magazine*.[41] This was in line with Blackwood policy of promoting new serializations by placing them at the top of the table of contents, and was in fact the usual arrangement at most journals featuring major fiction.[42] Furthermore, Blackmore was urged in the early summer to complete work quickly on initial sections in order to insure that the piece could be published in the August issue. The rationale for this decision was simple – based on past experience and anticipation of the dispersal of audiences for summer holidays, the Blackwoods felt that Blackmore's work would be read and reviewed more widely if it appeared earlier. As John Blackwood noted on deciding the matter, 'We had better start the *Maid of Sker* in August No. It is a better month to begin than September when people are all separated.'[43]

Judging the likely effect of appropriate placement of subsequent material also proved a serious matter; it was frequently deliberated by the London and Edinburgh staffs. For the September 1871 issue, the editors exercised themselves over which serialized work to feature first in the table of contents. On the one hand, there was the need to continue promoting their 'new' author, Blackmore. Having led off the August issue with the first part of *The Maid of Sker*, they thought it seemed reasonable to continue the story as the lead piece in September. On the other hand, also ready to print was the latest section of Laurence Lockhart's *Fair to See*, the serialized work previously promoted and then displaced by Blackmore's entrance. The Blackwoods debated whether the increased literary and aesthetic value of the latest section merited giving Lockhart back the *'place d'honneur.'* William Blackwood pondered at length before inclining in favour of Blackmore at Lockhart's expense – '[Lockhart's] part is so good I am almost inclined to think it should begin the No.,' he wrote to John, 'but yet it has made itself so well known that people are sure to go to it at once & it is very desirable to hook them on to The Maid by giving it the place d'honneur.'[44] The team agreed and John, who was organizing the contents for that month, ordered compositors to make up Blackmore's work to start off the issue.[45]

'*Place d'honneur*' was not the only editorial metaphor employed by the Blackwoods and their team in their daily discussions. Peppered throughout their correspondence is the concept of material 'opening the ball.'[46] For the Blackwoods, the editorial function was frequently compared to that of arranging the intricate dance sequences of a society function, where participants were offered a dance card upon which partners were noted, and through which they engaged in a prioritized, structured, and ranked progression of quadrilles and set pieces. The magazine's contents were similarly monitored, ranked, and adjusted to reflect changing fortunes and emphasis. Serialized novel parts usually headed the table of contents, but authors could find their installments honoured by heading the table of contents in the first month, only to see the succeeding parts moved further down the contents list when critical reception proved less than positive or there was need to promote another submission. Thus the third and fourth sections of the *Maid of Sker* were moved down to make way for the penultimate and concluding sections of *Fair to See* in October and November 1871.

Alternatively, later instalments might be reinstated at the head of the list if the editors found that subsequent events, reviews, or the quality of the section recommended a promotion. Blackmore's novel impressed the Blackwoods enough for sections 5 and 6 to merit *place d'honneur* in

December 1871 and January 1872. Over the next four months, the placement of the piece whipsawed up and down the contents, moving from middle of the issue to top of the class depending on the editors' reactions to each part. When the editors found sections written to their liking, they set them to 'open the ball,' as in the case of sections 9 and 11. About the latter part, both John and William concurred that its literary merit was sufficient for a promotion to opening spot. 'The next part of the Maid is I think first class & I am making it up to begin,' William wrote in justifying the decision. 'Old Digs [Blackmore] comes out with some wonderfully good things & I often turned back to read them or the pages over again which is I think a capital sign.'[47] 'I was greatly taken with the Maid also,' John concurred.[48] As was the case with Lockhart's serial, the concluding section of the *Maid of Sker* was featured at the top of the table of contents in the July 1872 issue.

Keeping sections strictly separated was also a concern, although William was more sensitive to the need for separation than John. William believed that placing serialized parts of novels close together would dilute the effect each was meant to have on the reader. John Blackwood's view was more sanguine. Perhaps he was less committed to the notion that readers read *seriatim*, or possibly he had a higher opinion either of readers' discrimination or of the distinctiveness of each fiction. In any case, he was – on some occasions at least – less worried about juxtaposing novels. With regard to William's concerns about arranging intervening materials between part three of George T. Chesney's *The Dilemma* and the barrister Julian Sturgis's story *Under the Mask* in the July 1875 issue, he replied: 'You can make up the Dilemma to begin the No. & follow it with Julian Sturgis' story. I do not see that the two stories coming together much signifies but you may interject Paulo Post Mortem which I have kept over too long.'[49] William did run the two pieces seriatim without any intervening post mortem.

But editors were not the only ones arranging copy text. From Dickens and Bentley to the end of the twentieth century, compositors have played a crucial role. Yet the material constraints that sometimes affect the make-up of a publication – 'putting a quart into a pint bottle' John Blackwood complained[50] – are rarely if ever noticed, except on those occasions when annotated copytexts survive indicating that the compositors forced cuts. Anthony Curtis, literary editor on the *Financial Times* (1970–91), recalls that until 1987 his pages were set up in hot metal. He would stand by the compositor as the articles were cast into type, and the 'compositor – or stone-hand, as he was called – told [me] how many lines [I] needed to cut from a review to make it fit; this information would be given usually in the intervals of conversation about football or holiday plans.'[51] Likewise, designers, illustrators, and advertisers might squeeze letterpress into a fraction of its original length. So much for the sanctity of copytext and editorial authority.

Buying and Selling Advertising

Advertising and sales might be thought to be the task of the publisher rather than the editor. Several magazines were started by publishers just so they could 'puff' their own works, even if running costs led to a net loss. As William Tinsley remarked on learning his journal *Tinsley's Magazine*, begun in 1867, was losing money, 'What cheaper advertisement can I have for twenty-five pounds a month? It advertises my name and publications; and it keeps my authors together.'[52]

Other magazines had announced policies against such puffing. Vicious *ad hominem* reviews inaugurated a complete revamping of *Blackwood's* in October 1817: that was the issue in which the infamous 'Chaldee Manuscript' and Lockhart's first instalment of 'The Cockney School of Poetry' appeared. Such virulent attacks might be expected to get the publisher in trouble with authors, advertisers, and other publishers. But not in this case. William Blackwood paid off anyone who threatened to sue, and circulation of the newly revamped periodical went through the roof. At other times William used the pages of Maga to drum up interest in texts not yet realized, as in the sly case of John Gibson Lockhart's *Peter's Letters to his Kinfolk* (1819). In February 1819 there appeared in Maga a positive notice of this book, a collection of letters supposedly written by a Welsh doctor and published in Aberystwyth. The following month a Maga review heaped further praise upon it, going on to attack booksellers who had not yet stocked up on this virtuoso text. Needless to say, the work did not exist; not, that is, until it was brought out shortly afterwards by Blackwood as a 'second' (i.e., first) edition due to 'popular demand.' Such economy of truth was an early experiment in marketing that was refined upon and inventively amplified in future years by other firms in their own periodicals.

For the Blackwood firm, book advertisements were an important commercial statement by those whose livelihoods depended on the public's consumption of new texts. Successful works required continual promotion, much like any other sales product, in order to retain public interest and to refresh relevant publishing portfolios. Joseph Munt Langford, Blackwood's London manager, repeatedly made explicit the link between commerce and the literary marketplace. Commenting on the need for frequent advertisement to insure that the firm's most valuable asset, George Eliot's novels, would sell in industrial quantities, he noted in 1877 that 'George Eliots [sic] books sell more like Holloways Pills than like books and it pays to keep them before the public by advertising.'[53] The Blackwood family agreed with the sentiment and the method: 'By all means keep them well before the public,' William Blackwood replied, 'and in much the same way as Holloway does his Pills.'[54] Langford repeated the formula a few years later. 'Her works are like Patent Medicines in the respect that they should always be kept under the eye of the public,' he wrote in 1879 to John Blackwood, forwarding suggested advertisement copy for use in promoting Blackwood's edition of her collected works.[55] Blackwood, by then head of the firm, agreed and published Langford's text in competitors' journals during the run-up to the Christmas shopping season. In turn, Blackwood's sold advertising space in their books and journals, welcoming the extra revenue such material generated.

By the late 1830s, journal proprietors were increasingly conscious of the value of maintaining strong turnover in advertising revenue. Hugh Fraser, for example, worked hard to draw in material from both the book and general trade as advertising coordinator for *Fraser's Magazine* in the late 1830s. Seeking to manoeuvre a post as London agent for Blackwood's in 1839, he boasted that under his management *Fraser's* advertising revenue had doubled in six months. 'When I tell you that I have done this without deviating in <u>one instance</u> from our scale charges,' he concluded, 'I dare say you will give me credit for doing as much as almost any one could do in my situation.'[56] Rather than contract independently for such work, Blackwood's chose instead to set up its own London office in 1840 under direct control of the family.

The advertising pages were not always benign sites – Blackwood's sometimes saw rivals use that space to promote poached works. This was the case when, in 1862, George Smith sent Blackwood's an advertisement ('bill') that trumpeted his prize acquisition of George Eliot's latest novel *Romola*, which he had unceremoniously snatched from the Blackwood firm's grasp through 'ungentlemanly' direct contact and an unbeatable offer that included a high advance and royalty share. 'They are sending over a bill for Maga to which in the first flint of temper I thought you should refuse insertion,' sputtered Langford to John

1 Line engraving portrait of William Blackwood I (1776–1834), founder of the Edinburgh publishing firm and its pioneering monthly literary journal *Blackwood's Edinburgh Magazine*.

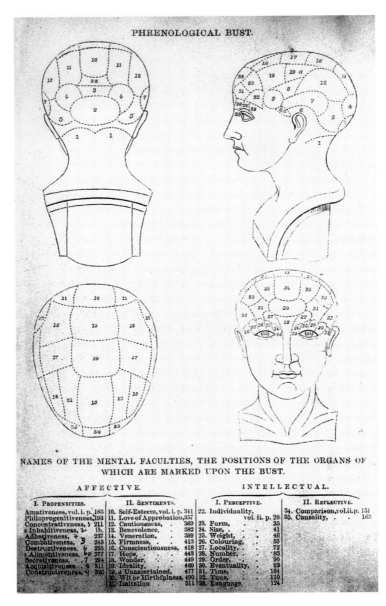

2 'Phrenological Bust' illustration, taken from George Combe's *A System of Phrenology*, fifth edition, 1853.

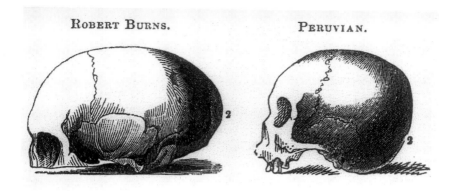

3 'Robert Burns – Peruvian' illustration, taken from George Combe's *A System of Phrenology*, fifth edition, 1853.

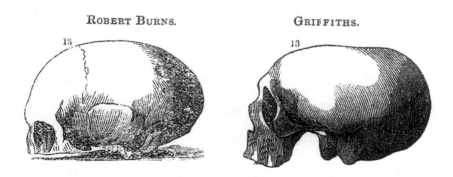

4 'Robert Burns – Griffith' illustration, taken from George Combe's *A System of Phrenology*, fifth edition, 1853.

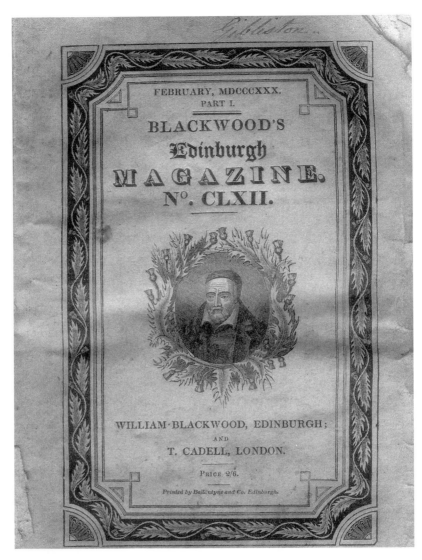

Gibliston...

FEBRUARY, MDCCCXXX,
PART I.

BLACKWOOD'S
Edinburgh
MAGAZINE.
Nº. CLXII.

WILLIAM·BLACKWOOD, EDINBURGH;
AND
T. CADELL, LONDON.

PRICE 2/6.

Printed by Ballantyne and Co. Edinburgh.

5 Cover of an 1830 *Blackwood's Edinburgh Magazine,* showing an example of the stern George Buchanan image that graced every issue of 'Maga' from October 1817 until its demise in 1980. *Edinburgh* was quietly dropped from the magazine's title in 1905, making official what it had been called in practice for many years: *Blackwood's Magazine.*

6 Advertising supplement page example from November 1884 issue of *Blackwood's Magazine*.

7 An example of inside front cover ads from November 1884 issue of *Blackwood's Magazine.* The ad for L.B. Walford's works occupies the space that would have been reserved for the announcement of Lady Martin's book in May 1885.

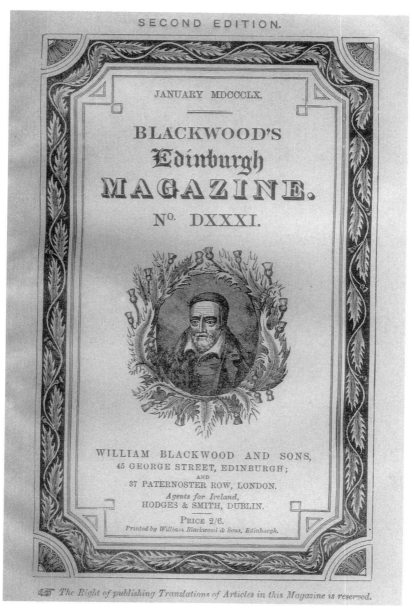

SECOND EDITION.

JANUARY MDCCCLX.

BLACKWOOD'S
Edinburgh
MAGAZINE.

Nᵒ. DXXXI.

WILLIAM BLACKWOOD AND SONS,
45 GEORGE STREET, EDINBURGH;
AND
37 PATERNOSTER ROW, LONDON.
Agents for Ireland,
HODGES & SMITH, DUBLIN.
PRICE 2/6.
Printed by William Blackwood & Sons, Edinburgh.

The Right of publishing Translations of Articles in this Magazine is reserved.

8 Cover of *Blackwood's Magazine,* January 1860.

9 Cover of the *Cornhill Magazine*, January 1860.

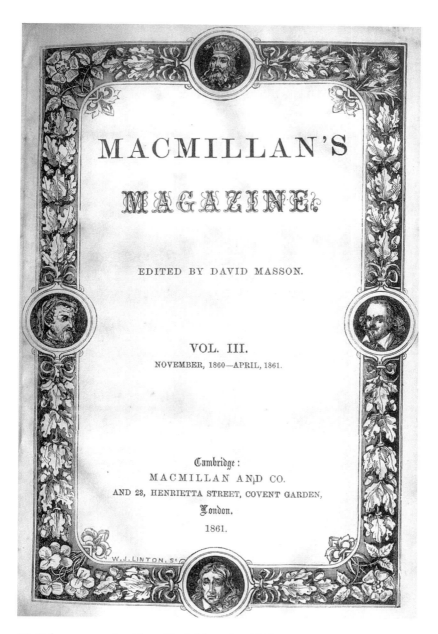

MACMILLAN'S

MAGAZINE.

EDITED BY DAVID MASSON.

VOL. III.

NOVEMBER, 1860—APRIL, 1861.

Cambridge :
MACMILLAN AND CO.
AND 23, HENRIETTA STREET, COVENT GARDEN,
London.
1861.

W. J. LINTON, S

10 Volume cover for *Macmillan's Magazine,* 1860.

MACMILLAN'S MAGAZINE.

NOVEMBER, 1860.

THE LIFE AND POETRY OF KEATS.

BY THE EDITOR.

KEATS was born in Moorfields, London, in October, 1795, the son of a livery-stable keeper of some wealth, who had attained that position by marrying his master's daughter and so succeeding him in the business. There were five children, four sons and a daughter, of whom John was the third. The father, who is described as an active, energetic little man of much natural talent, was killed by a fall from a horse at the age of thirty-six, when Keats was in his ninth year; and the care of the children devolved upon the mother, a tall, large-featured woman, of considerable force of character. There was also a maternal uncle, a very tall, strong, and courageous man, who had been in the navy, had served under Duncan at Camperdown, and had done extraordinary feats in the way of fighting. Partly in emulation of this uncle, partly from constitutional inclination, the boys were always fighting too—in the house, about the stables, or out in the adjacent streets, with each other, or with anybody else. John, though the shortest for his years, and the most like his father, was the most pugnacious of the lot; but with his pugnacity he combined, it is said, a remarkable sensibility, and a great love of fun. This character he took with him to a boarding-school at Enfield, near London, kept by the father of Mr. Charles Cowden Clarke, then also a boy, not much older than Keats, receiving his education under his father's roof.

No. 13.—VOL. III.

At school, Keats, according to the recollections of Mr. Clarke and others of his schoolfellows, was at first a perfect little terrier for resoluteness and pugnacity, but very placable and frolicsome, very much liked, and, though not particularly studious, very quick at learning. There would seem to have been more of pleasant sociability between the family of the master and the scholars in the school at Enfield, and more of literary talk at bye-hours, than was then common at private English schools. At all events, when, by the death of his mother, of lingering consumption, in 1810, the guardianship of Keats, his two surviving brothers, and his only sister, devolved on a Mr. Abbey, a London merchant who had known the family, and when Mr. Abbey thought it best to take two of the boys from school and apprentice them to professions, it was felt by Keats to be a very happy arrangement that he was apprenticed to a surgeon-apothecary at Edmonton, so near to Enfield, that he could still go over when he liked to see the Clarkes. He was then fifteen years of age. The share of the family property held for him by his guardian till he came of age, was about 2,000l.; and his apprenticeship was to last five years.

From Edmonton, Keats was continually walking over to Enfield to see his young friend, Cowden Clarke, and to borrow books. It was some time in 1812 that he borrowed Spenser's "Faery

B

THE

CORNHILL MAGAZINE.

JANUARY, 1860.

𝔉ramley 𝔓arsonage.

CHAPTER I.

"OMNES OMNIA BONA DICERE."

WHEN young Mark Robarts was leaving college, his father might well declare that "all men began to say all good things to him," and to extol his fortune in that he had a son blessed with so excellent a disposition.

This father was a physician living at Exeter. He was a gentleman possessed of no private means, but enjoying a lucrative practice, which had enabled him to maintain and educate a family with all the advantages which money can give in this country. Mark was his eldest son and second child; and the first page or two of this narrative must be consumed in giving a catalogue of the good things which chance and conduct together had heaped upon this young man's head.

His first step forward in life had arisen from his having been sent, while still very young, as a private pupil to the house of a clergyman, who was an old friend and intimate friend of his father's. This clergyman had one other, and only one other, pupil—the young Lord Lufton, and, between the two boys, there had sprung up a close alliance.

While they were both so placed, Lady Lufton had visited her son, and then invited young Robarts to pass his next holidays at Framley Court. This visit was made; and it ended in Mark going back to Exeter with a letter full of praise from the widowed peeress. She had been delighted, she said, in having such a companion for her son, and expressed a hope that the boys might remain together during the course of their education. Dr. Robarts was a man who thought much of the breath of peers and peeresses, and was by no means inclined to throw away any advantage which might arise to his child from such a friendship. When, therefore, the young lord was sent to Harrow, Mark Robarts went there also.

12 Sample text from the *Cornhill Magazine*, January 1860.

13 *Blackwood's Magazine advertiser, November 1884, 14–15.*

Blackwood. However, second thoughts prevailed: 'but it would certainly be more dignified to insert it.'[57] In contrast, 'quackery adverts' were second class and second rate, tolerated for the revenue they brought in, but certainly not worthy of placing on the same page as prestigious publication notices.

When the *Spectator* seemed to slight Maga in the 1880s, William Blackwood III wondered whether it would have been better 'to have stopt sending Maga altogether or have taken no notice.' Stopping advertising in the rival periodical was, he considered, ineffective: if sales held up anyway, advertisements 'were useless,' and if sales declined as a result, 'you injure the firm's other publications by ceasing to advertise.'[58] He stayed alert to free 'word of mouth' commendations, too. 'Have you seen yesterday's Pall Mall' he asked his uncle in May 1871. 'In Occasional Notes it has a most capital one upon the Battle of Dorking & we are going to advertise the No. as enclosed & hope you approve. [George] Simpson says it just requires that to set the Ball rolling [a different 'ball' metaphor]. Before I knew of it I had been looking thro' the Maga notices & was perfectly disgusted with them.'[59] Three weeks later he saw that *The Times* correspondent in Rome had given Chesney's *Battle of Dorking* a long notice, and that with some recent letters to the papers about it sales might revive.[60]

No detail was too trivial, no publicity expedient too minor, to evade editors' attention. John Blackwood was particularly pleased to 'win' Bulwer Lytton back to *Blackwood's* with *The Parisians*, Lytton's last, unrevised novel and one that expresses his mature political views and opposition to French romanticism of the sort exemplified by Victor Hugo. The eminence of the writer and the coincidence of the novel's ideology with Maga's made this catch 'a very great triumph' that John thought would 'prove most satisfactory. It should make a great sensation.' But he was puzzled 'how to announce it. Should a paragraph be set afloat [to the effect that] in Blackwood for October will appear the first part of a new Tale by the Author of the Coming Race[?] Let me hear,' he asked his nephew, 'what ... you think.'[61] These matters occupied William the moment he got back into town. Getting a notice into the *Athenaeum* was one expedient; inserting slips promoting new work in the Maga issues was another one. But William worried about the wording of the advertisement for Bulwer's novel: 'Is not tale too trivial a word & the word <u>new</u> is better we think wanting so as to make this appear the author's first novel.'[62] In short, there is abundant evidence that editors as well as publishers paid attention to every aspect of advertising – not only the publicity about their own journals but also, as we saw at the opening of this essay, the advertisements the journal itself carried.[63]

Supervising Quality

Slack editing, poor writing, and uninspired topics and formats could depreciate the value and sales of a magazine. The decline of *Bentley's*, *Ainsworth's*, and other magazines testifies to the symbiosis between energetic and imaginative editing and success. But then history summons up a witness for the other side. William Jerdan was doing fine with the *Literary Gazette*, having effectively wrested control from the indecisive and expedient Colburn, until in 1830 Maginn went down from Edinburgh and started the monthly *Fraser's Magazine*. At the same time Charles Wentworth Dilke revamped the weekly *Athenaeum*, making it a journal that strove to cover a broad range of fields judiciously rather than in a fiercely partisan spirit. It did not help the competition that in 1831 Dilke cut the price of the *Athenaeum* in half, multiplied his subscriber base, and strengthened his finances.[64] Jerdan had an increasingly hard time staying even with sassier, better financed, or more authoritative publications, no matter how much attention he paid to quality.

All scholars who write about *Blackwood's Magazine* agree that its strongest, most creative and influential periods came under the management of William Blackwood I between 1817 and 1832 and under the custodianship of John Blackwood between 1845 and 1879. During these years management practices included both collective editing with trusted advisers and confirmed 'Blackwoodians,' and strong, individual leadership promulgating Blackwood's Conservative political and editorial vision. Other articles in this volume, by Ian Duncan, Michael Michie, Robert Morrison, and Charles Snodgrass, explore these issues in more depth. But it is also important to note that all the family members who ended up as editors of the journal brought a sense of duty and commitment to their work. Driven by family traditions and a strong work ethic, they all devoted a great deal of time to ensuring that the material prepared for the magazine was consistent and well edited. Such commitment to business is typified by this characteristic confession of guilt from William Blackwood III after he indulged in a three-day holiday: 'A great deal seems to have occurred during [the] last few days & the pile of letters [George] Simpson had awaiting me was most alarming & makes me feel regret at having gone away.'[65]

Editors did, for a variety of reasons, lose interest in their publications. But even when they continued to be as devoted and conscientious as the Blackwoods, competition, changing times, fickle readers, and deep pockets might compromise standards. Repeatedly in the 1880s and 1890s the Blackwoods knew that other journals were paying more for high profile contributors. But William opposed 'running after such men as Anthony Hope (author of "The Indiscretion of a Duchess" a vile book) & John Davidson or even S. R. Crockett or Ian Maclaren.' 'Experience of past years goes to show,' he reflected ruefully, 'that no special article from some popular idol of the day or hour repays the extra premium that has to be paid.'[66] Resistance, however, regardless of noble motives, was sometimes commercially disastrous. On 10 April 1877 Joseph Munt Langford, the London manager, went to see Charles Mudie, owner of Mudie's Select Library, London's biggest distributor and purchaser of books, hoping to arrange more purchases of Blackwood publications. He was largely unsuccessful. Mudie sang his old tune about the exorbitant price charged for three-volume novels: he could not make money buying them wholesale at more than 5 shillings a volume. And as for taking more copies of Maga? No, the first number of the *Nineteenth Century* had lessened demand for other established periodicals. 'I am inclined to think,' Langford – always somewhat dour and pessimistic – reported, 'that trading on these lists of popular names is the most powerful opposition we have ever had to Maga.' But, he advised William, who certainly agreed, 'it is not to be met by taking any notice or giving way to the practice but by quietly going on in our own way and by keeping up the high character of Maga in anonymous articles.'[67] Thus for *Blackwood's* the practice of keeping up quality entailed 'going on in our own way.' A resolute and stalwart course, no doubt, but one increasingly uncompetitive. Even maintaining a journal's 'high character' could be a way of condemning it to a slow death

Giving the Periodical a Distinctive Character

It would seem that editors ought to be responsible for the character of their publications. True enough: Leigh Hunt oriented the *Examiner* and the *Champion* to his own radical politics, as Thomas Wooler did with *The Black Dwarf*. William Blackwood III pushed imperialism in the 1880s and 1890s Maga. The *Edinburgh Review* was political and Whig for 127 years, taking 'positions on every major issue in British politics.'[68] The *Quarterly* was unremittingly Tory, conservative, Augustan, anti-Romanticism, and establishmentarian, though Sir Walter Scott thought it went too far in those directions at the outset. But these facts prove the opposite of the proposition that editors determined the character of their publications: the politics of these journals, and of the *London and Westminster Review*, were less established and maintained by editors than by a whole congeries of forces, including the proprietors, stable of contributors, subscribers, advertisers, the importance of continuity, changing political circumstances and markets, and new commercial opportunities.

Even an editorial revamp of the look of a journal did not guarantee its distinctiveness or necessarily instance significant editorial agency. *Blackwood's* altered in 1817, eliminating the old formal divisions; immediately the *New Monthly* imitated the change, and when John Scott designed his *London Magazine* in 1820 he too copied *Blackwood's* new format. However, Scott went out of his way to deny any debt to Maga, loudly claiming originality and superiority for his periodical over rivals emanating 'from secondary towns of the Kingdom.'[69]

Maga pioneered in the publication of serials, though their instalments were not particularly well designed for that mode of issuance. Frederick Marryat is usually given credit not only for publishing fiction in instalments in his *Metropolitan Magazine* from 1830 on, but also for paying attention as editor and contributor to the aesthetic and structural implications of serialization. But he was quickly overset by Dickens and Ainsworth's editing of *Bentley's Miscellany*. G.W. Nickisson is often blamed for being a publisher who could not sustain the feisty spirit of *Fraser's* when he succeeded as publisher in 1842; but then, he succeeded in the first years of the Hungry Forties, when many of the original *Fraser's* men were dead or had aged into far more conservative thinkers and writers.

Innovations were not confined to expensive monthlies and quarterlies. In February 1832, the Chambers brothers launched *Chambers's Edinburgh Journal*, a penny weekly aimed at the literate middle classes and artisans with aspirations for self-improvement. London based Charles Knight entered in direct competition a month later with the weekly *Penny Magazine*, backed by the religiously based SDUK (Society for the Diffusion of Useful Knowledge). Both editor/publishers worked hard to open up the market for inexpensive periodicals, but while the Chambers brothers stuck to soberly packaged text, Knight was aesthetically innovative, sprinkling the *Penny Magazine* with liberal doses of vivid illustrations to accompany the morally sound text. *Chambers's* flourished – within two years it was averaging a circulation of 50,000 –

but Knight's lively hand stirred audiences more: in its first year it reached an astounding circulation of 200,000. Knight's experiment lasted twelve years, ceasing in 1846 due to high production costs and an inability to sustain initial enthusiastic reading audiences with the uninspired diet of dull, didactic text, no matter how livened up they were by accompanying illustrations. The Chambers brothers saw their journal move into the august survivor category, lasting through to late in the twentieth century.[70]

Conclusion

So what, having conducted a summary historical investigation, might we conclude about 'What do editors do?' Not much, though we can surmise that if the question was rephrased, 'What did X editor do?' there is a great deal of data for some editors, though little or nothing for others. One consequence of our investigation so far is that we probably need to be fairly circumspect in offering generalizations about the genus of editor or editor-function. One principle suggested in a previous work that is 'likely to figure in any new paradigm of publishing history' is 'the principle of mediation.' That is, 'Increasingly through the [nineteenth] century, the direct connections between author and publisher, publisher and printing house, and press and audience were moderated by the interposition of other agencies: literary agents, fiction bureaus, and the Society of Authors between author and publisher; technologies between publisher and printing house; distribution and evaluation systems between press and audience.'[71] That principle of mediation seems to apply to editing in nineteenth-century Britain particularly well. It was a time when, on the whole, editors were more directly connected to publishers, writers, copytexts, and production at the beginning of the century than at the end, always, of course, with notable exceptions at both ends of the spectrum and the century.

Even in the limited case where the publisher *was* the editor, as, say, with John and/or William Blackwood III from 1845 to 1912, there were many people in subsidiary positions, serving the business, production, and editorial sides. In most instances through the century publishers tended to specialize, either in terms of the kind of journals they produced or the kind of work they reserved for themselves: Bradbury and Evans printed but were not consistently eager to publish journals, Robert Chambers, Archibald Constable, Henry Colburn, Richard Bentley, John Murray, Alexander Macmillan, George Smith, increasingly got caught up in finance and administration, hiring deputies, foremen, and other factotums to manage the actual printing and publication. There were 120 persons involved in the Chambers brothers printing house in 1845. In most instances the single editor, like the single publisher, proliferated into multiple deputies. In the case of *Chambers's Edinburgh Journal*, for instance, William Chambers was succeeded by Robert as joint editor, and Robert hired Thomas Smibert, then W.H. Wills, then Leitch Ritchie, who rose from unnamed assistant to co-editor; then James Payne, who rose from co-editor to editor. Richard Bentley tried to co-edit his journals with Jerdan, Dickens, and Ainsworth; then as he expanded he took on the assistance of Edward Morgan as chief clerk and advisor, William Shorberl (who returned to Colburn in the early 1840s), Charles Ollier to 1839, replaced as literary advisor by R.H. Barham to 1843, and bookkeeper Eliza Ketteridge. Increasingly, literary advisors rather than overworked editors read the manuscripts submitted to the press: John Forster, Margaret Oliphant, Elizabeth Rigby, Geraldine Jewsbury, and George Meredith.

And the advent of authors' agents infuriated publishers. 'Middlemen like AP Watt & W. Morris Colles are to be avoided,' William minuted. 'MSS sent in by them unsolicited must have same careful consideration as accorded to others but to solicit contributions through them is to court mortification. Their business & interest is to get the highest possible price for their clients and these generally run far beyond what any old established self respecting house would be justified in paying.' However, William's hard-headed realism acknowledged the changing conditions of publishing: 'At same time I must admit these middlemen are necessary evils due to the ever increasing number of publishers & also the increasing desire of authors to be saved all personal trouble of negotiations.'[72]

A second application of this principle of mediation might be by way of Pierre Bourdieu's formulation of 'field,' a nexus of discursive and non-discursive practices specific to a particular activity that partly conditions that activity.[73] The Bourdieusian field has been deployed recently by book historians, notably by Peter D. McDonald in his *British Literary Culture and Publishing Practice, 1880–1914*, to account for ways in which publishing is both a commercial and a literary activity. A 'field' is a set of dynamically changing practices conditioned by the internal structures and laws of the field, and also a body of practices indirectly conditioned by forces moving outside the field. Bourdieu's theory of the 'field,' McDonald explains, 'stands precisely at the perilous junction between culture and society.'[74] Bourdieu's conceptualization of relational fields of practice permits us in book history to analyse not only paradigms of linear material production and distribution such as Robert Darnton and others have posited, but also how the structure of the field itself confers status and symbolic capital and serves as a dynamic mediator between the marketplace, on the one hand, and the production of literature on the other.

Thus we can understand that 'editors,' while operating within the field of practices developed for their work, are also impacted by a whole host of material and ideological conditions not necessarily directly connected to publishing but nonetheless inescapable: Constable's bankruptcy, for instance, had nothing to do with the quality of the books and journals he was producing. On the other hand, practices within the field, not directly connected to things outside, also condition particular acts. Take the ideological positions of periodical reviewers in the nineteenth century. R.G. Cox in 1939, Alvin Sullivan in 1983, and many others have argued that beneath the apparent political and aesthetic disputes of the Romantic and Victorian magazines lie strains of continuity and tradition extending back to Plato and Aristotle, discursive traditions that exert a powerful constraint on truly radical revaluations.[75] Almost all editors and reviewers in the nineteenth century, this argument goes, would, conditioned by the practices of their field, have subscribed to a mimetic theory of art – though differing in what was being imitated; to connections between literature and human experience, be those experiences memorial, sensational, cognitive, emotional, or otherwise; and to the social utility and value of writing, albeit those values were for some calculated rationally and for other intuited imaginatively. Hence editors might be seen as collectively participating in the practices of a field itself responding to both external and internal forces.

But such a field paradigm, with its dynamic mediations of forces inside and outside, should not obscure those cases where strong-mindedness or invention or luck (good or bad) produced a result that could not be predicted simply by vectoring abstract forces, trends, and practices. Take John Scott as a limit case: his success as an editor is surely in part due to his untimely death. We don't know whether his imitation of *Blackwood's*, his distinguished list of contributors, and his firmness on ethical issues would have lasted out changes in publishers, market forces, political events, personal differences with writers, and so forth. Or take another set of cases where the quality of the product cannot be predicted solely by the study of impersonal forces: the reviews by John Forster in the *Examiner* and by George Eliot in the *Westminster* are among the best in the century. Credit in the first instance needs to be granted to Forster as his own editor, and in the second to John Chapman, who, whatever else his faults, managed to recognize and keep George Eliot as a contributor. In short, the Bordieusian field does serve a useful purpose if it alerts us to the ways practices within literature mediate, and are mediated by, practices in other fields, notably the economic and the ideological. But even with this understanding of the increasing mediations effected as journal publishing expands in the later nineteenth century, it would not serve the extraordinary achievements of certain figures to be reduced to nothing more than resultants of predictable causes.

Having by now historicized and theorized beyond our boundaries, let us close by offering a very old-fashioned notion of what an editor does. It comes from Anthony Curtis's recent book, *Lit Ed*, the best account since John Gross's, and more up to date, about what a British man of letters did in the twentieth century.[76] Curtis's survey leaves one feeling that what a literary editor must do is cultivate talent, wherever it is found, and even if the cost is very high. Ford Madox Ford recognized Rebecca West's talent when she was barely twenty. In return, West said of Ford: 'I think first-rate editors are rarer than first-rate writers ... To have the real feeling where good writing is coming from, and to know how to foster it, is a very great gift, and Ford had it.'[77] According to a recent memoir of the *New Yorker* editor William Shawn, he too had that 'very great gift.'[78]

Beyond that, an editor must have a wide circle of able friends. Bruce Richmond, the original editor of the *Times Literary Supplement*, had an extraordinary ability to recognize and nurture talent and turn them into 'regulars.' It was he who hunted out the TSE who had been penning book reviews for Middleton Murry's *Athenaeum*, who persuaded TSE – that is, Thomas Stearns Eliot – to write on Tudor and Stuart drama, who discovered over lunch that Eliot was interested in Lancelot Andrewes and so commissioned a leader on that obscure sixteenth-century divine, and who provided Eliot with the model for his own editorial practices at the *Criterion*.[79]

Editors need to know anyone who can write, and to cultivate those relationships assiduously. Although William Blackwood's friends were increasingly old-fashioned and somewhat out of touch with rising men of letters, he staunchly supported them, and they reciprocated. William's Scots blood boiled at paying the high prices rising literary stars were earning: 'I would suggest rather than trying to get hold of men who command fancy prices far beyond their intrinsic merits,' Maga should 'go to the more beneficial & not nearly so costly extra expenses of giving over quantity,' in short, publishing fewer pages, of the same high quality. And these pages should be written by those who 'are to be cherished as Maga's true friends.'[80]

Occasionally an editor can observe a direct correlation between his hands-on hiring and editing and some stupendous result. The October 1817 *Blackwood's*, William Blackwood's first number, is one instance. Another is the surprise success of *Blackwood's* May 1871 issue, featuring the anonymously penned invasion scare novella *The Battle of Dorking*. Subsequently denounced by William Gladstone as a panic-mongering work, 'mischievous as well as mad, heaping together a mass of impossible or incredible suppositions,'[81] *The Battle* provoked spirited political debate about its graphic depiction of the dangers awaiting a militarily weakened Britain. Controversy stimulated demand: sales rose by 65 per cent that month, from 5,300 to 8,100 copies. Capitalizing on the novella's *éclat*, the Blackwoods reprinted it as a sixpenny pamphlet, hired street hawkers and 'sandwich board' men to publicize it, and quietly congratulated themselves as sales topped 100,000 copies within six months.[82]

There were several models to choose from in assembling contributors to a journal. Leaving aside the practice at *Notes and Queries*, characteristic of many periodicals that depend on unsolicited material, editors can write most of the copy themselves, form a group of regulars, or seize whatever the momentary issue and literary star are and pay them enough to secure copy. The middle course was most often successful. The *Edinburgh Review*, the *Quarterly*, *Blackwood's*, *Fraser's*, Dickens's periodicals, along with more specialized journals addressing niche audiences, prospered by cultivating a set of writers whose pens could flow on any topic and in the assigned editorial direction. Some of these literary collaborations are famous even now. Probably the most celebrated, most remembered, and most successful of all editorial round tables was a deal table ('the Mahogany Tree') in a back room of Bradbury and Evans's premises, where Mark Lemon presided over the most influential company of artistic and literary wits of the nineteenth century.[83] A light humorist and playwright himself, Lemon also had the capacity not only to negotiate with his publishers and turn them into friends, bankers, and genial hosts, but also to negotiate almost all of the political, social, religious, aesthetic, and temperamental differences among his staff, to adjust Mr Punch's vitriol and obscenity without damping his authors' creative fires, and to carry on at a pace that would have killed many others. The Victorians paid tribute to his decency, to 'the purity and good nature of Lemon's singularly amiable and honest mind,'[84] although conversations around the table and some of *Punch's* treatments exhibit a greater range of sensibility, from obscenity and prejudice to powerful empathy for the downtrodden. Like many other nineteenth-century editors, Lemon not only got the weekly issue together; he also performed as an actor and lecturer, composed jest books and novels and fairy tales, and circulated among the journalists and governing classes who increasingly gathered in London as the centre for print media.

The Blackwoods, by comparison, seem a little dull and provincial. With editorial authority divided between London and Edinburgh, with stolid conscientious managers in both locations, and with a cohort of regular contributors capable of manufacturing on request copy on the subjects of their expertise, they sustained an excellent magazine for more than a century. They had their share of triumphs, and seized on the lions of the day expeditiously. But they didn't engage in the high-level clubbing practised by William I and other periodical proprietors and editors, and they never wrote themselves, established independent reputations as men of letters, or were quite willing to relinquish editorial control, even to the most able of their steady colleagues, Margaret Oliphant. Sober Scots publishers of conscience and probity, considerate to their employees and public spirited, they did all that editors do. Yet, over time, others, possibly less gifted or responsible, proved to be more innovative and even more successful.

NOTES

Robert L. Patten delivered portions of this paper as a keynote address to the Research Society for Victorian Periodicals in July 1998. David Finkelstein cites from material collected while organizing the catalogue of the Blackwood Papers in the National Library of Scotland. The authors are grateful to both institutions for permission to use these materials. We are also indebted to Patrick Leary and Martin Conboy for their advice, amplifications, and corrections. The remaining errors and misjudgments are ours.

1 Algar Labouchere Thorold, *The Life of Henry Labouchere* (London: Constable, 1913), quoted by Christopher Kent, in *Innovators and Preachers: The Role of the Editor in Victorian England*, ed. Joel H. Wiener, Contributions to

the Study of Mass Media and Communications 5 (Westport, Conn.: Greenwood Press, 1985), 460–1.

2 Laurel Brake, for example, has written extensively on the manner in which the lack of such 'intertextuality' has shaped scholarly appraisals of nineteenth-century periodical production, most recently in *Print in Transition, 1850–1910: Studies in Media and Book History* (Basingstoke: Palgrave Macmillan, 2001). As she notes, our reception of serialized fiction via bound, collected issues has resulted in the 'omnipresence of the volume in our libraries, and in our scholarship' (Laurel Brake, 'Star Turn? Magazines, Part-issue, and Book Serialisation,' in *Print in Transition, 1850–1910*, 29). See also Graham Law, *Serializing Fiction in the Victorian Press* (Basingstoke: Palgrave, 2000), and Laurel Brake, Bill Bell, and David Finkelstein, eds., *Nineteenth-Century Media and the Construction of Identities* (Basingstoke: Palgrave Macmillan, 2000).

3 William Blackwood to Thomas Henderson, Blackwood Papers, National Library of Scotland, 24 April 1885, MS 4467, fol. 61. The layout would have been similar to that of figure 7 from the November 1884 issue, in which advertisements for Tonic and Pears' Soap appear above an announcement for Lucy B. Walford's novels.

4 'Conducting' as a euphemism for 'editing' may have originated with the artist George Cruikshank, who was the 'Conductor' of his *Omnibus*, an 1841–2 miscellany. Dickens 'conducted' his periodicals, 1850–70, George Augustus Sala 'conducted' *Temple Bar*, 1860–3, and in the autumn of 1863 Anthony Trollope projected a new weekly that he would conduct (N. John Hall, *Trollope: A Biography* [Oxford: Clarendon Press, 1991], 269).

5 William Blackwood III to John Blackwood, Blackwood Papers, 24 May 1868, MS 4229, fol. 108, our emphasis.

6 For further information on nineteenth-century British publishing trends and shifts, see Lee Erickson, *The Economy of Literary Form: English Literature and the Industrialisation of Publishing, 1800–1850* (Baltimore, Md.: Johns Hopkins University Press, 1996); William Secord, *Victorian Sensation: The Extraordinary Publication, Reception and Secret Authorship of 'Vestiges of the Natural History of Creation'* (Chicago: University of Chicago Press, 2000); and John Feather, *A History of Publishing* (London: Routledge, 1989).

7 William Hazlitt, 'The Periodical Press,' in *The Complete Works*, ed. P.P. Howe, 21 vols. (London: Dent, 1930–4), 16:220.

8 In August 1861, the publisher John Maxwell, seeking to capitalize on the *Cornhill* model, offered Anthony Trollope £1,000 a year to contribute a novel and edit *Temple Bar*, assuring him that '[a]ll the real work of editorship will be performed – as heretofore – by Mr. Edmund Yates.' Trollope refused. Walter Houghton et al., eds., *The Wellesley Index to Victorian*

Periodicals, 1824–1900, 5 vols. (Toronto: University of Toronto Press, 1966–89), 3:387–8.

9 For more on this subject, see Law, *Serializing Fiction in the Victorian Press*.

10 The first series was published in March 1857, a second series in May 1878, and a third produced in June 1891. With the decision to concentrate on military and imperial audiences at the turn of the century, a new series (*Tales from the Outposts*), fulfilled the same compendium collection role from 1908 onwards.

11 For a brief comment on the transaction, see Joseph Munt Langford to William Blackwood, 24 December 1878, Blackwood Papers, MS 4377, fol. 270.

12 In 'Salesmen, Sportsmen, Mentors: Anonymity and Mid-Victorian Theories of Journalism,' *Victorian Studies* 41, 1 (Autumn 1997), 31–68, Dallas Liddle expertly summarizes the mid-century debate over anonymity versus signed articles, but we still lack a full treatment of the consequences of that debate, namely the changes in editorial practice, reading, authorship, publicity, and sales that the signature system introduced.

13 Walter Bagehot, 'The First Edinburgh Reviewers' (1855), in Bagehot, *Literary Studies*, ed. Richard Holt Hutton, 3 vols. (London: Longmans, Green, and Co., [1895], new impression, 1910), 1:175; quoted in Joanne Shattock, 'Showman, Lion Hunter, or Hack: The *Quarterly* Editor at Midcentury,' in Wiener, *Innovators and Preachers*, 161–83.

14 Wiener, *Innovators and Preachers*, xvi–xvii.

15 Anthony Curtis, *Lit Ed* (London: Carcanet Press, 1998), 123.

16 Charles Dickens, *Letters*, ed. Madeline House et al., British Academy/Pilgrim edition, 12 vols. (Oxford: Clarendon Press, 1965–2002), 9.343.

17 William E. Buckler, '*Once a Week* under Samuel Lucas, 1859–65,' *PMLA* 67, no. 7 (December 1952), 924–41.

18 Among the tasks Langford had to undertake in this context were regular tours round major London publishing houses, booksellers, and other book and magazine retail agents to gather advance subscriptions and sales for Blackwood books (and its Magazine). Although a tedious activity, it did afford Langford invaluable opportunity for gauging market interest in the firm's products and evaluating reactions to the Magazine's contents, as well as for keeping abreast of the latest trade gossip and business news. For further information on this, see David Finkelstein, *The House of Blackwood: Author–Publisher Relations in the Victorian Era* (University Park: Pennsylvania State University Press, 2002), 44–6.

19 Anthony Trollope, *An Autobiography*, 2 vols. (Edinburgh: William Blackwood and Sons, 1883), 2:121.

20 Ibid., 2:123.

21 Ibid., 2:124–5.

22 K.K. Collins, 'The British and Foreign Review,' in *British Literary Magazines. The Romantic Age, 1789–1836*, ed. Alvin Sullivan (Westport, Conn.: Greenwood Press, 1983), 53–7, 54. For information on British journals and publishers, we have used, in addition to the previously cited Wellesley Index, Sullivan's *Romantic Age* and its successor, *British Literary Magazines: The Victorian and Edwardian Age, 1837–1913* (Westport, Conn.: Greenwood Press, 1984); and Patricia J. Anderson and Jonathan Rose, eds., *British Literary Publishing Houses*, Dictionary of Literary Biography 106: 1820–80, 112: 1881–1965 (Detroit: Gale Research, 1991).

23 Quoted in Jerold J. Savory's entry on *Vanity Fair*, Sullivan, *The Victorian and Edwardian Age*, 439.

24 More on Blackwood's response to the *National Review* can be found in Finkelstein, *House of Blackwood*, 98–101.

25 In this and the following discussion of female editors we are indebted to Barbara Onslow, *Women of the Press in Nineteenth-Century Britain* (Basingstoke: Macmillan, 2000), which brings together earlier scholarship on the subject and adds significant new research and conclusions.

26 Carl Woodring, *Victorian Samplers: William and Mary Howitt* (Lawrence: University of Kansas Press, 1952).

27 See Robert Lee Wolff, 'Devoted Disciple: The Letters of Mary Elizabeth Braddon to Sir Edward Bulwer Lytton, 1862–1873,' *Harvard Library Bulletin* 22 (January–April 1974): 5–35, 129–61, his *Sensational Victorian: The Life and Fiction of Mary Elizabeth Braddon* (New York: Garland, 1979), and Onslow, *Women of the Press*, 121–4, where Braddon is identified as 'one of the most effective female periodical editors of the century' (121).

28 Richard D. Altick, *Punch: The Lively Youth of a British Institution, 1841–1851* (Columbus: Ohio State University Press, 1997), 394–5.

29 Onslow, *Women of the Press*, 230.

30 *Saint Paul's* 1 (October 1867), 4.

31 Christopher Kent, 'The Editor and the Law,' in Wiener, *Innovators and Preachers*, 99–109, 104.

32 Finkelstein, *House of Blackwood*, 10.

33 Patrick Leary, 'James Fraser,' *Carlyle Encyclopedia*, ed. Mark Cumming (Cranbury, N.J.: Farleigh Dickinson University Press, 2004), 171–4.

34 Quoted without attribution in Sullivan, *Romantic*, 292.

35 For a full listing of Oliphant's contributions to *Blackwood's Magazine*, see the *Wellesley Index*, 1:1033–5.

36 Miriam M. Thrall, *Rebellious Fraser's: Nol Yorke's Magazine in the Days of*

Maginn, Thackeray and Carlyle (New York: Columbia University Press, 1934), argues that Yorke is a collaborative *nom de plume*, but Leary, 'Fraser's,' thinks Maginn was almost solely responsible.

37 See M.H. Spielmann, *The History of 'Punch'* (New York: Cassell, 1895), Altick, *Punch*, and Michael Slater, *Douglas Jerrold, 1803–1857* (London: Gerald Duckworth, 2002).

38 Patrick Leary, 'A Victorian Virtual Community,' *Victorian Review* 25, no. 2 (Winter 2000), 62–79.

39 Dickens, *Letters*, 1:303, 339–40.

40 See appendix 1 for the table of contents for Maga issues from August 1871 through July 1872.

41 The Blackwoods nicknamed Blackmore the 'Market Gardener' after receiving his explanation for delays in producing copy. He blamed it on the pressures of the strawberry season: 'Strawb., Strawb., strawb., is my whole work now from 4 a. m. to 9 p. m.; &, if one can get a good crop, they pay much better than literature. I have 4 cwh now to weigh; and must be off acc[ording]ly.' R.D. Blackmore to William Blackwood, 26 June 1871, Blackwood Papers, MS. 4270, fols. 105–6. 'He is a character,' chortled John Blackwood in response to the excuse (29 June 1871, Blackwood Papers, MS 4270, fol. 210).

42 Possibly the most famous instance of placing a new serial at the beginning of a periodical and then displacing it applies to Charles Lever's *A Day's Ride: A Life's Romance*. It dragged down circulation of *All the Year Round* so disastrously that Dickens had to rush into weekly instalments of the work he had thought of publishing in monthly parts or possibly in volumes, *Great Expectations*. Lever was pushed to the back of each number. Chagrinned, he told Dickens that he regretted being a 'misfortune' to him and his journal. See Dickens, *Letters*, 9:321–2 and 327–8.

43 John Blackwood to William Blackwood III, 21 July 1871, Blackwood Papers, MS 4270, fols. 222–3.

44 William Blackwood III to John Blackwood, Blackwood Papers, 14 August 1871, MS 4271, fols. 104–7.

45 Maga rarely held the first position for a leading fiction throughout its magazine run. During its serialization, *Scenes of Clerical Life* occupied positions 1, 2, 5, 1, 1, 3, 4, 4, 4, 5, and 1 respectively; *Miss Marjoribanks* occupied positions 1, 3, 1, 4, 3, 1, 4, 2, 2, 2, 2, 0 (no instalment in January 1866), 7, 5, 4, and 6, despite the editors' delight in many of the parts; *John Caldigate*, 1, 1, 3, 1, 2, 2, 4, 3, 2, 2, 1, 2, 3, 3, and 3; *Saracinesca*, forgotten now, started out bravely in May 1886 in first position, and was subsequently run 1, 1, 1, 2, 2, 1, and 2 for the rest of 1886. In January 1887 it dropped to

6, then 5, 5, and 1 for the last, April, instalment. Conrad's *Heart of Darkness* never opened an issue: it was placed second in all three months (February–April 1899). His *Lord Jim*, after taking head place for the first instalment in October 1899, slipped to the bottom of succeeding issues: 5, 5, 4, 6, 7, 6, 5, 5, 8, 6, 4, 6, and 6.

46 See, for examples, William Blackwood III to John Blackwood, Blackwood Papers, 13 February 1868, MS 4229, fol. 12; 30 May 1870, MS 4256, fol. 36; and 14 July 1870, MS 4256, fol. 68.

47 William Blackwood III to John Blackwood, Blackwood Papers, 16 May 1872, MS 4286, fol. 5.

48 John Blackwood to William Blackwood III, Blackwood Papers, 22 May 1872, MS 4285, fol. 84–5. The novel remained Blackmore's favourite.

49 John Blackwood to William Blackwood III, Blackwood Papers, 14 June 1875, MS 4327, fols. 158–9.

50 John Blackwood to William Blackwood III, Blackwood Papers, 20 August 1872, MS 4285, fols. 144–5.

51 Curtis, *Lit Ed*, 10.

52 Quoted in Barbara Quinn Schmidt, 'Novelists, Publishers, and Fiction in Middle-Class Magazines, 1860–1880,' *Victorian Periodicals Review* 17 (Winter 1984), 143.

53 Joseph Munt Langford to William Blackwood, 26 July 1877, Blackwood Papers, MS 4361, fols. 228–9.

54 William Blackwood to Joseph Munt Langford, 27 July 1877, Blackwood Papers, MS 4355, fols. 91–2.

55 Joseph Munt Langford to John Blackwood, 20 September 1879, Blackwood Papers, MS 4393, fol. 169.

56 Hugh Fraser to William Blackwood and Sons, 20 May 1839, Blackwood Papers, MS 4048, fols. 268–9. We are grateful to Patrick Leary for drawing this source to our attention.

57 Joseph Munt Langford to John Blackwood, 23 May 1862, Blackwood Papers, MS 4171, fols. 151–2. For further information on the negotiation and publication of *Romola*, consult Roland Anderson, '"Things Wisely Ordered": John Blackwood, George Eliot, and the Publication of *Romola*,' *Publishing History* 11 (1982), 5–39, Gordon S. Haight, *George Eliot: A Biography* (Oxford: Oxford University Press, 1968), 354–74, and Finkelstein, *House of Blackwood*, 27–9.

58 William Blackwood III, undated memorandum, Blackwood Papers, National Library of Scotland, MS 30073.

59 William Blackwood III to John Blackwood, Blackwood Papers, 4 May 1871, MS 4271, fol. 13.

60 William Blackwood III to John Blackwood, Blackwood Papers, 28 May
    1872, MS 4286, fols. 13–14.
61 John Blackwood to William Blackwood III, Blackwood Papers, 13 August
    1872, MS 4285, fol. 136.
62 William Blackwood III to John Blackwood, Blackwood Papers, 14 August
    1872, MS 4286, fol. 93.
63 Some attention has been paid to the relation between advertisements and
    texts with respect to serial fiction, where the 'thingness' of the world is
    instantiated by both the advertising paratexts and the texts. See Bernard
    Darwin, *The Dickens Advertiser* (London: Elkins Mathews and Marrot,
    1930), Gerard Curtis, 'Dickens in the Visual Market,' in *Literature in the
    Marketplace: Nineteenth-Century British Publishing and Reading Practices*, ed.
    John O. Jordan and Robert L. Patten (Cambridge: Cambridge University
    Press, 1995), 213–49, and Curtis, *Visual Words: Art and the Material Book in
    Victorian England* (Aldershot, Hants: Ashgate, 2002).
64 Leslie A. Marchand, *The Athenaeum: A Mirror of Victorian Culture* (Chapel
    Hill: University of North Carolina Press, 1941), 34–7.
65 William Blackwood III to John Blackwood, Blackwood Papers, 14 August
    1872, MS. 4286, fol. 92.
66 William Blackwood III, undated memorandum, Blackwood Papers,
    National Library of Scotland, MS 30073.
67 Joseph Munt Langford to William Blackwood III, Blackwood Papers,
    10 April 1877, MS. 4361, fols. 173–4.
68 Sullivan, *The Victorian and Edwardian Age*, 140.
69 Quoted in David Finkelstein, 'The Maga Mohawks,' *Scottish Book Collector*
    7, no. 5 (Autumn 2002), 20. See also Mark Parker, *Literary Magazines and
    British Romanticism*, Cambridge Studies in Romanticism 45 (Cambridge:
    Cambridge University Press, 2000).
70 More information on both Chambers's and Knight's periodical experi-
    ments can be found in William Secord, *Literature*, 67–9.
71 Jordan and Patten, *Literature*, 12.
72 William Blackwood III, undated memorandum, Blackwood Papers, Na-
    tional Library of Scotland, MS 30073.
73 A field is 'a structured space with its own laws of functioning and its own
    relations of force independent of those of politics and the economy, except,
    obviously, in the cases of the economic and political fields. Each field is
    relatively autonomous but structurally homologous with the others ... A
    field is a dynamic concept in that a change in agents' positions necessarily
    entails a change in the field's structure': Randal Johnson, 'Editor's Intro-

duction,' Pierre Bourdieu, *The Field of Cultural Production*, ed. Johnson (New York: Columbia University Press, 1993), 1–25, 6.

74 Peter D. McDonald, *British Literary Culture and Publishing Practice, 1880–1914* (Cambridge: Cambridge University Press, 1997), 10.

75 R.G. Cox, 'Nineteenth Century Periodical Criticism: 1800–1860,' PhD diss., Cambridge University, 1939; Sullivan, *Romantic Age* and *Victorian and Edwardian Age*.

76 John Gross, *The Rise and Fall of the Man of Letters: A Study of the Idiosyncratic and the Humane in Modern Literature* (New York: Macmillan, 1969).

77 Curtis, *Lit Ed*, 43.

78 For instance, Ved Mehta, *Remembering Mr. Shawn's 'New Yorker': The Invisible Art of Editing* (Woodstock, N.Y.: Overlook Press, 1998).

79 Curtis, *Lit Ed*, 146.

80 William Blackwood III, undated memorandum, Blackwood Papers, National Library of Scotland, MS 30073.

81 William Ewart Gladstone, *Diaries*, ed. M.R.D. Foot and H.G.C. Matthew, 14 vols. (Oxford: Clarendon Press, 1968–94), 7:500.

82 For further comment on this episode, see I.F. Clarke, *Voices Prophesying War*, 2nd ed. (Oxford: Oxford University Press, 1992); Darko Suvin, 'The Extraordinary Voyage, The Future War, and Bulwer's *The Coming Race*: Three Sub-Genres in British Science Fiction, 1871–1885,' *Literature and History* 10, no. 2 (Autumn 1984), 231–48; and David Finkelstein, 'From Textuality to Orality: The Reception of *The Battle of Dorking*,' in *Books and Bibliographies: Essays in Commemoration of Don McKenzie*, ed. John Thomson (Wellington, NZ: Victoria University Press, 2002), 87–102.

83 The best biography is Arthur A. Adrian, *Mark Lemon: First Editor of 'Punch'* (London: Oxford University Press, 1966), and the best account of Lemon's early *Punch* years is by Richard D. Altick, *Punch*.

84 J[oseph] A. H[atton], 'Mark Lemon,' *Dictionary of National Biography*.

Maga, the Shilling Monthlies, and the New Journalism

LAUREL BRAKE

Introduction

This is a piece about the impact of distinctive types of competition on *Blackwood's Magazine* between 1860 and 1895, and how the definition of the magazine as a genre changes over those years in Britain. From its inception in 1817, *Blackwood's* presented itself as an exemplar of a *type* of periodical – the magazine – as distinct from the upmarket, high culture reviews of the day. Accordingly it welcomed and circulated the sobriquet 'Maga,' by which affectionate term it was known to its editors, contributors, and readers. As an exemplar at its origin of a genre whose defining characteristics are breadth, heterogeneity, and inclusiveness, Maga was a *miscellany* of politics and literature, and accordingly porous. It is not surprising then that it flourished and survived several generations of serials – magazines, weeklies, and reviews – as well as considerable political change in Britain.

In the nineteenth century the genre of the magazine is in a continuing process of transformation. Was the longevity of Maga the result of stability and/or change? How did it respond to the accretion of modernity in its many guises? Initially alert to Maga's tenacious adherence to varieties of anonymity long after the onset of celebrity journalism, I found that my hypothesis of *Blackwood's* stubborn stability had to be qualified. Anonymity was a single feature in a complex model of variables in print media. Like many journal titles that survive the breadth of a century – the *Spectator* is another – the character of even this relatively stable journal changes, though the title, like Dorian Gray's face, remains the same. It is both the adjustments in the journal and the interplay between a specific title and the genre that are my remit.

Conversely, the lineaments of transformation of the nineteenth-century magazine between 1860 and 1895 emerge by comparison between the relatively stable layout, concept and contents of *Blackwood's* over this period, with some of its successors' attempts to re-launch and refresh this type of periodical for a niche market of middle-class readers. How does the 'meaning' of Maga change in light of the new definitions of the magazine around it? I write of 'successors' rather than 'rivals' for a reason. *Blackwood's* did, within its first fifteen years, prompt at least one southern rival/imitator in *Fraser's Monthly Magazine for Town and Country*, and possibly two.[1] Like *Blackwood's, Fraser's* was a monthly costing 2/6; it was Tory in politics, ludic in mode, and its layout was in two columns. Unlike Maga, it was occasionally illustrated, and it did not emphasize or carry fiction to the same degree as its rival. The scarcity of fiction is evident: in volume 2 in the 'Monthly list of New Publications. London' in August 1830, in which works of 'Poetry, Drama, &c' (p. 120) begin the list, fiction is only included toward the end (p. 121) in a general category called 'Literary Intelligence,' and in the index of volume 3 which covers six months, only ten stories are listed in a category called 'Tales and Narratives.' Likewise, in the February 1831 number, 22 novels are reviewed in one article, the beginning of which furnishes an explanation of *Fraser's* contents and an implied critique of *Blackwood's* association with serial fiction: 'We believe that since novel-writing has become a trade, never was it lower than at present.'[2] Rather *Fraser's* specialized in satire as a spice to its politics, and Thackeray's serialized 'Yellowplush Correspondence,' Men's Wives,' and 'Fitz-Boodle's Confessions' characteristically appeared in its pages.

Blackwood's was literally imported into the *Fraser's* project from its inception. William Maginn, *Fraser's* founder and first editor, had been a frequent contributor to Maga from 1824 to 1826, and was himself a collaborator in the authorship of *Noctes Ambrosianae* under the pseudonym Christopher North or C.N. *Blackwood's* nickname 'Maga' was matched by *Fraser's* 'Regina' and *Blackwood's* pseudonymous Christopher North by *Fraser's* Oliver Yorke.[3] In 'L'Envoy' to its first anniversary issue in Jan 1831, *Fraser's* identified its rivals in the monthly market by distinguishing itself from them. Unlike Colburn's *New Monthly* that was well known for its puffing of its publisher's titles, *Fraser's* strenuously denies puffing, while exposing its workings in detail.[4] It excuses its vehemence on this matter on the basis of [Colburn's] practices: 'We know that some have considered us rather too severe every now and then ... [but] we have a constant and daily provocation to our spleen, in the flourishing vigour of the puff system,' with 'daily' provocation referring to Colburn's system of 'paid paragraphs,' reviews of titles on his list written by his staff and inserted as reviews in other papers.[5] From *Fraser's* close imitation of Maga, its rivalry would have been clear to all analysts of the press, but Maginn identifies *Blackwood's* as *Fraser's* most formidable rival in 'L'Envoy' by equating the high quality of *Fraser's* with that of Maga, but also boasting that *Fraser's* circulation outpaced its prestigious rival: 'No Magazine within our memory, ever made its way so successfully in so short a time. We are now ... fixed and recognised, as leading members of the highest class of periodicals ... we sell considerably more than three times the number sold by Blackwood at the end of his first year.'[6] In the following month, in 'Novels of the Season,' *Fraser's* attacks *Blackwood's* author John Wilson, by taking issue with Wilson's critique of *Tristram Shandy* and publicly 'identifying' Wilson as 'Christopher North,' the author of *Noctes*. This seems particularly disingenuous as Maginn had himself written *Noctes* under this pen name, and was well aware that its real signatories were plural and collaborative.[7]

However, apart from *Fraser's*, I believe that most of the magazines that followed *Blackwood's* were successors rather than rivals. Once the domination of the paradigm of *Blackwood's* was successfully challenged in the 1860s by the shilling monthlies – which *began* as a response to Maga and its descendants, the paradigm of the new monthlies displaced that of its ancestors. A distinct middle-class market niche opened, largely composed of younger, more metropolitan consumers of shilling monthlies. *Their* successors, quintessential mainstream and popular 'magazines' of the 1890s such as the 6d *Strand* or the *Pall Mall*, develop this niche. Dedicated to entertainment, avoiding politics, heavily illustrated, cheap, accessibly laid out and 'got up,' with named celebrity authors and personal journalism, these titles hardly betray their ancestry in Maga. *Blackwood's*, while necessarily responsive to these developments, as I shall show, adhered to its target group of preponderantly old-market readers: Tory gentlemen: the clergy, their families and parishioners; and old-money gentlewomen. Looking at Maga of the 1890s, one sees that its market niche appears increasingly to engage with a new cultural and physical geography – the framework of Empire and readers in the colonies, rather than its mid-century readership base in Edinburgh/Scotland and English parishes. While some of the latter reader groups are retained, the expanding readership seems to be elsewhere.

Let us begin with the advent of the shilling monthlies in the 1860s. *Macmillan's Magazine* and the *Cornhill* set off the avalanche of that subgenre of the magazine in 1859/60, and the plethora of other middle-class, 'light,' cheap, and entertaining titles that followed. At two other points later in the century, new clusters of journals drew on the Maga formula, as well as impacted on it. First, the *monthly* reviews between 1865 and 1882 (comprising the *Fortnightly*, the *Contemporary*, the *Nineteenth Century*, and the *National*) looked to the *monthly magazines* for their re-conceptualization of the review beyond the limits of the by now venerable *quarterly* reviews. This new generation of reviews impinged on another of Maga's primary characteristics, its robust political orientation. The *Blackwood's* of the 1890s, now an antiquated figure at the banquet of modernity, compared poorly with new journalism magazine products such as the *Strand Magazine*.

The impact of these new titles on the circulation of Maga may be gauged from the sales figures for *Blackwood's* compiled by David Finkelstein,[8] bearing in mind that enhancement of sales may be achieved through greater expenditure on advertising,[9] as well as from lure of editorial matter, illustrations, and price. Following the dates of the intervention into the market of these successive reconfigurations of the magazine genre, sales of *Blackwood's* fall, mirroring the multiplication and thus fractionalization of niche markets in middle-class periodical consumption. Thus, between June 1860 and April 1861, soon after the two new shilling monthlies appear, sales per number of *Blackwood's* begin to falter, falling from an average of 8222 per issue 1859/60, to 8065 in 1860/1. Then in the next four years, between May 1861 and June 1865, sales per issue manage to hold their own, hovering around a lower average of 7200 per issue, before taking big dips in annual sales (of 1500 and 4545) in the years ending June 1866 and June 1867. These were, respectively, the year immediately following the appearance of two of the new reviews, the *Fortnightly* (1865) and *Contemporary* (1866), and the year during which the *Fortnightly* went monthly.[10] From June 1868 annual sales move gradually downward. There are sharp dips in the years when both the *Nineteenth Century* and the *National Review* commence, of 3967 sales per year between June 1877 and June 1878 in the throes of the *Nineteenth Century*, and of 1674 between June 1883 and June 1884 when the *National Review* entered the market. The startling 'loss' of nearly 4000 sales in the year 1877–8 is largely accounted for by the striking *rise* of sales, by 3393, in the year before.[11] This success exactly coincided with the appearance in Maga of Charles Reade's *A*

Woman Hater, a thirteen-part serial published between June 1876 and June 1877. As David Finkelstein explains,[12] Reade's novel was a controversial intervention in the current argument for the opening up of medical education to women and, in August 1876 during the novel's run, 'amendments to the Medical Act were passed ... removing gender restrictions in the examination procedure.'[13] Between June 1885 and June 1890, annual regular sales dropped from 60,130 to 55,831, a loss of about 4300 copies, but for the year June 1890–June 1891, the year after the launch of the *Strand*, the reduction in copies sold was 1500! There was a larger dip of 2568 copies annually between June 1892 and June 1893, and the trend both in circulation and profits was downward, although revenue from American sales, enjoyed by the Scottish firm from June 1891 helped boost profits after that date.

The Magazine as a Genre in 1817

In order to assess the degree to which the magazine genre changes over the period, I propose to suggest some 'core' elements of the early form of *Blackwood's*, qualities that are arguably associated with conditions of consumption and production of media publication in the pre-Victorian period. High on this list are the prominence of national identity/ Scottishness, and a related but not identical regional identification with the North of Britain rather than the South. This stems from not only the ethnicity of the particular proprietors of Maga but from a critical mass in Scotland in the early nineteenth century, and especially in Edinburgh following the Scottish Enlightenment, of publishers, journals, writers, institutions such as universities, libraries, and churches, and a relatively educated population of readers and disputants, well acquainted with intellectual controversy and ideas. It is a cluster propitious to print culture.

Specifically, it was the weight and sway of the quarterly and Whig *Edinburgh Review* and the platform it provided for Constable, its Scottish publisher who was also the Blackwoods' chief rival in Edinburgh, which prompted William Blackwood to initiate his periodical project. Its prime media targets as well as its geographic location are evident in its earliest title, the *Edinburgh Monthly Magazine*, which alludes to local and national competitors, to the *Edinburgh Review*, and to Henry Colburn's *New Monthly Magazine*, which was London based. Central too is the strong Tory political identity of the fledgling Blackwood's publication, not only as an ideological alternative to the Whiggish

Edinburgh Review, but also as a supplement/competitor to Tory rivals of the *Edinburgh* – the *Quarterly* and the *New Monthly Magazine*. Both of these journals were relative newcomers, the *Quarterly* having been launched in 1809 and the *New Monthly* in 1814, just three years before *Blackwood's*. London-based like the *New Monthly*, the *Quarterly* was published from its inception by John Murray[14] in Albemarle Street. The *Quarterly*'s southern location might have contributed to William Blackwood's low opinion of its effectiveness, and to have fostered the notion that on *two* counts – the dominance in Scotland of the *Edinburgh* as well as the English base and readership of the *Quarterly* – there was room for a Scottish, Tory intervention.

This Tory dimension of *Blackwood's* is retained throughout the century. A good mid-century example is its campaign against free trade in the early months of 1850. The January number of that year begins with a notably lengthy piece for Maga of forty-two pages entitled 'British Agriculture and Foreign Competition.' Although there is nothing in the January heading to suggest that this is the first of a series, the February number included a second part to the article and a 122-page 'Appendix,' 'Blackwood on the Agricultural Question and the Free Press.' Beginning with an editorial note, the appendix claims that despite Maga's best efforts, no pro–free trade paper could provide adequate answers to their statement: although the *Times* and provincial papers quote the article, the *Times*, lacking any effective defence of Protectionism, 'discredited the facts adduced by the writer ... and has resorted to falsification of facts, and bad reasoning.'[15] What is now clearly a campaign by *Maga* is pursued in the March number by a third article with an agricultural slant, 'Agriculture, Commerce, and Manufacturers: Opening of the [Parliamentary] Session.' It occupies the slot of the last piece in the number, a space regularly occupied by current political affairs, by which means Maga has continued its assault on free trade. An advert for the March number of *Blackwood's* in the *Athenaeum* (23 February 1850), which lists this article, is published adjacent to Blackwood's March list of publications, among which is their agricultural journal, the *Journal of Agriculture and the Transactions of the Highland and Agricultural Society of Scotland*. The publisher's larger commercial interest in agriculture and the Scottish dimension of that interest partner its political campaign against free trade nationally in Maga.

Also central to *Blackwood's* was the miscellany that characterized its contents, the format that distinguished a magazine from a review. From its inception in 1817, it was an admixture of politics, general articles, and literature. To emphasize its distinctive, non-quarterly and non-review genre, Maga advertised its magazine identity. While it included occasional book reviews and, initially, a Register (eventually dropped) in imitation of the early quarterlies and monthlies, it also featured 'original' papers, that is writing that did not originate in previously published works as reviews did, nor reports copied from other sources. Its contents were thus freed up from an agenda confined and attached to new books of the day, evaluation of these books, and the concomitant and potentially controversial commercial engagement with the lists of fellow publishers and the works of contemporary authors that reviewing involved. Like the principal *Magazines* of the day, this model allowed for both stand-alone pieces on topical, critical, or insouciant subjects, original literary works (English poetry and poetry in translation for example in the case of the *Monthly Magazine*) and, crucially, serialized works, such as belles lettres and fiction, which the infrequency of the quarterly reviews ruled out. While the length of individual numbers of the monthly was necessarily shorter than that of the quarterlies,[16] reflecting *Blackwood's* greater frequency and the shorter intervals available between numbers to read it, the brevity and high number of articles in the new monthly meant that each number offered a *variety* comparable to that of the longer quarterly numbers. Thus there were nineteen articles in *Blackwood's* March 1817 number of 120 pages, and nine articles in the *Edinburgh Review* of that month. The quicker pacing of *Blackwood's* contents mirrored its higher frequency of publication, suggesting a lightness in comparison with the quarterlies. So did its price, 2/6 per issue, compared with the quarterlies' 6/0.

The 'original papers' in the magazine format, both fiction and non-fiction, also contributed to this lightness of tone, through the element of humour, which could attach to the subject matter as well as the style of writing on which the quarterly reviews had to rely for their injection of humour. It should be noted that in the early years of *Blackwood's* the proportion of belles lettres far outstripped the incidence of serialized novels, which appeared only sporadically up to the late 1840s.[17] The first appearance (anonymously) of Bulwer Lytton's and Margaret Oliphant's fiction, in March 1848 and July 1852 respectively, can be seen to occur at the beginning of *Blackwood's* more intensive publication of serialized novels. Perhaps it was to reinforce this lightness, and to open up the new venture to a readership habituated to lighter literature normally denied consumers of the 'heavy' quarterlies, that the layout of Maga – the divided page set in two tall, unruled columns – facilitated the ease of reading, and signalled its distinction from the undivided pages and lengthy articles of the quarterlies.

So, in the early years of *Blackwood's*, the lightness of tone and of appearance, the variety of topics, the pacing of each number, and the inclusion of serialized belles lettres and fiction had implications for the composition of the readership of the new magazine: these features increased the likelihood of new readers beyond that of the quarterly audience: first middle- and upper-class women of Scotland and England, who could be counted among the projected community of *Blackwood's* readers, and secondly more insouciant (and perhaps younger) male readers reaching deeper into the lower middle classes who looked to journals for amusement. There is no doubt that the yoking of *belles lettres* and serial fiction to monthly magazines both in this period and later, in the shilling monthlies and fiction papers, succeeded in attracting high numbers of women readers, as the advertisements in *Blackwood's* addressed to female consumers attest (see fig. 7).[18]

That *Blackwood's* did have wrappers, and a monthly Advertiser should also be noted. Although very few editions of the journal survive intact with these paratexts,[19] at least one library in Edinburgh has such holdings. They remind us of the origins of the income derived by publishers of journals, from advertisements as well as the cover price, and the vehicle of free advertising that wrappers offered to a publisher like Blackwood, who had a monthly list of other publications to circulate and sell. Clearly, that *Blackwood's* was monthly, was tailored not only to its publisher's monthly lists, but to the commercial world at large which enjoyed more frequent and timely opportunities to advertise its products to potential consumers than it did in quarterly publications.

A quality of *Blackwood's* in these early years to which it stuck tenaciously late into the century was the anonymity of its individual contributors. In this respect it mimicked the quarterlies of the early nineteenth century, whose authors were necessarily anonymous due to the association of some of their number with government, party politics, and/or the professions; anonymity also protected them in the event of libel or slander charges.[20] However, the monthly magazines made limited moves toward formulaic signatures that distinguished characteristic 'personalities' either of recurring authors or serial features by which successive numbers of the journal could be anticipated.[21] Thus there were generic signatures for authors, such as Y.Y.Y. (David Robinson), 'The English Opium Eater' (De Quincey), and 'The Ettrick Shepherd' (James Hogg), all *Blackwood's*, and for series or columns

(*Noctes Ambrosianae* and *Horae Germanicae*) in *Blackwood's*. I even found one example, in an appendix to the February 1850 number, in which *Blackwood's* contrived a way to divulge the name of a contributor of one of its most controversial pieces, which appeared in the previous issue. It simply published the name by quoting commentary on the January article from a rival paper, *John Bull* (5 January): 'Rarely has the cause of free trade been more seriously damaged than by the masterly article, entitled "British Agriculture and Foreign Competition," from the pen, we believe, of Mr Henry Stephens, the author of "The Book of the Farm," in the January number of *Blackwood's Magazine*.'[22]

In the case of the early *Blackwood's*, in more than one instance different writers authored a recurring feature (such as 'Noctes' and the 'Letters of Timothy Tickler'), suggesting that even this gesture to signature was reluctant and playful rather than informative or a guarantee of responsible journalism. This ludic quality surrounding the tease of pseudonyms and identity of columnists is itself an attitude towards authorship that distinguishes the monthly magazines from the quarterly reviews. The latter do not traffic with signature in any guise except to withhold it. Thus there are few playful sobriquets. Nor can their quarterly review format accommodate the serial bait of recurring columns; formally, it is limited to the recurring pattern of 'and,' 'and,' 'and,' with one book review of a new book following another.[23] While both quarterly and monthly editors exercise selection of material through commissioning articles, the editing and 'make-up' of quarterly numbers differ from the monthlies, where shaping and structuring of issues are more flexible, as pointed out above in Patten and Finkelstein's essay. Where the quarterly editor deals with a series of lengthy articles, each edited and perfected in its own right, the monthly editor is more free to edit the number as a composite *issue*, including complementary and diverse articles, columns that recur month to month, and the tease of half 'signature.' But perhaps my/our emphasis on the anonymity of individual authors is mistaken, a predictable and retrospective desire stemming from the culture of celebrity, which became a significant discourse from the mid-1860s and the onset of the 'new journalism.' The main point to make about *Blackwood's* may be another aspect of the meanings of anonymity rather than on failure to name the individual – the emphasis on the corporate sign of the journal – in its title, so that the literary authority of the journal derives from the name of the publishing house (Blackwood) and the collective genre of the Magazine.[24]

So, how did the advent of the shilling monthlies in late 1859

(*Macmillan's Magazine*), and early 1860 (*Cornhill Magazine*), change the model of the magazine as a genre – its design, contents, and quiddity – from the models that *Blackwood's*, now over forty years old, and its southern imitator from 1830, *Fraser's*, offered?

Maga and the Shilling Monthlies

Macmillan's and *Cornhill* were both (publishing) 'house' journals like *Blackwood's*, produced respectively by Macmillan and Smith, Elder, & Co. Both firms had extensive monthly lists of publications, among which their respective shilling monthlies figured. Between them, these journals lowered the price of the monthly from 2/6 to a shilling and began to bring signature and 'star' authors into view, *Macmillan's* through outright signature, and *Cornhill* by a celebrity editor and coy signature for certain elements of the magazine. *Cornhill* added lavish illustrations. Together, they transformed the generic 'image' of the middle-class magazine, making it still 'brighter' journalistically – through attractive cover designs on quality coloured paper and more modern contents, as well as cheaper.

  Cornhill's modernity consisted in its emphasis on, and high proportion of quality fiction by tried and thinly veiled (though ostensibly anonymous) authors,[25] enhancing the element of fiction and belles lettres that *Blackwood's* by now featured in its 'magazine' formula of miscellany. While it included fiction, the early *Macmillan's* did not make fiction its distinctive note of modernity, which was rather its avowed policy of signature, the virtues of which were debated in its pages, the distinction of its celebrity authors, and the high quality of the writing. *Macmillan's* and *Cornhill* take different pathways from their common model of the *Blackwood's/Fraser's* miscellany: the early *Cornhill* targets fiction, producing an undivided page with a high incidence of illustration, making the journal physically resemble literary production, which offers a reading experience akin to that of reading fiction in book or part-issue; in particular, part-issues often carried illustrations, a quality mimicked by Smith's journal, which like many part-issues, cost a shilling. *Cornhill*, then, is quite distinct physically from the divided page that *Macmillan's* appropriates from *Blackwood's* along with the dearth of illustration: *Macmillan's* is more akin to the male medium of the daily newspaper and its politically driven contents of news and information.

  Like the fiction in *Cornhill*, the columns in *Macmillan's* represent an enhancement of its *Blackwood's* model; however, if anything, *Macmillan's* columns are longer and more densely printed than *Blackwood's* and, unrelieved by illustration, the lightness achieved by *Blackwood's* and *Cornhill* is sacrificed. Instead of opening with a novel instalment as *Cornhill* does, the first number of *Macmillan's* begins with a review of domestic and foreign politics. Certainly this difference of design between the pages of *Cornhill* and *Macmillan's* and the different character of the lead articles indicate the distinct gender orientations of the two journals, the one ruling out politics and controversy, and affiliating itself typographically with the literary production of fiction (*Cornhill*) with an eye, famously, to women and family readership, and the other priding itself on the high quality, essay/article which is topical, political, related to news, and typographically more akin to a public print (*Macmillan's*).

The other point about this pair of early shilling monthlies is that they both attempted to define their markets through forms of non-party politics: Thackeray in *Cornhill* deliberately addressed women and children by ruling out party (and indeed all) politics, philosophy, religious controversy, and any (sexual) impropriety, all of which were alleged to render reading unsuitable for the family circle to which the magazine professed to address itself. If *Macmillan's* by its high quality writing and moral rectitude also wished to signal the centrality of respectability to its project, its targeted readership was narrower, promulgating as it did in its early years Christian Socialism as opposed to the old Whig or Tory party politics. While overlapping with *Cornhill* in its *inclusion* of fiction, its gender address was never aimed preponderantly at women *readers*; rather it characterized itself in these early years by identification of its group of principal (male) *contributors*, appropriate for a journal which championed signature; these were known as the 'Tobacco Parliament.' However, like most periodicals the nuanced character of *Macmillan's* varied with the identity of the editor, and fiction and literature flourished more under George Grove (May 1868–April 1883) than it had under David Masson (November 1859–April 1868) at the inception of the journal or under John Morley and Mowbray Morris in the 1880s and 1890s.

The sales of both journals were predictably good but diverse, reflecting the degree of popular appeal of their contents (120,000 copies for early numbers of *Cornhill* and 8,000 to 9,000 for early issues of *Macmilan's*).[26] On their appearance, both of their circulation figures overtook that of *Blackwood's*. David Finkelstein shows that in the two-year period from June 1860 to June 1862 Maga had lost an average of

816 sales *per issue* (from 7,538 to 6,722), and by June 1863 annual sales had fallen from 90,444 in June 1860 to 79,353 in June 1863.[27] By rethinking and refreshing the magazine genre – its appearance and price as well as its contents – these two early shilling monthlies expanded the market significantly beyond the limitations of *Blackwood's* readers. They identified niche markets of middle-class readers based on a lower price[28] and the expansion of the appetite for fiction, and the capacity of monthlies to supplement the weeklies. Even in the wake of the *Saturday Review* in 1855, *Macmillan's* offered, with moderate success at circulation, an admixture of political commentary/analysis, entertaining, well-written essays, and a bit of fiction and poetry to boot.

Just months before *Macmillan's* appeared in November 1859, *Blackwood's* published an anonymous, two-part article, 'Popular Literature – the Periodical Press,' in which the fractionalization of the middle-class monthly market (that is, the *Monthly* Magazine, the *New Monthly*, *Blackwood's*, and *Fraser's*) is identified and limned: 'periodical literature is essentially a classified literature. No matter on what principle the classification proceeds, the result is … to divide and subdivide this kind of literature more and more. It is the rarest thing in the world for a periodical to succeed which does not either represent a class of readers or select a class of subjects.'[29] E.S. Dallas, the anonymous author, concludes that periodicals fail 'because of the want of a speciality,'[30] a characteristic that he welcomes as insurance against 'superficiality.' While Dallas admits that this weakness may be a concomitant danger of the 'frequency' of periodical writing, he denies its *necessity* in this form of popular literature. This argument for specialism in *Blackwood's* seems to tell against its own miscellany, a generality which both *Cornhill*, with its high value on entertainment and its avoidance of politics, and *Macmillan's*, with its serious attachment to current affairs, have narrowed and honed. This implicit juxtaposition of Maga's overall format and the arguments of a contributor is an example of the unacknowledged tension between the character of the brand (the journal) and the opinions of its individual if anonymous journalists that journals without signature generate. However, on anonymity, another key characteristic of Maga, Dallas's defence of the practice is in complete harmony with the title for which he is writing.

The two *Blackwood's* articles on popular literature by Dallas appear in the early months of 1859 in the immediate aftermath of two similarly anonymous pieces by Margaret Oliphant and Wilkie Collins, on the popular press, both of which appeared in August of 1858[31] and together elicited a wide response, of which Dallas's is part: this Dallas makes clear in his reference to 'publications for the million,'[32] a phrase used by both Oliphant and Collins. Oliphant's, appearing in Maga the previous summer, expressed understanding but also dismay at the number and standard of such a readership.[33] Her alarm about the lower classes' vulgarity of taste is transferred to a vehement contempt for the journalists who satiate it: 'in the underground, quite out of sight and ken of the heroes, spreads thick and darkly an undiscriminate multitude,' their fame consisting of 'a certain singular low-lying Jack-o-lantern celebrity, ... the oddest travestie and paraphrase of fame.'[34] Indeed, in its open attempt to distance and decimate writers of popular fiction who pose a threat to the respectability of a genre that was still regarded as 'light,' Oliphant's piece is a close parallel to Marian Evans's/George Eliot's 'Silly Novels by Lady Novelists' in the *Westminster* two years before.[35] On this level, both Maga and the *Westminster* – as high culture serials that published and/or reviewed contemporary literature – had an interest in policing the boundaries of respectable fiction.

Behind the anonymity, these pieces arise out of similar circumstances of the individual journalists writing in this niche as well. Evans (born 1819) and Oliphant (born 1828) were of roughly the same generation, but Evans began to write and publish fiction late in life, just after 'Silly Novels' appeared. Both women were associated with Blackwood's firm, as authors published in Maga and in volume form, Evans/Eliot from 1858 and Oliphant from 1852. Like Eliot, Oliphant was writing her article out of a perceived threat to her own fiction, although she was a seasoned novelist, with some seventeen works of published fiction by 1858, four of them in Maga. However, many of Oliphant's titles seem to fit into visible strands of popular, if middle class, fiction, such as historical fiction, fictional autobiography, etc. The border with working-class, popular fiction, as published in the penny weeklies, had to be made clear to Maga's readers.

In 1858 in 'Byways,' Oliphant notes ironically (and wisely) the taste for fiction that these readers of working-class popular journals share with their betters, and she dismisses as outmoded and misdirected the attempts made by publishers earlier in the century to channel such readers into 'useful knowledge' and spiritual uplift. Her solution is intriguing, in that it bypasses print altogether, by recommending public performances of oral story-telling of high quality fictional narratives – 'Suppose Mr Thackeray and Mr Dickens, instead of monthly numbers yellow and green, had a monthly assembly, and gave forth the story to a visible public.'[36] It is certainly true that Oliphant, in keeping with the clerical base of *Blackwood's* readership, explicitly takes the environs and circle of an Anglican cathedral as the trope of the safety net in which respectable reading is situated, albeit fiction and literature. Even though Oliphant concludes with limning a see-saw relation between the virtues of the old and draw of the new, the piece begins and ends with an image of 'those fair religious walls.'[37] But, for Dallas the function of journalism with respect to working-class readers is unabashedly to teach and lead the way, like clergy with their congregation: 'the true working clergy of the British Isles are the authors and journalists' of the press.[38] The displacement of the clergy in his model, in which journalists occupy the pulpit, is calculated to shock *Blackwood's* readers, and to contrast visibly with the article [by Oliphant] that appeared six months earlier.

The address in Maga to a common topic in close succession by two anonymous contributors whose emphases differ also exposes the tensions of an apparently univocal journal, pounded inexorably by the waves of personality and individual opinion in the early 1860s, before the full case for signature was made afresh by the *Fortnightly* in 1865. All of the titles under consideration here are part of a trajectory of expanding middle-class readership, which does not take in the working-class audience detected anxiously by Oliphant and Collins. However, where *Macmillan's* and *Cornhill* might be viewed as cautious if direct responses to the phenomena of an expanding readership and the fragmentation of the market – in their low price, bright journalism, avoidance of party politics, approach to signature and, in *Cornhill*, large dollops of illustration and fiction, what was *Blackwood's* response to the challenge to expand its share of the beckoning market?

Immediately before the rolling out of the shilling monthlies, from November 1859, the profile of *Blackwood's* was not one in which fiction was predominant. It took the position of the lead article only once in that year (in January); there was usually one serial novel a month, and occasionally two, but in one number there was none. There was a regular inclusion of book reviews (eleven appeared in seven numbers) which included fiction, poetry, theology/religious history, foreign affairs, and Classical literature. International and domestic politics were both ingredients of every issue, with the position of the last article always reserved for politics, as a kind of leader. Its counterbalance, the lead or first article, was divided among military (two), literature (two), Scottish history (one), London art exhibitions (one), and international travel (two). Its targeting of English and Scottish readers, and of men and women is evident from this profile, and its (Tory) politics is pervasive.

From the profile of *Blackwood's* in 1860, it might be argued that it positioned itself primarily as a rival to *Macmillan's*, but inside it had its eye on rivalling the *Cornhill* as well. Serial novels were in the lead only in two numbers, January and February of that year, at the launch of the *Cornhill*. Presumably that launch was the reason January carried three fiction titles, but one or two was the pattern in the issues that followed, with one number (May) having none at all. But there is a significant element of supporting literary criticism which, combined with the fiction, makes the 1860 profile significantly more literary than that of 1859. After February, however, Maga led with articles calculated to attract male readers, on military topics, on domestic and foreign politics, and (unusually) on science (G.H. Lewes in 'Seeing is Believing'). Other articles continue the topics already established as characteristic of *Blackwood's*: international and domestic politics; military topics; Scottish history and culture; Protestant/religious history; and visual art.

The 1860s might be characterized as the period of the second wave of signature, following that of Henry Colburn's eye for the commerce of celebrity in his *New Monthly Magazine* (1814 onwards), with its famous, publicized editors and editorial treatment of famous writers,[39] and *Blackwood's* and *Fraser's Magazine's* development of an array of indicators of authorship short of transparent signature in the ensuing forty years. Two new media enterprises staked their fortunes to signature in the second wave. The first of the shilling monthlies, *Macmillan's Magazine*, when it first appeared in the autumn of 1859, included signature in its prospectus,[40] and six years later a liberal journal of quite a different kind – a review, published *fortnightly* – similarly adapted signature, and even more publicly attacked anonymity. However, the progress of signature was slow. Debate continued for decades among journalists, and in a variety of guises, surfacing for example in charge and counter-charge with respect to 'puffing' and 'log-rolling.'[41]

The Reviews

The appearance of the *Fortnightly Review* in 1865, and the new reviews that followed it (the *Contemporary* in 1866, its successor the *Nineteenth Century* in 1877, and the *National* in 1883) also had an impact on the monthly magazine, in two other respects. The fortnightly interval of the first of the new reviews gave way to monthly publication within a year, and all of the subsequent reviews were issued monthly. Reviews now entered into direct competition with magazines in the monthly market. Moreover, these new reviews did not confine themselves to reviews of new titles, but resembled magazines in the catholicity and variety, indeed the miscellany of their contents. Thus the distinguishing characteristics of the older, expensive reviews – their quarterly frequency and their tie to review articles – gave way in the new reviews to monthly publications that resemble magazines far more than their forebears, including the publication of serialized fiction and poetry, as well as literary reviews. The new reviews still, however, purport to be 'weightier' than magazines, and expensive, costing at least double the price of the shilling monthlies. According to Finkelstein's overall sales figures, *Blackwood's* lost a total of 1,500 sales between June 1865 and June 1866, and another 4,500 between June 1866 and June 1867, which seems to suggest that readership of *Blackwood's*, with its archaic cover and adhesion to anonymity, was vulnerable to the lure of the monthly reviews, in which controversy and signature were freely proclaimed. Each manifesto of the successive new journals offered different cases for a reshaping of the serial as a form, with the *Fortnightly* refuelling the argument for signature, and the *Contemporary* intending to provide a medium for debate of theological questions as they pertain to the common subjects of public discourse. While it might be thought that neither of these directly impinge on *Blackwood's*, these new reviews appropriate the characteristic *miscellany* form of the magazine along with its frequency. The monthly market is not only significantly more crowded and competitive,[42] but also entered by a genre whose format, once quite distinctive generically and distant from the magazine, now resembles it.

   The collapse of the review as a genre into a new rhythm of monthly issue in the 1860s should be seen as part of a well-established blurring of genres, with titles appearing at more than one frequency. Thus weeklies had long been available in weekly and monthly editions; even an advertisement in the *Athenaeum*, for *Once a Week*, a publication whose periodicity is part of its title, states baldly '"Once a Week" is published in Weekly Numbers, price 2d, early on Wednesday Mornings, in time for the Morning Mails; and in Monthly Parts.'[43] And, the move of the *Fortnightly Review* towards yet another genre – that of the daily newspaper – is evident in its initial and preferred fortnightly frequency of publication; it only settled for monthly latterly as second best, and after the monthly *Contemporary Review* emerged as the first of the new *monthly* reviews of the 1860s. Another example of this tendency on the part of publishers to maximize their markets by transformation of one media form into that of another is *Good Words*, a monthly costing 6d. It advertises itself as 'The Serial of Serials' because it is made up of, not 'separate papers,' but 'serial works by the most eminent living authors,' 'each [annual] volume of GOOD WORDS forming a complete *book*.'[44] This transformation of serial to book is commonplace, both in part-issues which result in a complete book, observable both in fiction and reference works, but also generally in periodicals themselves, which routinely publish volumes at six- or twelve-month intervals for libraries, or issue boards for private readers to bind their accumulated parts. Another element of the *Good Words* advertisement reminds us, reading retrospectively in the knowledge of the authorship of *Blackwood's* contributors, that anonymity masked the shared pool of authors which the nineteenth-century titles drew upon, meaning that the same authors contributed to a range of journals. Thus, E.S. Dallas is prominently advertised as the editor of *Once a Week*, while at the same time he may have been writing anonymously for other titles. This draws our attention to the needs of the publishing industry at the time, whose members warmed to more frequent publication which provided more opportunity for paid work and a living. So, while the older quarterly reviews appeared every fourth month, the new ones appear every month; while the quarterlies confined themselves to reviewing, the new reviews had the same mobility as magazines to respond relatively quickly and topically to public debate, and the flexibility to serialize fiction, columns, and articles, in order to capture readers for successive issues. Moreover, the new reviews cost a fraction of the old, and roughly the same as *Blackwood's*.

When the *Fortnightly Review* began in 1865 on 15 May, it featured signed articles by respected figures such as Walter Bagehot, Trollope, George Eliot, Moncure Conway, G.H. Lewes, Frederic Harrison, and F.T. Palgrave. The variety of subjects matched the miscellaneous character of any magazine one could name, and included constitutional law, current American politics, science (biology and physics), literary criticism, and trade unions. There were reviews of philosophy and new books generally, and there was a serialized novel by Trollope. Strahan's *Contemporary Review* with a theological/literary remit began six months later in January 1866, and is alleged to have been 'the *Fortnightly* of the Established Church' by design.[45] While it carried no fiction in these early numbers, its regular treatment of visual art from the first number (which included a piece on Christian art), music, aspects of religion such as 'Sunday' and hymn books, as well as theology, might attract the more serious woman reader, who was also addressed by one-off articles on the education of women, Trollope and the clergy, and a review of Browning's poetry. The *Contemporary*'s orientation to theological issues develops what is a regular topic in Maga, but not a filter through which other material is viewed. If the *Contemporary* was pitched as an up-market sister to Strahan's popular magazines for the religious market niche, it represented both an upmarket and specialized alternative to Maga as well.

By comparison, *Blackwood's* of 1866, as seen in a sample of its March and November issues, seems decidedly weighted towards fiction, per-haps with *Cornhill* prominently in mind. Both numbers locate double doses of fiction at the front of the journal; in March a review of a religious novel is followed by an instalment of serial fiction, and the November number is led by successive serial parts of two novels; each number includes three novels in all, accompanied by almost equal weighting of politics, domestic and foreign. The last slot in each num-ber is allocated to politics. Other significant topics are American Civil War memoirs, historical biography, and religion. On this profile, with a high proportion of fiction, the presence of religion in each issue, and the inclusion of historical biography, *Blackwood's* could be said to be target-ing women readers as well as men, and to make an appeal to family readers comparable to *Cornhill* rather than to largely male readers as might be extrapolated from both *Macmillan's Magazine* and the *Fort-nightly*, with their high proportion of politics, science and economics.

By 1867, however, the prominence if not the proportion of fiction in *Blackwood's* has significantly dropped. The lead positions are occupied by the second part of a series on military history (March) and fiction (November). In March the fiction element is delayed with the two novel instalments back to back just before the last political piece. Thus the number looks more immediately inviting to male readers, and more of a match, in its own way, to *Macmillan's* and even the *Fortnightly*. The military is a consistent thread of copy in *Blackwood's*, as are some of the other topics of the 1867 tranche, such as the history of Scotland, foreign travel, and domestic and international politics. As in *Macmillan's* and the *Fortnightly* in the 1860s, American politics is a recurring subject. Rather than a 'literary' magazine, *Blackwood's* is at this point finely balanced between arts and humanities and politics/social science. This balance arguably reflects its primary competition in the mid 1860s, the belles lettrist *Cornhill* and the more political *Macmillan's* and *Fortnightly*

Review. While these proportions change throughout the century in response to the market, and other elements come and go, the ingredients of *Blackwood's* remain relatively consistent. Thus *Blackwood's* was never a preponderantly 'literary' journal, in the narrow twentieth-century sense of literary. In an important article on the Romantic press in 1993, Marilyn Butler has an apt phrase for upmarket serials such as *Blackwood's*, which she calls 'culture's medium.'[46] In this piece she is making an argument to extend the notion of what constitutes the 'literary,' to include consideration by critics of the non-fictional materials which fill the magazines and reviews that have been appropriated by English literary critics to the field of English Literature. I want to extend her nomenclature to serials at all levels of the market (cultures' media), and to endorse her argument that the study of the periodical press requires approaches tailored to the whole of periodical texts.

By 1877 the proportion of serial fiction in *Blackwood's* drops to two serials per number in a sample of March and November (five out of fourteen articles in total), but both the March and November issues lead with it. However there is a new preponderance of articles with an international element (Montenegro, India, Asia, Russo/Turkey), two articles out of seven in March and four out of seven in November; of these a high proportion pertain to travel abroad. Military topics make up a quarter of the November number, with no arts balance except the fiction, whereas the fiction in March is bastioned by a critical article on Balzac. Literature, then, holds its own in March, beside two travel articles, and two political. This admixture of fiction, military subjects, and Tory politics, always in the context of Scotland, the London Parliament, and the Empire, is a fair indicator of the profile of *Blackwood's* for the duration of the century. In the 1877 March and November sample, similar Scottish, military, political, and international topics are recurrent, with a slightly smaller proportion of literary contents (fiction and criticism) – five articles out of a total of seventeen. Still, the mixture clearly signals that the target readership includes both male and female readers, in both domestic and imperial locations, with a still discernible appeal to Scottish readers, whether at home or abroad. It should also be noted that *Blackwood's* makes few if any concessions to the new journalism in the type of article it publishes; interviews, personalities, and more personal journalism are not in much evidence, nor are illustrations or signature introduced.[47] However, as Laurence Davies points out later in this collection in '"A sideways ending to it all": G.W. Steevens, Blackwood, and the *Daily Mail*,' the irony is that despite its resistance to such brash, new journalist forms of literary reportage, *Blackwood's*, in publishing work by George W. Steevens, would become a major promoter of the career of one of the most vibrant new journalists of the *fin-de-siècle* period.

Snapshot 1868: The *Athenaeum Adverts*

It is useful to examine a horizontal slice of advertisements for journals in the *Athenaeum* in 1868, after the shilling monthlies had bedded in, and with the added competition of the initial crop of new Reviews. I have selected an issue at the beginning of a month, when notices for monthly journals tend to appear. Advertisements for monthly journals issued that week fall into two categories, those that foreground the *topics* of articles to supplement the draw of the title of the journal and those that feature the authorship of articles, the former being (still) anonymous and the latter advertising the new lure of signature. Thus the anonymous *Chambers's Journal* – like *Blackwood's*, Scottish and long established, *Cornhill*, a most successful pioneer of the shilling monthlies, and Maga itself rely solely in their advertisements on the unembroidered type of marketable topics such as 'Cigarettes' (*Chambers Journal*), 'A Dialogue on Finality' (*Cornhill*), and 'Clever Women' (*Blackwood's*). Representatives of the signature camp, which stretches on this page from the popular shilling monthly *London Society* to the intellectually abrasive and expensive *Contemporary Review: Theological, Literary and Social*, tend to rely on the names of their contributors, who include the authoritative Dean of Canterbury writing 'The Church of the Future' (*Contemporary Review*), the names of an array of medical experts whose names precede the titles of their articles in the advertisement for the *Journal of Mental Science*, and the celebrity-like Robert Buchanan[48] writing in *London Society*. It is notable that journals attached to scientific/medical fields and theology, which were developing rapidly as professions by this date, are among the first to call on accountable individuals of status to bastion their claim to the authority and truth of specialist knowledge disseminated by the journals. Titles that address a wider, heterogeneous readership and openly dedicate themselves to entertainment (as well as instruction) draw on celebrities – in so far as they do, not as guarantors of knowledge but primarily for consideration of business, of sales. So, what are we to make of the *Blackwood's* phenomenon?

According to the *Wellesley Index*, the line-up of authors writing for

Blackwood's in the October 1868 number advertised here includes two well-known novelists of the day, Margaret Oliphant and Charles Lever, a prolific economist and academic (Bonamy Price), the Chaplain General to the Forces, G.R. Gleig, and the experienced journalist, Anne Mozley, on 'Clever Women.' However, the attribution of authorship to named individuals is neither permitted by the Blackwoods to subvert or supplement the authority of the firm's name that the journal bears, nor its affiliation with Scotland, to which its antiquarian logo of George Buchanan on the cover refers.[49] The magazine functions then as the firm's flagship, displaying its name prominently, trailing (and financially supporting) its authors, and carrying free advertising for its lists on which these authors appear in the regular monthly issues. Examination of these lists shows that of the authors published anonymously in the October 1868 issue, a large majority were published in volume form by Blackwood, sometimes under their own names and sometimes anonymously.[50] The co-presence of authors in Maga and on the Blackwood list is a strong indicator that the functions of the journal from the firm's point of view were primarily viewed in the 1860s (and perhaps more generally backward and forward) within the framework of the publishing firm as a whole, rather than as a freestanding journal, as the advertisement implies.

In this respect it is germane that two other journals, *Macmillan's Magazine* and the *Fortnightly Review*, similarly located within publishing firms and potential 'flagship' journals, are advertised in this issue of the *Athenaeum* in conjunction with adverts for their respective house lists. It is notable that these are the two journals promulgating signature most vigorously at the time, and that the attribution of authorship in the journals takes its place beside the named authors in the respective publishers' lists of Macmillan and Chapman and Hall. Blackwood's list, not advertised here, is interestingly more likely to publish anonymous volumes that echo its journal practice. Their issue of the first and second series of Anne Mozley's essays, for example, in 1864 and 1865, is anonymous, with the 1864 edition entitled *Essays on Social Subjects from the 'Saturday Review,'* and an 1892 edition called *Essays from 'Blackwood,'* similarly anonymous. That Anne Mozley's journalism may have been anonymous through strong authorial preference[51] does not weaken the point that this mode of publication continued to be favoured by and characteristic of the *firm*[52] as well as the author, at a time when commercially 'names' were beginning to attract readers and purchasers.

In both the monthly reviews and the *Strand*, the new journalism of the 1880s and 1890s personalized journalism, introducing individual authorial signature and foregrounding authorial names over that of the 'house.' The interview and further illustration were other popular ingredients added to fiction in the magazines. These and the collapse of the three-volume novel from 1894 which re-enforced the shift to short fiction in the magazines, evident already in the *Strand*, impacted on the Maga model of monthly serial fiction, still largely unsigned. By the end of the century, weeklies had taken over many of the political functions that Maga had served in the past, and a brighter, racier, more demotic new journalism marked monthly magazines such as the *Strand* which, at 6d, was considerably cheaper than Maga or indeed the shilling monthlies.

Conclusion

Looking at two sample issues of *Blackwood's* in 1895 in March and November, there are few concessions to the new journalism. It retains its characteristic elements: the military, travel articles including one on ballooning, strong international interest, a modicum of fiction, and Scotland, but there are differences. The Scottish element is very strong, with three pieces in one issue (March) and two in the other; this may not only be a renewed bid for indigenous Scots, but also for the many abroad in the church, in business, or in the Foreign Service in the Empire. The fiction element is modest in comparison, and includes a short story, reflecting the enhanced interest in that form of fiction evident in the periodical market as well as the recent collapse of the three-volume format of novel publication. Novels themselves were shrinking to accommodate what would soon be the dominant one-volume format. What seem to me most indicative in *Blackwood's* of the impact of the new journalism are the muted element of politics, which in these sample issues retains a token presence in the last slot in each number, and a high incidence of signature, which creeps in, in ones, twos, threes, and fours per number from the mid-1880s.[53] But through 1895 anonymity and signature co-exist in Maga, apparently dependent on the author's preference. Margaret Oliphant, a veteran contributor to Maga, largely holds out for anonymity, but in the January 1896 number for example, to which she contributes two pieces, she does not sign the lead short story, but 'The anti-marriage league,' situated in the penultimate slot of the number, is signed with initials, M.O.W.O. In obscuring its reliance on a single author for two contributions to the same number, the journal serves its own as well as the author's interests: she does not appear as a hack, and their pool of contributors does not appear deficient or biased.

Nevertheless, comparison of the *Strand*, one of the new journalism's quintessential products, with *Blackwood's* of 1895 suggests that the latter's protracted abandonment of anonymity and its halting moves toward signature do not prevent its contents, design, and make-up from appearing as a vestige of an earlier tradition of literary journal publishing. Serving the Empire, Tory rural readers, and Scotland, Blackwood's turned to its old reading community and faced away from the new. From the perspective of the mass market about to be mobilized by the creation of the *Daily Mail* in 1896, of which the *Strand* is a sign, *Blackwood's* appears expensive, unillustrated, and essentially non-urban, a pioneer of the magazine genre that eluded modernity. T.H. Escott, writing the retrospective review 'Thirty Years of the Periodical Press' in *Blackwood's* in October 1894, appositely called his host 'the most historic of all our periodicals.'[54]

NOTES

1 The *London Magazine* (1820–9) was undoubtedly a rival, as may be seen in its initial robust critique of *Blackwood's* tone, style, and anonymity. Its imitation of *Blackwood's* appears limited, except in so far as its own conduct is presented as the obverse of *Maga's*. Mark Parker agrees (Mark Parker, *Literary Magazines and British Romanticism* [Cambridge: Cambridge University Press, 2000, 137]), while noting that they 'share one premise: that politics and literature cannot be separated.'

2 *Fraser's Magazine* 2 (1831), 95.

3 For this and further comparison between the two journals, see J. Don Vann, 'Fraser's Magazine,' in *British Literary Magazines: The Romantic Age, 1789–1836*, ed. Alvin Sullivan, 4 vol. (Westport, Conn.: Greenwood, 1983), 2:171–5.

4 This is an account of puffing which merits reading in its own right.

5 *Fraser's Magazine* 2 (1831), 745.

6 Ibid.

7 See 'Blackwood's Magazine,' *Wellesley Index to Victorian Periodicals*, ed. Walter E. Houghton (Toronto and London: University of Toronto Press and Routledge, 1966), 1, Item #36 and #64, for example.

8 David, Finkelstein, 'Appendix 2,' in *The House of Blackwood: Author–*

Publisher Relations in the Victorian Era (University Park: Pennsylvania State University Press, 2002), 165–6.

9 This may be seen in the period June 1864/June 65 when the shilling monthlies were bedded in and the *Fortnightly Review* arrived: advertising went up to a peak of £355/4/3 and loss of sales was limited to 185 over the year; for the same period profits rose to over £5000, a figure to which it never returned, once this dual market of the shilling monthlies and the new Reviews appeared. Similarly, a modest rise of £36 in advertising costs between June 1869 and June 1870 (part of a steady rise of advertising expenditure 1868–72) results in holding sales from the previous year (minus seventy-four copies) and a modest rise in profits (of £64). Other factors in the rise of profits not visible here include the costs of production and the revenue from advertisements in the *Blackwood's Advertiser.*

10 Annual sales in these years are 77,872 for the year ending June 1866, and 73,327 for the year ending June 1867 (Finkelstein, *House of Blackwood* [2002], 165). By June 1869, the figure is 68,982. The *Fortnightly* went monthly from January 1867.

11 Sales soared from 65,595 in the year ending June 1876 to 68,988 in the year ending June 1877.

12 Finkelstein, *House of Blackwood*, 76–90.

13 Ibid., 88.

14 Murray was, however, a Scottish publisher gone south.

15 'Appendix,' *Blackwood's Magazine* 67 (February 1850), 9.

16 The sample pagination that follows shows that the quarterlies were at least twice the length of *Blackwood's* monthly numbers: *Blackwood's Magazine:* 120 pages (April 1817), 124 pages (January 1868); *Edinburgh Review:* 273 pages (March 1817), 300 pages (January 1868); *Quarterly Review:* 240 pages (February 1817), 286 pages (January 1868).

17 The earliest example listed in *Wellesley* (which only begins its index of *Blackwood's Edinburgh Magazine* in 1825) is March 1825, in which G.R. Gleig's *The Subaltern*'s first of seven instalments began. Afterwards, further serial fiction commences in January 1827, August 1830, March 1834, etc; in the 1840s similar intervals between serial fiction occurs: February 1842; September 1844 (two parts only); December 1846; April 1848. By comparison, there are regular and numerous serialized belles lettres articles from the beginning.

18 This trend was present in *Blackwood's* advertising throughout the late nineteenth century. Advertisements in the 'Blackwood's Advertiser' for November 1884, 12–15, for example, indicate through their address to

women consumers that the proportion of women among Maga's readers was sufficiently high to warrant expenditure on gendered products. Specifically, the advertisement for Fry's Cocoa on p. 15 is accompanied underneath by display adverts for Brussels (knitting) wool, 'artistic wall-papers,' and 'Southall's Sanitary Towel for Ladies.' A different type of appeal may be found in Hurst and Blackett's list on p. 13. All of their titles listed here are popular, from *The Life and Adventures of Peg Woffington* to *The Pictorial Press: Its Origins and Progress*, and could address Maga's consumers of 'light' reading of both sexes, but appended to these 'New Works' is a list of 'New and Popular Novels' titles, including *Joy, Love and Mirage, Cyclamen,* and *We Two,* which seem particularly addressed to women.

19 I could find no such copies in either the British Library or the Senate House Library, University of London.

20 It should be noted that the occasion of the dual between representatives of *Blackwood's* and the editor of the rival *London Magazine* (1820–9), John Scott, turned on the anonymity policy of Blackwood's. Scott accused Lock-hart publicly in the *London Magazine* of hiding behind anonymity, as both editor of *Blackwood's* and author of various scurrilous remarks on living writers that appeared routinely in the journal. Scott was fatally wounded in the dual in February 1821. For pertinent critique of the dual and the relationship of *Blackwood's* with the *London Magazine,* see Parker, *Literary Magazines,* 135–7. For more on the *London Magazine,* see Helen B. Ellis, 'The London Magazine,' in *British Literary Magazines,* ed. Sullivan, 288–96.

21 For interesting work on the meaning and ploys of journals of this period, see David Higgins on 'personality' and pseudonyms in Maga, and his quotation of Peter Murphy: '*Blackwood's Edinburgh Magazine* and the Con-struction of Wordsworth's Genius,' *Prose Studies* 25 (April 2002), 123–4. For other very interesting current work on anonymity in journals of romanti-cism, see also Mary Poovey, 'Forgotten Writers, Neglected Histories', *ELH* 71 (2004), 436–7, Margaret Russett, *De Quincey's Romanticism* (Cambridge: Cambridge University Press, 1997), and Peter T. Murphy, 'Impersonation and Authorship in Romantic Britain,' *ELH* 59 (1992), 625–49.

22 'Appendix,' *Blackwood's Magazine* 67 (February 1850), 90.

23 .Quarterly editors did attempt to create as much latitude as they could within this form through careful *selection* of publications for review, and also the generic freedom of turning reviews into essays, as Walter Bagehot famously noted in 'The First *Edinburgh* Reviewers,' *National Review* 1 (October 1855), 253–84.

24 The force of this identity may still be seen today when on book jackets or theatre or film posters, favourable quotations from reviews are often attributed to the *Times*, or the *Guardian*, and not to Claire Tomalin or Michael Billington.

25 Thackeray revealed his own and Trollope's authorship of the two serialized novels carried in the first number in his editorial 'Roundabout Paper' with which that issue ended.

26 More on the origins of *Macmillan's* may be found in George Worth, *Macmillan's Magazine* (Aldershot, Hants: Ashgate 2003) from which these figures are quoted (15).

27 Finkelstein, *The House of Blackwood*, 165.

28 *Longman's Magazine*, a 6d monthly which rivalled *Macmillan's*, only appeared over thirty years later in November 1882, just a few months before the advent in March 1883 of a new Tory monthly, the *National Review*, that threatened to reduce the readership of *Blackwood's Magazine*.

29 *Blackwood's Magazine* 85 (January 1859), 103.

30 Ibid.

31 The anonymously published pieces are Wilkie Collins's 'The Unknown Public,' *Household Words* (21 August 1858), 217–22 and Margaret Oliphant's 'Byways of Literature: Reading for the Million,' *Blackwood's Magazine* 84 (August 1858), 200–16.

32 *Blackwood's Magazine* 85 (January 1859), 101.

33 See [Oliphant], 'The Byways of Literature,' 200–16.

34 Ibid., 204.

35 [Marian Evans], 'Silly Novels by Lady Novelists,' *Westminster Review* 66 (1856), 442–61. It is notable that Oliphant also makes the gender link between middle-class fiction and women, stating as her first observation about the nature of serials in popular 6d journals such as the *London Journal* that 'The lowest range, like the highest range, admits no women,' unlike 'the fiction feminine, which fills with mild domestic volumes the middle class of this species of literature' ([Oliphant], 'The Byways of Literature,' 206).

36 [Oliphant], 'The Byways of Literature,' 206.

37 Ibid., 216.

38 *Blackwood's Magazine* 85 (January 1859), 110. Compare W.T. Stead's trope for the press in 1885, 'Government by Journalism.' For Stead, the social institution displaced by journalism was parliamentary government, rather than the Church. Given *Blackwood's* earlier date (pre Darwinian) and Tory affiliation, the Church is both apposite and predictable.

39 Editors of the *New Monthly Magazine* who were public figures included the poet Thomas Campbell (1821–30), Bulwer (1831–3), Theodore Hook (1837–41) and Thomas Hood (1841–3). Many 'original papers' were publicly attributed through the use of initials, pseudonyms, or reference to 'By the author of,' while other feature articles such as the series 'On the Cockney School of Prose' (1818–19), which echoed *Blackwood's* naming and coverage of the Cockney School of poetry, supplemented *New Monthly Magazine's* fledgling signature by trailing the famous in more conventional ways. For more on the *New Monthly Magazine* see W. Paul Elledge, in *British Literary Magazines*, ed. Sullivan, 331–9.

40 Thomas Hughes was a strong advocate of signature. See George J. Worth, *Macmillan's Magazine, 1859–1907* (Aldershot, Hants: Ashgate, 2003), 9.

41 For more on these issues see Laurel Brake, *Subjugated Knowledges* (Basingstoke: Macmillan, 1994), 19–32.

42 The monthly market continued to hold its own as one of the dominant frequencies for print culture of the nineteenth century. In addition to the monthly magazines and the new monthly reviews, new books lists from publishers appeared monthly, as did many of those works that appeared in part-issue, such as some of Dickens's and Thackeray's fiction, and works of reference such as Encyclopaedias and Dictionaries.

43 *Athenaeum* 2100 (25 January 1868), 114.

44 Ibid., 140, my emphasis.

45 'The *Contemporary Review*, 1866–1900,' *Wellesley Index to Victorian Periodicals*, ed. Walter Houghton (Toronto and London: University of Toronto Press and Routledge, 1966), 1:211.

46 Marilyn Butler, 'Culture's Medium: The Role of the Review,' in *The Cambridge Companion to British Romanticism*, ed. S. Curran (Cambridge: Cambridge University Press, 1993), 120–47. There are a number of issues in this suggestive piece that merit discussion; its signposts for future scholarship are many and varied. One relevant point here is that where Butler deploys 'review' as a general term for Romantic journals, I am distinguishing formally between the review and the magazine.

47 One part of the magazine that may well reflect the new journalism is the adverts of the 1880s onward. I have not examined the advertisers.

48 Robert Buchanan (1841–1901) was a Glaswegian, who came to London in 1860, and published poetry, fiction, and criticism. By 1868 he had venomously (and anonymously) attacked Swinburne's work in a poem in the *Spectator* (1866), and had published eight volumes of poetry (1862–8), a collection of critical essays, and a biography of J.J. Audubon.

49 George Buchanan (1506–82) was tutor to James VI and I, a convert to

Protestantism, and an enemy of Mary Queen of Scots. He is probably best known as the writer in Latin of an early history of Scotland.

50 Of the six contributors to the October 1868 number, five either were past and/or future authors published in volume form by Blackwood: R.E. Francillon's novel *Earl's Dene* was published serially in Maga, and then in volumes in 1870, and Oliphant's *Historical Sketches of the Reign of George the Second* appeared in volume form in 1869. For the publication by Blackwood of Gleig, Mozley, and Lever see n. 52 below.

51 Mozley, the daughter of a bookseller and publisher herself, was eight years older than *Blackwood's* in 1868. Writing anonymously throughout her career, as a poet, children's author, editor, and journalist for a variety of papers, this woman of letters (b. 1809) avoided publicity like many other women of her generation, including Charlotte Brontë (b. 1816), George Eliot (b. 1819), and Harriet Martineau (b. 1802).

52 Of the six authors published in the October 1868 number of Maga, three appeared anonymously in Blackwood volumes, including Mozley's. Charles Lever's series, *Cornelius O'Dowd*, had appeared previously in three anonymous Blackwood volumes in 1864–5, and G.R. Gleig's *The Subaltern*, published anonymously by the firm over forty years before in 1825 reappeared anonymously from Blackwood in 1872. Gleig's piece on Disraeli in the October 1868 number was part of a regular series of anonymous articles on contemporary politics that he wrote for Maga in the wake of the Second Reform Act between December 1867 and December 1868, having commented on the Reform Bill itself in the May 1867 number. Parts of this series may have been subsumed into his *Letters on the Irish Question* (Rivington, 1868).

53 Oscar Wilde's 'Portrait of Mr. W.H.,' which appeared as the lead article in July 1889, for example, was one of five signatures in that number.

54 T.H. Escott, 'Thirty Years of the Periodical Press,' *Blackwood's Magazine* 156 (October 1894), 532–42.

PRESERVING STATUS

At the Court of *Blackwood's*: In the Kampong of Hugh Clifford

LINDA DRYDEN

Of the writers who contributed imperial stories to *Blackwood's Edinburgh Magazine* in the late nineteenth and early twentieth centuries, Sir Hugh Clifford was in good company: Joseph Conrad had contributed imperial fiction to 'Maga,' notably, *Heart of Darkness* (1899) and *Lord Jim* (1900); and Sir Frank Swettenham was also a regular contributor. What singles out Clifford from his close friend Conrad, however, is the fact that Clifford's stories were almost exclusively concerned with life in the Malay Archipelago during the period of British governance in the province. While Conrad, through his experiences as a merchant seaman, was writing stories that dealt largely with the white man's struggle to maintain European 'civilization' in the backwaters of empire, Clifford was trying to convey to his readers the sense of Malay life as he had experienced it, first as secretary to the Resident of the region, and later as Resident of Pahang himself. Clifford had a far more intimate and comprehensive knowledge of Malaya than did Conrad, and his writings remain valuable because of the detail in which he describes, in the words of Anthony Stockwell, his 'activities in Malaya together with his descriptions of Malay society, his analysis and response to it, and his views on the role of Europeans in the East.'[1]

Clifford found considerable favour with *Blackwood's* because his subject matter was very much in convergence with the conservative atmosphere of Maga: while his tales of Malays and their governing Europeans were sympathetically drawn from life, they rarely questioned the legitimacy of British rule in the region. Since the magazine was staple reading for British officers in the colonies, Clifford's stories of endurance, and his 'authentic' Malay tales were particularly appropriate. Those serving in the far-flung empire recognized his experiences as their own, and those at home were enthralled by the seemingly exotic reality of Clifford's contributions. Further, as J. de V. Allen points out, Clifford's literary offerings 'set him apart, historically speaking, from his contemporaries': 'He wrote hardly at all in the Maugham vein about white colonists and their problems; far more about the relationships between Europeans and Malays, or, in some short stories, about Malays or Chinese alone or even Aborigines: a daring topic which only Clifford, perhaps, would at the time have been prepared to tackle.'[2] For William Roff, Clifford's stories of the native peoples of the Malay Archipelago are observed 'so far as Clifford was able, with sympathy and insight.'[3] It was for this reason that Clifford, for a time, found himself being compared favourably with Conrad. Harry Gailey goes so far as to suggest that Blackwood and John Murray 'considered him to be in the first rank of practicing writers.'[4] This is high praise for one whose primary career was that of imperial officer.

Clifford's career as a colonial representative, and later as Governor, Straits Settlements, and then High Commissioner, Malay States, has been well documented.[5] His long and close friendship with Conrad has also been explored in some detail.[6] Except for the recent work of Philip Holden, Clifford's literary career has received scant attention, and collections of his stories, many of which were published in *Blackwood's*, are hard to come by in Britain. The following discussion will explore Clifford's work for *Blackwood's* and suggest the reasons why he was regarded with such approval by Blackwood and John Murray. Doing so also offers insight into the imperial context of *Blackwood's Edinburgh Magazine* and the editorial policy of its editors. Blackwood's correspondence with Clifford reveals significant respect for his work, and underlines how Clifford was actively courted by the editor because of the nature of his work. In the light of such approbation, Clifford's published stories in Maga are significant in that they exemplify the atmosphere of imperial preoccupation that typified the magazine in the late nineteenth and early twentieth centuries.

Clifford, Malaya, and Literature

Clifford's first published collection of fiction, *East Coast Etchings*, initially appeared in *The Straits Times* in 1896, and was later expanded into *In Court and Kampong* (1897). In his preface to the 1897 edition of the latter, Clifford claims that he has 'striven throughout to appreciate the Malay point of view, and to judge the people and their actions by their own standards, rather than by those of the white man living in their midst.' With more than a hint of sad regret, he states that the conditions of life in the Independent Malay States about which he writes 'are rapidly passing away.'[7] By the time Clifford wrote his preface to the 1927 edition of the volume he can claim for his work a significance that reaches beyond traditional perceptions of literary value: 'Today my tales are to be valued, not only as historical, but as archaeological studies.'[8] In many ways this is a remarkable realization, prefiguring as it does the postmodern recognition of the relationship between literature and cultural history; but, more to the point, Clifford's statement is mingled with sadness and regret for a culture which he saw as irrevocably changed by the imperialist project. Having been one of the most respected of imperial administrators, Clifford left Malaya for the last time in 1927 disillusioned and deeply doubting the cause to which he had devoted his life.[9]

Clifford was a remarkable man. He was first and foremost an officer in the colonial service, and only secondly a writer; and it was his firsthand knowledge of the life and peoples of the Malay Archipelago that led him to write so many stories from the point of view of the 'native' subject. Like his friend Joseph Conrad, Clifford had a desire to 'make you see,' and he became a friend of Conrad's after the latter's review of *Studies in Brown Humanity* (1898), 'An Observer in Malay.'[10] Conrad's article is eloquent and sensitive in its appraisal of Clifford's evocation of Malaya: 'And of all the nations conquering distant territories in the name of the most excellent intentions, England alone sends out men who, with such a transparent sincerity of feeling, can speak, as Mr. Clifford does, of the place of toil and exile as "the land which is very dear to me, where the best years of my life have been spent" – and where (I would stake my right hand on it) his name is pronounced with respect and affection by those brown men about whom he writes.'[11] Whilst drawing attention to his ability to convey 'the very breath of Malay thought and speech,'[12] Conrad makes it quite plain that he believes that Clifford's skills lie more in colonial administration than literary achievement. Thus he concludes: 'The Resident of Pahang has the devoted friendship of Ûmat,[13] the punkah-puller, he has an individual faculty of vision, a large sympathy, and the scrupulous consciousness of the good and evil in his hands. He may as well rest content with such gifts. One cannot expect to be, at the same time, a ruler of men and an irreproachable player on the flute.'[14] Clifford, Conrad avers, has 'gifts of his own, and his genius has served his country and his fortunes in another direction.'[15] Despite their resulting firm friendship, in September of the same year Clifford wrote an article in which he deplored Conrad's 'complete ignorance of Malays and their habits and customs,'[16] and Conrad himself recalls how, on their first meeting, Clifford accused him of not knowing 'anything about Malays.'[17] Conrad claims he responded to this with, 'Of course I don't know anything about Malays. If I knew only one hundredth part of what you and Frank Swettenham know of Malays I would make everybody sit up.'[18] Conrad was referring, of course to Clifford and Swettenham's long careers as colonial administrators which provided them with an in-depth knowledge of the Malay Archipelago and its people.

Clifford was originally destined for the army but, on the death of his father, he was invited by Frederick Weld, his father's cousin and Governor of the Straits Settlements, to embark on a colonial career. Clifford was immediately appointed secretary to the Resident of Perak, Hugh Low, in September 1883. Between 1896 and 1899 Clifford was the Resident of Pahang, with a brief spell as Governor of North Borneo from February 1900 until March 1901 when he returned to his post in Pahang.[19] Prolonged illness forced him to return to England in 1901.[20] He convalesced at Hampton Court until September 1903 when he set sail for Trinidad to take up the post of Colonial Secretary at the request of Joseph Chamberlain. He was knighted for his services to the Empire in 1909 and returned to Malaya in 1927 as Governor of the Straits Settlements. By then, however, according to J. de V. Allen, Clifford was disillusioned: 'His principles were compatible with the early imperialistic faith in regeneration; but the new imperialism, or rather colonialism, no longer a creed or an ideology but a social and economic structure designed to reorientate men's ways of life to accommodate a racial oligarchy and a humming, Twentieth Century economy, was not for him.'[21] Thus, in the words of William Roff, Clifford 'began to have serious doubts about part at least of the very ideology of Imperialism which explained and justified his own presence in Malaya.'[22] Clifford remained only two years in Malaya, returning permanently to England in 1929 in failing health and unable to reconcile this new direction colonialism had taken in Malaya with his own deeply held convictions. He died in 1941 after a long illness, as Stockwell notes, just 'as the Japanese were invading the Malay Peninsula.'[23] Long before these doubts had set in, however, Clifford had forged a parallel career as a writer of stories and reminiscences based on his experiences in Malaya. It was these tales that found favour with Maga: despite Conrad's reservations, Clifford's writing was convergent with *Blackwood's* agenda, and he became a regular contributor to the magazine in the early years of the twentieth century.

Clifford and Blackwood: First Contact

William Blackwood was keen to publish Clifford's short stories and reminiscences of his time as a colonial administrator. The collections of 'classic' stories from *Blackwood's*, entitled *'Blackwood': Tales from the Outposts*, published in twelve hardback volumes in 1932, contain numerous offerings from Clifford, signalling his place among *Blackwood Magazine* luminaries. In his time Clifford was a respected author, yet today his voice is hardly audible outside the circle of literary academia that deals with the literature of empire. While many of *Blackwood's* authors, notably George Eliot, Joseph Conrad, and John Buchan, continue to enjoy literary celebrity, Clifford remains relatively unknown. This may partly be accounted for by the fact that he wrote almost exclusively about Malaya, thus restricting the range of his artistic imagination. It may be that his literary talent was, as Conrad noted, limited. But it may also be due to the fact that Clifford's material, colonial Malaya, had a cultural relevance in the late nineteenth and early twentieth centuries that has waned in the years that followed. Clifford's relationship with *Blackwood's* thus gives us an insight into the type of readership William Blackwood anticipated for Maga, and how Blackwood went about commissioning appropriate material to appeal to such an audience.

The first archival evidence of Clifford's contact with *Blackwood's* comes in the form of a letter from his mother, Lady Clifford. Written on 13 September 1897 from Hampton Court Palace, the letter had accompanied the manuscript of the story 'The Death-March of Kulop Subing.' Lady Clifford explains that because her son is away in distant lands she is acting on his behalf, and mentions that his recently published work, *In Court and Kampong*, 'has been well received.'[24] There is no reply to this offer, and Clifford himself follows up with a letter dated 23 May 1898 from the British Residency in Pahang. Enquiring politely on the fate of the short story his mother had sent 'with a view to its insertion in Maga,' Clifford tries to pressure Blackwood to a decision, hinting that if the answer is negative 'he may be able to place it elsewhere.' Blackwood replies affirmatively on 21 June, accepting 'The Death-March' for Maga and immediately requesting further material of the same nature. Clifford duly sent 'Mina – A Daughter of the Muhammadans.' 'The Death-

March' appeared in the October edition of the magazine and Clifford received £15 for it. This was evidently Clifford's first attempt at placing a story with *Blackwood's*.[25] He had found the ideal publisher for his work. In the years that followed, Clifford was to express his gratitude to Blackwood on a number of occasions, in a manner revealing of the way in which 'Blackwoodian' authors were nurtured and encouraged. For example, on 23 June 1900, Clifford writes: 'Your letters always bring me a little whiff of encouragement in my literary work, and make me wish to produce better stuff. That, I take it, has always been part of the tradition of the House of Blackwood in its dealings with its more obscure writers, and even a giant like George Eliot shows in her letters that she experienced a similar filip [sic] from a like cause.'[26]

It is worth noting Lady's Clifford's efforts on her son's behalf. In his first letter Clifford had asked Blackwood to direct any correspondence to Lady Clifford at Hampton Court Palace. Having seen the proofs, Lady Clifford herself corresponded with Blackwood on 22 August 1898, pointing out an error in the title of 'The Death-March' – it had been wrongly transcribed as 'The Wrath March.' It was Lady Clifford who forwarded the cheque and the October edition of Maga containing 'The Death-March' to Clifford in Pahang, and it was she who undertook the early proofreading and correcting of Clifford's manuscripts, thus acting as her son's factotum and literary agent in his early literary career. She was herself an author, who in her time had known Dickens and contributed to *Household Words*: as such she was in a good position to advise her son and act on his behalf.

Clifford transferred his literary affairs to J.B. Pinker in 1899 while he was on leave in England. Writing from his mother's address at Hampton Court Palace, Clifford informed Blackwood of this change in his financial affairs: 'Like the hero of "All for Love," I have recently sold myself to a Demon. In other words I have placed all my literary work in the hands of Mr. Pinker of Effingham House, Arundel Street, Strand, and any cheques that may be payable to me in the future will have to pass through his hands.'[27] David Finkelstein has noted how Pinker became a 'major supplier of valued literary property for Blackwood's firm and its magazine' in the early years of the twentieth century, and notes in particular the role of Pinker in advancing Joseph Conrad's career.[28] In fact it was Clifford who persuaded Conrad to transfer his literary dealings to Pinker, and interestingly, it was Clifford who was instrumental in securing Conrad's literary future by recommending him to James Gordon Bennett of the *New York Herald* when Bennett was on a visit to Ceylon where Clifford was stationed.[29]

Clifford's second manuscript, 'Mina,' appeared in the famous thousandth 'Special Double Edition' of Maga as 'A Daughter of the Muhammadans: A Study from the Life.' On 17 March 1899 Clifford wrote to Blackwood thanking him for a copy of Maga and owning to a 'feeling of diffidence at finding [himself] in such distinguished company.' He also owned up to a sense of pride that the Malay Native States Civil Service contributed two pieces to that edition – Conrad's 'The Heart of Darkness' had also begun serialization in the thousandth edition, and Clifford's pleasure at being included was most likely heightened by the fact that he was being published alongside Conrad, with whom he had already corresponded.[30] At this point, after accepting two stories, it would seem that Blackwood was keen to encourage Clifford and to ask for more of his work. 'Your kind praise of my story pleased me greatly, and I must thank you for the very real encouragement which you have given me,' says Clifford, before revealing that he had two more manuscripts 'which I propose to forward to you for your consideration shortly, in accordance with the suggestion which you have made.'[31] What that suggestion could have been is unknown, but we can speculate that Blackwood was encouraging Clifford to write more stories along the lines of his first two for Maga. Certainly their relationship was convivial and not marred by the acrimony that characterized Conrad's dealings with Blackwood in later years. In the October 1899 letter to Blackwood where he mentions Pinker, Clifford makes his feelings about Blackwood's personal commitment to authors quite clear: 'I have, however, specially reserved to myself the right of conducting all my business with you at first hand, as you have always made our relations so pleasant that I was loath to abandon a correspondence which has contained for me nothing but interest and enjoyment.'[32]

Clifford's stories were based on his own experiences and acquaintances in the East. 'A Daughter of the Muhammadans' was, Clifford told Blackwood, taken directly from life, and told the story of a woman whose home is 'within a few miles of the place from which I now sit writing to you.'[33] Thus Clifford's literary life and his life as a colonial governor began to intersect. His third piece for Blackwood's was 'Father Rouellot,' a tale of a 'French missionary's saintly devotion to his task in Pahang and the Malayan Archipelago.'[34] Clifford's description of it to Blackwood in April 1899 is very similar to Conrad's description of Lord Jim in a letter to Clifford. Of 'Father Rouellot' Clifford writes, 'Like most of my stories and sketches this is a study drawn from the life, but in the present case it is more in the nature of a composite photograph than an individual portrait.'[35] On 13 December 1899 Conrad writes to Clifford about *Lord Jim*: 'I want to put into that sketch a good many people I've met – or at least seen for a moment – and several things overheard about the world. It is going to be a hash of episodes, little thumbnail sketches of fellows one has rubbed shoulders with and so on. I crave your indulgence; and I think that read in the lump it will be less of a patchwork than it seems now.'[36]

It is hardly surprising that these two writers of colonial tales were speaking to each other in similar terms: it is known that they discussed their work in detail and gave each other sight of their manuscripts.[37] In fact some literary rivalry is in evidence, as we shall see later in this piece. As with Conrad's early work, it is Malaya and its exoticism that occupies Clifford, and by the time 'Father Rouellot' had been accepted Clifford was confident enough to make judgments on the suitability of his other stories for Maga. On 13 June 1899 he offered Blackwood another story, adding this rider: 'It is the record of a personal experience, which, however, is not of a very blood-curdling kind, and I do not in the least know whether it is the sort of thing that Maga can make use of.'[38] What this tale was is unclear, but stories like 'The Death-March of Kulop Subing' and 'Wan Beh, Princess of the Blood' are infused with that exoticism and mythic quality that so absorbed the late nineteenth-century imagination hungry for tales from the far flung reaches of Empire. Alternatively, stories like 'In the Heart of Kalamantan' and 'At the Court of Pelesu' deal with the white man's experience of an alien and exotic culture, while such sketches as 'The East Coast' and 'In Chains' are a celebration of the land and its people. In such stories Clifford satisfies the desires of his readers at home in Britain by presenting Malaya in the style of the *Arabian Nights*. His love of the country and its people is expressed in the more documentary-style contributions which seek to present to the uninitiated the conditions and customs of an Eastern people, while those who have served in the Far East would be expected to identify with his imperial adventurers and administrators who fall foul of, but eventually overcome a hostile 'native' tribe. The exotic exudes from every page, like this passage from 'In Chains' (1899):

> It would not be easy to conceive a life more delightful for a healthy youngster blessed with a keen interest in the much which he was learning, and in the little which he was slowly and cautiously teaching. A hurried meal soon after the dawn had broken; a long tramp from village to village while daylight lasted; a swim in the river; a huge plate of rice

and curry, of a sort, eaten with a hunter's appetite; a smoke and a yarn with the elders of the village, picturesque figures grouped gravely in a circle chewing betel-nut as the placid cattle masticate the cud; a dispute or two, perhaps settled between smoke and smoke, without any magisterial formalities; a little information picked up here and there upon matters which would some day be of importance – and then sound soul-satisfying sleep, an early waking and another long day of labour and of life. By boat and raft on rivers great and small; tramping through gloomy depths of forest, or across rice-swamps sizzling in the heat; camping at night-time in a headman's house, beneath the peaked roof of a little village mosque, or in some crop-watcher's hut, on the ground in the dead jungle with a green palm-leaf shelter above my head to ward off the worst of the drenching dews – however I travelled, wherever I stayed or halted, no matter who the strange folk with whom I consorted, I tasted to the full the joys of a complete independence, the delights of fresh open air, hard exercise and enough work for the intellect to keep the brain as fit and supple as the limbs. I had been jerked out of the age in which I had been born, out of the security and the bustle of European life, into a wild unfettered freedom among a semi-civilised people, where nature still had her own way unchecked by man's contrivances, where the blood ran merrily and the heart was made glad to overflowing.[39]

Clifford's love of Malaya and Malay life is laid bare here, and it is prime material for Maga: it is little wonder that Clifford found immediate favour with Blackwood.

It was not just Clifford's writing that Blackwood entertained: Clifford associated with William Blackwood at the social level too. In March 1899, Clifford informed Blackwood that he would be on leave in England shortly, during which he hoped to have the opportunity of meeting Blackwood, a sentiment he reiterated in a letter in June 1899. By 12 July 1899 Clifford was ensconced in Egerton Mansions in London, and wrote to Blackwood about the proofs of 'In Chains,' requesting information on when 'Father Rouellot' would appear. He mentions lunching with Sir George Warrender and the fact that the Cliffords would be Scotland with the Warrenders in the autumn. In a letter to Blackwood in September, he accepts a luncheon invitation on behalf of himself and his wife, and it is here that the first reference to Conrad appears. We also begin to see signs of Conrad and Clifford discussing their literary output. As Clifford writes: 'Conrad told me something of his new tale, & showed me a page or two, but I am longing to see the whole.'[40] In a letter of

2 October Clifford goes even further in his response to *Lord Jim* saying that it interested him but compared it unfavourably with *Heart of Darkness*.[41]

In the letters to Blackwood subsequent to their lunch in Edinburgh, Clifford becomes much more familiar in style of address and decidedly more verbose. Frequently he addresses Blackwood as 'My Dear Mr Blackwood.' In April 1900, he writes at length about the war in South Africa and imperialism in general. Here he predicts the end of Cecil Rodes's company and hopes that all Chartered Companies 'will be allowed to come into being under the auspices of the old Flag.' He criticizes Chartered Companies in general saying that 'As we view things now-a-days, the only justification for white rule over brown or black folk is the improvement which we are able to effect in the condition of the latter.' In another long letter of 23 June 1900 he offers his opinion on the May number of the magazine and singles out the articles that he particularly enjoyed. He also mentions his wife's fall from her pony and discusses Roberts and Kitchener.

Clifford, Conrad, and Blackwood's Colonial Network

John Blackwood, William Blackwood III's uncle, had created a particular type of magazine: the works he serialized 'were aimed at a mainstream, essentially middle-class reading public. It was an audience thought likely to vote Conservative, an audience that was viewed as suspicious of change and unwilling to tolerate challenges to the literary and social status quo.'[42] William Blackwood overlaid onto this matrix material aimed solidly at the colonial reader and, with the help of David Storr Meldrum who joined the firm in 1896, actively sought out writers such as Clifford and Conrad in order to develop a circle of specialists on colonial fiction to complement the other networks of writers that *Blackwood's* had nurtured. Finkelstein notes that Conrad was 'invited to lunch with Blackwood's "colonial writers",' and points out how Blackwood assiduously courted 'colonial' figures such as Roger Casement for the journal. Blackwood wrote to Casement in 1905 expressing how he would be 'happy to hear' from him if he were 'willing to contribute to [his] Magazine on subjects connected with The Congo': 'I daresay you know very well the kind of article which suits Blackwood,' William comments disingenuously, 'but I may mention that even where political matters are under discussion, that the method I prefer is one dealing with matters from a firsthand picturesque point of view combined with interest for the general reader.'[43] No doubt, given Casement's connections with Conrad and his knowledge of the Congo, Blackwood was thinking of Conrad's 'The Heart of Darkness'; he may also have had in mind the colonial stories of the likes of Clifford and Frank Swettenham.

While Casement never actually published anything in Maga, Clifford's contributions were an immediate success with readers of *Blackwood's Magazine*, and his literary star rose swiftly. So successful was he as a storyteller that a reviewer of *Tales of Unrest* in the *China Mail* of 25 May 1898 assumed 'Conrad' to be a pen-name for 'Clifford.'[44] This conflation of the two writers is indicative of the success of Blackwood and Meldrum in attracting top-rate writers of colonial fiction. It is perhaps understandable that the two should have been fused in this reviewer's mind, given they were both writing about colonial Malaya, and in a distinctly romantic vein. Conrad had not yet flexed his modernist muscles, although unmistakable evidence of some of the tensions, contradictions, and scepticism of his later work appears in the early Malay tales. It is evident in the work of both Clifford and Conrad that these were writers trying to convey the very essence of the territory about which they were writing; and of course this is why they disagreed over authenticity.

Yet their literary careers were to move in very different directions: Conrad fell out with Blackwood in 1902–3 after a series of unsuccessful attempts to secure advances and loans from the firm. On 31 May 1902, over lunch Blackwood had told Conrad that he was a loss to the firm. Exasperated, on arrival home, Conrad immediately wrote to Blackwood complaining: 'I am *modern*, and I would rather recall Wagner the musician and Whistler the painter ... They too have arrived. They had to suffer for being "new."'[45] After that he was to publish only 'The End of the Tether' and two shorter chapters from *The Mirror of the Sea* with Blackwood. Although the final break seems to have been over money, Conrad was right in distinguishing himself from writers who had gone before, and his exhortation to Blackwood to regard his writing as 'modern' probably betrays Conrad's suspicion that he was artistically and aesthetically moving away from the conservative, colonial fiction fraternity that Blackwood and Meldrum had clustered him within. Conrad's literary eye was roaming nearer to Europe and domestic matters, as evidenced by *The Secret Agent*, *Under Western Eyes*, and *Chance*, hardly novels that would have cemented his reputation as a member of Blackwood's colonial 'family.'

Clifford, on the other hand, was deeply committed to writing about

Malaya. As de V. Allen observes: 'Perhaps the most striking thing about Clifford is that through all his years of absence from Malaya he scarcely wrote a word about any other part of the world.'[46] For Conrad the Malay Archipelago was just the starting point; for Clifford it was the beginning and the end – it was his life. Even before his quarrel with Blackwood, Conrad was content to let Clifford lead the vanguard of writers of Malay fiction. To his credit, and without a trace of resentment, Conrad, on receipt of Clifford's *In a Corner of Asia* (1899), wrote to the author: 'Of course the matter is admirable – the knowledge, the feeling, the sympathy ... It is all sterling metal, a thing of absolute value. There can be no question of it, not only for those who know, but even for those who approach the book with blank minds on the subject of the race you have, in more than one sense, made your own.'[47]

By the turn of the twentieth century, the colonial markets, particularly those in India and Australasia, were becoming lucrative ones for British publishers, and Blackwood joined the ranks of publishing houses issuing novels in Colonial Libraries for consumption only in the British colonies. Clifford's initial works were almost guaranteed to find in Blackwood's an appreciative publisher, given its 'firsthand picturesque' qualities, and its evident colonial context: the titles alone promised tales of exotic adventure in faraway lands that would strike a chord with a colonial audience, and thrill those readers at home eager for stories of Eastern exoticism that they believed offered a taste of lands where they would never set foot. As Conrad was later to write to Pinker in reference to *Blackwood's Magazine* and its perceived readership, 'There isn't a single club and messroom and man-of-war in the British Seas and Dominions which hasn't its copy of Maga.'[48] A recent critic endorses this view, commenting on life in early twentieth-century colonial Malaysia: 'culturally, as so many visitors remarked, the range was small: Savoy Operas and *Blackwood's Magazine* were characteristic fare.'[49]

The exotic colonial tale thus had a dual appeal: it fictionalized the familiar for those living and serving in the colonies, just as the domestic novel did (and still does) for those at home; and it satisfied a thirst for romantic adventure stories set in the far-flung colonial territories. In Edward Said's sense of the term, such stories endorsed an 'orientalist' perspective on the Far East. It was presented in all its exotic otherness and frequently figured as fixed in time, an unchanging landscape and populace, colorful, luxuriant, and inscrutable. Clifford's portrayal of the country and its peoples, however, speaks of his deep affection for the region and its culture, and his desire to figuratively capture what he believed to be the essence of the land before it disappeared forever under the exorable march of imperial 'progress.' As Clifford himself had recognized, his works constituted a kind of cultural archaeology in which future generations could catch sight of Malaya as it was perceived in the closing years of the nineteenth century. As Roff says of Clifford's years as a colonial official in Malaya, '[H]e came to discover the frightening fascination of living completely immersed within a culture alien to his own, and coming to accept in some measure an alien system of values. It is this twin impulse – the need to look more closely at what may be called the moral effects of colonial rule and the need to explore the innermost character of the people he was set to govern and of his relationship with them – which underlies much of Clifford's writing.'[50]

Furthermore, Clifford's attempts to portray the region and its culture as through the eyes of the Malay subject are to be commended: even if his sketches were not wholly successful aesthetically, they at very least were drawn with a respect for the indigenous people and its culture that was too often lacking in contemporary colonial fiction.[51]

Establishing a Reputation

Clifford's next offering to Maga was 'Bush-Whacking,' a story that seems to mark the high water mark of his career at *Blackwood's*. He had been due to return to Malaya in the autumn but as he had accepted the Governorship of British North Borneo his leave in England was extended: this presumably gave him time to work on the first part of 'Bush-Whacking.' On 31 October 1899 Clifford enclosed his manuscript of the story, with a covering letter already mentioned. On the margin of this letter Blackwood wrote: 'This is a tip top sketch & will come in famously for January no.'[52] 'Bush-Whacking' was given the 'place of honour' in the January 1900 issue, appearing before the latest instalment of Conrad's *Lord Jim*. As Patten and Finkelstein note above, the placement of material in Maga's pages was a nuanced and hierarchically informed process, with the starting slot in the table of contents reserved for significant contributions. Conrad's 'The Heart of Darkness,' for example, received pride of place in the thousandth edition of Maga, a key position and indicative of the value accorded it by Maga's editors. Other Clifford work would be accorded similar honours, such as 'The Quest for the Golden Fleece,' which started the January 1903 issue of Maga.

The magazine was staple reading in the colonies, eagerly awaited by those anxious for reading material, and in all likelihood it would indeed have been read cover to cover. Certainly Clifford was an avid reader and commented regularly on the articles in Maga in his increasingly voluble letters to Blackwood. For example on 11 April 1900 he comments: 'I must thank you again for the copies of Maga which have reached us so regularly, and have furnished us with so much delightful reading. The political articles upon South African affairs have appealed specially to me.'[53] The mixture of literary, documentary, and political articles in Maga suited it especially for a colonial audience, allowing those serving abroad to engage with Tory inflected political commentary of home affairs while at the time offering much needed diversion. Clifford frequently uses comments on political articles in the magazine as a means of introducing his own reactions to political situations in the empire. He would also report details to Blackwood on the avidity with which colonial residents engaged with Maga's contents, as evidenced from the following comment in a letter dated 2 March 1900: 'We have old Admiral Sir Harry Keppel staying with us, and it may, perhaps, please your authors to know that the old man has been quite delighted with the two articles on the War Operations and the War Policy, more especially the latter. He has done nothing but talk about it for days, and says that it is the best article on The subject that has been or could have been written. What an admirable sketch the Cold Day in Canada is!'[54]

That accolade then of being the first author in the magazine, coupled with the fact that this was the first *Blackwood's Magazine* of the twentieth century, must have been very encouraging to Clifford. Indeed in the letter mentioned above, he seems to have been quite overwhelmed by his success with the story, declaring: 'I was very proud to find my "Bush-Whacking" leading the van.'[55] In fact the next and the concluding instalment of the story appeared consistently before instalments of *Lord Jim*.

The concluding part of 'Bush Whacking' was written on board ship, en route to Borneo, and represented for Clifford 'a considerable amount of patient labour, and an honest attempt to draw things as they are, and as I have seen and known them.'[56] On 11 April 1900 Clifford writes: 'Thank you for the cheque for £21 – sent to Mr. Pinker on my behalf. Your payment for my work is always most generous. "Bush-Whacking" alone has brought me in more money than any one of my published books!'

The Governorship of North Borneo was a demanding undertaking, and the acceptance of Clifford's submissions to *Blackwood's*, not surprisingly, declined in number from this time. In the period September 1902 to March 1904, for example, *Blackwood* ledgers reveal that Clifford had sent its editors no less than nine offerings. Of these only four were accepted: 'Romance of a Scots Family' in December 1901; 'Problems of the Pacific' in March 1902; 'Sally' in December 1902; and 'The Earliest Exile of St Helena' in February 1903. Of the five rejected pieces one notable offering stands out: 'A Freelance of Today' was rejected in September 1901. This was later to be published as a book in its own right. During this period Clifford was back home in England convalescing after an illness, so he presumably had plenty of leisure time to devote to writing. Finkelstein's *Index to Blackwood's Magazine, 1901–1980* details Clifford's publications in *Blackwood's* from 1901. He published in twenty-seven volumes of Maga, finishing in June 1927 with a piece entitled 'Promotion.' Two of his stories are published in serial form: '"Sally": A Study' from November 1903 to February 1904, and 'Saleh: A Sequel' from May to August 1908. On 2 March 1900, Clifford wrote to Blackwood that 'my own little disturbances are at an end' as Muhamed Saleh had been killed. One of Clifford's comments in the letter to Blackwood of 11 April 1900 sheds further light on the publication of these two stories. Blackwood had clearly picked up on the story of Muhamed Saleh as providing good material for a story, for Clifford says: 'Yes; Muhamed Saleh had his points, and some day, perhaps, I may turn him into copy. At present, however, I do not think I could do so without showing up the British North Borneo Company and the mistakes which it and its officials have made in their dealing with this and other native Chiefs, which would not be fair.'[57] Thus it is evident that Clifford had to be very careful in his fiction not to allow his role as author and as colonial governor to come into conflict. Clearly, by the time 'Sally' reached the *Blackwood's* offices in 1902 either things in Borneo had changed or Clifford, convalescing in England, had changed his mind.

By this time, Clifford was enjoying a healthy reputation as a writer. Gailey notes that it is 'certain that Clifford was viewed by his literary peers as a solid, sometimes inspired craftsman': 'Further evidence of Clifford's growing literary reputation can be seen in the hundreds of reviews of his books and stories. There was hardly a reputable newspaper or periodical in the world which did not carry reviews of his works. The *Singapore Free Press*, *New York Times*, *St Louis Post Dispatch*, and even a newspaper from Duluth, Minnesota joined the *Pall Mall Gazette*, *Spec-*

tator, Review of Reviews, and all the major newspapers in taking note of Clifford, the author. Most of these reviews were laudatory, praising particularly the plots and the glimpse Clifford gave to the reader of life in a strange and alien land.'[58]

'In the Heart of Kalamantan' went to Blackwood on 2 March 1900, and appeared in the October number of the magazine. It seems that around this time Clifford was using his connections to help Blackwood's nephew to be elected to the Wellington Club where, on his home leave, Clifford was often to be found in the company of Conrad or Frank Swettenham. Perhaps the 'old boy' network was further proof of Clifford's credentials as a writer for *Blackwood's*! In any case it would appear that Clifford now felt comfortable among the ranks of celebrated writers. Swettenham was a regular contributor to *Blackwood's* too, and Conrad, although not yet receiving the acclaim he deserved, was nevertheless feted among the literary circles, with friends such as Henry James, Ford Madox Ford, and Stephen Crane.

Being published alongside Conrad, and even superseding him in such cases as 'Bush-Whacking,' may well have caused Clifford to regard himself as an up-and-coming artist, one capable of making critical judgments of the work of fellow writers. As *Lord Jim* began its serialization in *Blackwood's* in 1899, Clifford begins including critical appraisals of Conrad's work in his letters to Blackwood. In October 1899, for example, Clifford notes: 'Please accept my best thanks for the October number of Maga ... It is capital – <u>cela</u> <u>va</u> <u>sans</u> <u>dire</u>; and Conrad's story interested me much, tho' judging as well as I may by a first instalment, it is not to me quite as attractive as the magnificent "Heart of Darkness."'[59]

As a postscript to a letter of 11 May 1900 to Blackwood's nephew congratulating him on his election to the Wellington club, Clifford asks: 'By the way; how does "Lord Jim" suit your taste?'[60] The question seems designed to elicit criticism of his friend's novel, a fact that his letter of 23 June to William Blackwood appears to substantiate: 'Conrad's last instalment appears to me to be on a far higher level of excellence than most of the previous chapters of Lord Jim. Your methodless Muser hits out straight from the shoulder as usual. I always enjoy his strong opinions and his forthright expression of them.'[61] If H.A. Gailey is correct in asserting that Blackwood and John Murray 'considered him to be in the first rank of practising writers,'[62] Clifford may have been given the impression that he could stand alongside Conrad as an author of outstanding talent. The manuscript for 'In the Heart of Kalamantan' went to Blackwood in March 1900, and it is tempting to speculate that Clifford may have been comparing his own story with Conrad's. After all, Clifford's story appeared while *Lord Jim* was in the middle of its serialization, and as we have seen Clifford and Conrad had discussed *Lord Jim* while Conrad was in the midst of writing it. Furthermore, as I have already shown in my article on Clifford and Conrad in *The Conradian*, there are certain thematic similarities in the two tales that suggest Clifford may have been attempting to emulate Conrad, or at least utilize some of his themes.

Interestingly too, during this period Conrad was severing his association with *Blackwood's* for various reasons, not the least being William Blackwood's refusal to loan him any more cash. But perhaps it is also important to note that while Clifford maintained the imperial theme to his fiction throughout his writing career, Conrad was moving in other directions and thus his work was no longer suitable for Maga. After *Lord Jim* he published only one or two pieces with the magazine, finishing in 1906 with 'Initiation.' Indeed, commenting on the tone of Conrad's letter to Clifford of 13 December 1899, Allan Hunter notes that Clifford had achieved 'public recognition, and was being published alongside Conrad in *Blackwood's Magazine*': 'Furthermore, he was considerably younger than Conrad (thirty-three to Conrad's forty-two), and his successes may possibly have caused Conrad a certain amount of concern as to his own lack of progress.'[63] Be that as it may, it is certain that despite possible early literary rivalry Clifford did finally acknowledge Conrad's greatness and his own literary inadequacies. Years after they had differed over the issue of Conrad's knowledge of Malays, Clifford made this deferential 'apology' to Conrad: 'I have often, during the years that have supervened, told the story you tell tho' in rather different fashion: – How I had the temerity to deplore the fact that you did not know more about Malays, & how *you* (with only too much justification) deplored the fetters imposed upon my knowledge finding any adequate expression by my woefully imperfect mastery over my own language. No man can doubt upon whose side the balance of the advantage lay.'[64]

In the autobiographical preface to the 1927 edition of *In Court and Kampong* Clifford writes:

> From first to last my pen, or I should more properly say my type-writer, has made me very little money, but the fashioning of my books has brought much pleasure into my life. It has brought me, moreover, many

friends, especially in the literary world, whom I otherwise should never have known; and there have been times when the resulting cheques seemed to me and my wife to make all the difference between poverty and affluence.

But, best of all, I think, there are to be found in the pages of my books a singularly faithful picture of life among the Malays and the wild hill-tribesmen of the States of the East Coast Peninsula as it was forty years ago and as it can never be again. Today my tales are to be valued, not only as historical but as archaeological studies.[65]

The rather melancholy tone of this may well be accounted for by the circumstances Clifford witnessed on his return to Pahang after many years' absence. In 1927 he returned as Governor of the Straits Settlements. By then, however, according to J. de V. Allen, Clifford's 'time had come.'[66] Thus, in the words of William Roff, Clifford 'began to have serious doubts about part at least of the very ideology of Imperialism which explained and justified his own presence in Malaya.'[67] Clifford published nothing more with *Blackwood's* from this time on, a fact that may be accounted for by this disillusionment: he no longer had the heart for imperial fiction.

NOTES

In preparing this paper I am grateful to the Trustees of the National Library of Scotland and to Mr Hugo Clifford Holmes for kindly granting permission to use quotations from Sir Hugh Clifford's letters.

1 A.J. Stockwell, 'Sir Hugh Clifford's Early Career (1866–1903): As Told from His Private Papers,' *Journal of the Malaysian Branch of the Royal Asiatic Society* 49 pt 1 (1976), 89–112.

2 J. de V. Allen, 'Two Imperialists: A Study of Sir Frank Swettenham and Sir Hugh Clifford,' *Journal of the Malaysian Branch of the Royal Asiatic Society* 37, pt 1 (1964), 41–73.

3 Hugh Clifford, *At the Court of Pelesu and Other Malayan Stories*, ed. William Roff (Kuala Lumpur: Oxford University Press, 1993), xvii.

4 Harry A. Gailey, *Clifford: Imperial Proconsul* (London: Collins, 1982), 38.

5 See, in particular, Stockwell, 'Sir Hugh,' and Gailey, *Clifford*.

6 See, for example, Stockwell, 'Sir Hugh,' and Linda Dryden, 'Conrad and Hugh Clifford: An "Irreproachable Player on the Flute" and "A Ruler of Men,"' *Conradian* 23, no. 1 (1998), 51–73.

7 Clifford, *In Court and Kampong* (Singapore: Graham Brash [Pte], 1989), 194.

8 Ibid., 219.

9 See J. de V. Allen for a full discussion of Clifford's career in Malaya, and for a discussion of his opinion on imperialism, Indirect Rule and the project of Malay regeneracy.

10 Conrad's famous statement 'to make you see' comes from the Preface to *The Nigger of the 'Narcissus'* (1897). 'An Observer in Malay' was published in *Academy* on 23 April 1898. It is reprinted as 'An Observer in Malaya' in *Notes on Life and Letters* (London: Dent, 1949). It was requested by the *Academy* following their award to him of a £50 prize, and Conrad rose to the occasion.

11 'An Observer in Malay,' 58–9.

12 Ibid., 60.

13 Clifford was Resident of Pahang at the time of publication of his book. Ûmat is a character in one of the book's sketches.

14 Ibid.

15 Ibid., 59.

16 'The Trail of the Bookworm: Mr Joseph Conrad at Home and Abroad,' *Singapore Free Press*, 1 September 1898; quoted in Norman Sherry, *Conrad's Eastern World* (Cambridge: Cambridge University Press), 139.

17 Clifford's comments appear in his article 'The Genius of Mr Conrad,' *North American Review* (1904), 842–52. Conrad gives an elaborate account of how this 'misapprehension' came about and how he actually did come to write in English in his 'Author's Note,' *A Personal Record* (London: Dent, 1919), v–vii. I would not like to comment on whether Conrad's famously unreliable 'memory' of such personal details is evident. Certainly he is wrong about the date of publication of Clifford's article, which in *A Personal Record* he cites as probably 1898.

18 This is Conrad's version of a friendly discussion at the beginning of their friendship which he recounts in the 'Author's Note,' *A Personal Record*, iv. The original interchange probably took place some time in 1899. Interestingly, in a letter to Blackwood of 22 August 1899, in which he mentions Clifford's visit, Conrad reiterates these statements. Speaking of Clifford, Conrad says: 'His knowledge is unique. If I only knew one hundre[d]th part of what he knows I would move a mountain or two' (*The Collected Letters of Joseph Conrad*, ed. Frederick R. Karl and Laurence Davies, 4 vols. [Cambridge: Cambridge University Press, 1983–90], 2:194).

19 See Stockwell, 'Sir Hugh,' for a full discussion of Clifford's first appointments in Malaya. See also Gailey, *Clifford*, for a fuller biography of Clifford, and Allen, 'Two Imperialists,' for an analysis of Clifford's approach to his appointments in Malaya and his attitude to the Malays.

20 Clifford had been poisoned by ground glass placed in his food and only recovered through determination and a rigorous regimen. See Stockwell, 'Sir Hugh,' 97, and Gailey, *Clifford*, 34–5, for an account.

21 Allen, 'Two Imperialists,' 70–1. Allen's comments on regeneration are worth noting. Unlike Frank Swettenham, Clifford did not regard Malay civilization as essentially degenerate. Rather, Allen argues that 'In the Malays' *ancien regime*, he stressed, was to be seen a remarkably exact counterpart to the European feudalism of five or more centuries earlier. He believed that Britain's role was to terminate the rule of the chiefs, "liberate" the people, and introduce a new order' (Allen, 'Two Imperialists,' 58); see also 55–8, for a fuller discussion.

22 *At the Court of Pelesu*, ed. Roff, xvi.

23 Stockwell, 'Sir Hugh,' 41.

24 National Library of Scotland, MS 4656/no. 252.

25 He was also publishing in the *Cornhill* and *Macmillan's* magazines during this period.

26 National Library of Scotland, MS 4698, fol. 110.

27 Ibid., fol. 105.

28 David Finkelstein, *The House of Blackwood: Author–Publisher Relations in the Victorian Era* (University Park: Pennsylvania State University Press, 2002), 132.

29 Bennett subsequently commissioned *Chance* (1913), the novel that changed Conrad's literary and financial fortunes.

30 His correspondence with Conrad began in 1898 and his visit to the Conrads in the summer of 1899 marked the start of a long friendship.

31 National Library of Scotland, MS 4686/no. 84

32 Ibid., MS 4698, fol. 105.

33 Ibid., MS 461, fol. 252.

34 Allan Hunter, 'An Unpublished Letter from Conrad,' *Notes and Queries* (December 1984), 503–4 (504, n. 10).

35 National Library of Scotland, MS 4686, fol. 86.

36 *Collected Letters*, 2:226–8.

37 See Conrad's letters to Clifford in *Collected Letters*.

38 National Library of Scotland, MS 4686, fol. 87.

39 Clifford, 'In Chains,' in *'Blackwood' Tales from the Outposts IV: Pioneering*, ed. Lieut.-Colonel L.A. Bethel (London: Blackwood, 1946), 57–8.

40 National Library of Scotland, MS 4686, fol. 99.

41 Ibid., fol. 102.

42 Finkelstein, *House of Blackwood*, 77.

43 Ibid., 108.

44 I am indebted to Professor Anthony Stockwell for this information (private

correspondence). After their initial correspondence in 1898, Clifford eventually visited Conrad in the summer of 1899 while on leave in England. They thereafter met frequently during Clifford's brief visits to England, sometimes at the Conrads' family home at Pent Farm and sometimes at the Wellington Club in London, along with Frank Swettenham.

45 31 May 1902, Conrad to William Blackwood, in *The Collected Letters*, 2:418.
46 Allen, 'Two Imperialists,' 55.
47 Jean Aubry, ed., *Joseph Conrad: Life and Letters*, 2 vols. (Garden City, N.Y.: Doubleday, 1927), 279.
48 *Collected Letters*, 4:130.
49 Anthony J. Stockwell, 'The White Man's Burden and Brown Humanity: Colonialism and Ethnicity in British Malaya,' *Journal of the Malaysian Branch of the Royal Asiatic Society* 10, no. 1 (1982), 49.
50 *At the Court of Pelesu*, xiii.
51 See Linda Dryden, *Joseph Conrad and the Imperial Romance* (Basingstoke: Palgrave Macmillan, 1999) for further discussion of the impact of imperial romance on the reading public.
52 National Library of Scotland, MS 4698, fol. 105.
53 Ibid., MS 4686, fol. 105.
54 Ibid., MS 4698, fol. 104.
55 Ibid., MS 4698, fol. 104. This is said in the context of a visit to the Cliffords from Admiral Sir Harry Keppel with whom it seems they discussed articles dealing with the Boer War. In fact much of this letter is taken up with a discussion of the war.
56 National Library of Scotland, MS 4686, fol. 103.
57 Ibid., fol. 105.
58 Gailey, *Clifford*, 37–8.
59 National Library of Scotland, MS 4686, fol. 102.
60 Ibid., MS 4698, fol. 108.
61 Ibid., MS 4698, fol. 111. 'Methodless Musings' was the title of a regular column in the magazine often containing numerous articles on a wide range of issues.
62 Gailey, *Clifford*, 38.
63 Hunter, 'An Unpublished Letter,' 505.
64 Letter to Conrad from Government House, [Lagos,] Nigeria, of 31 May 1921, in *A Portrait in Letters: Correspondence to and about Conrad*, ed. J.H. Stape and Owen Knowles (Amsterdam: Rodopi, 1996), 179.
65 *In the Court and Kampong*, 219.
66 Allen, 'Two Imperialists,' 70–1.
67 *At the Court of Pelesu*, xvi.

'A sideways ending to it all': G.W. Steevens, Blackwood, and the *Daily Mail*

LAURENCE DAVIES

To see the importance of George Warrington Steevens to the House of Blackwood, one might look no further than his sales. No other author of the 1890s was as profitable. By June 1902, *With Kitchener to Khartum* (1898) in its various editions (priced from sixpence to six shillings) had sold 189,438 copies for a total profit of £6,524. By the same date, *From Capetown to Ladysmith* (1900, posthumous and uncompleted) had made £1,863 from a total of 35,272 copies, despite yielding extraordinarily lavish advance royalties.[1] Nevertheless, to dwell on Steevens's ability to write best-selling reports of famous campaigns in far-off places would be to emphasize what became the most contentious as well as the most lucrative of his dealings with the firm. A regular contributor to 'Maga,' Steevens provided essays that crystallized the magazine's belief in Britain's imperial calling; it was, he argued, necessary on the grounds of national aptitude and tradition, admirable on account of the scope of the challenge and the strenuousness of the response, yet also, thanks to the corrosions of modernity, all too fragile. Although most of his contributions appeared anonymously, his authorship was an open secret.[2] Blackwood's had a modern legend on their hands, a man who in all but his dealings with the ha'penny press seemed more an old Athenian than a Londoner. He was the don who had left the niceties of history, philology, and philosophy, where he had held his own with ease, to gallop with the lancers, or forage in ruined Thessalian villages, or trek across the deserts of the Nile; the star reporter for the *Daily Mail* whose accounts of Omdurman and Spion Kop earned a passing status as high literature; the scholar who brought the figures of ancient history to life as vividly as he did the Boers, the Mahdists, and the Bashi-bazouks; the stylist who freshened the course of English prose and died unpleasantly but gallantly of enteric fever during the siege of Ladysmith. According to Fleet Street tradition, he perished holding a glass of champagne, and his last words were 'This is a sideways ending to it all!'[3]

The tributes at his passing honoured his coruscating prose and his insouciant behaviour on campaign. 'Brave, not for show of courage' Kipling wrote of him '– his desire / Truth, as he saw it, even to the death.'[4] A fellow-campaigner in South Africa testified that 'at Eland's Laagte he went forward on horseback with the Highlanders when every other man was dismounted.'[5] W.E. Henley, his former patron,[6] saw Steevens as a national figure: 'he had identified himself so keenly and so intimately with the greatness of England that, reporter as he was, he had come ... to be her chosen craftsman.'[7] An obituarist in the *Academy* recalled the first book, *Monologues of the Dead* (1896), a vigorous reanimation of characters from Roman, Greek, and Medean history that shows both the heft of his classical learning and his spirited refusal to let it weigh him down: 'A man who, having such a wonderful University record as Mr. Steevens, could do such work then, and in his late twenties could become the trump card of the leading London democratic newspaper, must have had a great and unique career before him.'[8] In the obituaries, the idea that Steevens might have flowered as a great literary writer or an unusually astute and knowledgeable statesman became a commonplace. So, however, did the suggestion that his work for Alfred Harmsworth at the *Daily Mail* (which he carried out with immense enjoyment) was a little too 'democratic' for his own good. In Henley's words, 'Brains apart, assuredly the best of our dear George Steevens is not in his books. For one thing, he saw too easily, and wrote too brilliantly – he filled his Editor's bill too well.'[9] Writers for *Blackwood's* took Harmsworth's paper, Imperialist though it was, as the epitome of fickle, cheap-jack politics. Soon after Steevens's death, for example, Charles H.T. Crossthwaite found a distressing lack of constancy among the public: 'This is an age, however, which does not favour steadfastness. The mass of the people are sensation-fed by a cheap press. Popular enthusiasm is strong, but it is short-lived in proportion to its strength. Nothing seems able to hold the attention of the public for more than a few weeks: it will become bored with the war, weary of the "Absent-Minded Beggar," weary of Kipling, weary even of the "Daily Mail" itself.'[10]

For the last three and a half years of his life, Steevens had balanced the requirements of William Blackwood against those of Alfred Harmsworth: one the seasoned proprietor of a High Tory institution, the other an unabashed populist whose ideas were as new as his money. By writing for a monthly magazine with a circulation of around 5,000 and for a daily whose readership burgeoned in his time from a quarter of a million to a million, largely thanks to his own brilliance as a special correspondent, Steevens bestrode two very different literary turfs.

Like the obituarists in the serious weeklies, Charles Whibley, *Blackwood's* fearsome critic-in-residence, celebrated Steevens's work for the daily press only to put it in its place:

> Ripe learning, alert and masterly power of observation, a rarely trenchant style – all these attainments (modestly and without advertisement) Mr Steevens brought to his chosen work, a work generally, and not always wrongly, regarded as the refuge of those who have failed in literature and art. The antagonism between literature and the press is an old source of epigrammatic comment; but the antagonism is still well rooted in reality, and Mr Steevens was one of the very few who reconciled the difference ... the general and not always generous public will remember Mr Steevens as the vivacious historian of Khartum ... But to the smaller number to whom popular success is not the first and last criterion of literary merit, Mr Steevens will also be remembered for the astonishing quantity, variety, and excellence of work which he crowded into a lifetime of thirty years. In pure literature undoubtedly his greatest achievement was his 'Monologues of the Dead.'[11]

Would, in other words, that Steevens, that good Imperialist fallen among Philistines, had stuck to dazzling revisions of the classics. Steevens, after all, had been the 'Balliol Prodigy,' a star pupil at the City of London School, then under the aegis of Edwin Abbott Abbott (one of the greatest Victorian headmasters), and a winner of the most coveted scholarship at Oxford's most demanding college. After taking a double first in classics and philosophy, he became a fellow by examination at Pembroke College. Encouraged by Oscar Browning, a master of connections in the academic world, Steevens soon moved to Cambridge, where he co-founded the *Cambridge Observer*, a review of literature and politics much given to satire.[12]

In full accord with Henley's cult of strenuousness, an article for his *National Observer* shows how impatient Steevens became with the company of 'The Futile Don': 'His colleges are castles of somnolence, palisaded off from all the world of men and things ... Rarely there passes over his coffin a gust from the roaring world that stirs him to a moment of galvanic life.'[13] One such gust swept him off to London, where he joined the staff of the *Pall Mall Gazette*, the evening paper then edited by Harry Cust, a resolute Tory. The don marked out by his restlessness and his bohemian connections became a 'sub' known for admiring Zola, Ibsen, and Wagner, and understanding German Idealist philosophy. In 1894, he married Christina Rogerson (née Stewart), a Scottish widow twenty years his senior, a friend of Margaret Oliphant, and an occasional contributor to Maga. Henley's account of the courtship of a man given to praising the 'savage virtues' (*Things Seen*, 17) is too revealing in its possibly unwitting ironies to pass over: 'In the early days of our acquaintance he came to lunch with us. He was silent and shy, but he could not escape the eye of the serenest and sincerest thing that ever lived; and in the course of the afternoon she proposed to him, and he was finally taken into her exquisite and beautiful little life' ('Memoir,' xi, n. 1). Within two years, she had become her husband's most dauntless advocate, dealing with William Blackwood and his staff as an unofficial agent every bit as exacting as Sophia Jex-Blake or J.B. Pinker.[14] Unemployed after a change of editors at the *Pall Mall Gazette* and alert to the endless quest for bigger guns and thicker armour-plating, Steevens began a comparative study of European naval policies. His first article on this topic so pleased William Blackwood that he took it immediately, giving it the place of honour in the issue of May 1896.[15] During this crucial year, Methuen published *Naval Policy* and *Monologues of the Dead*, while Blackwood published *The Land of the Dollar*, Steevens's impressions of the United States during a presidential election. The latter was the first of the Blackwood titles compiled from columns in the *Daily Mail*. Its successors were *With the Conquering Turk* (1897), *Egypt in 1898*, *With Kitchener to Khartum* (both 1898), *In India* (1899), and *From Capetown to Ladysmith* (1900). In 1899, Harper's brought out *The Tragedy of Dreyfus*, using material from *McClure's* and *Harper's Magazine*. Very soon after his death, his widow persuaded Blackwood to assemble a memorial edition which included *Things Seen* (1900) and *Glimpses of Three Nations* (1901), collections made up of articles for *Blackwood's*, the *Daily Mail*, the *National Observer*, and the *National Review*.

Working at the *Daily Mail*

When Alfred Harmsworth started the *Mail*, which made its debut on 4 May 1896 after several dummy issues, he was determined to make a row: 'Talking-points every day! Every day our pebble must be thrown into the pond.'[16] Hired to lob his pebbles from the comfort of the leader-writers' room, Steevens soon proved a better marksman in the field.[17] His gift for rapid, incisive analysis (which created an impression of easy self-confidence not always confirmed by his modesty in person), was all the more forceful when combined with his talent for breathless narrative and flamboyant description. As Harmsworth's star reporter, he made more waves than ripples. His major assignments included the American election, the Graeco-Turkish war, the expedition to retake Khartoum (and avenge the killing of General Gordon), the inauguration of Curzon as Viceroy of India, and the Anglo-Boer war. In these forty or so months of following big stories, he also covered the Dreyfus trial for *Harper's*, and filled in odd moments at the *Mail* by reporting on 'The Feast of Saint Wagner' at Bayreuth (he was fluent in German as well as French), German military manoeuvres, country life in Prussia, a famine in Ireland (seen through disconcertingly sceptical eyes), the Broadmoor asylum for the criminally insane, the Derby, the Cesarewitch, and, most famously, the celebrations of the Diamond Jubilee. His portrayal of the Queen's arrival at Saint Paul's became canonical, a masterly show of regal ideology, the begetter of a thousand imitations.

> And there was a little, plain, flushed old lady. All in black, a silver streak under the black bonnet, a simple white sunshade, sitting quite still, with the corners of her mouth drawn tight, as if she were trying not to cry. But that old lady was the Queen, and you knew it. You didn't want to look at the glittering uniforms now, nor yet at the bright gowns and the young faces in the carriages, nor yet at the stately princes ... You couldn't look at anybody but the Queen. So very quiet, so very grave, so very punctual, so unmistakably and every inch a lady and a Queen ... When the other kings of the world drive abroad, the escort rides close in at the heels of the carriage; the Queen drove through her people quite plain and open, with just one soldier at the kerbstone between her and them. Why not? They are quite free; they have no cause to fear her; they have much cause to love her ... We know now what that which had come before all stood for; we knew as we had never known before what the Queen stands for. The empire had come together to revere and bless the mother of the empire. The mother of the empire had come to do homage to the one Being more majestic than she. (*Things Seen*, 196–7)

Whatever one may think of all this (a Republican or a Nationalist who was not English might be tempted to say that once again the Devil has the catchy tunes; a modern Conservative might wonder where the tunes have gone), Steevens clearly had the power of articulating or creating cultural master-narratives. His work spoke both to and for the readership of the *Daily Mail*, providing not so much talking points as talking patterns.

His work for *Blackwood's Magazine*, especially 'From the New Gibbon' (1899), presents a more sceptical persona, concerned lest the Empire might in some not so far distant time fall apart, but in his pieces on the Jubilee (the occasion, after all, of Kipling's 'Recessional,' a poem Steevens admired greatly), everything is bright, and clear, and glorious. With impressive rhetorical cunning, Steevens turns even the Queen's frailty into a strength. Indeed this is a classic example of his journalistic work, with its remarkable sense of pace and timing, its precisely rung changes on the pronouns (the engaging *you* was a favourite informality), its dramatic, some might say cinematic changes of perspective, and its characteristic shifts from blur to sharpness: 'All in black, a silver streak under the black bonnet, a simple white sunshade.'[18]

The appearance of the *National Review* in the 1880s as the other Tory magazine was a shock to Maga's system.[19] The emergence in the 1890s of the *Daily Mail*, a cheap and vastly popular newspaper with views that at first glance might seem similar to its own and a proprietor willing to shower cash on the liveliest Conservative writers became another challenge. It became yet another competitor for Blackwood to contend with, the rival for Steevens's attention if not inevitably his affection.

In practical terms, however, the magazine and the newspaper established a virtually symbiotic pairing. Harmsworth paid Steevens lavishly to send back from his almost constant travels punctual yet vigorous reports of what he saw, and smelled, and heard. Harmsworth was generous with expenses too, and, like most of his fellow correspondents, Steevens liked to travel well prepared.[20] After the *Mail* had done with his letters, as they were called by all concerned, he was free to make a book of them and sell it where he pleased. Thirty-three such letters, for example, stitched together with a minimum of thread, went into *The Land of the Dollar* (published as noted earlier by Blackwood). H.G. Wells, a fellow-oarsman in the 'Henley Regatta,' was much impressed by the author's ability to turn these pieces, written 'with a sense of unity,' into 'a single and complete work of art.'[21] Practising verbal husbandry, Steevens also used his American jaunt to make an article for Maga.[22] The Blackwood books were up-to-the-minute in every sense, appearing almost as rapidly as the 'instant books' of our own time. The Battle of Omdurman was fought on 2 September 1898; it forms the climax of *With Kitchener to Khartum*, published in Edinburgh on 27 September A note in the first edition explains that had the original plan of setting 'the concluding chapters of this book from telegraphic reports' been followed, it would have come out the previous week. The reference to 'concluding chapters' holds the secret of the book's extraordinarily rapid appearance. Twenty-seven of its thirty-six chapters consist largely of despatches written for the *Mail* between April and mid-August, when the last regiments moved south from Atbara for the march on Khartoum. Once published, copy could go straight on to Scotland for house-styling and immediate setting. Meanwhile Steevens was also sending back narrative links and extra military and political analyses, either to his wife, one of the few people able to read his execrable handwriting, or directly to the unlucky compositors in Edinburgh. Whatever the campaign's outcome, victory, defeat, or stalemate, most of this material was to stand.[23] In February, before a word of it had been written, Christina Steevens referred to the book as 'How we took (or failed to take) Khartoum.'[24]

Much of Steevens's journalism appears in the book verbatim. Blackwood's, a house normally given to strict editorial discipline, handled his work with a light touch. This passage from the book, for instance, differs from its source in the *Daily Mail* of 13 April 1898 only in the substitution of a dash for a comma: 'Halfa clangs from morning till night with rails lassoed and drawn up a sloping pair of their fellows by many convicts on to trucks; it thuds with sleepers and boxes of bully-beef dumped on to the shore. As you come home from dinner you stumble over strange rails, and sudden engine-lamps flash in your face, and warning whistles scream in your ears. As you lie at night you hear the plug-plug of the goods engine, nearer and nearer, till it sounds as if it must be walking in at your tent door. From the shops of Halfa the untamed Sudan is being tamed at last. It is the new system, the modern system – mind and mechanics beating muscle and shovel-head spear' (8). Steevens, who had a sharp eye for the latest technology and felt quite at home with the demands of modern newspaper production,[25] was a part of this 'new system, the modern system' himself – and, by virtue of their connection with him, so was the House of Blackwood.

This newness pulses through his style. With its reliance on muscular verbs in the present tense ('clangs ... thuds ... flash ... scream'), precisely chosen, onomatopoeic nouns ('the plug-plug of the goods engine'), aggressive similes, and buttonholing pronouns ('till it sounds as if it must be walking in at your tent door'), this is prose for the 'busy man' whom Harmsworth saw as the natural reader of the *Mail*.[26] It is also prose distinctive enough to parody, as G.K. Chesterton does for over twenty pages of *The Napoleon of Notting Hill*, his mock-heroic novel of urban insurrection. Faced with describing the Battle of Campden Hill, the special correspondent of the *Court Journal* tries several modes, all unsatisfactory, before he settles on 'old Steevens and the *mot juste.'*[27] Steevens is 'old' because the book is set eighty years into the future (the time is 1984), but of all the flamboyant journalists of his day, he is the one remembered. In the report of skirmishes around West London, *mots justes* gleam and similes flourish: 'I saw the blue cloudy masses of Barker's men blocking the entrance to the high-road like a sapphire smoke' (225). Chesterton even captures Steevens's relish of the gruesome and his willingness to put himself in the picture:[28] 'I write with some difficulty, because the blood will run down my face and make patterns on the paper ... If you ask me why blood runs down my face, I can only reply that I was kicked by a horse. If you ask me what horse, I can reply with some pride that it was a war-horse. If you ask me how a war-horse came on the scene in our simple pedestrian warfare, I am reduced to the necessity, so painful to a special correspondent, of recounting my experiences' (230). By the time of the Sudan campaign, Steevens's reports were appearing in the *Daily Mail* under his signature rather simply as by 'Our Special Correspondent.' In the world of the popular press, star journalists were becoming as much a commodity as the news they reported. Steevens was valuable to his editors and publishers for the immediacy of his writing. Like such American reporters as Nelly Bly and Richard Harding Davis, he had a name that sold papers.[29]

Late nineteenth-century journalism shrank both space and time. The introduction of the telephone (used by armies as well as metropolitan businesses), the expansion of the cable network and its increasing technical sophistication speeded up the circulation of the news. Datelines and dates of publication were converging. The need to insist on the remoteness and exoticism of newsworthy events (not to mention the journalist's own intrepidity) meant that the concomitant shrinkage of psychic distance was not as great or sudden. But even so, special correspondents needed to find some common ground between 'I am here' and 'thanks to my verbal magic, you are here.' Steevens was a master of this space. Whether in columns for Harmsworth or books for Blackwood, he offered his readers a vivid and intensely dramatic illusion of taking part in soldier's work, and he offered it with a dose of imperial ideology: 'But the cockpit of the fight was Macdonald's ... Every tactician in the army was delirious in his praise; the ignorant correspondent was content to watch the man and his blacks. "Cool as on parade," is an old phrase; Macdonald Bey was very much cooler. Beneath the strong, square-hewn face you could tell that the brain was working as if packed in ice' (*With Kitchener*, 278). To the appetite for knowledge and vicarious experience, he catered most obligingly; one chapter of *With the Conquering Turk* is called 'What War Is Like.' He presented himself not as a don turned adventurer but as a town-bred man who chanced his life at the front writing for those who stayed at home.[30]

His primary audience in the *Mail* was civilian, made up not so much of armchair warriors as warriors of the desk and counter.[31] He expected the purchasers of Blackwood titles to be more prosperous[32] and would have recognized that many of them knew the Empire at first hand. Yet, in the transformation from newspaper copy to book, he made no attempt to change his implied reader, who always enjoys a vigorous imaginary. On his first military campaign, he discovered that 'everything artificial, conventional, social, had vanished, and you were left the bare, natural man.'[33] Shifting from the *you* that stands in for *one* or *I* to the *you* that means *you, the reader of Mr Blackwood's book or Mr Harmsworth's paper*, he adds: 'It is in this return to the naked state of nature that consist both the charm and the devilishness of war. The charm you will understand readily' (*With the Conquering Turk*, 311–12). His signature fancy for the second person further complicates itself in a passage from *With Kitchener*. Here, in a striking aporia, the appeal to voyeurism lurking in his work becomes an open contradiction. The scene is the *zariba* (fortified encampment) of Atbara immediately after the Anglo-Egyptian victory. 'Now fall in, and back to the desert outside. And unless you are congenitally amorous of horrors, don't look too much about you.' Having coloured in a grisly picture of the charred and broken corpses of jihadi and their beasts of burden, Steevens goes on: 'don't look at it. Here is the Sirdar, who created this battle, this clean-jointed, well-oiled, smooth-running, clockwork-perfect masterpiece of a battle. Not a flaw, not a check, not a jolt; and not a fleck on its shining success. Once more, hurrah, hurrah, hurrah!' (151) Who is the *you* who sees and does not see the dreadful mess, who turns from the ruined bodies to admire Kitchener, Sirdar or Commander-in-Chief of this 'well-oiled' operation? The soldiers, who must literally fall into line, the readers, who are told to do so metaphorically, or Steevens himself, whose line is supposed to be an editorial one? Who looks and who does not, and who among the lookers can ignore what they have seen?

What Steevens could have ignored when covering the Sudan campaign, but did not, was the enormous superiority of Anglo-Egyptian firepower. In the 1890s, like their successors in the next two centuries, journalists covering punitive expeditions and imperial wars had several options. Without any mention of the enemy's far inferior equipment, they could exult in the bravery of their own troops; feeling the disproportion, they might restrain the bragging and the gloating; or they might acknowledge suffering and courage on all sides. Then as now, the middle option would be the least tempting to proprietors, editors, and reporters with a name to make. With the public in aggressive mood as, with the calls for avenging General Gordon's death, it was in 1898, the third option would be only slightly more tempting, yet this was the option Steevens took. A cynic might of course argue that to honour the boldness of a foe is to make the victory all the sweeter, but the so-called 'fog of war' does not confine itself to battlefields, and, especially when the enemy is alleged to be less civilized or even less human than citizens of the imperial heartland, the immediate gratification of total victory attracts more eyes than any scruples about giving honour where honour is due.

Here is Steevens reflecting on the Battle of Atbara and the experience of the Jehadia, Mahdist troops from far southern Sudan: 'If their fire seemed bad to us, what hell must ours have been to them! First an hour and a half of shell and shrapnel – the best ammunition, perfectly aimed and timed, from some of the deadliest field-pieces in the world; then volley after volley of blunted Lee-Metford and of Martini bullets, delivered coolly at 300 yards and less, with case and Maxim fire almost point-blank. The guns fired altogether 1500 hundred rounds, mostly shrapnel; the Camerons averaged 34 rounds per man' (*With Kitchener*, 158). Spears and antique firearms against quick-firing artillery and the latest rifles shooting blunted bullets, all 'delivered coolly' at close range: not for the first time or the last, the world of millenarianism and the world of statistics collide head on. At Omdurman, five months later, forty-six British and Egyptian soldiers died, and over 11,000 Mahdists. 'It was not a battle,' Steevens wrote, 'but an execution' (264). This is his description of the final moments:

From the green army there now came only death-enamoured despera-
does, strolling one by one towards the rifles, pausing to shake a spear,
turning aside to recognise a corpse, then, caught by a sudden jet of fury,
bounding forward, checking, sinking limply to the ground. Now under
the black flag in a ring of bodies stood only three men facing the three
thousand of the Third Brigade. They folded their arms about the staff and
gazed steadily forward. Two fell. The last dervish stood up and filled his
chest; he shouted the name of his God and hurled his spear. Then he stood
quite still, waiting. It took him full; he quivered, gave at the knees, and
toppled with his head on his arms and his face towards the legions of his
conquerors. (283)

The Boers had better guns than the Mahdists, but a worse press.
Although not every newspaper concurred,[34] in general, they were said
to be stiff-necked, ruthless, crude, yet diabolically cunning. The *Daily
Mail* led the charge. Yet Steevens refers to the treatment of the thousand
British soldiers who surrendered at Nicholson's Nek like this: 'The
Boers had their revenge for Dundee and Elandslaagte in war; now they
took it, full measure, in kindness' (*From Capetown*, 79).[35] After Steevens's
death, some obituarists and reviewers wondered if his heart and his
hand had followed different loyalties.[36] Whether or not he practised
that duality, Steevens's prose matches his sense of modernity, even in its
sudden gestures and its moments of ambivalence.

In his writing for what Henley called 'the experimental, novel, irre-
sistible "Daily Mail,"'[37] Steevens shows a literary kinship with the innovators of his time. Obvious influences in their vividness and directness
are Kipling's books of reportage, such as *From Sea to Sea* and *The City of
the Dreadful Night*. The closest equivalents to his war writings are Stephen
Crane's stories and despatches from Cuba. Like Crane, Steevens is
much taken with the incongruous, preferably ironic, detail and the
unexpected simile. These are examples from *With the Conquering Turk*:
'During the first battle of Velestino I saw a hen go, business-like, into a
barn, and after a little while came out, her cackle shrilling triumphantly
over the grinding musketry and banging guns' (314). Skirmishers converge on a battlefield: 'It began to be so full that the men seemed to be
standing still and the field to be drawn slowly back through them, like
the great brown roll of a musical box through the black teeth' (171).[38] In
some of his techniques, he appears to share the project of Conrad and
Ford. Particularly, Steevens favoured what is now called 'delayed de-

coding,' giving first the effect and then the cause: 'In front of the city stretched a long white line – banners, it might be; more likely tents; most likely both. In front of that was a longer, thicker black line – no doubt a zariba or trench ... Only as we sat and ate a biscuit and looked – the entrenchment moved. The solid wall moved forward, and it was a wall of men' (*With Kitchener*, 256).[39] Steevens writes not only what he sees but how he sees it, making the search for the story part of his narrative. Certain reviewers and obituarists called him a literary impressionist, an apt term for a writer so attentive to what art historians would call the conditions of seeing.[40] Vernon Blackburn, in his obituary, goes on to place Steevens in the context of an even fresher art-form: 'In a scientific age his style may be described as cinematographic. He was able to put vividly before his readers, in a series of smooth-running little pictures, events exactly as he saw them with his own intense eyes.'[41] This is not the place to chart the affiliations of literary impressionism and proto-modernism, let alone their connections to early cinema. At best this would be an act of taxonomic strangulation. Suffice it to say that one can see the decades on either side of 1900 as a period of epistemological turbulence, surging around the radical instability of observer and observed. As a writer, Steevens rode the eddies of this turbulence.

It is true, however, that Steevens often writes as a man utterly sure of himself and his ideas; whether in Maga, or a Blackwood book, or a column for the *Daily Mail*, he rallies his readers with a well-placed *we*, precipitates their convictions, finds the sharp, the peremptory words for what they might have been suspecting all along. On his way to Egypt, for instance, he watches Lascars working his ship, and finds them collectively 'a specimen of the raw material' of Empire. 'Their very ugliness and stupidity furnish just the point. It is because there are people like this in the world that there is an Imperial Britain. This sort of creature has to be ruled, so we rule him, for his good and our own' (*Egypt in 1898*, 16). This, then, is the opinionated Steevens, all the more seductive to his public and all the more deplorable for the cramping of his mind.

Poised against the rigidity of his axioms is another Steevens immersed in the moment's flux, where being yields to seeming, certainty to confusion. As the poets and novelists of the First World War were to show, combatants spend a great deal of their time in a most unmystical cloud of unknowing. Steevens's prose combines certitudes with their contraries; his style is by nature heterogeneous, his narratives veer unpredictably. It is in these ways that he was a modern writer, even an incipient modernist.

In the late Victorian and Edwardian period, fictional and non-fictional prose enjoyed a lively symbiosis. Novelists like Conrad, Ford, and James admired Turgenev's *Sportsman's Notebook*, which is only barely fictional, and the nature writings of W.H. Hudson; techniques flowed over or around generic boundaries; such Crane stories as 'The Open Boat' come very close to fragmentary memoir. Steevens was no Crane, let alone a Conrad, and, his acquaintance with Wells excluded, he had nothing to do with the extraordinary group of writers settled around Rye and Winchelsea, but he was in a sense part of the same enterprise.[42] Aside from Conrad and Crane (a few of whose war pieces appeared in Maga), Steevens was Blackwood's most artistically daring author.

The novelty of Steevens's work seems not to have troubled William Blackwood.[43] What he did find difficult was its value as a commodity, as something to be fiercely bargained for. When proposing books, George Steevens combined diffidence with a shrewd sense of the competition. Concerning his work on *With the Conquering Turk* he wrote: 'My criticism of it would be that it inclines to fall between the two stools of history, and a picture of campaigning, but after all the American book [*In the Land of the Dollar*] was equally mixed and as I see from your advertisement in your last Maga that it has attained a third edition there is perhaps a public which does not mind mixing its brimstone with treacle ... I don't know whether you have seen Clive Higham's book ... I have great confidence in being able to turn out not only a vastly more amusing book, but also a more accurate one.'[44] Christina Steevens, who handled most negotiations, was far more aggressive about every aspect of publication, from royalties to marketing. Planning in advance for the 'Khartoum book,' she announced that her husband 'would make efforts to get it out <u>before anyone else</u>. A great point must be made of this.'[45] After publication, she told Blackwood: 'I have written to everyone I can think of to review the book <u>quickly</u> [.] I am glad you approved of sending a copy to the Queen. You will surely publish her acceptance if such there be?'[46] Her progress report on sales reached Edinburgh a few days later: 'It is all most encouraging! We cannot get a copy anywhere yet! None have reached Smith's bookstalls yet! Several publishers have already asked for George's next book!! He cannot promise you an article for <u>December</u> as he is kept very hard at work & is half promised both to the Fortnightly & McClure, but he will see what the next ten days bring forth. Would it not be judicious to press the American sale while yet it is in the mouths of the people.'[47] At the head of this letter, William Blackwood wrote: 'a most ungrateful woman,' adding below: 'He was under promise to me long before the Fortnightly ever thought of him.' Ungrateful or not, she poured on the flattery: 'Delighted am I that the time honoured House of Blackwood is having some part of the success it merits[.] Such unfailing rectitude & courtesy <u>must</u> surpass the sharp practise [*sic*] of so many who <u>try</u> to rival it!'[48] This courtesy was challenged by the haggling over *In India* the following year. On 5 February, Mrs Steevens asked for £400 on publication and a 25 percent royalty: 'I feel I must make [a] decision now as several publishers have applied for it offering higher terms than that – but there is no publisher like Mr. Blackwood.'[49] By 11 February, Blackwood had agreed to these terms, but she had had an offer of £1,000 down and 28 per cent: 'Please do not think in any way I am receding from our "bargain" – I only want you not to think I was unreasonable.' On this letter, William Blackwood pencilled a note to George: 'What do you and Meldrum think of this. It is a cracker – I wonder who the idiot is that makes it.' As war in South Africa approached, Christina Steevens raised the stakes again, undeterred when the formidable J.B. Pinker, now her husband's agent, failed to make headway against Blackwood, who was taking a stern line against literary auctions: 'Several publishers have written to me asking for George's next book (?) I have uniformly made the same answer that the first offer of his book wd. always be made to you. Mr. Heinemann – a friend or acquaintance of our – wrote & offered £3500 for English & colonial rights 25p/c on 1st 10,000 & 30p/c after.'[50] Having announced that another publisher had topped this bid with the prospect of £5,000, she continues: 'Now comes yr. letter to Mr. Pinker & his conversation with Mr. Meldrum & I am driven to the conclusion that you decline to make an offer at all lest it shd. be used in – to my thinking – a most dishono[u]rable manner. I am very much upset by the whole thing & have cabled & written to George begging for definite instructions. I trust I have written nothing improper in this letter – but if I have, I pray you hold me excused, for I write with a sad & anxious heart, only desirous to do the best I can for the most punctilliously [*sic*] hono[u]rable gentleman I ever knew.' How, then, were Blackwood and the Steevens to regard each other? As gentlefolk bound by shared beliefs and mutual obligations, or as contenders, loyal only to the market? Either she was confused, or Christina Steevens tried to twist both Blackwood's arms at once. Yet any confusion was his as well. William Blackwood conducted his business with a delicate balance of shrewdness and noblesse oblige. Though solicitous for the welfare of his authors, whenever confronted with what he considered unreasonable demands, he baulked at them. Dealing with a writer as famous and as profitable as G.W. Steevens quite upset the equilibrium.

Contributing to Maga

Like many others, Steevens was doubly a Blackwood's author, a contributor to Maga as well as a substantial presence in their list of publications. Between 1896 and 1899, he wrote ten articles for the magazine on subjects such as Russian foreign policy, strengthening the navy, arbitration, and German country life. One of the naval articles anticipates and the others supplement his *Naval Policy* (Methuen, 1896); articles on the American election and the war in Thessaly are longer than anything he could write for the *Daily Mail* and set out ideas taken further in *The Land of the Dollar* and *With the Conquering Turk*.[51] Writing for *Blackwood's Magazine*, that is to say, gave his arguments more latitude than a run of columns could afford.

Two of his articles assailed the daily press. 'The New Humanitarianism' (January 1898) condemns an excess of pity in the treatment of the criminal and the sick. Indeed, he comes close to lumping the two together: 'Parents should be taught to be ashamed of crippled children ... the only way to palliate ill-health is to ignore it' (*Things Seen*, 4); 'A wiser humanitarianism would make it easy for the lower quality of life to die. It sounds brutal, but why not? We have let brutality die out too much' (13). The ideas were commonplace in Henley's circle, but as if to show that he for one revels in healthy barbarism, Steevens puts them with uncommon vigour. They come from a moment when Nietzsche, Social-Darwinism, and the old-fashioned stoicism of country house and public school converge;[52] Steevens framed them as a challenge to Liberal and Radical editorialists: 'I have had some thoughts of writing a criticism on and denunciation of the newest kind of humanitarianism – as seen in the "Daily Chronicle" & 'Star' – the sort of spirit that regards death and pain as the greatest of all evils.'[53] The targets here are the 'Cocoa' press (the *Daily Chronicle* and *Daily News*, owned by Quaker confectioners) and papers situated farther left, such as the *Star*. In another piece, 'From the New Gibbon,' Steevens disparaged the whole institution of popular journalism, including cheap magazines as well as dailies. He offered this agenda to William Blackwood: 'Reflections upon the bad effect upon the nation of huge businesses, cheap uniform goods, everlasting[ly] the same thing, worship of money shown equally well by such different things as Chamberlain's colonial policy & the success of Harmsworth's magazine ... something rather good could be knocked together on these lines – perhaps more or less in the style of Gibbon as a dangerous symptom of decline in the midst of an apparent prosperity ... as time is limited I will not start anything you do not fancy.'[54] Along with Part 1 of *Heart of Darkness*, which has its own reflections on colonial policy and the worship of money, not to mention popular journalism and cheap goods, 'From the New Gibbon' appeared in the thousandth number (February 1899).[55] As the letter to Blackwood promised, the New Gibbon regards the popular press as only one swamp in an unkempt landscape, part of a drainage system dug by Chamberlain, linking business with imperialism. 'The student of that age will find melancholy evidence of degeneration in the printed records, and especially in the newspapers, of that time. The reported speeches of public men, the tattling of the parasites of fashion, the statistics of the markets, the very advertisements, bear unanimous testimony to the debased ideas which then enjoyed a ready and unprotested currency. The empire, that magnificent fabric founded upon the generous impulse to conquer and to rule, was now formally regarded as a mere machine for the acquisition of pounds sterling (*Things Seen*, 24).[56] The squalor of the press, moreover, is but one aspect of bad writing in 'this age of mediocrity': 'With the vast increase of readers promoted by the spread of elementary education, the social standing, as the monetary rewards, of authorship increased in equal proportion; but this cause, while it lowered the standard of taste, at once inflamed the cupidity and diverted the ambitions of men of letters; and what once had been a single-minded devotion degenerated into a trade, pursued rather for its accidental emoluments than for its intrinsic charm' (35).

What sense can we make of this sinner seeming to castigate his own sins? If he was simply venal, he would not be the first journalist or intellectual to offer up his gifts to cash or power, nor would he be the last – the very notion of a 'last' is risible. For a lapsed don, however, romance, danger, and the daring proof of manliness might be even more seductive than the money; Harmsworth was paying him to have adventures.

As I remarked earlier, speculations flew around after his death that his fervent imperialism was a pretence. Yet he had not necessarily succumbed to what Julien Benda was to call *la trahison des clercs*. His assault on Joseph Chamberlain in the 'New Gibbon' suggests another possibility: he was not *that kind* of imperialist. The Blackwood family embraced an imperialism characterized, as they saw it, by honour, duty, justice, self-denial, courage, and love of country;[57] at the mention of profits, they stared purposefully towards the horizon. Steevens admired new technology a great deal more than they did, but otherwise he shared their views of empire, including the view expressed in the 'New Gibbon' that, because even the strongest, most austere society is liable to degenerate, the survival of the British Empire never could be taken for a certainty. That idea owes as much to Juvenal or Tacitus as to Nordau or to Herbert Spencer. Steevens's classicism never left him. He was not, however, saving the right doctrine for the few, like some premature Straussian. Steevens's inner life is enigmatic, but one can argue that he saw his role at the *Daily Mail* as that of a writer who taught as he excited, preaching the higher imperialism in the forecourts of the lower.[58] He was negotiating a political landscape where patrician Tories claimed tradition and the party's conscience, Chamberlainites dug up the money, and the Harmsworth brothers charmed plebeian votes. This was the quandary of Conservatism in a democratic age, and one that perplexed the Blackwoods: how to reconcile privilege with popularity, how to make the first amenable to the second without the lure of bread and circuses. Steevens worried less about party loyalties and less about decorum.[59]

With a century's worth of hindsight, the distinction between the duty to serve an empire and the impulse to make money from it looks like a bad case of false consciousness. The Chamberlainites also invoked glory, duty, and racial fitness, and for the devotees of self-sacrifice, we might remember Marlow's remark to his aunt: 'I ventured to hint that the Company was run for profit.'[60] Yet, however fuzzy this distinction between soul and wallet becomes, to elide it altogether means overlooking important variations in colonial praxis[61] and being deaf to the period's cultural dialect. The moral grandstand, what is more, offers only a wobbly perch, since our own moment is all too similar to Steevens's. He worked in what historians would call the long twentieth century, which has yet to let us go. Most of what is most repellent in his work has its counterparts today: cocksureness, callousness, bellicosity, the gift for crystallizing general prejudices, the ready a priori statements about race and nation, the rendering of war as spectacle. The same is also true of his more attractive features, such as his freshness, his eye for odd, significant connections and his sense of the absurd extending even to himself. Very much a modern, and in literary style a proto-modernist, he did not always play along with what the public might have wanted, nor inevitably obey his masters' voices. Although William Blackwood did not entirely see what he had done, by taking Steevens on, he had embraced modernity.

NOTES

1 National Library of Scotland, Blackwood Papers, Publication Ledgers, MS 30862–6; see also David Finkelstein, *The House of Blackwood: Author–Publisher Relations in the Victorian Era* (University Park: Pennsylvania State University Press, 2002), appendix 1, 163–4.
2 Charles Whibley confirmed these attributions in his 'Musings Without Method,' *Blackwood's Magazine* 167 (February 1900), 167, 287.
3 Bernard Falk, *Bouquets for Fleet St.* (London: Hutchinson, 1951), 344.
4 Kipling's memorial quatrain, originally written for *The Friend* (Bloemfontein), 24 March, is the epigraph to W.E. Henley's 'Memoir' of Steevens, in the posthumous collection *Things Seen*, ed. G.S. Street (Edinburgh: William Blackwood and Sons, 1900).
5 Henley, 'Memoir,' xxvi, n. 1.
6 Spotting his talent while Steevens was still at Oxford, Henley sent Maga a story that was too long for the *National Observer*: Henley to William Blackwood, 18 May 1891, *The Selected Letters of W.E. Henley*, ed. Damian Atkinson (Aldershot, Hants: Ashgate, 2000), 201–2.
7 Henley, 'Memoir,' xxv.
8 *Academy*, 27 January 1900, 88.
9 Ibid., xxvii.
10 'After the War – What Then?' *Blackwood's Magazine* 167 (March 1900), 325.
11 *Blackwood's* 167 (February 1900), 286. For Whibley's role at Maga, see Stephen Donovan's chapter in this volume.
12 The sources of this biographical sketch are Henley's 'Memoir,' Vernon Blackburn's 'The Last Chapter' (the postscript to *From Capetown to Ladysmith* [Edinburgh: William Blackwood and Sons, 1900], 144–80), and the entry in the *New DNB*. For fuller information about his career and personal history, see H. John Field, *Toward a Program of Imperial Life* (Westport, Conn.: Greenwood, 1982), 119–201 and R.T. Stearn, 'G.W. Steevens and the Message of Empire,' *Journal of Imperial and Commonwealth History* 17 (1988–9), 210–31.

13 20 May 1893; collected posthumously in *Things Seen*, 133.

14 For Blackwood's struggles with agents amateur and professional, see Finkelstein, *House of Blackwood*, 129–49.

15 Annotation by Blackwood on National Library of Scotland, MS 4562, G.W. Steevens to William Blackwood, 15[?] May 1896.

16 Quoted by Hamilton Fyfe, *Northcliffe: An Intimate Biography* (London: Allen and Unwin, 1930), 79.

17 Ibid., 89.

18 'He had all the child's watchfulness, the child's curious interest in the little details of life' (*Academy*, 27 January 1900, 87).

19 Finkelstein, *House of Blackwood*, 98–101.

20 His field kit for the Upper Nile campaign included a folding bed, bath, chair, and table with set of table-linen, not to mention 'a cracking lunch-basket, a driving coat, and a hunting-crop' (*With Kitchener to Khartum* [Edinburgh: William Blackwood and Sons, 1898], 31). At the height of the Anglo-French crisis a month after Omdurman, Harmsworth sent Steevens to Paris at a moment's notice, chartering a tug to get him there as fast as possible (National Library of Scotland, MS 4682, Christina Steevens to William Blackwood, 28 October 1898).

21 *Saturday Review* 83 (1897), 273–4. This review delighted Steevens (National Library of Scotland MS 4667, G.W. Steevens to William Blackwood, 14 March 1897).

22 'The Presidential Election As I Saw It,' *Blackwood's Magazine* 160 (December 1896), 859–75. He wrote it on the voyage home (National Library of Scotland, MS 4652, Christina Steevens to William Blackwood, 17 September [1896]).

23 With occasional emendations in the light of victory. The first chapter ends by characterizing the Sudan as a 'murderous devil ... The man-eater is very grim, and he is not sated yet. Only this time he was to be conquered at last' (10). The corresponding sentences in the *Daily Mail* are: 'This man-eater is very grim, and he is not sated yet. Only this time he will be conquered at last' (13 April 1898).

24 National Library of Scotland, MS 4682, Christina Steevens to William Blackwood, 2 February 1898.

25 One of his essays, rich in technical detail, celebrates the monotype machine (*Things Seen*, 69–79).

26 He launched the *Mail* with the slogans: 'The Busy Man's Daily Newspaper' and 'A Penny Newspaper for One Halfpenny.'

27 *The Napoleon of Notting Hill* (London: John Lane, The Bodley Head, 1904), 225.

28 For example: 'Half the officers were down; the men puffed and stumbled on. Another ridge – God! Would this cursed hill never end? It was sown with bleeding and dead behind; it was edged with stinging fire before. And now it was surely the end. The merry bugles rang out like cock-crow on a fine morning. The pipes shrieked of blood and the lust of glorious death' (*From Capetown to Ladysmith*, 54). This bloodthirstiness was not universally popular. The Liberal and Labour press frequently took issue with such writing. Robert Blatchford, for instance, who had served in the army and was neither a pacifist nor a Little Englander, often used his editorial columns in the *Clarion*, a popular Socialist weekly, to denounce the popular journalistic blend of swagger, jocularity, and callousness: see, e.g., his remarks on Kipling, 13 March 1897, 82.

29 Writing on 'The Halfpenny Morning Press,' J.S.R. Phillips, who was editor of the *Yorkshire Post*, credits Steevens with much of the *Daily Mail*'s 'earlier attractiveness': *The Cambridge History of English and American Literature*, ed. A.W. Ward and A.R. Waller (Cambridge: Cambridge University Press, 1907–21), vol. 14, sect. 4, 36.

30 Nicely matching Harmsworth's populism, Steevens's persona as a journalist was that of a cheeky Londoner, brilliant and successful, but loyal to his roots. He came from the South-East London suburbs and, according to Henley, never tried to hide his accent ('Memoir,' x, n. 1). Thomas Pakenham calls him the 'jauntiest' of the correspondents in South Africa: *The Boer War* (New York: Random House, 1979), 277.

31 In *An Imperial War and the British Working Class: Working Class Attitudes and Reactions to the Boer War, 1899–1902* (London: Routledge, 1972), 132–77, Richard Price argues that the most fervent jingoism broke out in middle and lower middle class men, especially the clerks and shop assistants – two of Harmsworth's most important readerships: Such readers would have seen themselves as a cut above 'the street-bound masses, the men on the corners in their shirt sleeves' who, according to H. John Field, constituted Northcliffe's public (Field, *Toward a Program*, 190).

32 Regarding sales of *The Land of the Dollar*, he predicted that 'the price will be rather above the heads of the 250,000 readers of the "Daily Mail" who either did or did not read the letters originally' (National Library of Scotland, MS 4667, G.W. Steevens to William Blackwood, 24 January 1897).

33 *With the Conquering Turk* (Edinburgh: William Blackwood and Sons, 1897), 311.

34 The only newspapers which consistently questioned the purpose and conduct of the war were the *Manchester Guardian*, the *Morning Leader*, and the *Star*: the editor of the *Daily Chronicle*, another sceptic, lost his job:

Phillip Knightley, *The First Casualty: The War Correspondent as Hero and Myth-maker from the Crimea to Kosovo* (Baltimore: Johns Hopkins University Press, 2nd ed., 2000), 75.

35 Steevens suggests they were returning the kindness shown Boer prisoners captured earlier on. Possibly he assumed that a war between white men should elicit mutual respect – which would be to deny both centuries of history and the complex racial make-up of the armies – but in any case, his recognition of what happened, even in the face of a humiliating defeat, was unusual for the jingo press.

36 For example, Sir Charles Dilke in an unsigned review of *From Capetown to Ladysmith* for the *Athenaeum*: 'Another suggestion of the memoir is the question, What would have been Steevens's judgment upon the whole war had he lived to pronounce it? And would he have given the public his real judgment or a conventional judgment intended for daily newspaper consumption? Our impression is that in his interior self Steevens had remained a disciple of the naval school [which advocated a strong navy and a small, easily mobile army] and a Radical attached to peace all through his warlike and even Jingo writing for the *Daily Mail*' (3 March 1900, 265). Later that year, Vernon Blackburn wrote: 'We discussed the impending war, and he was eagerly looking forward to going with the troops. I dare not tell his views on the political question of the war. They would surprise most of his friends and admirers' ('The Last Chapter,' 164). Henley challenged such claims on the grounds that 'He was too good an Englishman and too poor a hypocrite' ('Memoir,' xvii, n. 1).

37 'Memoir,' xxiv.

38 For features such as these in Crane's fiction and his war-reporting, see Orm Øverland, 'The Impressionism of Stephen Crane,' in *Americana Norvegica*, ed. Sigmund Skard and Henry H. Wasser, vol. 1 (Oslo: The American Institute, 1966), 239–85.

39 To illustrate his maxim that the novelist should 'render: never report,' Ford gives the example of a man facing a gun: 'instead of writing "He saw a man aim a gat at him"'; you must put it: "He saw a steel ring directed at him": *Critical Writings of Ford Madox Ford*, ed. Frank MacShane (Lincoln: University of Nebraska Press, 1964), 67.

40 On this topic, Blackburn quotes the *Outlook*, whose obituarist makes the common distinction between Steevens as a writer for the few and for the many: 'Where the elect chiefly admired a scarcely exampled grasp and power of literary impressionism, the man in the street was learning the scope and aspect of his and our imperial heritage, and gaining a new view of his duties as a British citizen' ('The Last Chapter,' 166).

41 Blackburn, 'The Last Chapter,' 176. Some of the first newsreels would include fake or real footage of the war in which Steevens died: Knightley, *First Casualty*, 78.

42 Steevens did indeed begin a novel in 1899: National Library of Scotland, MS 4695, Christina Steevens to William Blackwood, 2 May 1899.

43 Nor was he troubled by *Heart of Darkness*, which he considered 'very powerful and a wonderful piece of descriptive word painting,' or the challenging narrative technique of *Lord Jim*: William Blackburn, ed., *Joseph Conrad: Letters to William Blackwood and David S. Meldrum* (Durham, N.C.: Duke University Press, 1958), 49, 91.

44 National Library of Scotland, MS 4667, G.W. Steevens to William Blackwood, 2 August 1897. To be 'amusing' was part of his literary persona.

45 National Library of Scotland, MS 4682, Christina Steevens to William Blackwood, 6 May 1898.

46 Ibid., 30 September.

47 Ibid., 8 October.

48 Ibid., 3 November.

49 National Library of Scotland, MS 4695. Grant Richards, who believed *With Kitchener* had been promised to him, was bitterly disappointed to find that Mrs Steevens had sent it to Blackwood: 'when the manuscript was ready she handed it over to him, just as if I and the promise to me had never existed. That was her way.' Grant Richards, *Author Hunting* (London: Hamish Hamilton, 1934), 215.

50 National Library of Scotland, MS 4695, 9 December 1899.

51 In the case of the article on the war, Steevens took care to ask if his pro-Turkish sympathies would be acceptable: National Library of Scotland, MS 4667, G.W. Steevens to William Blackwood, 8 June 1897.

52 As early as 1890, the novelist Mrs Lynn Linton denounced 'The Vice of Pity' in the *Daily Graphic*; her three-column letter appeared the day after Christmas (6). Further convergences and mutations of such ideas in the twentieth century have of course had vile results, such as the widespread vogue for sterilizing the 'unfit' and the Nazi 'euthanasia' program.

53 National Library of Scotland, MS 4667, G.W. Steevens to William Blackwood, 5 November 1897. He delivered the manuscript on 8 December, giving the house carte blanche with corrections: 'Sign it or not as you like; whoever is responsible for it will come in for a good deal of abuse, I should say; but I think it was time some such protest was made.' Blackwood printed it without a signature.

54 National Library of Scotland, MSS 4682, 1 December 1898.

55 Conrad told William Blackwood: 'I was delighted with the number. Gibbon especially fetched me quite': *The Collected Letters of Joseph Conrad*, ed. Frederick R. Karl, Laurence Davies, et al., 9 vols. (Cambridge: Cambridge University Press, 1983–2007), 2:162.

56 His opinion of the French and American popular press was harsher still. Reporting on the second Dreyfus trial for *Harper's*, for example, he observes: 'the cheapest rag in New York would blush for the recklessness, gullibility and foulness of the baser French press' (*The Tragedy of Dreyfus* [New York and London: Harper Bros., 1899], 302).

57 A view shared by many of their authors. In this context, see Linda Dryden's chapter above on Sir Hugh Clifford.

58 Another passage of 'From the New Gibbon' returns to the triviality of popular journalism (*Things Seen*, 35). Steevens would not have considered his principal topics – war, nationality, the social fabric – trivial. In his extensive and nuanced discussion of Steevens as a careerist, H. John Field argues that: 'In regard to his general audience Steevens was essentially cynical, realizing, as he once wrote [Grant] Richards, that he must make his work "as vulgar as I can, as that is the first rule of the game"' (Field, *Toward a Program*, 143). Nevertheless, 'Steevens was both artfully expedient and dutifully hyperproductive in writing to order, but he was also deeply engaged personally in propounding the new meaning of empire' (ibid., 186).

59 A clue to his own allegiances appears in a letter thanking William Blackwood for the November 1897 Maga: 'The paper on Tennyson is especially refreshing; I am not personally so complete a Conservative as "Maga" but it is good to read an article so robustly sure of its own mind' (National Library of Scotland MS 4667, 30 October 1897). J.H. Millar's article insists that the once-Liberal Tennyson became a sound Tory, a staunch imperialist, and a man who 'must be reckoned in the ranks of faith' (*Blackwood's Magazine* 162 [1897], 625). This account of the poet's later beliefs was unusual chiefly for its tone of fierce partisanship. The 'New Gibbon,' on the other hand, played down the differences of politics: 'The distinction of Conservative and Liberal preserved the name of party government without its substance' (*Things Seen*, 22).

60 Joseph Conrad, *Heart of Darkness and Other Tales*, ed. Cedric Watts (Oxford: Oxford University Press, 1990), 113.

61 Stephen Donovan, '"Figures, Facts, Theories": Conrad and Chartered Company Imperialism,' *Conradian* 24, no. 2 (1999), 31–60.

The Muse of *Blackwood's*: Charles Whibley and Literary Criticism in the World

STEPHEN DONOVAN

[W]e can but look forward with an insecure hope to the day when the critic shall remember that he owes a duty to truth as well as to generosity, and, stern in the conviction of a just cause, dares to revive the forgotten art of invective.
—'Musings Without Method,' *Blackwood's Magazine*
186 (July 1909), 123–36, 127

'Ah! dear Charles Whibley! What a reactionary! Is he not amusing? I love to read him – I am glad there is a Whibley! To force my opinions on others, that I could not do ... But I am glad there is a Whibley!'
– Joseph Conrad as recalled by Vio Allen[1]

If only for sheer prolixity, Charles Whibley's monthly causerie in *Blackwood's* must rank as one of the monuments of twentieth-century literary journalism. Published almost continuously between February 1900 and December 1929, 'Musings Without Method' exceeded the magazine's combined serialization of George Eliot, John Buchan, George Warrington Steevens, Hugh Clifford, and Joseph Conrad, a sprawling corpus of two million words or the equivalent of four and a half annual volumes.[2] Whibley's adherence to the mid-Victorian convention of journalistic anonymity, by this time as ostentatious a badge of conservatism as his quill pen, meant that 'Musings Without Method' appeared without a byline; yet its author's identity was as open a secret as the esteem in which he was held by the Blackwoods.[3] 'Whibley very interesting – very appreciative, very fair,' Joseph Conrad confided to William Blackwood in February 1899, alluding to an article in which the critic had coolly remarked upon Arthur Rimbaud's slave trading and gun-running activities in Africa: '[I]t is not difficult to understand the rare and aristocratic temperament, at once generous and insolent, which inflicts pain on the unworthy as easily as it succours those who demand legitimate aid.'[4] Like his appreciative description of Rimbaud as having 'declared war on journalism,' Whibley's valuation carried distinctly autobiographical echoes. For him, the 'aristocratic temperament' described a nobler affiliation than simple genealogy – Herbert Asquith's oration to Edinburgh University students, he declared in February 1907, 'breathes a spirit of intellectual aristocracy' – and in 'Musings Without Method' he made its exposition into his life-project.[5] In tireless pursuit of this ideal, as the obituarist in Maga conceded, 'he flogged our shams without mercy,' preaching belligerent Toryism in a coruscating, classical prose that eminently qualified him to speak for a magazine which, in Conrad's corruption of Tennyson, 'changeth not.'[6] Indeed, as the same author's emphases 'very interesting – very appreciative, very fair' attest, Whibley's voluminous commentaries offered Maga's contributors and readers nothing less than a shibboleth for their own collective identity during three tumultuous decades spanning the Dreyfus Affair and the Zinoviev Letter, the 'Khaki Election' and the General Strike, the death of Queen Victoria and the rise of Mussolini.[7]

Since column inches and circulation figures make poor measures of literary influence, as Whibley himself frequently pointed out, any re-evaluation of the significance of 'Musings Without Method' for Blackwood's and the early twentieth century literary field needs to start with the several kinds of cultural capital that Whibley brought to the column in his own right. Born the eldest son of a prosperous Kent merchant in 1859, he studied at Bristol Grammar School before winning a scholarship to Jesus College, Cambridge, where his prodigious talents enabled him to take a First in Classics in 1883. In spite of (or perhaps because of) his middle-class origins, Whibley adopted patrician cultural tastes and disdain for 'that strange form of government known as democracy' with all the fervour of a religious convert.[8] Embracing Cambridge elitism may have contained an element of psychological compensation, too, since he seems to have cut a rather unattractive and unhappy figure even in later years. Cynthia Asquith recorded in her diary how she had fended off 'Whibbles' in the back of a London taxi – 'I don't believe he is in the least conscious of being a gnome,' she noted mordantly – and Max Beerbohm mocked his meagre physical attributes in a caricature titled 'An Authority on the Dandies: Mr Charles Whibley, c.1900.'[9] Fundamentally, however, Whibley's ultraconservatism should be seen as part of a wider intellectual reaction to the advent of social modernity, in particular, the growth of the state and municipal government, the extension of the education system, and the rapid proliferation of what would later be called mass culture. He was drawn naturally into W.E. Henley's literary circle, whose at times incoherent espousal of British imperialism, masculine authority, and romantic anti-capitalism was, like its attachment to antiquated categories of 'genius' and 'man of letters,' firmly grounded in hostility towards literary professionalization and the burgeoning market for print.[10] Indeed, Whibley's contributions to Maga reveal him as clinging to the Henleyite banner long after the *New Review* and the *National Observer* had become defunct, an institutionalized avant-gardist or vanishing mediator between the literary configurations of the late-Victorian era and those of the Modernist 1910s and 1920s. Together with Kipling, Jerome Hamilton Buckley notes, 'Whibley carried [Henley's] battle into the new century, where they lived to see the defeat of the aesthetic doctrine made final and the victory of neo-realism assured.'[11]

Whibley's appointment as *Blackwood's* columnist at the age of forty-one represented the crowning achievement of an already brilliant career and was a much sought-after prize among the cadres of classically trained journalists whose impending obsolescence had inspired George Gissing's tragic portrait of Alfred Yule in *New Grub Street* (1891).[12] Recommended by Frederick Greenwood as a successor to Margaret Oliphant's 'Looker-On' column, he came to the post with strong credentials as a conservative political commentator. In July 1890, his venomous review of *The Picture of Dorian Gray* in the *Scots Observer* – 'Mr Oscar Wilde has again been writing stuff that were better unwritten; ... if he can write for none but outlawed noblemen and perverted telegraph-boys, the sooner he takes to tailoring (or some other decent trade) the better for his own reputation and the public morals' – had driven Wilde to protest in print at being attacked by a critic whom he dubbed 'Thersites.'[13] In the *Nineteenth Century* of April 1897, Whibley had denounced the attempts by reformers to enable Cambridge University to confer degrees upon women (whom he mystifyingly called 'the middle sex'), goading W.T. Stead, the voice of Britain's Nonconformist conscience, to propose that his stuffed corpse be labelled 'THIS IS CHARLES WHIBLEY' and put on display at the Natural History Museum at Kensington 'among other bipeds who have halted at vicious stages in the onward march towards a complete humanity.'[14] And in one of his first articles for Maga, published in March 1899, Whibley had delivered a searing indictment of Forster's Education Act of 1870 for creating a readership hungry only for sensationalist ephemera and its baneful complement, 'the worst periodical press that Europe has ever known,' to which he cannily counterposed *Blackwood's* as a model of the 'old-fashioned magazine' whose editor 'forced [readers] to accept the good things which he found for them' and whose integrity accorded it 'the right and the faculty to exert an influence.'[15] Whibley's credentials in contemporary literature, publishing, and academia were no less impressive. From 1894 to 1897 he had been Paris correspondent for the *Pall Mall Gazette*, now safely Tory again after its excursus into Radicalism under the editorship of Stead and John Morley, during which time he had become acquainted with Stéphane Mallarmé, Marcel Schwob, Paul Valéry, and James Whistler; and he would cultivate personal relationships with the rising stars of subsequent generations, among them D.H. Lawrence, T.S. Eliot, and Robert Graves.[16] Moreover, in addition to publishing *In Cap and Gown* (1889), *A Book of Scoundrels* (1897), and *Studies in Frankness* (1898) – a bibliography that would eventually run to seventy books, including monographs, biographies, translations, scholarly editions, and introductions – he had worked in Cassell's editorial department, assisted Henley and J.M. Barrie with the *Scots Observer*, briefly co-edited Lady Randolph Churchill's *Anglo-Saxon Review*, and established an affiliation with Macmillan as publisher's reader that would last for many years. Finally, he had retained a close and valuable connection to his alma mater, which would lead, in turn, to a commission from *The Cambridge History of English Literature* in 1909, the award of an Honorary Fellowship by Jesus College in 1912, and an invitation to give the university's prestigious Leslie Stephen Lecture in 1917.[17]

'Musings Without Method' was a belated continuation of William Hamley's unsigned column of the same name, which had appeared in six irregular instalments between April 1885 and September 1887.[18] The difference between the newcomer and its predecessor could hardly have been greater. A septuagenarian former army officer who had contributed stolid articles to *Blackwood's* on military and parliamentary matters, Hamley had clearly struggled with the looser format of the causerie. Beginning with palpable awkwardness, 'If, O reader, you have known what it is to pass years in a faraway land ...,' the series had concluded with a tacit concession of failure: '[A]s my ruminations do not seem to lead to an understanding of my subject ... perhaps I had better turn to something else.'[19] Indeed, his 'Musings Without Method' contained some disconcertingly candid admissions: that his argument has 'drifted'; that the reader '[p]robably ... thinks that a break in this yarn is well timed'; and, worst of all, that 'by a glance at the clock, I learn that I must give over my musings, and betake myself elsewhere.'[20] Not only were Hamley's hackneyed subjects – wrestling, mad dogs, early nineteenth-century army reforms, the rules of cricket[21] – un-enlivened by any scholarship (the few literary quotations are clichés, the solitary Greek epigram obviously transcribed), they were padded shamelessly with melodramatic and hokey dialect-filled vignettes of his own invention. Maga's conservative readers would likely have been discomforted by his tactless reference to a slave-owning family friend, and taken little cheer from his tepid criticisms of Joseph Chamberlain and French republicanism or his feeble proviso: 'there may, of course, be differences in opinion as to the precise nature and extent of the changes which may still be made with advantage to the community.'[22] Far from being self-effacing, the title 'Musings Without Method' was grimly accurate as a description of the fireside reminiscences of a writer who apparently believed that Blackwood's readership was interested in such topics as the availability of tropical fruit in London.

Whibley set himself the infinitely more ambitious task of reinventing the late-Victorian bookman as a public intellectual.[23] His 'Musings With-out Method' would integrate literature and political commentary using the critical lexicon not of genteel amateurism but of academic history and philosophy. More than just a source of cultural gravitas, his formi-dable erudition would be pressed into buttressing Maga's conservative values against the growing dangers of liberalism and socialism. For Whibley, Hamley's equivocations on the merits of flogging and British attitudes towards America, like his confession to a factual error, would have been unthinkable.[24] Indeed, to appreciate the extent to which Whibley excluded the very possibility of reasoned dissent from his opinions, one need only compare their respective defences (Hamley's qualified, Whibley's unapologetic) of the 'rotten' boroughs of the pre-1832 electoral system. Most importantly, Whibley's violent advocacy of the past effectively shifted Maga's editorial position from one of simple nostalgia to a peculiarly twentieth-century form of reaction.

'Musings Without Method' under Whibley's authorship did not lend itself to easy categorization or skim-reading. Its text, unlike that of its namesake, was unrelieved by crossheads or (for the most part) subdivi-sions, and its prefatory list of short titles gave few clues to the topics or trajectory of the dozen or so pages that followed. For example, its bill of fare for May 1907, 'A WAVE OF SENTIMENT – THE ADMIRATION OF THE

CRIMINAL – THE TRIUMPH OF THE BUSYBODY – THE AGRICULTURAL LABOURER – THE GOVERNMENT AND IRELAND' variously described: a societal tendency towards maudlin empathy with the unfortunate; public calls for clemency in the recent case of the parricide Horace Rayner; Liberal qualms about capital punishment; the reissue of a political tract, Thomas Kebbel's *The Agricultural Labourer*; and a new work of social anthropology, Ernest Iwan-Müller's *Ireland: To-day and To-morrow*. With his trademark directness, Whibley announced the Olympian purview of this fusion of *Kulturkritik*, leader column, book review, and political-aesthetic manifesto in his opening sentence: 'A mighty wave of sentiment is sweeping over the world.'[25] Moreover, for all its title's connotations of inconclusiveness and serendipity, 'Musings Without Method' was highly structured and programmatic in the selection and organization of its subject matter. Whibley's obituary in *Blackwood's* described him as enjoying 'discursive freedom ... in an age of critical anarchy' yet it would be more accurate to say that his position was defined by the discursive responsibilities of representing Maga to its readers and to the world at large.[26] After President William McKinley's assassination in 1901, it was Whibley who delivered a eulogy in a black-bordered 'Musings Without Method,' just as it was he who boasted portentously (and paradoxically) in a signed article commemorating Maga's centenary in April 1917: '*Blackwood's Magazine* has ever had a corporate life of its own. It is not a mere medley of heterogeneous articles. It is a single work, conducted by a single mind, for a single purpose.'[27]

Whibley's obscurity today is made all the more remarkable by the fact that his influence was acknowledged within a few years of his death by two of the twentieth century's most distinguished literary critics: T.S. Eliot and Richard Altick. Interestingly, each man saw Whibley as exemplary of a moribund tradition. In 'Charles Whibley,' a lecture given to the English Association in 1931 and included in the first edition of his *Selected Essays* (1932), Eliot located his old friend in a lineage of English prose stylists that counted Swift, Defoe, and Newman in its number, generously describing 'Musings Without Method' as 'the best sustained piece of literary journalism that I know in recent times.'[28] Learned, self-controlled, and always ready 'to say bluntly what everyone else is afraid to say,' Whibley's writing had displayed a mastery of invective, Eliot argued, which surpassed even that of Charles Maurras and Léon Daudet (the far-right and virulently anti-Semitic propagandists of *Action Française*).[29] Whibley's '*conversational style*,' he stressed, revealed the 'essential connexion between the written and the spoken word' which characterized all literature of lasting value, including 'the most recent writing of Mr. James Joyce.'[30] As Eliot noted approvingly, '[W]hat makes his own prose hold one's attention, in spite of, perhaps indeed emphasized by, its relation to remote models in the history of English literature, is that it is charged with life.'[31] In an era of deteriorating literary and ethical standards, Whibley's verbal energy, coupled with the 'moral integrity' inherent in 'genuine *plain speaking*,' had breathed new life into the classical values of the seventeenth and eighteenth centuries. On these grounds alone 'Musings Without Method' amply deserved to be anthologized before it became relegated to the dustbin of literary history, only ever to be consulted, in Eliot's memorable phrase, 'by some scholarly ferret into a past age.'[32]

Richard Altick's assessment, appearing during the dark days of 1942 and focusing upon Whibley's political views, started from a quite different premise. For Altick, the fact that 'Musings Without Method' had preached 'the gospel of die-hard Toryism' with such violence for so many years in 'one of the oldest and most respectable periodicals in the Empire' afforded disturbing evidence of 'a phenomenon which historians of contemporary Britain cannot afford wholly to ignore,' namely, the existence of a large English-speaking audience in sympathy with an ideology that was both morally despicable and politically bankrupt.[33] Recording how 'Musings Without Method' moved from anti-French jingoism in its first years to virulently anticommunist paranoia in the late 1920s, Altick followed Whibley through tirade after tirade against a never-ending stream of targets: republicans, Liberals, Radicals, social democrats, trade unionists, suffragettes, Bolsheviks, Germans, Irish nationalists, American philanthropists, and even Conservatives who fell short of his exacting standards. For Whibley, the old age pension was state-licensed beggary, unemployed miners were pampered idlers, and the progressive extension of the franchise had been a historic catastrophe without parallel. A book compiled only of Whibley's attacks on David Lloyd George, Altick speculated, 'would be without doubt the most vituperative volume in modern English history,' whilst the anti-Semitism of his final decade prompted Altick to end with a provocative counterfactual question: 'How would he have reconciled his very apparent sympathy with many of the tenets of fascism with his rabid Germanophobia?'[34]

Altick describes 'Musings Without Method' as 'British journalism's busiest whipping-post,' and the fact that Whibley's writing was dominated so spectacularly by a single rhetorical mode, the polemic, raises an important theoretical issue in the critical history of *Blackwood's* between 1900 and 1930.[35] To be sure, the necessarily reactive and negative character of polemic would appear to fit awkwardly with *Maga's* longstanding commitment to the promotion of Conservative political values and cultural authority through approval or endorsement.[36] And, as Pierre Bourdieu has argued in *The Field of Cultural Production*, although polemics are a standard feature of the struggles that both constitute and are constituted by 'the space of literary or artistic position-takings,' they remain intrinsically problematic as a strategy of engagement for the professional gatekeepers of cultural and political capital whom he calls 'symbolic bankers.'[37] '[P]olemics imply a form of recognition,' he writes, '[because] adversaries whom one would prefer to destroy by ignoring cannot be combated without consecrating them.'[38] Indeed, as Bourdieu notes elsewhere, polemics are extreme instances of the very systems of expression which 'create the objects that are worth talking about.'[39] At the same time, Altick is surely right when he points out that the Rabelaisian character of Whibley's denunciations – in which critics of the Anglo-Boer War are 'radical cannibals,' the Board of Education is 'a vast machinery of spies,' and Herbert Asquith 'the Marinetti of the House of Commons' – rules out any possibility that his thirty-year-long running commentary was seriously intended 'to instruct in the reactionary theory of government.'[40] To suggest that Whibley's reliance upon the polemic was merely a foible, a disagreeable symptom of cantankerousness, similarly fails to convince. On the contrary, the polemic should be seen as integral to Whibley's larger ambition to carve out an unassailable position separate from and superior to the flow of current events and warring ideologies, analogous to what he saw as the successful tactic adopted by 'our universities' (that is, Oxford and Cambridge) in defending their 'ancient character' against the predations of 'women, democrats, headmasters, and other faddists.'[41] Seen from this perspective, the *omnium gatherum* of Whibley's spleen, in which urgent questions of the day were often juxtaposed with matters of essentially trivial or antiquarian interest (the general election alongside a work titled *How to Write for the Magazines*, Japan's defeat of the Russian navy alongside Beerbohm Tree's staging of *The Tempest*), begins to makes more sense.[42] Such a position, which, as Bourdieu contends, frustrates any simplistic and moralizing definition as self-interest or co-optation, draws strength precisely from its unlimited capacity to find fault.[43]

The polemical mode of 'Musings Without Method' ought therefore to be seen as performing an act of symbolic withdrawal akin to the physical seclusion of Whibley's own favourite spaces – the Senior Common Room, the London club, the university library, and, above all, the scholar's study – whose synecdochic equivalence to a particular kind of unhurried reflection is the real significance of the word 'musings.' *This* was how Whibley envisioned his role: to supply Maga's readers with literary criticism that was in the world (as evidenced by his many treatments of mundane topics like taxation, parliamentary business, and legal rulings) yet not of the world, that is to say, not constrained by party allegiance, popular opinion, or even common humility. 'May we not be forgiven a little arrogance when we receive as fellow-subjects Gurkhas and Sikhs, Pathans and Rajputs, Mahrattas and Afridis ...?' he asked, with a revealing choice of pronoun and verb, on the eve of Edward VII's coronation in 1902.[44] This perspective provides a way of thinking about 'Musings Without Method' as not merely a series of (literally reactionary) commentaries upon an arbitrary selection of topics but, rather, as the exercise of a rhetorical mode ideally suited to apostrophizing Maga's virtual community, those readers in officers' messes and colonial clubhouses whom Conrad famously extolled as 'the good sort of public.'[45] It further enables us to understand Whibley's lifelong attraction to those on the fringes of society, whether at the top or the bottom, as more than just naive romanticism or individualism. In their defiance of convention and even the law, underworld figures and elite political coteries constituted the supreme units of social organization in his eyes, deferring only to their own codes of honour and the force of individual personalities (elective affinities that, not coincidentally, approximated closely to Whibley's conception of class): unrepentant criminals such as the serial poisoner Madame de Brinvillier, whose life he described as marked by 'courage and dignity'; aristocratic rakes such as John Law of Lauriston, the eighteenth-century Scottish gambler whose career he summed up as 'a fairy tale of splendour'; or Tory statesmen such as Benjamin Disraeli, who knew full well 'that influence in a democratic state must be won at the outset not by worth but by notoriety.'[46] As Whibley explained of his favourite historical subject: 'The romance of the high toby is imperishable. To bestride a well-bred mare and to carry a brace of pistols in your holster appeared of itself the action of a gentleman.'[47]

Pace Altick, Whibley's polemics were not simply an expression of frustrated rage at a world moving inexorably towards some kind of socialist dystopia. Rather, they served him as a means of rallying Maga's readers around a shared set of prejudices. Altick deprecates Whibley's outbursts as 'hymns of hate,' yet in exactly the same way as the ideological banality of the First World War propaganda song to which he alludes was less important than the collective act of singing it – in Ernst Lissauer's infamous lyrics, 'Wir lieben vereint, wir hassen vereint' ('We love as one, we hate as one') – so, too, was the unifying function of 'Musings Without Method' equal in importance to anything its author had to say on a particular subject. And he welcomed the same 'fine fury,' as he once described Hazlitt's critical outbursts, in his adversaries.[48] Whibley's most heartfelt term of abuse was 'pedantry,' a term that, for him, denoted bureaucratic insistence on factual accuracy at the expense of passionately held convictions, and so he thought it no inconsistency to praise a political enemy such as William Morris for proving himself (in Johnson's phrase) a 'good hater': 'When he hated, he hated with a splendid vigour. Herbert Spencer, Ferguson the architect, Pearson, and the whole race of restorers, he denounced with incomparable energy and cogent argument.'[49] Similarly, in order to highlight Kaiser Wilhelm II's manifest inadequacy in this field, Whibley quoted Napoleon's scathing attack on Jerôme, King of Westphalia, paying tribute to the French Emperor's ability to 'endow the simplest words with ferocity': 'Every syllable of this tirade breathes truth and rage ... He found the right words at once, and let them scourge and whip with all the ferocity that was in his mind.'[50]

If 'truth and rage' neatly summarizes the formula of Whibley's own polemicizing, it should not be assumed that all Maga's readers shared in his indignation. As Conrad's affectionate remarks in the second epigraph to this essay indicate, 'Musings Without Method' gave pleasure to some precisely by virtue of its rhetorical extravagance. Indeed, a full survey of Whibley's diatribes brings to light a host of memorable one-liners, often unintentionally comic: on medieval England ('Feudalism no doubt, had its hardships; but in spite of injustice it was the realisation of a generous dream'); on Mark Twain's *A Connecticut Yankee in the Court of King Arthur* (1907) ('His book gives you the same sort of impression you might receive from a beautiful picture over which a poisonous slug had crawled'); or on Liberal demands for an increase in the rate of income tax ('It is as though a highwayman, having demanded your purse and got it, should shoot you through the head because it was not full enough').[51] He could be particularly witty in debunking pretentiousness and third-rate scholarship. When a credulous American writer claimed to have found a lost work by Francis

Bacon (patently an inferior forgery) confirming his authorship of Shakespeare's plays, Whibley's irony was merciless: '"I have made great progress in cipher-writing," [Bacon] assures Mrs Gallup on one occasion, "finding it pleasing at first, – I may say, many times mildly exciting." Mildly exciting! We thank thee, Bacon, for teaching us that word! Would that the pages, mildly exciting to write, were mildly exciting to read! But, alas! it is only when he confesses his interest in Mrs Gallup that we are aroused to even a mild excitement.'[52]

More seriously, the incommensurability of Whibley's targets raises questions about the extent to which readers regarded his polemics as entertaining performances as much as statements of principle. In lambasting the journalist Emily Hobhouse for her exposé of squalid conditions in British concentration camps during the Anglo-Boer war, he undoubtedly gave voice to the anger felt by a majority of Maga's readers.[53] Likewise, his hilarious review of Marie Corelli's *The Master-Christian* (1900) ridiculed the intellectual posturings of a popular novelist whose works no self-respecting *Blackwood's* reader would ever admit to having purchased. 'Miss Corelli, then, has genius, and plenty of it – *cela va sans dire,* as she would say herself,' he commented acidly before moving into *recusatio,* the lawyer's favourite rhetorical device:

> If she did not possess the supreme gift, we might perhaps object to her sanguine temerity. We might suggest, for instance, that a formal attack upon all the Churches should not be made by an unlettered lady, who knows not the rudiments of theology or criticism. We might point out in all modesty that to give your characters high-sounding names, and to put such speeches in their mouth as would shame an orator of Hyde Park, is wicked irreverence. We might prefer a slight knowledge of English grammar to miles of obvious rhetoric ... But that is the advantage of genius: it need understand nothing; it may parade knowledge which it does not possess; it may commit every sin against taste and truth; and all the same it is genius, or, if it isn't, what becomes of the manifold protestations which have secured, we are told, to 'The Master-Christian' so many thousands of readers?[54]

Whibley's jeremiads against speed-loving drivers, by contrast, must have grated upon the motoring enthusiasms of his predominantly affluent, male readership (in whose ranks Conrad, for example, must be counted).[55] And in his lengthy enumeration of the modern plutocrat's character flaws, he betrayed a resentment of wealth that could easily have pained or embarrassed parts of his audience: 'Of course [the millionaire] can purchase more champagne than his fellows; of course he can enlarge his racing-stable, until it includes all the horses not already purchased by rival millionaires. Of course, also, he may buy books, and pictures, and houses; but the excitement of the genuine collector is not for him. A book or a picture that has caused no sacrifice and entailed no forethought cannot have the same value as a book or a picture that has been feverishly watched and bought with coins that are hardly spared.'[56]

Its first instalment in February 1900 established the paradigm to which 'Musings Without Method' would adhere for the next quarter century. Ranging with deceptive ease across a series of seemingly disconnected topics (a vogue for publishing diaries, three new memoirs, music-hall jingoism, newspaper coverage of the Anglo-Boer war, and the death of George Warrington Steevens), Whibley teased out the strands of his overarching theme – the journalization of public discourse.[57] At every stage in the essay, he took pains to underscore the superiority of the 'dear, dead conventions of the past' (282) to those of 'these prosaic times' (282). The newly published diaries of Sir Mountstuart Grant Duff, Sir Algernon West, and William Rossetti could not hold a candle to Charles Greville's celebrated *Memoirs* (1874–87); the 'inapposite patriotism' (282) and vulgarity of the new West End music-halls made poor substitutes for the 'old enchantments' (282) of traditional Christmas pantomime; and the current manipulation of public opinion by newspapers was a national disgrace unheard of in the days of empire-building or Wellington's Peninsula Campaign. And yet, for Whibley, these contemporary failings were not merely indices of historical decadence. In their reliance upon speed, shock, and the homogenization of experience, they expressed a deeper transformation of urban life, one that had given rise to a new subjectivity among audiences and an obsession with spectacle or 'the performances of the whole world' (275).[58] From the publicity-seeking diarists who thought nothing too intimate for print, to the music-hall dancers wearing petticoats made from Union Jacks, and the journalists whose reckless advertising of disharmony in the ranks constituted an incitement to mutiny, Whibley's anatomy of what he elsewhere called '*surface-culture*' anticipated, albeit in embryonic form and from a high Tory stance, the Frankfurt School's critique of reification and alienation.[59] In flattering Maga's readers as 'the smaller number to whom popular success is not the first and last criterion of literary merit' (286), he reminded his audience of the monthly review's special value as a corrective to a world of distortion.

Coherency is not consistency, however, and Whibley's essay abounds with internal contradictions. A memoirist's revelation of 'trivial secrets' (277) is, by definition, not an 'indiscretion' (281) of any consequence, just as dancing girls in Union Jacks are surely evidence of the strength of imperialist sentiment, not its attenuation. Whibley's claim that 'Fleet Street and the war correspondents are no more essential to the empire than the parasites who hope to loot our camps' (283) was patently untrue, as were his suggestions that Lord Roberts was practising 'censorship of news' (283) and that the *Times* had assisted the enemy during the Crimean War so that its editor might 'stultify a weak Government' (285).[60] His excoriation of 'the common journalist' (279), a prejudice he would never tire of reiterating, might have puzzled readers who knew of his work for the *Pall Mall Gazette* and *Scots Observer* (to which he would add stints at *The Spectator* and *Daily Mail*); later 'Musings Without Method' make reference to receiving letters from readers seeking advice on how to enter the profession. Yet all such troubling considerations were swept aside by Whibley's intellectual bravura and a magisterial prose style studded with classicisms and Gallicisms ('Amphitryonic statistics' (279), 'aestivate' (282), 'patriotard' (282), *'raconteur'* (279), *'revue'* (281)) as well as unattributed quotations and a torrent of compound adjectives calculated to intimidate: 'the frippish conversations of titled nobodies' (275); 'a shapeless mass of undigested "copy"' (276); 'appallingly dull' (277); 'heroically amiable' (277); and a 'squalid, insignificant life' (281). All the while, a fugue-like repetition of motifs served to amplify the contribution made by each item to Whibley's overall attack on cultural debasement. Thus each sub-section foregrounded the role of language: Duff's contemptible use of the word 'celebrities' (276); the pantomime's love of 'reckless, irresistable puns' (281); and journalistic exaggerations such as 'rain of lead' and 'a solid sheet of bullets' (285). Each offered a defence of the past in terms of an attribute simply termed 'manners' (281, 283, 285), and each stressed the historical novelty of present-day ills: the 'modern habit' of pandering to 'modern curiosity' (276); 'modern fashions' (281) in entertainment; and 'the sorriest spectacle of modern times' (283). And, in the wings of each, Whibley's Tory agenda could clearly be discerned: the ironic subtitle 'ONE MAN, ONE BOOK' (275); the unfavourable juxtaposition of Liberals West and Duff alongside the reactionary Roberts (soon to be President of the National Service League); the praise for the Liberal

Imperialist *Daily News*'s having 'valiantly set patriotism before party' (285); the veiled implications that journalists should be subject to the Army Act and conversation 'copyrighted by law' (281); and the snobbish quip that West's book had announced (in Cockney, no less): 'See how "genteel" I have always been! I've always been in a smart set, I have!' (279).[61]

As important as these structural homologies or the essay's framing notion of a lifetime's achievement is the skilful way that Whibley connected his individual subjects. Eliot praised these transitions in the highest possible terms when he defined the 'sudden transitions and juxtapositions of modern poetry' as being, when successful, 'an application of somewhat the same method without method,' and Whibley's confidently conjunctive 'Now, ...' (275), 'Now, ...' (278), 'Now, ...' (283), 'Again, ...' (280), 'Again, ...' (284) can perhaps be likened to Eliot's own deliberate repetitions: 'And a time for living ... / And a time for the wind ... / And to shake the wainscot ... / And to shake the tattered arras ...'[62] To this poetic variety of induction can be added Whibley's effective use of several other rhetorical devices. Some are familiar as the polemicist's tools in trade: rigid binaries (modernity–tradition, vulgarity–refinement, discretion–advertisement, patriotism–treason, public–private, scholarship–ignorance); hyperbole ('so long as his circulation is secure, [the journalist] will cheerfully witness the world in ashes' (284)); and plentiful superlatives ('bitterest' (276), 'busiest' (277), 'lightest' (278), 'most frivolous' (278), 'most distinguished' (278), 'greatest' (278), 'most assiduous' (279), 'smallest' (279), 'lowest' (282), 'noblest' (282), 'easiest' (282), 'sorriest' (283), 'staunchest' (284), 'most successful' (287), 'uttermost' (287), 'greatest' (287), 'most stirring' (287)). Others, such as Whibley's arresting similes and epigrams, are stamped with his own uniquely splenetic brand of humour:

The rare ones that have not joined what is called 'the ranks of our imaginative writers' may be pointed out in the street with confidence and precision. (275)

[N]or do we bear with patience a lesson in politics delivered by a young lady whose pink tights are obviously too small for her. (282)

If the speech of the Boulevards could project bullets, no nations save the French would live an hour; and if the pantomimes of London were translated into fact, a small, compact army of ballet-girls, wrapped round with the union-jack, would even now be marching to the conquest of the world. (283)

The foregoing analysis of Whibley's debut is intended to show how 'Musings Without Method,' unlike so many occasional writings in periodicals, can richly repay close analysis. The cluster of topics addressed in its first instalment are, moreover, a microcosm of the column's concerns in succeeding decades. The mediation of historic events according to 'the demand that has been created by the daily paper' (276) would emerge as one of Whibley's main preoccupations – in the final words of his very last essay he railed against the Viceroy of India for respecting 'the hasty opinions of a few special correspondents' – just as W.T. Stead, here invoked slightingly as journalism's 'most daring professor' (276), would remain Whibley's *bête noire* long after his influence had been eclipsed and even after his spectacular death aboard the *Titanic* (a media event that Whibley conspicuously ignored).[63] The same held true of the new reading public whose unwarranted intrusiveness and sentimentality became inextricably associated in Whibley's eyes with the enfranchisement and political organization of the lower middle and working classes; Ramsay MacDonald and Édouard Herriot, France's Radical-Socialist prime minister, were, he commented derisively in 1925, 'two middle-class sentimentalists.'[64] In the aftermath of the 'Black Week' of British defeats at Stormberg, Magersfontein, and Colenso in December 1899, perhaps only Whibley would have dared talk so casually about to how best to fight 'our next war' (286), but military conflict appealed to him, ideologically and professionally, almost as much as it did to Maga's uniformed readers, and later instalments of 'Musings Without Method' routinely considered the resolution of international disputes by force.[65] Furthermore, in its choice of subjects, as in its characteristic blend of jeremiad and *ubi sunt* lament, the essay looked ahead to Modernist aesthetics. Whibley's praise for the traditional variety show as 'a perfect vision of the past' (282) would be echoed by George Mair's observation in the *English Review* that the music hall 'has vitality, because it has its continuous history right back into the past,' and by T.S. Eliot's famous claim that Marie Lloyd had 'represented and expressed that part of the English nation which has perhaps the greatest vitality and interest.'[66] Lastly, Whibley's essay signalled a major departure from the conventional mode of reviewing in *Blackwood's*, in which a work of potential interest to Maga's readers served as the pretext for a literary survey and some brief speculative remarks on history and society. When not puffing works published by Blackwood or Macmillan, Whibley routinely performed a very different kind of operation, selecting works (often wholly insignificant) that allowed him to engage his real target.[67] An inferior memoir or a pink-hosed patriot accordingly held significance for him only as a 'symptom' (278, 282), and in sneeringly demanding what possible interest the minutiae of Gladstone's private life, detailed in the diary memoirs of his private secretary George A. West, could have for 'subscribers to a circulating library' (280), he betrayed the very premise of his review – that *Blackwood's* readers would form no part of the audience for West's diaries.

Although limitations of space preclude discussion here of Whibley's responses to the momentous political and cultural events during his long tenure at *Blackwood's*, some avenues for future research can usefully be indicated. Sixty years ago, in his short history of 'Musings Without Method' as political commentary, Richard Altick traced out the core ideological tenets that Whibley sought to promulgate or shore up among his readers, including Empire Free Trade, uncompromising hostility towards Germany, and opposition to female suffrage.[68] Since then, this vast archive of articulate Tory polemic, addressed to a readership in which opinion-makers and elite politicians were heavily overrepresented, has remained untapped by historians of the early twentieth century. Further investigation of 'Musings Without Method' will undoubtedly deepen our understanding of the role played by magazines such as *Blackwood's*, Leo Manxse's *National Review*, and Horatio Bottomley's *John Bull*, not least as influences on Conservative party policy during a period of revolutionary change.[69] And a similar trove of material relates to Whibley's friendship with the newspaper baron Alfred Harmsworth, Lord Northcliffe, whom he accompanied to the United States in summer 1906 (a trip that resulted in the columnist publishing half a dozen American sketches in *Blackwood's* between November 1906 and May 1907) and again to Provence in spring 1910. In 1908, Northcliffe lured Whibley away from the *Spectator* with the offer of his own *Daily Mail* column, 'Letters of an Englishman,' from which a two-volume selection was published anonymously in 1911–12 and republished under Whibley's name in 1915.[70] During the First World War, as David Finkelstein has shown, *Blackwood's* made a substantial contribution to the propaganda war effort through reportage items such as Sylvia Townsend Warner's 'Behind the Firing Line: Some Experiences in a Munition Factory' and popular fiction serials such as John Hay Beith's *The First Hundred Thousand*.[71] Whibley's involvement in this campaign raises some fascinating questions. What difference did it make to *Blackwood's* that its principal spokesperson had direct access to – indeed, as J.A. Hammerton noted, was deeply respected by – a man whose cynicism and efficiency as Director of Propaganda in Enemy Countries would later be an inspiration to the Nazi Party?[72] (When challenged about the veracity of German atrocity stories, Whibley is said to have shouted, 'I'm not looking for Truth! I'm looking for Hate, which for most Englishmen is at the bottom of a far deeper well than Truth!'[73]) How, too, should we interpret the fact that a feature article with his byline appeared alongside articles by two other *Blackwood's* men, John Buchan and Joseph Conrad, in the *Daily Mail* of 30 June 1919, a special gilt-edged number commemorating the Treaty of Versailles that sold one million copies?[74]

The tone of Whibley's polemics became steadily more shrill during the turbulent 1920s, his irascibility doubly exacerbated by neuralgia and an acute anxiety that the world had at last slipped beyond the reach of Toryism. Now overwhelmingly political in nature, the topics treated by 'Musings Without Method' in this final decade reflect their author's pessimism and fatigue. There are, to be sure, occasional glimpses of the old fury in his acerbic pronouncements on cultural and intellectual developments such as psychoanalysis ('the baleful superstition of Freud'), television ('what a word!'), Darwinism ('How miserable we should have been ... had we lived and died without knowing that we were descended from apes!'), and female enfranchisement ('THE FLAP-PERS' VOTE').[75] More frequent, however, are Whibley's complaints at the Conservative Party's failure to halt the tides of Liberalism and Communism; he praised the 'wholesome' counter-revolution of Mussolini's 'brave and competent' *Fascisti* and openly called for a new political party just one year before Oswald Moseley launched his New Party (later renamed the British Union of Fascists).[76] Disaster everywhere seemed imminent – from Mahatma Gandhi's treasonable declaration, 'Get ready soon for the war, and God will grant victory to India very soon,' to the 1922 Anglo-Irish Treaty in whose every clause, Whibley thundered, 'Destruction is written large.'[77] The mood of his 'Retrospective' on a quarter-century of 'Musings Without Method' in January 1925 – the first time, as he pointed out, that he had 'descend[ed] to the use of the first person singular' – was unusually bleak.[78] Neither his tirades against MacDonald and Herriot as pawns of Kerensky nor his (at times

acute) dissection of Communist theories of the dictatorship of the prole-
tariat could conceal the sense of defeat that accompanied his call for
another Aristophanes to take up the torch of satire and prevent Britain
from 'follow[ing] Athens to destruction.'[79] Tellingly, these years saw
Whibley increasingly turn to literature, not for illustration of a political
or sociological thesis, but for escape: 'It is pleasant to turn from the
confusion of politics to a book ...'; 'Aubrey Herbert's *Record of Eastern
Travel* is a pleasant relief from the tangle of politics.'[80] Three months
before his own death, he speculated darkly in a final 'Musings Without
Method' that the sentence of death passed upon Socrates by the Athenian democracy 'might, if the supremacy of the law be not restored, be
meted out to those who in the present day seem hostile to a democratic
regime.'[81]

The modern culture industry's targeting of niche audiences, what is
sometimes referred to as 'narrowcasting,' has its origins in the forma-
tive impact of advertising upon magazine production in the late
nineteenth century, and despite its august reputation *Blackwood's* was
no stranger to the concept of literary 'branding.'[82] Seen in this light,
Whibley's authorship of 'Musings Without Method' was a resounding
success, delivering an extremely stable product ('Whibley') to audiences around the globe for over a generation. In a world of ceaseless
change, Maga's readers could always rely upon his Cassandra-like
predictions, vehement reverse Whiggism, and, not least, supremely
self-confident opinions on literature. Among those who knew and loved
Whibley, wrote Maga's obituarist, were numerous readers who 'knew
not even his name, but have delighted in his wisdom, his humour, and
his wit.'[83] To this paratextual intimacy should be added his commanding status in the wider literary field, as the *New York Times*'s coining of
the term 'Whibley-ized' attests.[84] To be sure, Whibley's engagement
with the modern world remained limited to a negative dialectic that, as
even Eliot acknowledged, left no room for creative imagining of the
future, yet this was perhaps no more than a symptom – as Whibley
himself might have put it – of the severity of the challenges now facing
Maga's 'twin banners of sound criticism and Tory politics.'[85] In securing
the services of a critic who has been called 'the 1890s most eloquent
literary reactionary,' *Blackwood's* found a voice capable of articulating its
unique vision to an international audience.[86] The cultural historian
must resist imposing a false teleology upon the cultural and political
agendas pursued by *Blackwood's* in the twentieth century. Had fascism
found more fertile ground in Britain in the 1930s, the name Charles

Whibley would perhaps be as recognized today as that of Oswald Spengler.

NOTES

1 Vio Allen, 'Memories of Joseph Conrad,' *Review of English Literature* 8, no. 2 (April 1967), 77–89, 84.
2 Between 1898 and 1930, Whibley also published ninety-seven articles (totalling half a million words) in *Blackwood's*, mostly under his own name, and by 1900 he had already contributed over thirty articles to other reviews. 'Musings Without Method' (henceforth MWM) did not appear in the following months: August 1900, August 1903, August 1906, March 1921, April 1926, April and May 1928, and April–August 1929.
3 On anonymity in *Blackwood's*, see Laurel Brake, *Print in Transition, 1850–1910: Studies in Media and Book History* (Basingstoke: Palgrave Macmillan, 2001), 4–6.
4 Joseph Conrad, *Collected Letters*, volume 2, *1898–1902*, ed. Frederick R. Karl and Laurence Davies (Cambridge: Cambridge University Press, 1986), 162. Charles Whibley, 'A Vagabond Poet,' *Blackwood's Magazine* 165 (February 1899), 402–12, 409.
5 MWM, *Blackwood's Magazine* 181 (February 1907), 281–90, 283.
6 Anonymous [Sir Stanley Leathes], 'Charles Whibley by a Friend,' *Blackwood's Magazine* 227 (April 1930), 585–8, 586. See Joseph Conrad, *Collected Letters*, volume 1, *1861–1897*, ed. Frederick R. Karl and Laurence Davies (Cambridge: Cambridge University Press, 1983), 402. 'The old order changeth, yielding place to new,' reads Tennyson's 'The Passing of Arthur,' *Poems*, ed. Christopher Ricks, vol. 3 (Harlow, Essex: Longman, 1987), 559.
7 See, respectively, 'The Cries of Paris,' *Blackwood's Magazine* 163 (March 1898) 313–21; MWM, *Blackwood's Magazine* 222 (July 1927), 133–44, 133–40; MWM, *Blackwood's* 168 (November 1900), 757–67, 757–62; MWM, *Blackwood's Magazine* 220 (July 1926), 132–44, 132–7; MWM, *Blackwood's Magazine* 169 (March 1901), 418–28; MWM, *Blackwood's Magazine* 212 (December 1922), 825–35, 829.
8 MWM, *Blackwood's Magazine* 225 (February 1929), 278–90, 278.
9 Lady Cynthia Asquith, *Diaries 1915–1918* (London: Hutchinson, 1968), 310–11. John Gross gives a damning portrait of Whibley in *The Rise and Fall of the Man of Letters: Aspects of English Literary Life since 1800* (London: Weidenfeld and Nicolson, 1969), 154–5.

10 In addition to contributing numerous articles to the *New Review*, Whibley wrote the introductions for Henley's 'Tudor Translations' series in the late 1890s, and edited a second series himself in the 1920s. He was also Henley's literary executor. On Whibley's place in Henley's 'Regatta,' whose writers included Rudyard Kipling, H.G. Wells, Arthur Morrison, R.L. Stevenson, J.M. Barrie, Andrew Lang, George Saintsbury, George Wyndham, G.W. Steevens, and W.B. Yeats, see Peter D. McDonald, *British Literary Culture and Publishing Practice, 1880–1914* (Cambridge: Cambridge University Press, 1997), 47–52. The New York Public Library's copy of *Musings Without Method: A Record of 1900–01* (1902) contains the autograph dedication: 'To W. E. Henley with the affection and gratitude of Charles Whibley, 1902.'

11 Jerome Hamilton Buckley, *William Ernest Henley: A Study in the 'Counter-Decadence' of the 'Nineties* (Princeton, N.J.: Princeton University Press, 1945), 161. It has been suggested that Whibley was the model for Keneu the Great War Eagle in Kipling's *The Light That Failed* (1891) and the fascist politician Everard Webley in Aldous Huxley's *Point Counter Point* (1928).

12 See Nigel Cross, *The Common Writer: Life in Nineteenth-Century Grub Street* (Cambridge: Cambridge University Press, 1985), 230–2.

13 In *The Iliad*, Thersites is the most rancorous of the Greek warriors – and the ugliest; Whibley gamely used the sobriquet as his signature when replying to Wilde. See Merlin Holland and Rupert Hart-Davis, eds., *The Complete Letters of Oscar Wilde* (London: Fourth Estate, 2000), 438–9 and 446–9. Whibley also made several influential critiques of Ruskin's aesthetic principles during this period.

14 Charles Whibley, 'The Encroachment of Women,' *Nineteenth Century* 39/242 (April 1897), 531–7, 537; W.T. Stead, 'The Reviews Reviewed,' *Review of Reviews* 15 (April 1897), 371–2, 371. See also Whibley's 'The Encroachment of Women,' *Nineteenth Century* 41 (March 1896), 495–501.

15 'The Sins of Education,' *Blackwood's Magazine* 165 (March 1899), 503–13, 506. Whibley's notorious intransigence on this subject was immortalized in another Beerbohm caricature, 'Mr Charles Whibley consoling Mr Augustine Birrell for the loss of the Education Bill by a discourse on the uselessness of teaching anything whatsoever, sacred or profane, to children of the not aristocratic class.' See Max Beerbohm, *A Book of Caricatures* (London: Methuen, 1907), 28.

16 As a committee member of the Royal Literary Fund, Whibley was instrumental in helping D.H. Lawrence receive financial support, and he also arranged for Cynthia Asquith to make an anonymous donation to the novelist. '[H]e has guten Augen' (he is perceptive), Lawrence told Asquith appreciatively in November 1917. See James T. Boulton and Andrew

Robertson, eds., *Letters of D.H. Lawrence*, vol. 3 (Cambridge: Cambridge University Press, 1984), 187. Thomas Hardy inscribed copies of *Tess of the D'Urbervilles, Jude the Obscure*, and *Selected Poems* to Whibley.

17 Charles Whibley, 'Translators,' in *The Cambridge History of English Literature Volume 4*, ed. A.W. Ward and A.R. Walker (Cambridge: Cambridge University Press, 1909), 1–25. Whibley took Jonathan Swift, appropriately, as the subject for his University lecture.

18 MWM, *Blackwood's Magazine* 137 (April 1885), 528–48; MWM, *Blackwood's Magazine* 138 (October 1885), 517–34; MWM, *Blackwood's Magazine* 139 (March 1886), 351–69; MWM, *Blackwood's Magazine* 140 (August 1886), 231–50; MWM, *Blackwood's Magazine* 140 (December 1886), 735–54; MWM, *Blackwood's Magazine* 142 (September 1887), 355–72.

19 MWM, *Blackwood's Magazine* 137 (April 1885), 528–48, 528; MWM, *Blackwood's Magazine* 142 (September 1887), 355–72, 372.

20 MWM, *Blackwood's Magazine* 138 (October 1885), 517–34, 532; MWM, *Blackwood's Magazine* 140 (August 1886), 231–50, 250; MWM, *Blackwood's Magazine* 137 (April 1885), 528–48, 548.

21 MWM, *Blackwood's Magazine* 139 (March 1886), 351–69; MWM, *Blackwood's Magazine* 140 (August 1886), 231–50; MWM, *Blackwood's Magazine* 140 (December 1886), 735–54.

22 MWM, *Blackwood's Magazine* 138 (October 1885), 517–34, 532–4.

23 Whibley's project has been consistently misunderstood by literary historians. Typical is the unhelpful entry in the *Everyman's Dictionary of Literary Biography*, ed. D.C. Browning (London: Dent, 1979), 731: 'He has been described as an anachronism, belonging to the nineteenth century but publishing his works in the twentieth.'

24 MWM, *Blackwood's Magazine* 137 (April 1885), 528–48, 544–7; MWM, *Blackwood's Magazine* 139 (March 1886), 351–69, 369. As Altick observes of his attitude towards Tsar Nicholas II in 1917, events might force Whibley to change his position but he adamantly refused to admit to being fallible. Whibley's sarcastic dismissal of Wells's claims for the potential of atomic energy in MWM, *Blackwood's Magazine* 195 (June 1914), 854–64, was just one of countless sweeping assertions he did not live to see rebutted.

25 MWM, *Blackwood's Magazine* 181 (May 1907), 710–18.

26 Anonymous [Sir Stanley Leathes], 'Charles Whibley by a Friend,' *Blackwood's Magazine*, 587.

27 MWM, *Blackwood's Magazine* 170 (October 1901), 559–69; Charles Whibley, 'A Retrospect,' *Blackwood's Magazine* (April 1917), 433–46, 445.

28 T.S. Eliot, 'Charles Whibley,' *Selected Essays*, 3rd ed. (London: Faber, 1986), 492–506, 499.

29 Ibid., 498. In MWM, *Blackwood's Magazine* 222 (October 1927), 566–78, 569,

Whibley defended *Action Française* as being 'at once a gospel and a trumpet call,' and he again praised its 'courage and wisdom' in MWM, *Blackwood's Magazine* 224 (September 1928), 418–31, 426–29.

30 Whibley's friendship with Eliot merits a study in its own right. In a letter to Ezra Pound in 1922, Eliot included him among the 'good people' who 'write about something they know something about.' See Valerie Eliot, ed., *The Letters of T.S. Eliot*, volume 1, *1898–1922* (London: Faber, 1988), 593. In *The Criterion: Cultural Politics and Periodical Networks in Inter-War Britain* (Oxford: Oxford University Press, 2002), 179, Jason Harding notes that Whibley's celebration of traditional authority in the essays he contributed to *The Criterion* in the mid-1920s were representative of the magazine's politics at that time; Whibley also provided crucial financial support for Eliot's venture in 1928. In *Cynthia Asquith* (London: Hamish Hamilton, 1987), 323, Nicola Beauman points out that it was Whibley who recommended Eliot as a literary editor to Geoffrey Faber in 1925. Eliot wrote an introduction to his friend's edition of *Seneca: His Tenne Tragedies* (1927) and dedicated *The Use of Poetry and the Use of Criticism* (London: Faber 1933), originally given as his Charles Norton lectures at Harvard, to Whibley's memory. Eliot owned an (unpublished) caricature of Whibley by Beerbohm.

31 Eliot, 'Charles Whibley,' 498.

32 Ibid., 492, 497, 499. In 1902, the first two years of MWM were published pseudonymously by Blackwood as 'Annalist,' *Musings Without Method: A Record of 1900–01* (Edinburgh: Blackwood, 1902). An edited anthology of twenty-seven numbers of MWM was submitted as a doctoral thesis at the University of Pennsylvania in 1961 and published many years later. See Frederick R. MacFadden, ed., *Charles Whibley's 'Musings Without Method': A Critical Selection Edited with Biography* (diss., University of Pennsylvania, 1961), and Frederick Rankin MacFadden, ed., *Knight With Quill by Charles W. Whibley: Essays on British and European Literature and Littérateurs* (San Bernadino: Borgo Press, 1997). Strangely, MacFadden nowhere mentions Eliot's proposal.

33 Richard D. Altick, 'Toryism's Last Stand: Charles Whibley and His "Musings Without Method,"' *South Atlantic Quarterly* 41 (1942), 297–312, 297.

34 Ibid., 311, 312. Whibley's scabrous opinions of Jews, backed by references to *The Protocols of the Elders of Zion*, are articulated at length in MWM, *Blackwood's Magazine* 208 (November 1920), 681–92, 691–2; MWM, *Blackwood's Magazine* 210 (October 1921), 552–64, 557–62; and MWM, *Blackwood's Magazine* 218 (August 1925), 284–96, 293–6. 'For our part we dread the

tolerance which would admit an inferior race into equality with a superior,' he announced in MWM, *Blackwood's Magazine* 209 (May 1921), 694–704, 701.

35 Ibid., 311.

36 Even so, there was a strong tradition of conservative polemic at the firm. See David Finkelstein, *The House of Blackwood: Author–Publisher Relations in the Victorian Era* (University Park: University of Pennsylvania Press, 2002), 98–101.

37 Pierre Bourdieu, *The Field of Cultural Production: Essays on Art and Literature*, ed. Randal Johnson (New York: Columbia University Press, 1993), 30, 77.

38 Ibid., 42.

39 Pierre Bourdieu, *The Craft of Sociology: Epistemological Preliminaries*, ed. Beate Krais, trans. Richard Nice (Berlin: Walter de Gruyter, 1991), 77n.

40 MWM, *Blackwood's Magazine* 195 (January 1914), 138–48, 142; MWM, *Blackwood's Magazine* 182 (October 1907), 558–67, 563; MWM, *Blackwood's Magazine* 170 (July 1901), 135–45, 137; Altick, 'Toryism's Last Stand,' 302.

41 MWM, *Blackwood's Magazine* 167 (March 1900), 420–30, 427.

42 MWM, *Blackwood's Magazine* 168 (November 1900), 757–67; MWM, *Blackwood's Magazine* 176 (October 1904), 569–78.

43 Bourdieu, *Field of Cultural Production*, 94. In this, as in his implacable contempt for popular journalism, Whibley closely resembles the Viennese satirist Karl Kraus, who delivered an uninterrupted stream of invective on topical events and the cultural sphere in his magazine *Die Fackel* between 1899 and 1936. See Harry Zohn, ed., *In These Great Times: A Karl Kraus Reader*, trans. Joseph Fabry et al. (Manchester: Carcanet Press, 1984); and Edward Timms, *Karl Kraus, Apocalyptic Satirist: Culture and Catastrophe in Habsburg Vienna* (New Haven: Yale University Press, 1989), 35–41.

44 MWM, *Blackwood's Magazine* 172 (July 1902), 840–51, 146.

45 Joseph Conrad, *Collected Letters: Volume 4, 1908–1911*, ed. Frederick R. Karl and Laurence Davies (Cambridge: Cambridge University Press, 1990), 506. As Laurel Brake notes in *Print in Transition*, 229 and 245, Maga's readership was somewhat less masculine and uniformed than Conrad and others imagined.

46 MWM, *Blackwood's Magazine* 179 (May 1906): 710–21, 715; MWM, *Blackwood's Magazine* 183 (March 1908), 431–41, 431; MWM, *Blackwood's Magazine* 174 (November 1903), 684–95, 691. '[T]here is no crime which may not be described as political,' he declared in MWM, *Blackwood's Magazine* 217 (January 1925), 136–48, 136. Whibley described his fascination with the 'lettered vagabonds' of late-seventeenth-century England in 'An Underworld of Letters,' *Literary Studies* (London: Macmillan, 1919), 298–9.

47 MWM, *Blackwood's Magazine* 182 (December 1907), 845–55, 848.

48 MWM, *Blackwood's Magazine* 170 (December 1901), 852–64, 859.

49 Charles Whibley, 'William Morris,' *Blackwood's Magazine* 166 (July 1899), 16–26, 25. See also his 'The Hates of Napoleon,' *Fortnightly Review* 60os/62ns (October 1897), 559–70; and his enthusiasm for Eimar O'Duffy's 'hatreds' in MWM, *Blackwood's Magazine* 220 (November 1926), 704–16, 711–14.

50 MWM, *Blackwood's Magazine* 175 (February 1904), 262–72, 270.

51 MWM, *Blackwood's Magazine* 170 (July 1901), 135–45, 141; MWM, *Blackwood's Magazine* 182 (August 1907), 279–86, 283; MWM, *Blackwood's Magazine* 178 (August 1905), 279–87, 280.

52 MWM, *Blackwood's Magazine* 171 (February 1902), 264–77, 272.

53 MWM, *Blackwood's Magazine* 172 (November 1902), 703–13, 712. See Paula M. Krebs, *Gender, Race, and the Writing of Empire: Public Discourse and the Boer War* (Cambridge: Cambridge University Press, 1999), 32–54.

54 MWM, *Blackwood's Magazine* 170 (October 1900), 595–604, 600–1.

55 See MWM, *Blackwood's Magazine* 173 (June 1903), 847–56; MWM, *Blackwood's Magazine* 184 (September 1908), 397–407, 401–4; MWM, *Blackwood's Magazine* 218 (July 1925), 138–48, 138–9; and MWM, *Blackwood's Magazine* 224 (October 1928), 561–72, 565–8.

56 MWM, *Blackwood's Magazine* 170 (July 1901), 135–45, 142.

57 MWM, *Blackwood's Magazine* 167 (February 1900), 275–87. Further references to this instalment will be made parenthetically in the text.

58 Whibley denounced Marinetti and the cult of speed in MWM, *Blackwood's Magazine* 195 (January 1914), 138–48, 138–41. In *George Newnes and the New Journalism in Britain, 1880–1910* (Aldershot, Hants: Ashgate, 2001), 33, Kate Jackson notes that 'as the end of the century approached, there was a widely diffused sense that Britons were participating in the emergence of "modernity."' On the relation between journalism and modernity, see Ben Singer, 'Modernity, Hyperstimulus, and the Rise of Popular Sensationalism,' in *Cinema and the Invention of Modern Life*, ed. Leo Charney and Vanessa R. Schwartz (Berkeley: University of California Press, 1995), 72–99. On the broader theoretical stakes in periodizing the modern, see Frederick Jameson, *A Singular Modernity: Essays on the Ontology of the Present* (London: Verso, 2002), especially 141–60. Whibley's own interventions in contemporary debates over the shock of the new are discussed in Stephen Donovan, '"SHORT BUT TO THE POINT": Newspaper Typography in "Aeolus,"' *James Joyce Quarterly* 40, no. 3 (Fall 2004), 1–22, 12–13; and 'Dead Men's News: Joyce's 'A Painful Case' and the Modern Press,' *Journal of Modern Literature* 24, no. 1 (Fall 2000), 25–45, 32.

59 MWM, *Blackwood's Magazine* 171 (June 1902), 840–51, 845 (emphasis added).

60 On Roberts's cultivation of the newspapers, see Thomas Pakenham, *The Boer War* (1979; London: Abacus, 1997), 242–3.

61 The *Daily News* was bought by George Cadbury in late 1900 as a vehicle for Radical and pro-Boer views. On the political bias of press coverage during the war, see John Benyon, '"Intermediate" Imperialism and the Test of Empire: Milner's "Excentric" High Commission in South Africa,' in *The South African War Reappraised*, ed. Donal Lowry (Manchester: Manchester University Press, 2000), 84–103, 98–9.

62 Eliot, 'Charles Whibley,' 500; 'East Coker,' *Complete Poems and Plays* (1969; London: Faber, 1989), 177. Eliot identified Whibley's *Studies in Frankness* (1898) as his source for the quotation by Lucian that serves as the epigraph to 'Mr Apollinax' (1917). See Jane Worthington, 'The Epigraphs to the Poetry of T.S. Eliot,' *American Literature* 21.1 (March 1949), 1–17, 4.

63 MWM, *Blackwood's Magazine* 226 (December 1929), 859–70, 870. Whibley's many attacks on Stead included 'The Sins of Education,' *Blackwood's Magazine* 165 (March 1899), 503–13, 503 and 509; MWM, *Blackwood's Magazine* 168 (December 1900), 915–26, 920–1; and MWM, *Blackwood's Magazine* 217 (January 1925), 136–48, 147. In MWM, *Blackwood's Magazine* 175 (February 1904), 262–72, 262, he confessed to having a 'pathological interest' in Stead's career.

64 MWM, *Blackwood's Magazine* 217 (January 1925), 136–48, 137. See also MWM, *Blackwood's Magazine* 221 (April 1927), 555–66, 564.

65 The policy that Whibley proposed, to suppress war news by keeping 'all the correspondents kicking their heels at the coast' (286), would in fact seriously undermine the war effort in 1914–16. See Martin J. Farrar, *News From the Front: War Correspondents on the Western Front 1914–18* (Stroud, Gloucestershire: Sutton Publishing, 1998), 6–14 and passim.

66 G.H. Mair, 'The Music-Hall,' *English Review* 9 (August–November 1911), 122–9, 125. T.S. Eliot, 'Marie Lloyd,' *Selected Essays*, 456–59, 456. Whibley returned to the music hall in MWM, *Blackwood's Magazine* 176 (November 1904), 679–87, 685–7, and in MWM, *Blackwood's Magazine* 224 (August 1928), 277–88, 287–8. For detail on the relation between anti-decadent conservatism and early Modernist aesthetics, see Chris Baldick, *Criticism and Literary Theory 1890 to the Present* (London: Longman, 1996), 25–38.

67 In MWM, *Blackwood's Magazine* 186 (November 1909), 713–24, an inferior monograph on advertising in Addison and Steele's *The Spectator* leads Whibley, via a peroration on Hall Caine and Theodore Roosevelt, to the tax proposals of another notorious publicity-seeker, Lloyd George. In an

appreciative review of *A Book of Scoundrels*, the *New York Times* described Whibley as '[n]ever weary of exploring the waste places of knowledge.' 'Different Types,' *New York Times* (Book Review), 5 May 1912, 270.

68 Altick, 'Toryism's Last Stand,' 303–11.

69 See Bill Schwarz, 'Conservatism and "Caesarism,"' in *Crises in the British State, 1880–1930*, ed. Mary Langan and Bill Schwarz (London: Hutchinson, 1985), 33–62, especially 54–7.

70 Charles Whibley, *Letters of an Englishman* (London: Constable, 1911), 2 vols. Since it was the *Daily Mail* which famously popularized golf among the British middle class, the inclusion of an essay titled 'The Tyranny of Golf' further suggests that many readers viewed Whibley's polemics as diversion rather than persuasion. In his 1915 preface Whibley defined the essays' ideal as 'the Toryism, not of politics, but of life and letters' (2). In *Northcliffe* (New York: Frederick A. Praeger, 1959), 392, Reginald Pound and Geoffrey Harmsworth quote the peer's description of Whibley, whom he first met in the late 1890s, as 'very loving, delightful.' In turn, Northcliffe's obituary in MWM, *Blackwoods Magazine* 212 (September 1922), 414–24, 424, praised him as 'vastly superior to his press.' For detail on Whibley's curious friendship with the most successful popular journalist of his generation and a political ally of Lloyd George, see MacFadden, 'Charles Whibley's "Musings Without Method,"' 13–17. Whibley also delivered obsequious eulogies to the *Daily Express*'s owner, Lord Beaverbrook, in MWM, *Blackwood's* (December 1921), 832–42, 839–42, and MWM, *Blackwood's Magazine* 219 (February 1926), 281–92, 281–7.

71 See David Finkelstein, 'Literature, Propaganda, and the First World War: The Case of *Blackwood's Magazine*,' in *Grub Street and the Ivory Tower: Literary Journalism and Literary Scholarship from Fielding to the Internet*, ed. Jeremy Treglown and Bridget Bennett (Oxford: Oxford University Press, 1998), 91–111, especially 99–104. A special article by Whibley, titled simply 'The War,' appeared in *Blackwood's Magazine* 196 (September 1914), 413–24.

72 J.A. Hammerton, *With Northcliffe in Fleet Street: A Personal Record* (London: Hutchinson, 1932), 42. In *The Life and Death of the Press Barons* (London: Secker and Warburg, 1982), 122, Piers Brendon quotes Adolf Hitler's remark to Harold Harmsworth: 'Much in our Nazi propaganda methods is based on the tactics so successfully employed against us by your brother.' See also J. Lee Thompson, *Lord Northcliffe and the Great War, 1914–1919: Politicians, the Press, and Propaganda* (Kent, Ohio: Kent State University Press, 1999), passim.

73 Cynthia Asquith, 'Charles Whibley As I Remember Him,' BBC, Third

Programme, 22 January 1950. Quoted in MacFaddden, 'Charles Whibley's "Musings Without Method,"' 21. Long regarded as an Allied propaganda myth, the brutality of advancing German troops towards Belgian civilians has recently been documented by John Horne and Alan Kramer, whose account of the destruction of the towns Visé and Andennes in *German Atrocities, 1914: A History of Denial* (New Haven: Yale University Press, 2001), 24–5 and 30–5, bears out many of Whibley's claims in MWM, *Blackwood's Magazine* 197 (June 1915), 860–70, 863–8.

74 Charles Whibley, '"Some Former Treaties": What We Won in the Field and Lost in the Council Chamber,' *Daily Mail*, Golden Peace Number (30 June 1919), 3.

75 MWM, *Blackwood's Magazine* 219 (March 1926), 422–34, 433; MWM, *Blackwood's Magazine* 222 (October 1927), 566–78, 575; ibid., 576; MWM, *Blackwood's Magazine* 222 (November 1927), 710–22, 710. Whibley was especially provoked by the application of psychoanalysis to literary criticism. See MWM, *Blackwood's Magazine* 209 (January 1921), 125–35, 132–5, and MWM, *Blackwood's Magazine* 220 (September 1926), 421–32, 429–32.

76 MWM, *Blackwood's Magazine* 212 (December 1922), 825–34, 828 and 830. 'We would give anything to find a kind of Fourth Party skilled in guerilla warfare, tireless in attack, and well knowing how to strike its blows where they would be felt most bitterly,' he declared in MWM, *Blackwood's Magazine* 226 (December 1929), 859–70, 867.

77 MWM, *Blackwood's Magazine* 208 (August 1920), 262–72, 263. MWM, *Blackwood's Magazine* 211 (February 1922), 260–72, 263.

78 MWM, *Blackwood's Magazine* 217 (January 1925), 136–48.

79 Ibid., 146.

80 MWM, *Blackwood's Magazine* 215 (June 1924), 877–88, 855; MWM, *Blackwood's Magazine* 216 (November 1924), 717–28, 722.

81 MWM, *Blackwood's Magazine* 226 (December 1929), 859–70, 863.

82 Jackson, *George Newnes and the New Journalism in Britain, 1880–1910*, 12; Finkelstein, *The House of Blackwood*, 112. See also Richard Ohmann, *Selling Culture: Magazines, Markets, and Class at the Turn of the Century* (London: Verso, 1998), passim.

83 Anonymous [Sir Stanley Leathes], 'Charles Whibley by a Friend,' 585.

84 'Different Types,' *New York Times* (Book Review), 5 May 1912, 270.

85 T.S. Eliot, 'Perfect and Imperfect Critics,' in *The Sacred Wood: Essays on Poetry and Criticism* (London: Methuen, 1950), 37; Charles Whibley, 'A Retrospect,' 433.

86 McDonald, *British Literary Culture*, 94. In a full-page illustrated feature titled 'Hot Shot from England for Our Magnates,' the *New York Times* (Sunday Magazine), 21 July 1907, 2, reprinted what it described as Whibley's 'red-hot arraignment' of Andrew Carnegie in his article 'The American Millionaire,' *Blackwood's Magazine* 182 (July 1907), 93–102.

Appendix:
Blackwood's Magazine Table of Contents, August 1871–July 1872

November 1871

Fair to See, conclusion	Laurence Lockhart
A Century of Great Poets from 1750 Downwards: Samuel Taylor Coleridge	Margaret Oliphant
Nine Idylls of Bion	Henry King
Notes on Fortresses	J.H. Burton
More Roba di Roma: The Mausoleum of Hadrian, or the Castle St Angelo (part 3)	W.W. Story
French Home Life (no. 1): Servants	Frederick Marshall
The Maid of Sker (part 4)	R.D. Blackmore

December 1871

The Maid of Sker (part 5)	R.D. Blackmore
More Roba di Rome: The Mausoleum of Hadrian, or the Castle St Angelo (part 4)	W.W. Story
The Two Mrs Scudamores (part 1)	Margaret Oliphant
Cornelius O'Dowd (no. 41)	Charles Lever
Unreflecting Childhood & Age	F. Locker
Gerty's Necklace	F. Locker
French Home Life (no. 2): Children	Frederick Marshall
Illustration	Anne Mozley
The House of Lords	Bonamy Price

January 1872

The Maid of Sker (part 6)	R.D. Blackmore
French Home Life (no. 3): Furniture	Frederick Marshall
The Two Mrs. Scudamores, conclusion	Margaret Oliphant
The Nine-Hours Movement	Bonamy Price
Chersiphron	W.W. Story
The Haunted Enghenio	J.B. Gladwyn Jebb
A Sailors' Narrative of H.M.S. Megaera and Of the preservation of her crew on the Island Of St Paul	A.T. Thrupp and W.G. Hamley

February 1872

French Home Life (no. 4): Food	Frederick Marshall
A Century of Great Poets from 1750 Downwards: Robert Burns	Margaret Oliphant
Serpent Charming in Cairo	Richard Owen
The Maid of Sker (part 7)	R.D. Blackmore

Quinet's *Creation*   Robert B. Lytton
An Educational Experiment in Yorkshire   Daniel Robert Fearson
The Reasonable Fears of the Country   W.G. Hamley

March 1872
A True Reformer (part 1)   George T. Chesney
Voltaire   Margaret Oliphant
The Maid of Sker (part 8)   R.D. Blackmore
Autumnal Manoeuvres   Archibald Alison, Jr
The Manchester Nonconformists and
   Political Philosophy   Bonamy Price
General Lee   Francis Charles Lawley
Cornelius O'Dowd (no. 42)   Charles Lever
Ministers Before Parliament   W.G. Hamley

April 1872
The Maid of Sker (part 9)   R.D. Blackmore
A Century of Great Poets from 1750
   Onwards: Percy Bysshe Shelley   Margaret Oliphant
French Home Life (no. 5): Manners   Frederick Marshall
A True Reformer (part 2)   George T. Chesney
New Books   Margaret Oliphant
The Minister Parliament and the Country   W.G. Hamley

May 1872
French Home Life (no. 6): Language   Frederick Marshall
A True Reformer (part 3)   George T. Chesney
Church Reform   W. Lucas Collins
The Maid of Sker (part 10)   R.D. Blackmore
The Situation in France   Frederick Marshall
Statesmen in and out of Parliament   W.G. Hamley

June 1872
The Maid of Sker (part 11)   R.D. Blackmore
Haud Immemor: Thackeray in America   William B. Reed
Zanzibar [by R.F. Burton]   W.G. Hamley, J.A. Grant,
                                                       and C.P. Rigby
A True Reformer (part 4)   George T. Chesney
New Books   Margaret Oliphant
The Downward Course   W.G. Hamley

July 1872

The Maid of Sker, conclusion	R.D. Blackmore
The British Tourist in Norway	J.H. Burton
A Century of Great Poets from 1750 Downwards: Lord Byron	Margaret Oliphant
A True Reformer (part 5)	George T. Chesney
Old Maids	W.G. Hamley
Charles James Lever	Charles Neaves and John Blackwood

Bibliography

Adelman, Paul. *Gladstone, Disraeli and Later Victorian Politics*. London, New York: Longman, 1997.

Aird, Thomas. 'Memoir.' In *The Poetical Works of David Macbeth Moir*, edited by T. Aird. Edinburgh: Blackwood, 1852.

Alexander, J.H. '*Blackwood's Magazine* as Romantic Form.' *Wordsworth Circle* 15(2) (1984): 57–68.

– 'Learning from Europe: Continental Literature in the Edinburgh Review and Blackwood's Magazine, 1802–1825.' *Wordsworth Circle* 11(3) (1990): 118–23.

Alexander, J.H., ed. *Tavern Sages: Selections from the 'Noctes Ambrosianae.'* Aberdeen: Association of Scottish Literary Studies, 1992.

Alison, Archibald. 'Duties of the Conservative Party.' *Blackwood's Magazine* (1832): 139–43.

– 'The State of Public Feeling in Scotland.' *Blackwood's Magazine* (1832): 65–76.

– 'Experience of Democracy.' *Blackwood's Magazine* (1836): 293–303.

– 'British History during the Eighteenth Century.' *Blackwood's Magazine* (1845): 353–68.

– *Some Account of My Life and Writings: An Autobiography by the late Sir Archibald Alison*. Edited by L.J. Alison. 2 vols. Edinburgh: William Blackwood & Sons, 1883.

Alison Jr, Archibald. 'Democracy Beyond the Seas.' *Blackwood's Magazine* (1870): 220–37.

Allardyce, Alexander. 'The Ethics of Gladstonianism.' *Blackwood's Magazine* (1881): 634–45.

Allen, J. de V. 'Two Imperialists: A Study of Sir Frank Swettenham and Sir Hugh Clifford.' *Journal of the Malaysian Branch of the Royal Asian Society* 37, pt. 1 (1964): 41–73.

Allen, Robert. *The Clubs of Augustan London*. Cambridge, Mass.: Harvard University Press, 1933.

Altick, Richard D. 'Toryism's Last Stand: Charles Whibley and His "Musings Without Method."' *South Atlantic Quarterly* 41 (1942): 297–312.

– *Punch: The Lively Youth of a British Institution, 1841–1851*. Columbus: Ohio State University Press, 1997.

Anderson, Patricia J., and Jonathan Rose, eds. *British Literary Publishing Houses, 1820–1880*. Vol. 106. Detroit and London: Gale Research, 1991.

– *British Literary Publishing Houses, 1881–1965*. Vol. 112. Detroit and London: Gale Research, 1991.

Anderson, Roland. '"Things Wisely Ordered": John Blackwood, George Eliot and the Publication of *Romola*.' *Publishing History* 11 (1982): 5–39.

'Annalist.' *Musings Without Method: A Record of 1900–1901*. Edinburgh: William Blackwood and Sons, 1902.

Anon. *The Craniad: or Spurzheim illustrated: A Poem in two parts*. Edinburgh, 1817.

– 'On the Sculpture of the Greeks; On Greek Tragedy.' *Edinburgh Monthly Magazine* 1 (1817).

– 'Remarks on Schlegel's History of Literature.' *Blackwood's Edinburgh Magazine* 3 (1818): 479–511.

– 'Proposed National Monument at Edinburgh.' *Blackwood's Edinburgh Magazine* (July 1819): 377–87.

– 'Restoration of the Parthenon as the National Monument.' *Blackwood's Edinburgh Magazine* (November 1819): 137–48.

– *Tait's Edinburgh Magazine* 11 (1833): 58–9.

– 'Different Types.' *New York Times*, 5 May 1912, 270.

Arnold, Martin. 'Let's Book Lunch.' *Houston Chronicle*, 14 June 1988, 29.

Asquith, Lady Cynthia. *Diaries 1915–1918*. London: Hutchinson, 1968.

Atkinson, Damian, ed. *The Selected Letters of W.E. Henley*. Aldershot, Hants: Ashgate, 2000.

Aubry, Jean, ed. *Joseph Conrad: Life and Letters*. 2 vols. Garden City, N.Y.: Doubleday, 1927.

Bagehot, Walter. 'The First *Edinburgh* Reviewers.' *National Review* 1 (October 1855): 253–84.

– *Literary Studies*. Edited by R.H. Hutton. 3 vols. London: Longman, Green and Co., 1895.

Baines, Jocelyn. *Joseph Conrad: A Critical Biography*. London: Weidenfeld & Nicolson, 1960.

Baldick, Chris. *Criticism and Literary Theory, 1890 to the Present*. London: Longman, 1996.

Beasley, George Spencer. 'The Letters of John Galt.' Unpublished PhD thesis, Texas Technological College, 1951.

Beauman, Nicola. *Cynthia Asquith*. London: Hamish Hamilton, 1987.

Bell, Alan, ed. *Lord Cockburn: A Bicentenary Commemoration 1779–1979*. Edinburgh: Scottish Academic Press, 1979.

Bennett, Nell Wayne Carlisle. 'Three Irish Contributors to Blackwood's Magazine: Eyre Evans Crowe, George Downes, and Horatio Townsend.' Unpublished MA thesis, Texas Technological College, 1958.

Benyon, John. '"Excentric" High Commission in South Africa.' In *The South African War Reappraised*, edited by D. Lowry. Manchester: Manchester University Press, 2000.

Blackburn, William, ed. *Joseph Conrad: Letters to William Blackwood and David S. Meldrum*. Durham, N.C.: Duke University Press, 1958.

Bourdieu, Pierre. *The Craft of Sociology: Epistemological Preliminaries*. Translated by R. Nice. Edited by B. Krais. Berlin: Walter de Gruyter, 1991.

– *The Field of Cultural Production: Essays on Art and Literature*. Edited by R. Johnson. New York: Columbia University Press, 1993.

Brake, Laurel. *Subjugated Knowledges*. Basingstoke: Macmillan, 1994.

– *Print in Transition, 1850–1910: Studies in Media and Book History*. Basingstoke: Palgrave Macmillan, 2001.

Brake, Laurel, Bill Bell, and David Finkelstein, eds. *Nineteenth-Century Media and the Construction of Identities*. Basingstoke: Palgrave Macmillan, 2000.

Brake, Laurel, and Julie F. Codell, eds. *Encounters in the Victorian Press*. Palgrave Macmillan, 2005.

Brendon, Piers. *The Life and Death of the Press Barons*. London: Secker and Warburg, 1982.

Brodie, Alexander. *The Tradition of Scottish Philosophy: A New Perspective on the Enlightenment*. Edinburgh: Polygon Press, 1990.

Buckler, William E. 'Edward Walford: A Distressed Editor.' *Notes and Queries* 198 (December 1953): 536–38.

Buckley, Jerome Hamilton. *William Ernest Henley: A Study in the 'Counter-Decadence' of the 'Nineties*. Princeton, N.J.: Princeton University Press, 1945.

Butler, Marilyn. 'Culture's Medium: The Role of the Review.' In *The Cambridge Companion to British Romanticism*. Edited by S. Curran. Cambridge: Cambridge University Press, 1993.

Buzard, James. 'Translation and Tourism: Scott's *Waverley* and the Rendering of Culture.' *Yale Journal of Criticism* 8, no. 2 (1995): 31–60.

Campbell, Alexander. *Albyn's Anthology; or, A Selection of the Melodies and Local Poetry Peculiar to Scotland and the Isles, Hitherto Unpublished*. 2 vols. Edinburgh: Oliver and Boyd, 1816.

Cantor, Geoffrey, Gowan Dawson, Graeme Gooday, Richard Noakes, Sally Shuttleworth, and Jonathan R. Topham, eds. *Science in the Nineteenth-Century Periodical: Reading the Magazine of Nature*. Cambridge: Cambridge University Press, 2004.

Cartmell, Claire. 'The Age of Politics, Personalities, and Periodicals: The Early Nineteenth Century World of the "Noctes Ambrosianae" of *Blackwood's Edinburgh Magazine*.' PhD thesis, University of Leeds, 1974.

Chandler, James. *England in 1819: The Politics of Literary Culture and the Case of Romantic Historicism*. Chicago: University of Chicago Press, 1998.

Chesterton, G.K. *The Napoleon of Notting Hill*. London: John Lane, The Bodley Head, 1904.

Clifford, Hugh. 1894. *A Dictionary of the Malay Language, Malay–English A–G*. Taiping Perak: Government Printers, 1894.

– 'The Trail of the Bookworm: Mr Joseph Conrad at Home and Abroad.' *Singapore Free Press*, 1898.

– 'The Genius of Mr Conrad.' *North American Review* (1904): 842–52.

– 'In the Heart of Kalamantan.' In *Blackwood's Tales from the Outposts VIII: Jungle Tales*, edited by C.L.A. Bethel. London and Edinburgh: William Blackwood and Sons, 1946.

– *At the Court of Pelesu and Other Malayan Stories*. Edited by W. Roff. Kuala Lumpur: Oxford University Press, 1993.

Clyde, Robert. *Memorials of His Time*. Edited by K.F.C. Miller. Chicago: University of Chicago Press, 1974.

– *From Rebel to Hero: The Image of the Highlander, 1745–1830*. Lothian, Scotland: Tuckwell Press, 1995.

Coleridge, Samuel Taylor. 'Selections from Mr Coleridge's Literary Correspondence.' *Blackwood's Magazine* 10 (1821): 243–62.

– *The Collected Letters of Samuel Taylor Coleridge*. Edited by E.L. Griggs. 6 vols. Oxford: Clarendon Press, 1956–71.

– *Table Talk*. Edited by C. Woodring. 2 vols. Princeton, N.J.: Princeton University Press, 1990.

Collins, K.K. 'The British and Foreign Review.' In *British Literary Magazines: The Romantic Age, 1789–1836*. Edited by A. Sullivan. Westport, Conn., and London: Greenwood Press, 1983.

Collins, Wilkie. 'The Unknown Public.' *Household Words* (1858): 217–22.

Combe, George. *A System of Phrenology*. 5th ed. 2 vols. Edinburgh: MacLachlan and Stewart, 1853.

Conrad, Jessie. *Joseph Conrad and His Circle*. London: Jarrold's, 1935.

Conrad, Joseph. *A Personal Record*. London: Dent, 1919.

– *Lord Jim*. London: Dent, 1946.

– *Notes on Life and Letters.* London: Dent, 1949.
– *The Collected Letters of Joseph Conrad.* Edited by Frederick R. Karl, Laurence Davies, et al. 9 vols. Cambridge: Cambridge University Press, 1983–2007.
– *Heart of Darkness and Other Tales.* Edited by C. Watts. Oxford: Oxford University Press, 1990.
Cooke, Ann Kersey. 'Maginn-Blackwood Correspondence.' 2 vols. Unpublished MA thesis, Texas Technological College, 1955.
Cowell, Herbert. 'Liberty, Equality, Fraternity: Mr. John Stuart Mill.' *Blackwood's Magazine* (1873): 347–62.
– 'John Stuart Mill: An Autobiography.' *Blackwood's Magazine* (1874): 75–93.
– 'The Earl of Beaconsfield.' *Blackwood's Magazine* (1881): 674–82.
Cox, R.G. 'Nineteenth Century Periodical Criticism, 1800–1860,' PhD diss., Cambridge University, 1939.
Craig, Cairns. *Out of History: Narrative Paradigms in Scottish and British Culture.* Edinburgh: Polygon Press, 1996.
Cross, Nigel. *The Common Writer: Life in Nineteenth-Century Grub Street.* Cambridge: Cambridge University Press, 1985.
Curtis, Anthony. *Lit Ed.* London: Carcanet Press Ltd., 1998.
Curtis, Gerard. *Visual Words: Art and the Material Book in Victorian England.* Aldershot, Hants, and Brookfield, Vt.: Ashgate, 2002.
Curtis, Lewis Perry. *Esto Perpetua: The Club of Dr. Johnson and His Friends, 1764–1784.* Hamden, Conn.: Archon, 1963.
Dameron, J. Lasley, Pamela Palmer, and Kenneth J. Curry, compilers. *An Index to the Critical Vocabulary of Blackwood's Edinburgh Magazine, 1830–1840.* Conn.: Locust Hill, 1993.
Darwin, Bernard. *The Dickens Advertiser.* London: Elkins Mathews and Marrot, 1930.
Davies, Laurence. '"Free and Wandering Tales."' In *Conrad: Eastern and Western Perspectives,* edited by K. Carabine, O. Knowles, and Wieslaw Krajka. New York: Columbia University Press, 1992.
Davis, Leith. *Acts of Union: Scotland and the Literary Negotiation of the British Nation 1707–1830.* Stanford, CA: Stanford University Press, 1998.
De Quincey, Thomas. 'On the Approaching Revolution in Great Britain.' *Blackwood's Edinburgh Magazine* (1831).
– 'Political Anticipations.' In *The Works of Thomas De Quincey,* edited by R. Morrison. London: Pickering and Chatto, 2000.
– 'Dr Parr and his Contemporaries.' In *The Works of Thomas De Quincey,* edited by R. Morrison. London: Pickering and Chatto, 2001.
– 'Klosterheim.' In *The Works of Thomas De Quincey,* edited by R. Morrison. London: Pickering and Chatto, 2001.

- 'Professor Wilson.' In *The Works of Thomas De Quincey*, edited by E. Baxter. London: Pickering and Chatto, 2001.
- 'Sketches of Life and Manners [December 1840].' In *The Works of Thomas De Quincey*, edited by J. North. London: Pickering and Chatto, 2003.

Demata, Massimiliano, and Duncan Wu, eds. *British Romanticism and the 'Edinburgh Review': Bicentenary Essays*. Basingstoke: Palgrave Macmillan, 2002.

Dickens, Charles. *Letters*. Edited by M. House, et al. Oxford: Clarendon Press, 1965.

Donovan, Stephen. '"Figures, Facts, Theories": Conrad and Chartered Company Imperialism.' *Conradian* 24(2) (1999): 31–60.
- 'Dead Men's News: Joyce's "A Painful Case" and the Modern Press.' *Journal of Modern Literature* 24(1) (2000): 25–45.
- '"SHORT BUT TO THE POINT": Newspaper Typography in "Aeolus."' *James Joyce Quarterly* 40(3) (2004): 1–22.

Don Vann, J. 'Fraser's Magazine.' In *British Literary Magazines*, edited by Alvin Sullivan, vol. 2: 171–5. Westport, CT, and London: Greenwood Press, 1983.

Douglas, George. *The Blackwood Group*. Edinburgh: Oliphant, Anderson and Ferrier, 1897.

Dryden, Linda. '*An Outcast of the Islands*: Echoes of Romance and Adventure.' *Conradian* 20 (1995): 139–68.
- *Joseph Conrad and the Imperial Romance*. Basingstoke: Palgrave Macmillan, 1999.

Duncan, Ian. 'Edinburgh, Capital of the Nineteenth Century.' In *Romantic Metropolis: Cultural Productions of the City, 1770–1850*, edited by James Chandler and Kevin Gilmartin. Cambridge: Cambridge University Press, 2004.

Eliot, George [Evans, Marian]. 'Silly Novels by Lady Novelists.' *Westminster Review* 66 (1856): 442–61.

Eliot, T.S. *The Sacred Wood: Essays on Poetry and Criticism*. London: Methuen, 1950.
- *Selected Essays*. 3rd ed. London: Faber, 1986.

Eliot, Valerie, ed. *The Letters of T.S. Eliot*. Volume 1. *1898–1922*. London: Faber, 1988.

Elwell, Stephen. 'Editors and Social Change: A Case Study of *Once a Week* (1859–80).' In *Innovators and Preachers: The Role of the Editor in Victorian England*, edited by J.H. Wiener. Westport, Conn., and London: Greenwood Press, 1985.

Erickson, Lee. *The Economy of Literary Form: English Literature and the Industrialization of Publishing, 1800–1850*. Baltimore, Md.: Johns Hopkins University Press, 1996.

Escott, T.H. 'Thirty Years of the Periodical Press.' *Blackwood's Magazine* 156 (October 1894): 532–42.

Ezell, Margaret J.M. 'Reading Pseudonyms in Seventeenth-Century English Coterie Literature.' *Essays in Literature* 24 (Spring 1994): 14–25.

Falk, Bernard. *Bouquets for Fleet Street*. London: Hutchinson, 1951.

Farrar, Martin J. *News from the Front: War Correspondents on the Western Front 1914–1918*. Stroud, Gloucestershire: Sutton Publishing, 1998.

Feather, John. *A History of Publishing*. London: Routledge, 1989.

Ferris, Ina. *The Achievement of Literary Authority: Gender, History, and the Waverley Novels*. Ithaca, N.Y.: Cornell University Press, 1991.

Finkelstein, David. *An Index to Blackwood's Magazine, 1901–1980*. Aldershot, Hants: Scolar Press, 1995.

– 'Literature, Propaganda and the First World War: The Case of *Blackwood's Magazine*.' In *Grub Street and the Ivory Tower: Literary Journalism and Literary Scholarship from Fielding to the Internet*, edited by Jeremy Treglown and Bridget Bennet. Oxford: Oxford University Press, 1998.

– *The House of Blackwood: Author–Publisher Relations in the Victorian Era*. University Park: Pennsylvania State University Press, 2002.

– 'From Textuality to Orality: The Reception of *The Battle of Dorking*.' In *Books and Bibliographies: Essays in Commemoration of Don McKenzie*. Edited by J. Thomson. Wellington, NZ: Victoria University Press, 2002.

Finley, Gerald. *Turner and George the Fourth in Edinburgh*. London: Tate Gallery, 1981.

Fontana, Biancamaria. *Rethinking the Politics of Commercial Society: The Edinburgh Review 1802–1832*. Cambridge: Cambridge University Press, 1985.

Fyfe, Hamilton. *Northcliffe: An Intimate Biography*. London: Allen and Unwin, 1930.

Gailey, Harry A. *Clifford: Imperial Proconsul*. London: Collins, 1982.

Garside, Peter. 'Essay on the Text.' In *Walter Scott, The Black Dwarf*. Edited by Garside. Edinburgh: Edinburgh University Press, 1993.

Gere, Anne Ruggles. 'Common Properties of Pleasure: Texts in Nineteenth-Century Women's Clubs.' *Cardozo Arts and Entertainment Law Journal* 10(2) (1992): 647–63.

Gibbon, Charles. *The Life of George Combe, Author of 'The Constitution of Man.'* 2 vols. London: Macmillan, 1878.

Gleig, G.R. 'The Political Crisis.' *Blackwood's Magazine* (1866): 773–96.

– 'The Bill As It Is.' *Blackwood's Magazine* (1867): 245–56.

– 'The Reform Bill.' *Blackwood's Magazine* (1867): 633–48.

– 'The Ballot Bill.' *Blackwood's Magazine* (1871): 257–70.

Gordon, Ian A. *John Galt: The Life of a Writer*. Toronto: University of Toronto Press, 1972.

– 'Plastic Surgery on a Nineteenth-Century Novel: John Galt, William Blackwood, Dr. D.M. Moir and *The Last of the Lairds*.' *Library*, 5th series, 32(3) (1977): 246–55.

Gordon, Mary. *'Christopher North': A Memoir of John Wilson*. 2nd ed. Edinburgh: Grange Publishing, 1879.

Grave, S.A. *The Scottish Common Sense Philosophy*. Oxford: Clarendon Press, 1960.

Gray, Donald. 'George Eliot and Her Publishers.' In *The Cambridge Companion to George Eliot*, edited by George Levine, 181–201. Cambridge: Cambridge University Press, 2001.

Gregory, Richard L. *The Oxford Companion to the Mind*. Oxford: Oxford University Press, 1987.

Grierson, H.J.C., et al., eds. *The Letters of Sir Walter Scott*. 12 vols. London: Constable, 1932–7.

Gross, John. *The Rise and Fall of the Man of Letters: A Study of the Idiosyncratic and the Humane in Modern Literature*. London and New York: Macmillan, 1969.

Habermas, Jürgen. *The Structural Transformation of the Public Sphere: An Inquiry into a Category of Bourgeois Society*. Translated by T. Burger. Cambridge, Mass.: MIT Press, 1989. Original edition, 1962.

Haight, Gordon S. *George Eliot: A Biography*. Oxford: Oxford University Press, 1968.

Hall, N.J. *Trollope: A Biography*. Oxford: Clarendon Press, 1991.

Hammerton, J.A. *With Northcliffe in Fleet Street: A Personal Record*. London: Hutchinson, 1932.

Harding, Jason. *The Criterion: Cultural Politics and Periodical Networks in Inter-War Britain*. Oxford: Oxford University Press, 2002.

Hart, Francis R. *Lockhart as Romantic Biographer*. Edinburgh: Edinburgh University Press, 1971.

Hassan, M.A. 'The Major Romantic Poets and Their Critics in *Blackwood's Magazine*: 1817–1825.' Unpublished PhD thesis, University of Edinburgh, 1971.

Hawkins, Angus. *British Party Politics, 1852–1886*. New York: St Martin's Press, 1998.

Hayden, John O. *The Romantic Reviewers, 1802–1824*. Chicago: University of Chicago, 1969.

Hazlitt, William. 'On Public Opinion.' In *The Complete Works of William Hazlitt*, edited by P.O. Howe. London: Dent, 1930–4.

Henty, George A. *With Clive in India*. London and Glasgow: Blackie, n.d.

Hepker, Dale. 'Early Nineteenth-Century British Author–Publisher Relations.' Unpublished PhD diss. University of Nebraska, 1978.

Herbert, Christopher. *Culture and Anomie: Ethnographic Imagination in the Nineteenth Century*. Chicago: University of Chicago Press, 1991.

Higgins, David. 2003. '*Blackwood's Edinburgh Magazine* and the Construction of Wordsworth's Genius.' In *Romantic Periodicals and Print Culture*, edited by K. Wheatley, 122–36. London: Cass, 2003.

Hogg, James. *The Queen's Wake: A Legendary Poem*. Edinburgh: Longman, Hurst, Rees, Orme, Brown, 1813.

– *The Jacobite Relics of Scotland; Being the Songs, Airs, and Legends, of the Adherents to the House of Stuart*. 2 vols. Edinburgh: William Blackwood, 1819–1821.

– *The Royal Jubilee: A Scottish Mask*. Edinburgh: William Blackwood, 1822.

Holland, Merlin, and Rupert Hart-Davis, eds. *The Complete Letters of Oscar Wilde*. London: Fourth Estate, 2000.

Horne, John, and Alan Kramer. *German Atrocities, 1914: A History of Denial*. New Haven: Yale University Press, 2001.

Houghton, Walter, et al., eds. *The Wellesley Index to Victorian Periodicals, 1824–1900*. 5 vols. Toronto: University of Toronto Press, 1966–89.

House, Madeline et al., eds. *Charles Dickens, Letters*. Pilgrim edition. Vol. 1. Oxford: Clarendon Press, 1965.

Howe, P.P., ed. *The Complete Works of William Hazlitt*. London: Dent, 1930–4.

Hunter, Allan. *Conrad and the Ethics of Darwinism: The Challenges of Science*. London: Croom Helm, 1983.

– 'An Unpublished Letter from Conrad.' *Notes and Queries* (1984): 503–5.

Jack, Ian. *English Literature, 1815–1832*. Oxford: Oxford University Press, 1992.

Jackson, Kate. *George Newnes and the New Journalism in Britain, 1880–1910*. Aldershot, Hants: Ashgate Press, 2001.

Jameson, Frederick. *A Singular Modernity: Essays on the Ontology of the Present*. London: Verso, 2002.

Jeffrey, Francis. 'On Literature, Considered in its Relationship to Social Institutions.' *Edinburgh Review* 21 (1813): 1–25.

Johnson, Edgar. *Sir Walter Scott: The Great Unknown*. 2 vols. New York: Macmillan, 1970.

Jordan, John O., and Robert L. Patten, eds. 1995. *Literature in the Marketplace: Nineteenth-Century British Publishing and Reading Practices*. Cambridge: Cambridge University Press, 1995.

Kent, Christopher. 'The Editor and the Law.' In *Innovators and Preachers: The Role of the Editor in Victorian England*, edited by J.H. Wiener. Westport Conn., and London: Greenwood Press, 1985.

Kidd, Colin. *Subverting Scotland's Past: Scottish Whig Historians and the Creation of Anglo-British Identity, 1689–c. 1830*. Cambridge: Cambridge University Press, 1993.

Kilbourne, William. 'The Role of Fiction in *Blackwood's Magazine* from 1817 to 1845.' Unpublished PhD thesis, Northwestern University, 1966.

Klancher, Jon. *The Making of English Reading Audiences, 1790–1832*. Madison: University of Wisconsin Press, 1987.

Knightley, Phillip. *The First Casualty: The War Correspondent as Hero and Mythmaker from the Crimea to Kosovo*. 2nd ed. Baltimore: Johns Hopkins University Press, 2000.

Kraus, Karl. *In These Great Times: A Karl Kraus Reader*. Translated by J. Fabry. Edited by H. Zohn. Manchester: Carcanet Press, 1984.

Krebs, Paula M. *Gender, Race, and the Writing of Empire: Public Discourse and the Boer War*. Cambridge: Cambridge University Press, 1999.

Lamb, Charles. *The Letters of Charles and Mary Lamb*. Edited by E.V. Lucas. 3 vols. London: Dent, 1935.

Lang, Andrew. *The Life and Letters of John Gibson Lockhart*. 2 vols. London: John C. Nimmo, 1897.

Law, Graham. *Serializing Fiction in the Victorian Press*. Basingstoke: Palgrave, 2000.

Lawrence, D.H. *Letters*. Vol. 3. Edited by James T. Bolton and Andrew Robertson. Cambridge: Cambridge University Press, 1984.

Loch, James. *An Account of the Improvements on the Estates of Marquess of Stafford, in the Counties of Stafford and Salop*. London: Longman, Hurst, Rees, Orme, and Brown, 1820.

Lockhart, John Gibson. 'Remarks on the Periodical Criticism of England, by the Baron von Lauerwinkelk.' *Blackwood's Edinburgh Magazine* 2 (1818): 670–9.

– 'On the Revival of a Taste for our Ancient Literature.' *Blackwood's Edinburgh Magazine* 4 (1818): 264–6.

– *Peter's Letters to his Kinfolk*. 3 vols. Edinburgh: William Blackwood, 1819.

– 'Observations on "Peter's Letters to his Kinfolk."' *Blackwood's Edinburgh Magazine* 4 (1819): 612–21, 745–52.

– 'Noctes Ambrosianae, No. 1.' *Blackwood's Magazine* 11 (1822): 369–91 [pages misnumbered].

– 'Odoherty on *Don Juan*.' *Blackwood's Magazine* 14 (1823): 282–93.

– 'Lord Byron.' *Blackwood's Magazine* 17 (1825): 131–51.

– 'M.G. Lewis's *West Indian Journals*.' *Quarterly Review* 50 (1834): 374–99.

Lockhart, Laurence. 'The Late John Blackwood.' *Blackwood's Magazine* (1879): 772–5.

MacFadden, Frederick R. *Charles Whibley's 'Musings Without Method': A*

Critical Selection Edited with Biography. Diss., University of Pennsylvania, 1961.

MacFadden, Frederick Rankin, ed. *Knight with Quill by Charles W. Whibley: Essays on British and European Literature and Littérateurs*. San Bernadino: Borgo Press, 1997.

MacGregor, John. *British America*. 2 vols. Edinburgh: William Blackwood, 1832.

Mackay, Charles. 'The Principles and Issues of the American Struggle.' *Blackwood's Magazine* (1866): 17–27.

– 'Manhood Suffrage and the Ballot in America.' *Blackwood's Magazine* (1867): 461–79.

– 'The Working Classes.' *Blackwood's Magazine* (1867): 220–9.

Mackenzie, R. Shelton, ed. *Noctes Ambrosianæ*. 5 vols. New York: Redfield, 1854.

MacShane, Frank, ed. *Critical Writings of Ford Madox Ford*. Lincoln: University of Nebraska Press, 1964.

Maginn, William. 'Noctes Ambrosianae, No. IV.' *Blackwood's Magazine* 12 (1822): 100–14.

– 'Noctes Ambrosianae, No. VI.' *Blackwood's Magazine* 12 (1822): 695–709.

– 'Letters of Mr Mullion to the Leading Poets of the Age.' *Blackwood's Magazine* 16 (1824): 285–89.

Maginn, William, and John Gibson Lockhart. 'Maxims of Mr Odoherty.' *Blackwood's Magazine* 15 (1824): 597–605.

Mair, G.H. 'The Music-Hall.' *English Review* 9 (1911): 122–9.

Manners, Sir John. 'The End of the Struggle.' *Blackwood's Magazine* (1885): 144–54.

Mannion, Irene Elizabeth. 'Criticism "Con Amore": A Study of *Blackwood's Magazine*, 1817–1834.' Unpublished PhD thesis, University of California at Los Angeles, 1984.

Marchand, L.A., ed. *Letters and Journals of Lord Byron*. 12 vols. London: John Murray, 1973–94.

Martin, Carol A. *George Eliot's Serial Fiction*. Columbus: Ohio State University Press, 1994.

Masson, David. 'The Noctes Ambrosianae.' *National Review* 3 (1856): 175–200.

Maurice, F.D. 'The New School of Cockneyism, No. 1.' *Metropolitan Quarterly Magazine* 1 (1826): 34–62.

Mayo, Robert. *The English Novel in the Magazine, 1740–1815*. Evanston, Ill.: Northwestern University Press, 1962.

McDonald, Peter D. *British Literary Culture and Publishing Practice, 1880–1914*. Cambridge: Cambridge University Press, 1997.

McElroy, Davis. *Scotland's Age of Improvement: A Survey of Eighteenth-Century Literary Clubs and Societies*. Pullman: Washington State University Press, 1969.

McFarlane, Ian. *Buchanan*. London: Duckworth, 1981.

Mehta, Ved. *Remembering Mr. Shawn's 'New Yorker': The Invisible Art of Editing*. Woodstock, N.Y.: Overlook Press, 1998.

Michie, Michael. '"Mr Wordy" and the Blackwoods: Author and Publisher in Victorian Scotland.' *The Bibliotheck* 21 (1996): 39–54.

– *An Enlightenment Tory in Victorian Scotland: The Career of Sir Archibald Alison*. Kingston: McGill-Queen's University Press, 1997.

Mill, John Stuart. '*Poems, Chiefly Lyrical* [1830] and *Poems* [1833].' In *Tennyson: The Critical Heritage*, edited by J. Jump. London: Routledge and Kegan Paul, 1967.

Milne, Maurice. 'The Veiled Editor Unveiled: William Blackwood and His Magazine.' *Publishing History* 16 (1984): 87–103.

– 'The Politics of Blackwood's, 1817–1846.' Unpublished PhD diss., University of Newcastle, 1984.

Mitchison, Rosalind. 'The Highland Clearances.' In *A Companion to Scottish Culture*, edited by D. Daiches. London: Edward Arnold, 1981.

Morley, E.J., ed. *Henry Crabb Robinson on Books and Their Writers*. 3 vols. London: Dent, 1938.

Morrison, Robert. 'De Quincey, Champion of Shelley.' *Keats–Shelley Journal* 41 (1992): 36–41.

– 'John Wilson and the Editorship of *Blackwood's Magazine*.' *Notes and Queries* 46(1) (1999): 48–50.

– '"Abuse Wickedness, but Acknowledge Wit": *Blackwood's Magazine* and the Shelley Circle.' *Victorian Periodicals Review* 34(2) (2001): 147–64.

Morrison, Robert, ed. 'Richard Woodhouse's *Cause Book*: The Opium-Eater, the Magazine Wars, and the London Literary Scene in 1821.' *Harvard Library Bulletin* 9(3) (1998): 1–43.

Morrison, Robert, and Chris Baldick. 'Introduction.' In *Tales of Terror from Blackwood's Magazine*, edited by R. Morrison and Chris Baldick. Oxford: Oxford University Press, 1995.

– 'Introduction.' In *The Vampyre and Other Tales of the Macabre*, edited by R. Morrison and C. Baldick. Oxford: Oxford University Press, 1997.

Mozley, Anne. 'Mr. Mill on the Subjection of Women.' *Blackwood's Magazine* (1869): 309–21.

Mudie, Robert. *The Modern Athens: A Dissection and Demonstration of Men and Things in the Scotch Capital*. London: Knight and Lacey, 1825.

Muir, Edwin. *Scott and Scotland: The Predicament of the Scottish Writer*. London: Routledge, 1936.

Munday, Michael. 'The Novel and Its Critics in the Early Nineteenth Century.' *Studies in Philology* 79(2) (1982): 205–26.

Murphy, Peter. 'Impersonation and Authorship in Romantic Britain.' *ELH* 59 (1992): 625–49.

Nairn, Tom. *The Break-Up of Britain: Crisis and Neo-Nationalism*. London: New Left Books, 1981.

Neal, John. 'William Blackwood.' *Atlantic Monthly* 16 (1865): 660–72.

Nolte, Eugene A. 'The Letters of David Macbeth Moir to William Blackwood and His Sons.' 2 vols. Unpublished PhD thesis, Texas Technological College, 1955.

O'Sullivan, Noel. *Conservatism*. New York: St Martin's Press, 1976.

Ohmann, Richard. *Selling Culture: Magazines, Markets, and Class at the Turn of the Century*. London: Verso, 1998.

Oliphant, M.O.W. 'Byways of Literature: Reading for the Millions.' *Blackwood's Magazine* (1858): 200–16.

– 'The Great Unrepresented.' *Blackwood's Magazine* (1866): 367–79.

– *Annals of a Publishing House: William Blackwood and Sons*. 2 vols. Edinburgh: William Blackwood and Sons, 1897.

Onslow, Barbara. *Women of the Press in Nineteenth-Century Britain*. Basingstoke: Macmillan, 2000.

Orwell, George. *The Lion and the Unicorn*. Harmondsworth: Penguin, 1982.

Øverland, Orm. 'The Impressionism of Stephen Crane.' In *Americana Norvegica*, edited by Sigmund Skard and Henry H. Wasser. Oslo: American Institute, 1966.

Pakenham, Thomas. *The Boer War*. New York: Random House, 1979; London: Abacus, 1997.

Parker, Mark. *Literary Magazines and British Romanticism*. Cambridge: Cambridge University Press, 2000.

Patterson, R.H. 'The Crisis of the American War.' *Blackwood's Magazine* (1862).

'Pendragon, Berzelius' [pseudonym]. 'Pyne's History of the Royal Residences.' *Blackwood's Magazine* 5 (1819): 689–92.

Perry, Lewis Curtis. *Esto Perpetua: The Club of Dr. Johnson and His Friends, 1764–1784*. Hamden, Conn: Archon, 1963.

Phillips, J.S.R. 'The Halfpenny Morning Press.' In *The Cambridge History of English and American Literature*, edited by A.W. Ward and A.R. Waller. Cambridge: Cambridge University Press, 1907–21.

Poe, Edgar Allan. 'How to Write a Blackwood Article.' In *Collected Works of Edgar Allan Poe*, edited by T.O. Mabbott. Cambridge: Belknap Press of Harvard University Press, 1969–78.

Polk, Estus Cantrell. 'The Letters of Alaric Alexander Watts.' Unpublished PhD thesis, Texas Technological College, 1952.

Poovey, Mary. 'Forgotten Writers, Neglected Histories.' *ELH* 71 (2004): 436–7.

Pound, Reginald and Geoffrey Harmsworth. *Northcliffe*. New York: Frederick A. Praeger, 1959.

Pratt, Mary Louise. *Imperial Eyes: Travel Writing and Transculturation*. New York: Routledge, 1992.

Prebble, John. *The King's Jaunt: George IV in Scotland, August 1822; 'One and Twenty Daft Days.'* London: Collins, 1988. Repr. Edinburgh: Birlinn, 2000.

Price, Bonamy. 'Trade Unions, Part II.' *Blackwood's Magazine* (1870): 744–62.

Price, Richard. *An Imperial War and the British Working Class: Working Class Attitudes and Reactions to the Boer War, 1899–1902*. London: Routledge, 1972.

Raylor, Timothy. *Cavaliers, Clubs, and Literary Culture: Sir John Mennes, James Smith, and the Order of the Fancy*. Newark, N.J.: University of Delaware Press, 1994.

Redding, Cyrus. *Fifty Years' Recollection, Literary and Personal*. 3 vols. London: Skeet, 1858.

Redpath, Theodore. *The Young Romantics and Critical Opinion*. London: Harrap, 1973.

Richards, Eric. *A History of the Highland Clearances: Agrarian Transformation and the Evictions 1746–1886*. London: Croom Helm, 1982.

Robinson, Charles E. 'Percy Bysshe Shelley, Charles Ollier, and William Blackwood: The Contexts of Early Nineteenth-Century Publishing.' In *Shelley Revalued*, edited by K. Everest. Leicester: Leicester University Press, 1983.

Robson, Ann P., and John M. Robson. 'Private and Public Goals: John Stuart Mill and the *London and Westminster.*' In *Innovators and Preachers: The Role of the Editor in Victorian England*, edited by J.H. Wiener. Westport, Conn., and London: Greenwood, 1985.

Roe, Nicholas. 'A Cockney Schoolroom: John Keats at Enfield.' In *Keats: Bicentenary Readings*, edited by M. O'Neill. Edinburgh: Edinburgh University Press, 1997.

Roff, William. 'Introduction.' In *Hugh Clifford, At the Court of Pelesu and Other Malayan Stories*, edited by W. Roff. Kuala Lumpur: Oxford University Press, 1993.

Roper, Derek. *Reviewing before the 'Edinburgh,' 1788–1802*. London: Methuen, 1978.

Royle, Trevor. *Companion to Scottish Literature*. Detroit: Gale, 1983.

Rubenstein, William. *Britain's Century: A Political and Social History, 1815–1905*. London, New York: Arnold and Oxford University Press, 1998.

Ruddiman, Thomas. *Georgii Buchanani Scoti, poetarum sui seculi facile principis, opera omnia; ad optimorum codicum fidem summo studio recognita & castigata: nunc primum in unum collecta, ab innumeris pene mendis, quibus pleraeque omnes editiones antea scatebant, repurgata; ac variis insuper notis aliisque utilissimis accessionibus illustrata & aucta* ... 2 vols. Edinburgh: Robert Freebairn, 1715.

Ruggles, Anne Gere. 'Common Properties of Pleasure: Texts in Nineteenth-Century Women's Clubs.' *Cardozo Arts and Entertainment Law Journal* 10(2) (1992): 647–63.

Russett, Margaret. *De Quincey's Romanticism*. Cambridge: Cambridge University Press, 1997.

Sanders, Charles Richard, Clyde de L. Ryals, Kenneth Fielding, et al., eds. *The Collected Letters of Thomas and Jane Welsh Carlyle*. 29 vols. Durham, N.C.: Duke University Press, 1970–present.

Schlegel, Frederick. *Lectures in the History of Literature, Ancient and Modern*. Translated by J.G. Lockhart. 2 vols. Philadelphia: Dobson, 1818.

Schmidt, Barbara Quinn. 'Novelists, Publishers, and Fiction in Middle-Class Magazines, 1860–1880.' *Victorian Periodicals Review* 17(4) (1984): 142–52.

Schwarz, Bill. 'Conservatism and "Caesarism."' In *Crises in the British State, 1880–1930*, edited by Mary Langan and Bill Schwarz. London: Hutchinson, 1985.

Scott, John. 'Lord Byron: His French Critics: The Newspapers; and the Magazines.' *London Magazine* 1 (May 1820): 492–7.

Scott, Walter. *Hints Addressed to the Inhabitants of Edinburgh, and Others, in Prospect of His Majesty's Visit, by an Old Citizen*. Edinburgh: Manners and Miller, Archibald Constable and Co., William Blackwood, Waugh and Innes, and John Robertson, 1822.

– *The Letters of Sir Walter Scott*. Edited by H.J.C. Grierson. 12 vols. London, 1932.

– *The Journal of Sir Walter Scott (1826–32)*. Edited by W.E.K. Anderson. Oxford: Clarendon Press, 1972.

– *The Tale of Old Mortality*. Edited by D. Mack. Edinburgh: Edinburgh University Press, 1993.

Secord, William. *Victorian Sensation: The Extraordinary Publication, Reception and Secret Authorship of 'Vestiges of the Natural History of Creation.'* Chicago: University of Chicago Press, 2000.

Shand, Alexander Innes. 'Contemporary Literature III: Magazine Writers.' *Blackwood's Magazine* 125 (1879): 225–47.

Shattock, Joanne. *Politics and Reviewers: The 'Edinburgh' and the 'Quarterly' in the Early Victorian Age*. London: Leicester University Press, 1989.

Shattock, Joanne, and Michael Wolff, eds. *The Victorian Periodical Press: Samplings and Soundings*. Leicester: Leicester University Press, 1982.

Sherry, Norman. *Conrad's Eastern World*. Cambridge: Cambridge University Press, 1966.

– *Conrad and His World*. London: Thames and Hudson, 1972.

Singer, Ben. 'Modernity, Hyperstimulus, and the Rise of Popular Sensationalism.' In *Cinema and the Invention of Modern Life*, edited by Leo Charney and Vanessa R. Schwartz. Berkeley: University of California Press, 1995.

Slater, Michael. *Douglas Jerrold, 1803–1857*. London: Gerald Duckworth, 2002.

Smiles, Samuel. *A Publisher and His Friends: Memoir and Correspondence of the Late John Murray*. 3 vols. London: Murray, 1891.

– *A Publisher and His Friends: Memoir and Correspondence of the Late John Murray*. Edited by Thomas Mackay. London: John Murray, 1911.

Snodgrass, Charles. 'Advancing a Jacobite Patina: Hogg's Relics in Blackwood's House.' *Studies in Hogg and His World* 10 (1999): 27–39.

Spielmann, M.H. *The History of 'Punch.'* New York: Cassell, 1895.

Spivak, Gayatri Chakravorty. 'Problem with Thinking Ethics for the Other Woman.' Paper read at History and Ethics: The Question of the Other, at College Station, Texas A&M University, 20 February 1997.

Stape, J.H., and Owen Knowles, eds. *A Portrait in Letters: Correspondence to and about Conrad*. Amsterdam: Rodopi, 1996.

Stebbing, Henry. 'Periodical Literature.' *Athenaeum* 1 (1828): 334–7.

Steevens, George W. *With Kitchener to Khartum*. Edinburgh: William Blackwood and Sons, 1898.

– *Things Seen*. Edited by G.S. Street. Edinburgh: William Blackwood and Sons, 1900.

Sterling, John. 'The English Periodical Press.' *Athenaeum* 1 (1828): 695–6.

Stockwell, Anthony J. 'Sir Hugh Clifford's Early Career (1866–1903).' *Journal of the Malaysian Branch of the Royal Asian Society* 49(1) (1976): 89–112.

– 'The White Man's Burden and Brown Humanity: Colonialism and Ethnicity in British Malaya.' *Journal of the Malaysian Branch of the Royal Asiatic Society* 10, no. 1 (1982): 44–68.

Stones, Graeme, and John Strachan, eds. *Parodies of the Romantic Age*. London: Pickering and Chatto, 1999.

Strout, Alan Lang. 'The *Noctes Ambrosianae*, and James Hogg.' *Review of English Studies* 13 (1937): 46–63.

– *A Bibliography of Articles in Blackwood's Magazine, 1817–1825*. Lubbock: Texas Technological College, 1959.

Sullivan, Alvin, ed. *British Literary Magazines. The Romantic Age, 1789–1836*. Westport, Conn., and London: Greenwood Press, 1983.

- *British Literary Magazines: The Victorian and Edwardian Age, 1837–1913.*
  Westport, Conn., and London: Greenwood Press, 1984.
Swann, Elsie. *Christopher North <John Wilson>*. Edinburgh: Oliver and Boyd,
  1934.
Symonds, Barry. 'De Quincey to His Publishers: The Letters of Thomas De
  Quincey to his Publishers, and Other Letters, 1819–1832.' Unpublished PhD
  thesis, University of Edinburgh, 1994.
Tennyson, Alfred Lord. 'The Passing of Arthur.' In *Poems*, edited by C. Ricks.
  Harlow, Essex: Longman, 1987.
Thompson, J. Lee. *Lord Northcliffe and the Great War, 1914–1919*. Kent, Ohio:
  Kent State University Press, 1999.
Thompson, William Ross. 'The Letters of George Croly to William Blackwood
  and His Sons.' 2 vols. Unpublished PhD thesis, Texas Technological Col-
  lege, 1957.
Thorold, Algar Labouchere. *The Life of Henry Labouchere*. London: Constable,
  1913.
Thrall, Miriam M. *Rebellious Fraser's: Nol Yorke's Magazine in the Days of
  Maginn, Thackeray and Carlyle*. New York: Columbia University Press, 1934.
Timms, Edward. *Karl Kraus, Apocalyptic Satirist: Culture and Catastrophe in
  Habsburg Vienna*. New Haven: Yale University Press, 1989.
Tredrey, F.D. *The House of Blackwood, 1804–1954*. Edinburgh: William Black-
  wood and Sons, 1954.
Trela, D.J. ed. *Margaret Oliphant: Critical Essays on a Gentle Subversive*.
  Selinsgrae, Pa.: Susquehanna University Press, 1995.
Trollope, Anthony. *An Autobiography*. 2 vols. Edinburgh and London: William
  Blackwood and Sons, 1883.
Trumpener, Katie. *Bardic Nationalism: The Romantic Novel and the British Empire*.
  Princeton, N.J.: Princeton University Press, 1997.
Tutein, David W. *Joseph Conrad's Reading: An Annotated Bibliography*. West
  Cornwall, Conn.: Locust Hill Press, 1990.
Vann, J. Don. 'Fraser's Magazine.' In *British Literary Magazines*, edited by
  A. Sullivan. New York: Greenwood, 1983.
Wardle, Ralph. 'William Maginn and *Blackwood's Magazine*.' Unpublished PhD
  thesis, Harvard University, 1938.
Wells, H.G. *Saturday Review* 83 (1897): 273–4.
Wheatley, Kim, ed. 'Romantic Periodicals and Print Culture.' *Prose Studies*
  25 (2002).
- *Romantic Periodicals and Print Culture*. London and Portland, Ore.: Frank
  Cass, 2003.
Whibley, Charles. 'Translators.' In *The Cambridge History of English Literature*.

Volume 4, edited by A.W. Ward and A.R. Waller. Cambridge: Cambridge University Press, 1909.

- *Letters of an Englishman*. 2 vols. London: Hutchinson, 1911.
- 'A Retrospect.' *Blackwood's Magazine* 201 (1917): 433–6.

White, Andrea. *Joseph Conrad and the Adventure Traditions: Constructing and Deconstructing the Imperial Subject*. Cambridge: Cambridge University Press, 1993.

Wiener, Joel H., ed. *Innovators and Preachers: The Role of the Editor in Victorian England*. Contributions to the Study of Mass Media and Communications. Vol. 5. Westport, Conn., and London: Greenwood Press, 1985.

Willis, N.P. *Pencillings by the Way*. 3 vols. London: Macrone, 1836.

Wilson, John. 'Essays on the Lake School of Poetry, No. I. Wordsworth's *White Doe of Rylstone*.' *Blackwood's Magazine* 3 (1818): 369–81.

- 'Essays on the Lake School of Poetry, No. III. Coleridge.' *Blackwood's Magazine* 6 (1819): 3–12.
- 'Wordsworth's Sonnets and Memorials.' *Blackwood's Magazine* 12 (1822): 175–91.
- 'The Age of Bronze.' *Blackwood's Magazine* 13 (1823): 457–60.
- 'Noctes Ambrosianae, No. XIX.' *Blackwood's Magazine* 17 (1825): 366–84.
- 'Noctes Ambrosianae, No. XXIV.' *Blackwood's Magazine* 19 (1826): 211–27.

Wilson, John, and John Gibson Lockhart. 'Noctes Ambrosianae, No. LI.' *Blackwood's Magazine* 28 (1830): 383–436.

- 'Noctes Ambrosianae, No. LX.' *Blackwood's Magazine* 31 (1832): 255–88.
- 'Noctes Ambrosianae, No. LXVII.' *Blackwood's Magazine* 36 (1834): 258–88.

Wilson, John. 'Reformers and Anti-Reformers.' *Blackwood's Magazine* 29 (1831): 721–31.

Womack, Peter. *Improvement and Romance: Constructing the Myth of the Highlands*. Basingstoke: Macmillan, 1989.

Worth, George J. *Macmillan's Magazine, 1859–1907*. Aldershot, Hants, and Burlington, Vt.: Ashgate, 2003.

Worthington, Jane. 'The Epigraphs to the Poetry of T.S. Eliot.' *American Literature* 21, no. 1 (1949): 1–17.

Youngson, A.J. *The Making of Classical Edinburgh, 1750–1840*. Edinburgh: Edinburgh University Press, 1966.

Žižek, Slavoj. *Tarrying with the Negative: Kant, Hegel, and the Critique of Ideology*. Durham: Duke University Press, 1993.

Contributors

Laurel Brake is Professor of Literature and Print Culture at Birkbeck, University of London. She has published widely on aspects of nineteenth-century literature and culture, the press, and gender. Her books include two on the Victorian press, *Subjugated Knowledges* (1994) and *Print in Transition* (2001). She has co-edited various collections, some on that topic: *Investigating Victorian Journalism* (1990) with Aled Jones and Lionel Madden, and *Nineteenth-Century Media and the Construction of Identities* (2000) with David Finkelstein and Bill Bell; and *Encounters in the Victorian Press* (2005) with Julie Codell. She has been an active member of RSVP (The Research Society for Victorian Periodicals), as its president (2003–5). She is also a Fellow of the English Association, and on the editorial boards of *Victorian Periodicals Review* and the *Journal of Victorian Culture*. Other relevant work on the press includes a piece on W.T. Stead in *Marketing the Author*, edited by Marysa Demoor (2004) and a review of the field ('The State We're In,' *Journal of Victorian Culture*, 2001). She is currently the Director of the Arts and Humanities Research Council of the United Kingdom funded **ncse** project, a digital edition of six nineteenth-century journals, co-editor of a *Dictionary of Nineteenth-Century Journalism*, and writing a biography of Walter Pater.

Laurence Davies, formerly at Dartmouth College, USA, is now Senior Research Fellow at Glasgow University. With Cedric Watts, he is the author of *Cunninghame Graham: A Critical Biography* (1979). He is the general editor of *The Collected Letters of Joseph Conrad*, collaborating variously with Owen Knowles, Gene M. Moore, S.H. Stape, and the late Frederick R. Karl; Cambridge has published seven volumes, and the last two are in press. Davies also works on speculative fiction, European Modernism, the short story, the persistence of oral tradition, and the literatures of Scotland, Wales, and Ireland. He has held fellowships from the National Endowment for the Humanities, the National Endowment for the Arts, and the Woodrow Wilson Foundation.

Stephen Donovan is Lecturer in English at Uppsala University, Sweden. He has also been a visiting lecturer at Royal Holloway College, London, and the University of the Witwatersrand, Johannesburg. Donovan's work has appeared in *Journal of Modern Literature*, *James Joyce Quarterly*, the *Conradian* and *Conradiana*, as well as several essay collections. His *Joseph Conrad and Popular Culture* was published in 2005. He is currently working on a book on the late-Victorian imperial and chartered companies.

Linda Dryden is Reader in Literature and Culture at Napier University, Edinburgh. She has written extensively on Conrad, notably *Joseph Conrad and the Imperial Romance* (2000). Other work includes *The Modern Gothic and Literary Doubles: Stevenson, Wilde and Wells* (2003). Dr Dryden is co-editor, with Robert Hampson and Stephen Donovan, of *Joseph Conrad and Serialization*, a collection of essays that chronicles Conrad's publications in literary journals and magazines. Her work on Sir Hugh Clifford, entitled 'Conrad and Hugh Clifford: An "Irreproachable Player on the Flute" and "A Ruler of Men,"' was published in the *Conradian* in 1998. Essays on Conrad and Wells, Conrad and performance, and an edited book on Stevenson and Conrad are forthcoming. Dr Dryden is co-editor of the *Journal of Stevenson Studies* and a member of the executive committee of the Joseph Conrad Society (UK).

Ian Duncan is Professor of English and Department Chair at the University of California, Berkeley. He is the author of *Modern Romance and Transformations of the Novel* (1992) and has edited James Hogg's *Winter Evening Tales* (2002/2004) and novels by Walter Scott, Arthur Conan Doyle, W.H. Hudson and John Buchan (1996–8). He is a co-editor of *Scotland and the Borders of Romanticism* (2004) and *Travel Writing 1700–1830: An Anthology* (2005), and has published articles on a range of authors and topics in eighteenth and nineteenth-century British and Scottish literary history. Forthcoming works include essays on Edinburgh as Romantic metropolis, Scottish and Irish Romantic fiction, and Hugh

MacDiarmid and Scottish Modernism. He is completing a book called *Scott's Shadow: The Novel in Romantic Edinburgh.*

David Finkelstein is Research Professor of Media and Print Culture at Queen Margaret University College, Edinburgh. He is author of *An Index to Blackwood's Magazine, 1901–1980* (1995), *The House of Blackwood: Author–Publisher Relations in the Victorian Era* (2002), and co-author of *An Introduction to Book History* (2005). Other publications include co-editing *The Book History Reader* (2001; 2nd ed., 2006), *Thomas Nelson and Sons* (2001), *Negotiating India in the Nineteenth-Century Media* (2000), and with Laurel Brake and Bill Bell, *Nineteenth-Century Media and the Construction of Identities* (2000).

Michael Michie is Associate Professor in the School of Social Sciences, and Associate Dean, in the Atkinson Faculty of Liberal and Professional Studies, York University, Toronto. He is interested in British (especially Scottish) politics in the nineteenth century; the role of the periodical press in reform politics, and the politics of colonial emigration. He teaches courses in the history of Political Thought, and Modern Britain. He has published *An Enlightenment Tory in Victorian Scotland; the Career of Sir Archibald Alison* (1997) and articles in *The Bibliotheck* and *Scottish Studies*. He is presently working on a study of *Tait's Edinburgh Magazine.*

Robert Morrison is Professor of English literature at Queen's University, Kingston, Ontario. He is co-general editor of *The Selected Works of Leigh Hunt*, and editor of Hunt's essays, 1822–38 (2003). He edited three volumes of the *Works of Thomas De Quincey*, and co-edited a fourth (2000–3). He is editor of Thomas De Quincey, *On Murder* (2006), Jane Austen's *Pride and Prejudice: A Sourcebook* (2005), and 'Richard Woodhouse's *Cause Book*: The Opium-Eater, the Magazine Wars, and the London Literary Scene in 1821,' *Harvard Library Bulletin* (1998). With Chris Baldick, he edited *The Vampyre and Other Tales of the Macabre* (1997) and *Tales of Terror from Blackwood's Magazine* (1995). His articles have appeared in *Essays in Criticism*, *Romanticism*, the *Wordsworth Circle*, and *Victorian Periodicals Review.*

Robert L. Patten, Lynette S. Autrey Professor in Humanities at Rice University, Houston, Texas, writes on nineteenth-century British literature, art, and culture. He has published extensively on Charles Dickens and his modes of publication, on book illustration, and on the material formats in which cultural texts were circulated to Victorian audiences. Recipient of Fulbright, National Endowment for the Humanities, and Guggenheim Fellowships, he has been a Fellow at the National Humanities Center and an Associate at the Center for Advanced Study in the Visual Arts at the National Gallery of Art, Washington, DC. Professor Patten edits *SEL: Studies in English Literature 1500–1900*, and most recently has been publishing articles on the politics of Georgian caricature, the complexity of illustrating autobiographical fiction, the relation between a text's materiality and its thematics, and the formation of the 'industrial-strength' author. A contributor to both the Oxford and Cambridge companions to Charles Dickens, he is co-editor of *Palgrave Advances in Charles Dickens Studies* and author of many entries on publishers and artists for the *Oxford Dictionary of National Biography*.

Charles Snodgrass is an Assistant Professor of English at Xavier University in Cincinnati, Ohio, where he teaches British Romanticism. He has published articles on Sir Walter Scott, John Galt, and James Hogg in the *Scottish Literary Journal* and *Studies in Hogg and His World*. Along with Ian Duncan and Cairns Craig, he helped found the MLA Discussion Group on Scottish Literature. Since 1997 he has served as Associate Editor for *Romantic Circles Reviews* and was co-guest editor of the Spring 2001 special issue of *Studies in Romanticism*, 'Scott, Scotland, and Romantic Nationalism.' He is presently completing a book manuscript, *Scottish Romanticism: National Identity and the Novel in Blackwood's Circle*.

John Strachan is Professor of English at the University of Sunderland. He has published widely on the satirical literature of the Romantic period and is co-editor of *Parodies of the Romantic Age* (5 vols., 1999) and general editor of *British Satire 1785–1840* (5 vols., 2003). He has also edited Leigh Hunt's *Poetical Works* (2 vols., 2003). He is consultant editor and co-editor of *Blackwood's Edinburgh Magazine, 1817–25* (6 vols., 2006).

Index

Act of Union (1801), 102, 109, 131
Adelman, Paul, 134
advertising, 165–8, 191; in *Athenaeum*, 203–5
Age of Scott, 109
agents, authors', 172
Ainsworth, Harrison, 150, 154
Alexander, J.H., 26, 37, 94, 95
Alison, Sir Archibald, 11, 32, 119, 120, 122–6, 128–9, 140, 142, 160; article on effects of Reform Act, 130–1; articles written for *Blackwood's Magazine*, 122–3, 113n39; background, 122; *History of Europe*, 123–4, 129, 138; political position on reform, 128–32; *Principles of Population*, 123, 131; rejection of articles for *Blackwood's*, 124–5; as sheriff of Lanarkshire, 122, 123; on United States, 131–2
Alison Jr, Archibald, 133, 140–1, 160
All the Year Round, 153, 154, 180n42
Allardyce, Alexander, 121, 141, 142
Allen, J. de V., 216, 218, 226, 232
Altick, Richard, 264, 265–6, 268, 274
American Civil War, 132
Analytical Review, 7

Anglo-Irish Treaty (1922), 275
anonymity, and *Blackwood's Magazine*, 105, 108, 184, 191–2, 195, 199, 204, 208n20
Argosy, 150, 158
Asquith, Cynthia, 260
Asquith, Herbert, 260, 266
Atbara, Battle of, 245
Athenaeum, 159–60, 168, 189, 203–5
Austen, Jane, 22
Austin, Alfred, 156
authorship: cult of, 148; professionalization of, 12
Aytoun, William, 11, 120, 142

Bagehot, Walter, 152, 200
Baldwin, Robert, 29
Ballot Act (1872), 140
Balzac, Honoré de, 37
Banks, Percival Weldon, 161
Barham, R.H., 172
Barrow, Sir John, 160
Battle of Dorking, The, 175
Beaumont, Thomas Wentworth, 155
Beer, Rachel, 157
Beeton, Isabella, 157
Beeton, Samuel Orchart, 157

James, Henry, 230
Jeffrey, Francis, 6, 7, 26, 53–4, 64,
   74–5, 92, 152
Jerdan, William, 152, 154, 159, 160,
   168
John Bull, 274
Johnson, Edgar, 91
Johnson, Samuel, 91
Journal of Agriculture, 189

Keats, John, 26, 35, 64
Kemble, John Mitchell, 155
Kent, Christopher, 159
Kerr, Robert, 22
Ketteridge, Eliza, 172
Kidd, Colin, 103
Kilbourne, William, 36
'Killiecrankie,' 107, 115n60
Kinglake, Alexander, 12
Kipling, Rudyard, 246, 261
Kit-Kat Club, 93
Klancher, Jon, 32, 74
Knight, Charles, 170
Kraus, Karl, 281n43

Labouchere, Henry, 146
Lamb, Charles, 29
Landon, Letitia Elizabeth, 39, 156
Lang, Andrew, 160
Langford, Joseph Munt, 153, 166,
   169, 178n18
Law, John, 267
Lawrence, D.H., 262, 278n16
Leary, Patrick, 161
Lemon, Mark, 175–6
Lever, Charles, 3, 204, 211n52; *A
   Day's Ride*, 180n42
Lewes, George Henry, 153, 200
Liberals, 120, 133, 141, 142
Lincoln, Abraham, 132

Linton, Lynn, 257n52
literary advisors, 172
literary criticism and phrenology, 51
Literary Gazette, 168
Liverpool, Lord, 120
Lloyd, Charles, 27
Lloyd George, David, 265
Loch, James, 99
Lockhart, John Gibson, 9, 22, 27, 32,
   35, 55, 75, 95, 161; and Burns, 82;
   essay on Godwin's *Caleb Williams*,
   38; and *Noctes Ambrosianæ*, 106;
   'On the Revival of a Taste for our
   Ancient Literature,' 73; *Peter's
   Letters to his Kinsfolk*, 10, 28, 66n20,
   71–2, 76–86, 165; pseudonyms,
   111n20; and *Quarterly Review*, 152;
   visit to Germany (1817), 71; and
   Walter Scott, 71, 72
Lockhart, Laurence: *Fair to See*, 163
London Journal, 18, 35, 38
London Magazine, 29, 154, 159, 160,
   170, 206n1
London Society, 203
London Trades Council, 135
London and Westminster Review,
   154, 170
Longman's Magazine, 12, 209n28
Lytton, Bulwer, 126, 167; *The Pari-
   sians*, 167

MacColl, Norman, 160
McCrie, Thomas, 22
McDonald, Pete: *British Literary
   Culture and Publishing Practice*, 172
MacDonald, Ramsay, 273
Macdonell, Alastair Randalson, 95
MacGregor, John, 22
'*MacGregor na Raura*,' 107, 116n60
Mackay, Charles, 11, 132, 135–6, 140;

STUDIES IN BOOK AND PRINT CULTURE

General editor: Leslie Howsam

Hazel Bell, *Indexes and Indexing in Fact and Fiction*

Heather Murray, *Come, bright Improvement! The Literary Societies of Nineteenth-Century Ontario*

Joseph A. Dane, *The Myth of Print Culture: Essays on Evidence, Textuality, and Bibliographical Method*

Christopher J. Knight, *Uncommon Readers: Denis Donoghue, Frank Kermode, George Steiner, and the Tradition of the Common Reader*

Eva Hemmungs Wirtén, *No Trespassing: Authorship, Intellectual Property Rights, and the Boundaries of Globalization*

William A. Johnson, *Bookrolls and Scribes in Oxyrhynchus*

Siân Echard and Stephen Partridge, eds, *The Book Unbound: Editing and Reading Medieval Manuscripts and Texts*

Bronwen Wilson, *The World in Venice: Print, the City, and Early Modern Identity*

Peter Stoicheff and Andrew Taylor, eds, *The Future of the Page*

Jennifer Phegley and Janet Badia, eds, *Reading Women: Literary Figures and Cultural Icons from the Victorian Age to the Present*

Elizabeth Sauer, *'Paper-Contestations' and Textual Communities in England, 1640–1675*

Nick Mount, *When Canadian Literature Moved to New York*

Jonathan Carlyon, *Andrés González de Barcia and the Creation of the Colonial Spanish American Library*

Deborah McGrady, *Controlling Readers: Guillaume de Machaut and His Late Medieval Audience*

Leslie Howsam, *Old Books and New Histories: An Orientation to Studies in Book and Print Culture*

Elizabeth Driver, *Culinary Landmarks: A Bibliography of Canadian Cookbooks, 1825–1949*

David Finkelstein, ed, *Print Culture and the Blackwood Tradition, 1805–1930*